FIRST IMPRESSIONS

JANE AUSTEN'S SOUTHAMPTON CIRCLE

First Impressions

*Jane Austen's Southampton Circle
1780-1820*

CHERYL BUTLER

THE HOBNOB PRESS

First published in the United Kingdom in 2025

by The Hobnob Press,
8 Lock Warehouse, Severn Road, Gloucester GL1 2GA
www.hobnobpress.co.uk

© Cheryl Butler 2025

The Author hereby asserts her moral rights to be identified as the Author of the Work.

All rights reserved. No part of this publication may be reproduced, stored in a retrieval system, or transmitted in any form or by any means, electronic, mechanical, photocopying, recording or otherwise, without the prior permission of the publisher and copyright holder.

British Library Cataloguing in Publication Data
A catalogue record for this book is available from the British Library

ISBN 978-1-914407-84-0

Typeset in Adobe Garamond Pro, 11/14 pt
Typesetting and origination by John Chandler

CONTENTS

Dedication	vi
Acknowledgements	vi
Foreword	vii
Abbreviations and Short Titles	viii
Jane Austen in Southampton	1
The Watering Place of Southampton	16
Balls, Assemblies and other Entertainments	37
War	57
The Female Sphere	87
Georgian Ladies – Biographies of Ordinary Lives	113
Melicent Cropp Ballard	114
Ann Launce Newell	135
Anne Morse Middleton	149
Mary Hale Lewin	169
Mary Fitzhugh Lance & Charlotte Hamilton Fitzhugh	197
Elizabeth Austen Butler Harrison	236
End Note	260
Appendix One – The Letters of Melicent Ballard	267
Appendix Two – Correspondence relating to Elizabeth Butler Harrison and extracts from her household book	289
Appendix Three – Family trees	314
Bibliography	318
Index	330

To Sally Barton, direct descendent of Elizabeth Austen, for her generosity in giving access to the family archives
To Gloria Tack, my long time reader, friend and Austen fan
& to Anne 'Cassandra' Richardson
All dearly missed.

ACKNOWLEDGEMENTS

I WOULD like to thank the families and descendants for sharing their private archives with me, particularly Malcolm and the late Sally Barton, Dirk Fitzhugh, Colin Hyde Harrison, William Paton and Sarah Lewin. Also, thanks to Jo Smith archivist at Southampton City Council and to those historians and researchers whose interest in these women and generosity in sharing their research stimulated this book, particularly Stuart Drabble, Paula Downer and Garth Groombridge. I would also like to thank my readers Louise Fairbrother and Ken Farleigh.

FOREWORD

My interest in these Georgian women began whilst researching a book on Jane Austen's time in Southampton at the time of the Austen bicentenary in 2017. It grew when introduced to the Ballard and Butler Harrison families who had married into the Austen family and the discovery of the letters of Melicent Ballard and Elizabeth Austen; articles that I wrote on Jane Austen's neighbours turned up the story of Ann Newell, the plantation owning heiress of Castle Square; looking at the Austen connection with the East India Company brought to the fore Anne Middleton and Mary Lewin. Jane Austen's own letters introduced Mary Lance and the letters of Sarah Siddons, Charlotte Fitzhugh. It is often said that the characters in Jane Austen novels are so memorable because they are so real and that we all recognise them as being similar to those in our own circle. In looking at the lives of the Georgian women of Southampton they did feel familiar. Lady Bertram, Mrs Bennet, Miss Lambe, Lady Middleton are all reflected in the real women Jane knew whilst living in Southampton. Another comment made on Austen's work is that issues such as slavery, plantation ownership, war and colonial empire building are only tangentially mentioned but these issues are under the surface and not commented on enough. In looking at the lives of the women in this book the same comments could be made, on the surface the story is about balls, tea drinking, marriage and health but the issues of the day and the issues which are more to the fore in contemporary study are clearly there. Topics that at the time were so ubiquitous as not needing to be commented on directly, are woven between the letters, documents, paintings and family stories of these women. In choosing the women for this book it was important to find the original material which gave them a direct voice. For Melicent Ballard, Elizabeth Austen and Mary Lewin, we hear them through their letters; for Ann Newell and Anne Middleton, it is legal documents and contemporary newspaper articles which bring them to prominence; for the sisters-in-law Mary Lance and Charlotte Fitzhugh, it is from their celebrity friends, Jane Austen and Sarah Siddons. What we can see from all these sources are similar themes and topics: marriage and children; households and wealth; health and illness; networks and neighbourhoods.

Before delving into the women's stories, I wanted to revisit the town of Southampton in which they all lived, and put more emphasis on women's lives, from those leading society, the Marchioness of Lansdowne and the Princess Berkeley, to the daughters of the lawyer Thomas Ridding and those like Alicia Mant who, also, were writers and novelists.

ABBREVIATIONS & SHORT TITLES

SA	Southampton Archives
TNA	The National Archives
Jane Austen Letters	Deidre le Faye, *Jane Austen's Letters* (Oxford 2011)
Fitzhugh	Terrick FitzHugh, *Fitzhugh: the History of a family through six centuries* (Ottershaw 2001)
Lewin Letters	Thomas Herbert Lewin, *The Lewin Letters* Vol I & II (London 1909)
Patterson	A. Temple Patterson *A History of Southampton 1700-1914 Vol I An Oligarchy in Decline 1700-1835* (Southampton Records Series 1966)
Visitors' Descriptions	R. Douch *Visitors' Descriptions, Southampton: 1540-1956* (Southampton Papers No 2, reprinted 1978)

JANE AUSTEN IN SOUTHAMPTON

If that should be the case, we must remove to Canterbury, which I should not like as well as Southampton, Letter 8 January 1807

JANE AUSTEN WAS very familiar with the landscape of Southampton, a place where she spent time at three pivotal moments in her life. A place where she endured a near death experience; a place where the young flirtatious girl mixed with soldiers, sailors and the nouvelle riche; and finally, a place to escape the 'unmeaning luxuries of Bath' and to turn her thoughts once more to writing.[1]

As a seven-year-old child Jane Austen came to Southampton in 1783 with the woman entrusted with her early education, Mrs Cawley.[2] It was also, however, a military port, and although the sight of uniformed militia and regular soldiers, may have excited the imagination of young minds, there also lurked danger. An outbreak of typhus during their stay struck down Jane, her sister Cassandra and cousin, Jane Cooper, leading to their hasty removal

Jane Austen, National Portrait Gallery

---

1 "'Beware my Laura (she would often say) Beware of the insipid Vanities and idle Dissipations of the Metropolis of England; Beware of the unmeaning Luxuries of Bath and of the Stinking fish of Southampton'" Jane Austen *Minor Works* ed. R W Chapman revised London 1969 pp. 78-79

2 Mrs. Cawley was the sister of the Reverend Edward Cooper who had married the sister of Jane Austen's mother. Mrs. Cawley's husband, Ralph, had been Principal of Brasenose College, Oxford, but when he died his widow found herself in straightened circumstances. To supplement her income, she turned to tutoring young girls.

from the vicinity. Recent research has suggested that the girls had probably contracted endemic typhus, fortunately a disease from which the young could recover, unlike adult victims.[1] After a long illness Jane survived but her Aunt Cooper did not, after contracting the disease from her daughter and nieces. This childhood experience may had influenced the topics of fevers becoming a recurring motif in the novels: Marianne Dashwood in *Sense & Sensibility*, Tom Bertram in *Mansfield Park*, the concerns of Mr Woodhouse in *Emma*, and the characters who are sickly or imagine they are in *Pride and Prejudice* and *Sanditon*.

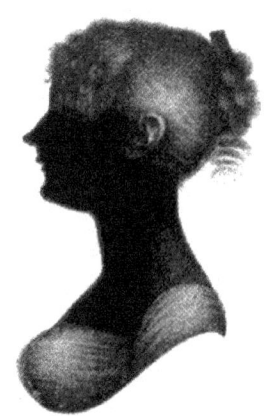

Cassandra Austen

The visit the young Austen's made to Southampton was short so it is unlikely, though not impossible, that the little party made the visit to the nearby popular visitor attraction of Netley Abbey. In 1783, however, it would

Netley Abbey, engraving by William Westall

1   Also called putrid throat or fever at the time, and a concern for Mr. Woodhouse in *Emma*, and why Mrs. Morland was concerned that Catherine wrapped up warm about the throat for her trip to Bath. See Linda Robinson Walker 'Jane Austen's Death: The Long Reach of Typhus?' *Persuasions On Line* 31.1(2010).

have required a lengthy walk and boat ride or a long carriage journey to cross the river Itchen over its only bridge at Mansbridge to reach the Abbey ruins.

When Jane was seventeen, an age which in *Love and Freindship* [*sic*] is described as 'one of the best of ages', she returned to Southampton for an extended visit.[1] Like the heroine of her novel *Northanger Abbey* Jane aged seventeen was extremely fond of Gothic novels, and was leaving her quiet village of Steventon to seek adventure abroad.[2] Her second stay in the town was much more pleasant and the company rather more prestigious. Jane's second cousin, Elizabeth Austen of Tonbridge in Kent, had married a wealthy and politically ambitious young man called John Butler Harrison II and their circle of friends included many of the East India Company families who were building houses and villas in the countryside around the town. The Butler Harrison household also included other Austen cousins, Elizabeth's sister Harriet and their brother Edgar. Similar in age to Jane, Edgar was then articled to the Southampton Town Clerk, Thomas Ridding, where he was training to be a lawyer. The recently married Elizabeth was also pregnant with her first daughter, Elizabeth Matilda, who would be born during Jane's stay and for whom she would stand as godparent.

Our knowledge of this visit is based on an aside in a letter Austen wrote some fifteen years later in 1808, by which time she was residing permanently in Southampton.[3] From this snippet we know that Jane had attended assemblies in the Dolphin Inn, which was sporting new bow windows said to be the largest in England at the time. No letters survive from this 1793 visit but, if a letter of 1795 is an indication,[4] Jane would have danced wearing silk stockings, pink silk underwear and white gloves and perhaps, like Silvianora, the heroine of the popular novel by Mrs. Sykes, be 'delighted at the prospect of exhibiting her pink dancing dress and wreath of white roses at so gay a place as Southampton' and where she promptly fell in love with a young naval officer.[5] Despite the threat of revolution and war we can only speculate that the Austen sisters took the opportunity to partake of the delights that Southampton had to offer, including the chance to visit Netley Abbey or at the very least to read of its

1 Jane Austen *Minor Works* ed. R W Chapman revised London 1969 p. 100.
2 Emily Auerbach has persuasively observed that *Northanger Abbey* was the most autobiographical of Austen novels *Searching for Jane Austen* University of Wisconsin 2004 pp. 43–44.
3 *Jane Austen Letters* p. 157
4 Claire Tomalin *Jane Austen a Life* London 2000 p. 114.
5 The author Mrs. Sykes, was well known to Jane Austen who certainly read her Gothic novel *Margiana*. Silvianora was the heroine of *Stories of Four Nations*. London 1813. See Vol II p. 127.

The Dolphin Inn

delights in the readily available pamphlets and booklets at Baker's circulating library.

In and around 1797, shortly after this extended visit to Southampton, followed by her first trip to Bath, the first version of the novel that became *Northanger Abbey* was written—a novel in which the seventeen-year-old heroine tastes the delights of a Spa and takes full advantage of the availability of Gothic novels. The manuscript, initially entitled *Susan*, was not prepared for publication until 1803 when Henry Austen persuaded the publisher Richard Crosby to take novel for a fee of £10. Unfortunately, it languished there and was not seen in print. In the meantime, in 1806, Jane Austen returned to Southampton as a resident. The move of the Austen family to Southampton was motivated primarily for monetary reasons. The widowed Mrs Austen and her two dependant daughters had been slipping down the social scale in Bath following the death of Mr Austen. Lodgings were changed to cheaper options but there was still pressure on finances and the ability to maintain a reasonable level of social engagement. When offered options to relocate which had narrowed to a move to Canterbury or to Southampton, it was Jane's preference to move to Southampton. The town had much to recommend it, not least of all its location in the county of Hampshire, the fact that it was a thriving spa and bathing resort (which must have appealed to the somewhat health obsessed Mrs Austen) and was near to the naval port of Portsmouth which was of importance to the other party in the move, Frank Austen.

The household of the widowed Mrs Austen, her two unmarried daughters and family friend Martha Lloyd joined forces with that of her son Frank and his new bride. After a short spell lodging on the main High Street – noted for its expensive rents – the family became tenants of the Marquis of Lansdowne. The pooled resources enabled them to rent a substantial property on Castle Square, which was overlooked by their landlord's overblown, pseudo medieval castle with its painting of the death of Marat which hung in the drawing room. The painting, according to the Skelton guidebook, was 'the very image of atrocity'.[1] The castle was described by *The Times* as a 'marine villa, in which, from dining hall and private bower to kitchen and scullery all was pure Gothic'.[2] The Austens could look over their garden wall and view the summer assembly rooms and baths on the West Quay. Their residence, an updated medieval tenement, was encircled by walls that were built in the Middle Ages. Although some of the towers and gates had been removed to facilitate the carriage traffic of the gentry, much of the medieval Gothic town survived, despite the fashion for covering monuments like the Bargate in stucco to make them appear more classical.

Old Southampton, by Tobias Young, Southampton Maritime and Local Heritage Collection

1 Skelton *New Edition of the Guide to Southampton; being a description of the Ancient & Present State of that Town & Neighbourhood 1816* p. 124.
2 *The Times* 2 February 1863.

The Austens were not intimates of the Marquis, but were close enough for him to offer the services of his painter Mr Huskett to make improvements to 2 Castle Square, 'Mr Huskett, Lord Lansdown'es Painter – domestic Painter I should call him, for he lives in the Castle . . . I suppose whenever the Walls want no touching up, he is employed about my lady's face.'[1] The Lady being Mary Arabella, Marchioness of Lansdowne.

The Austens began to renew old acquaintances including their cousins and made new ones like the Hills: 'Mrs Hill called on my Mother yesterday while we were gone to Chiswell' (Chessel, the home of David Lance).[2] Mrs Hill was trying to locate a Mrs Alford and her two daughters who had moved from Bath to Southampton on behalf of a Lady who had been doing some trimmings for them. Jane and her mother thought the Alfords were probably themselves: 'Mrs Hill had been applied to, as likely to give some information of them, on account of their probable vicinity to Dr Hill's Living'. Mrs Hill was the daughter of the Austens next door neighbour, Ann Newell. The Lance family are mentioned several times in Austens letters and their daughter Emma is specially referred to as she shared the name of a character Jane was working on at the time, Emma Woodhouse.

John Petty, Marquis of Lansdowne, National Portrait Gallery

Capt Francis Austen, courtesy of the Jane Austen Memorial Trust

Much speculation has been made as to why the Austens made an early acquaintance with the Lance family of Chessel House, a visit which included a river crossing and walk of some four miles to achieve, to a family to which they had no very close connection.

1 *Jane Austen Letters p. 119.*
2 *Jane Austen Letters p. 158*

Lance and his in-laws the Fitzhughs, were supercargoes for the East India Company in China and members of a whole coterie of Company families living in Southampton. Frank Austen's early naval career had taken place in the service of the East India Company, initially in India between the years 1789-93 but later in voyages to China. He went on to become the naval officer with most mentions in Company records, but at the time of the families move to Southampton he was owed money by the company. Why would Frank therefore not encourage his sisters to cultivate a relationship with influential company men such as the Lances and the Fitzhughs. That so many important company men had chosen to locate in Southampton may have contributed to the Austens deciding on the town as a place for them to reside. Not long before the family moved on from Southampton the Company voted the not unsubstantial sum of £420 to Frank to purchase a piece of plate in recognition of his services, so perhaps the possible ploy had worked.

Another Southampton based company family who would have been very familiar to the wider Austen clan were the Middletons. Nathanial Middleton was a very close associate of Warren Hastings and was resident at the court of Shuja ud-Daula, the Nawab of Oudh. Warren Hastings had been someone Jane's father knew personally and had sent his son to be educated by Mr Austen, and Hastings was the godfather and benefactor of Jane's cousin Eliza Hancock. Jane even wrote about the trial of Warren Hastings when she was just twelve years old the piece was called *The Mystery*. This was a trial in which Nathaniel Middleton was also heavily involved.

Another network of acquaintances the Austens were keen to bring into their social circle were the many captains and admirals of the Royal Navy who had also chosen to make Southampton their home. The way to progress up the naval ranks was more about who you knew than your naval competence. When Frank Austen began his career his exploits in India helped him to begin to climb the ranks making lieutenant at age eighteen, as Jane recorded in her dedication to him in her novella *Jack and Alice*.[1] In 1797 he served on the *Seahorse* captained by the friend of the family Edward Foote, Frank's sailor brother Charles owed his career advancement to Sir Thomas Williams, both these officers were also living in Southampton in the early 1800s.

> I think it would be very right in Charles to address Sir Tho. on this occasion; tho' I cannot approve of your scheme of writing to him (which you communicated to me a few nights ago) to request him to come home and convey you to

---

1 Jane Austen *Minor Works* ed. R W Chapman revised London 1969 p. 12.

Steventon. - To do you justice however, you had some doubts of the propriety of such a measure yourself.[1]

Another supporter of the brothers, Admiral Bertie, was also living in the town at the new development called The Polygon, which development was financed by the East India Company officer General Carnac. Carnac was a mutual friend of Jane's Aunt Philadelphia, and Margaret Clive, wife of Robert Clive. Carnac wrote to Margaret around the gossip circulating about the paternity of Philadephia's daughter Eliza, who some thought was the child of Warren Hastings.[2]

Vice-Admiral Sir Edward James Foote, National Maritime Museum, Greenwich

Philadelphia Austen Hancock, Courtesy of Rowan and Rowan

Frank was owed money by the navy in 1806, he had missed out in fighting at the battle of Trafalgar in 1805 but had been successful in seizing a prize ship, but had not received his percentage. That along with being put on half pay following the naval success at Trafalgar, which neutralized the French fleet for the foreseeable future, was another contributing financial factor to the joint household being set up in 1806. Jane and Cassandra kept up with the exploits of the navy but also those officers who could provide future support to their brothers' careers. Thomas Williams had been knighted after a successful naval engagement on *HMS Unicorn* in 1796, when Charles Austen was also part of the crew. He was a hero, was

1 *Jane Austen Letters p. 26*
2 "Would You believe it, Madam, Mrs. Hancock is pregnant. The scandalous chronicle gives the credit thereof to Hastings . . ." 1761.

wealthy and was also a widower after the tragic death of Jane Cooper, the Austen's first cousin and their former schoolmate, in a traffic accident in 1798. He had invested in a country property on the outskirts of Southampton called Brooklands, and perhaps was also considered a potential partner to one or other of the Austen sisters. His decision to marry after a few years as a widower

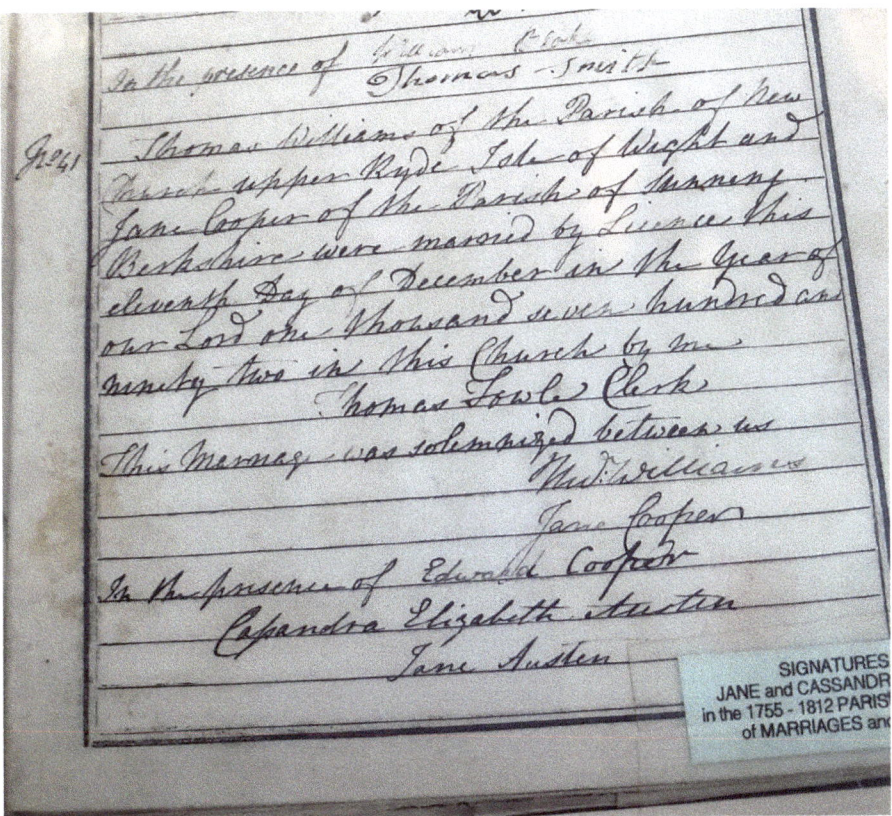

The Steventon Marriage Register, marriage of Jane Cooper & Thomas Williams

to a family of note within the church and legal profession but not at this point with naval connections was of considerable interest to the Austens. Would this marriage remove them from his sphere of interests, would members of his future bride's family the Wapshares have a better claim on him, would there be others whose careers would take precedence? There was much discussion in Jane's letters about the identity of the bride-to-be:

> It is reported at Portsmouth that Sir T Williams is to be married. - It has been reported indeed twenty times before, but Charles is inclined to give some credit

to it now, as they hardly ever see him on board, and he looks very much like a Lover.-¹

Mary Wapshare had been born in February 1777 and was christened in Salisbury Cathedral on 15th October 1778, the daughter of Charles Wapshare and Mary Sandford. Despite Jane's concerns that the lady not wealthy and was past her prime – she was twenty-three and her husband to be thirty-nine – the couple married in Salisbury Cathedral on the 12 December 1800. Their marital home was the recently refurbished Brooklands. Jane's letter of 1807 when the family were firmly ensconced in Southampton suggested the Williams were not as friendly as they might have been.

> ... and Captain Foote has a particular dislike to underdone mutton; but he was so good humoured and pleasant that I did not much mind his being starved. he gives us the most cordial invitation to his house in the country, saying just what the Williams ought to say to make us welcome. Of them we have seen nothing since you left us and we hear that they are just gone to Bath again, to be out of the way of further alterations at Brooklands.²

Like Frank, Williams was also employed in commanding a force of Sea Fencibles, local mariners under the command of a naval officer who were to provide a line of coastal defence should the French invade. Williams did introduce the Austens to his deputy Mr Edward-Walpole Browne, but only at that man's request: 'The Browns are added to our list of acquaintance; he commands the Sea Fencibles here under Sir Tho. and was introduced at his own desire by the latter when we saw him last week.'³ On the eve of their move to Chawton the family were still tracking Sir Thomas's career, but their disapproval of Mary was evident.

> A letter from Hamstall gives us the history of Sir Tho. Williams return; the Admiral, whoever he might be, took a fancy to the Neptune, and having only a worn out 74 to offer in lieu of it. Sir Tho. declined such a command, and is come home passenger. Lucky man! to have so fair an opportunity to escape. I hope his Wife allows herself to be happy on this occasion, and does not give all her thoughts to being nervous.⁴

1 *Jane Austen Letters p. 59*
2 *Jane Austen Letters p. 115*
3 *Jane Austen Letters p 121.*
4 *Jane Austen Letters p. 172*

The Austens welcomed visitors and relations to their new Southampton home and took some to Netley Abbey. The Abbey was even more popular as an attraction than during Jane's earlier visits. John Bullar had written *A Companion in a Visit to Netley Abbey*. There was even more poetry and prose, although not always of the highest calibre. William Lisle Bowles set his *Fairy Sketch*, with its references to Titania and Queen Mab, at Netley Abbey. Jane's niece Fanny Knight recorded 'We all except Grandmama, took a boat and went to Netley Abbey, the ruins of which look beautiful. We ate some biscuits we had taken, and returned home quite delighted.' Fanny extolled the virtues of Netley: 'never was there anything in the known world to be compared to that compound of every thing that is striking ancient and majestic'. She maintained they were all struck dumb with admiration, which may have been why Aunt Jane was quiet on the subject.[1]

The delights of Southampton as a watering place must have pleased Mrs Austen given her pre-occupation with her own health, and she would have been delighted to read that the town was 'well known' to the medical profession as being a highly suitable location for the 'first great class of invalids'; that is to say those affected with pulmonary diseases who were recommended to make it their winter residence.

The Austen household at Southampton had first hand evidence of the ravages of the disease of smallpox in the person of Martha Lloyd who had come to live with the family after the death of her mother. Martha and her siblings had contracted smallpox when they were children, her brother had died and she and her sisters were left with the tell-tale scars on their faces.[2] Jane Austen and her family and friends passed an evening entertaining themselves with readings from Edward Jenner's paper on the subject.[3] In 1813 Jane's niece Caroline met Jenner at Cheltenham and was revaccinated by him 'I had therefore the honour of a second operation from the hands of the great discoverer himself: and at the end of the whole process, he pronounced it had been all right before.'[4] They must have been pleased that Southampton had by subscription financed an inoculation programme aimed at the servants and working people of the town. The weather around their new home was often bracing and Jane wrote about Castle-Square weather with its strong winds from the North West and

---

1   David Selwyn *Jane Austen and Leisure* London 1999 p. 53
2   Irene Collins *Jane Austen: The Parson's Daughter* London 1998 p. 95
3   *Jane Austen Letters* p. 62
4   Valerie Grosvenor Myer *Jane Austen, Obstinate Heart: A Biography* New York 1997 p. 87

reported that her brother 'Frank has got a very bad cough, for an Austen'.[1] Later however Jane had her character Tom Parker pronounce 'where Bathing disagreed, the Sea Breeze alone was evidently designed by Nature for the cure'.[2]

The Austen family consulted with at least two doctors during their time in Southampton. Jane reported she had been cured by a prescription of Mr Lyford, a member of a large medical family of that name practising in Hampshire.[3] His treatments included oil of sweet almonds, still used today to treat burns and skin complaints, and in 1808 he also treated Jane for an ear infection.[4] Cassandra was also medicating herself with bark of cinchona, a patent medicine developed by the physician John Huxham, used for the treatment of putrid throat, probably in this case diphtheria or possibly Cassandra was also experiencing the long-term after effects of her childhood brush with endemic typhus; the bark is also a source of quinine.[5] Jane makes mention of a female chemist among their acquaintance, a Mrs Hookey.[6] Elizabeth Hookey was for some time in partnership with the chemist and druggist Charles Moon and when that partnership ended in 1807, as reported in the London Gazette (part II 1402), Moon went on to work with another chemist, Thomas Randall, before setting up on his own at 169 High Street. Moon planned to keep 'genuine articles, and charging moderate prices. Physicians' Prescriptions and Family Recipes will, as usual be attended to.' This illustrates that no difference was seen between medicines supplied by medical practioners and home cures handed down through families. Moon meanwhile also combined this duty as a druggist with being a dealer in British Wines as he advertised in the *Salisbury & Winchester Journal* on the 29th August 1808. Jane also reported that a new physician had arrived in the town and set up at 170 High Street, his name was Dr Percival, and he was the son of a renowned Manchester physician.[7]

The recipes for the medicines were closely guarded secrets and even led to disputes. William Randall who had produced his own medicine chest for the use of digestive problems, threatened his rival Mr Gillmore with the law for passing off a patent medicine of Randall's as his own. Mr Gillmore was in partnership at the time with Jane Austen's acquaintance Mrs Hookey, when Randall circulated a hand-bill accusing him of malpractice. Gillmore maintained, in a handbill of his own, that a customer had attended with an

1 *Jane Austen Letters* p. 123
2 Jane Austen *Minor Works* ed. R W Chapman revised London 1969 p. 373
3 *Jane Austen Letters* p. 140.
4 *Jane Austen Letters* p. 144.
5 *Jane Austen Letters* p. 127
6 *Jane Austen Letters* p. 161.
7 *Jane Austen Letters* p. 145

> CAUTION to the PUBLIC, to prevent their being deceived by Spurious and Counterfeit Medicines.
>
> *Dec. 1809.*
>
> Mr. GILLMORE (of the Firm of HOOKEY and GILLMORE, Chemists and Druggists, Southampton,) having taken the unwarrantable Liberty of preparing and selling a certain Medicine, purporting, by a printed Label, and Stamp on the Bottle, to have been prepared by WM. RANDALL, Chemist and Druggist, of the same Town ; and having refused to make a public Acknowledgment of the Impropriety and Injustice of such Conduct; Mr. RANDALL is obliged, in Justice to himself and the Public, to caution his Friends against any future Deceptions of a similar Nature. He also assures Mr. Gillmore, that, if such Practices are persisted in, a Prosecution must follow : but, *in Consequence of the Solicitation of an anonymous Friend of Mr. Gillmore, who pleads that he is a Young Man*, Mr. Randall will not proceed against him for the present Offence, being well persuaded that *Young Men have but little Experience.*
>
> BAKER and FLETCHER, Printers.

Randall & Gilmore advertisement

empty bottle, but with a Randall label, for a lotion for 'cutaneous eruption'. Gillmore had made up the lotion but 'in the hurry of business' omitted to change the label. In the end Randall, with some scathing comments on the ignorance of youth, accepted Gillmore's apology.[1]

One of Jane Austen's preferred remedies was the popular calomel treatment, this however had disturbing side effects as its main ingredient was powdered mercury which could cause loose teeth, an ashen appearance, and tremors of the face and even a change in personality.[2] Emma Clery suggests there was a strong possibility that she was self- medicating with calomel at the time of her death.[3] The Austens landlord the Marquis of Lansdowne died the same year that Jane Austen moved to Chawton, in November 1809, his ill-health was commented on by Jane in 1808, 'The Marquise has put off being cured for another year'.[4]

As Jane prepared to leave Southampton for her final home at Chawton, her thoughts turned to the manuscript of Susan still languishing with the publisher Crosby. Were those thoughts prompted by her return to Southampton, where she had danced, aged seventeen, enjoying the delights of a fashionable Spa? Or was it because she was living under the shadow of a Gothic Castle with an eccentric owner, whose wife, like a female John Thorpe, careered around the tiny Castle Square on her light phaeton?[5] Whatever prompted her, in 1809

---

1 Southampton Archives, Page & Moody collection, Handbill December 1809; Legal letter from Thomas Ridding to Mr Gillmore 15th December 1809; Handbill January 12th 1810. W Randall *Medical Observations, adapted to the Medicine Chests, fitted out by William Randall, Chemist, Southampton* 1795.
2 Lydia Kang *Quackery: A Brief History of the Worst Ways to Cure Everything* New York 2017.
3 Emma Clery *The Bankers Sister* London 2017, pp. 250, 299
4 *Jane Austen Letters* p. 142.
5 James Edward Austen-Leigh in his memoir of a visit to the Castle Square house described the Marchioness and her "light phaeton drawn by six, and sometimes

Chawton Cottage

she posted a letter from Baker's emporium on the Southampton High Street requesting the return of *Susan*.¹ The publishers in turn requested the return of their £10. Jane's brother Henry eventually retrieved the manuscript, and it was he who suggested the revised name, *Northanger Abbey*.

When Jane Austen began work on her last and sadly unfinished novel *Sanditon* and as her health failed, she must have reflected on her time spent in Southampton and other bathing and spa resorts, and remembered the extravagant promises made about the health-giving attributes of sea air and sea waters. Maybe she was hoping to again visit her Southampton relations and to convalesce by the water for as she made Tom Parker pronounce about Sanditon, the sea, and sea bathing: 'Nobody could catch cold by the Sea; nobody wanted appetite by the Sea; nobody wanted Spirits; nobody wanted Strength. Sea air was healing, softening, relaxing, fortifying and bracing.'²

There were several benefits to the Austens of living in a bustling town and the networking opportunities that this gave to them, at a time when who

    eight little ponies, each pair decreasing in size, and becoming lighter in colour, through all the grades of dark brown, light brown, bay and chestnut," which he described as a "fairy equipage" *Memoir of Jane Austen* London 1987 p. 83.
1 *Jane Austen Letters* p. 174-175.
2 Jane Austen *Minor Works* ed. R W Chapman revised London 1969 p. 373

you knew was of more importance that what you knew. These friends and neighbours could provide inspiration for an aspiring writer both in regard to characters and potential plots. In looking at the lives of contemporary women in her circle, it also goes someway to explaining what details Jane Austen could leave unsaid in her novels on the influence of war, of plantation wealth and the omnipotence of the East India Company that were so ubiquitous as to be unremarkable to a contemporary reader.

THE WATERING PLACE OF SOUTHAMPTON

I therefore have seen only enough of this place to dislike it. Its inhabitants are people connected with shipping - & sharking shopkeepers – its visitors the very top scum of aristocracy[1] Robert Southey

THE STORY OF Southampton in the eighteenth century is something of an aberration. In the hundreds of years before and in the centuries since, the town was always about the port and trade. It was the reason why it was founded and why it became wealthy and successful, but in the seventeenth century its trade had collapsed, and its economy was reduced. As Daniel Defoe commented 'Southampton was in a manner dying with age; the decay of the trade is the real decay of the town'. He did believe that the High Street was noble and the town could entertain great numbers of people.[2] The 1715 edition of Camden's *Britannia* reported that its fine houses, rich inhabitants and busy harbour were now things of the past.[3] To revive the town's fortune it was necessary to re-invent the ancient port and a growing interest in sea-bathing provided a new opportunity. The one thing the town did have was access to water which surrounded it to the east, south and west, even if at low tide, it was also marshy and a little malodourous as was reported later in the *Lady's Magazine* of July 1772:

> A SENTIMENTAL JOURNEY BY A LADY
> The rooms in which the balls are held, are very spacious, and capable of entertaining a great deal of company, but with regard to the architecture, I could see nothing worthy of praise. The prospect towards the New Forest is

1 Lynda Pratt, Tim Fulford & Ian Packer *The Collected Letters of Robert Southey: p. 218 Robert Southey to Grosvenor Charles Bedford 1797* www.romantic-circles/editions_letters 2009
2 *Visitors' Descriptions* p. 11.
3 E R Aubrey (ed) *Speed's History of Southampton* Southampton Record Society 1909, p. v.

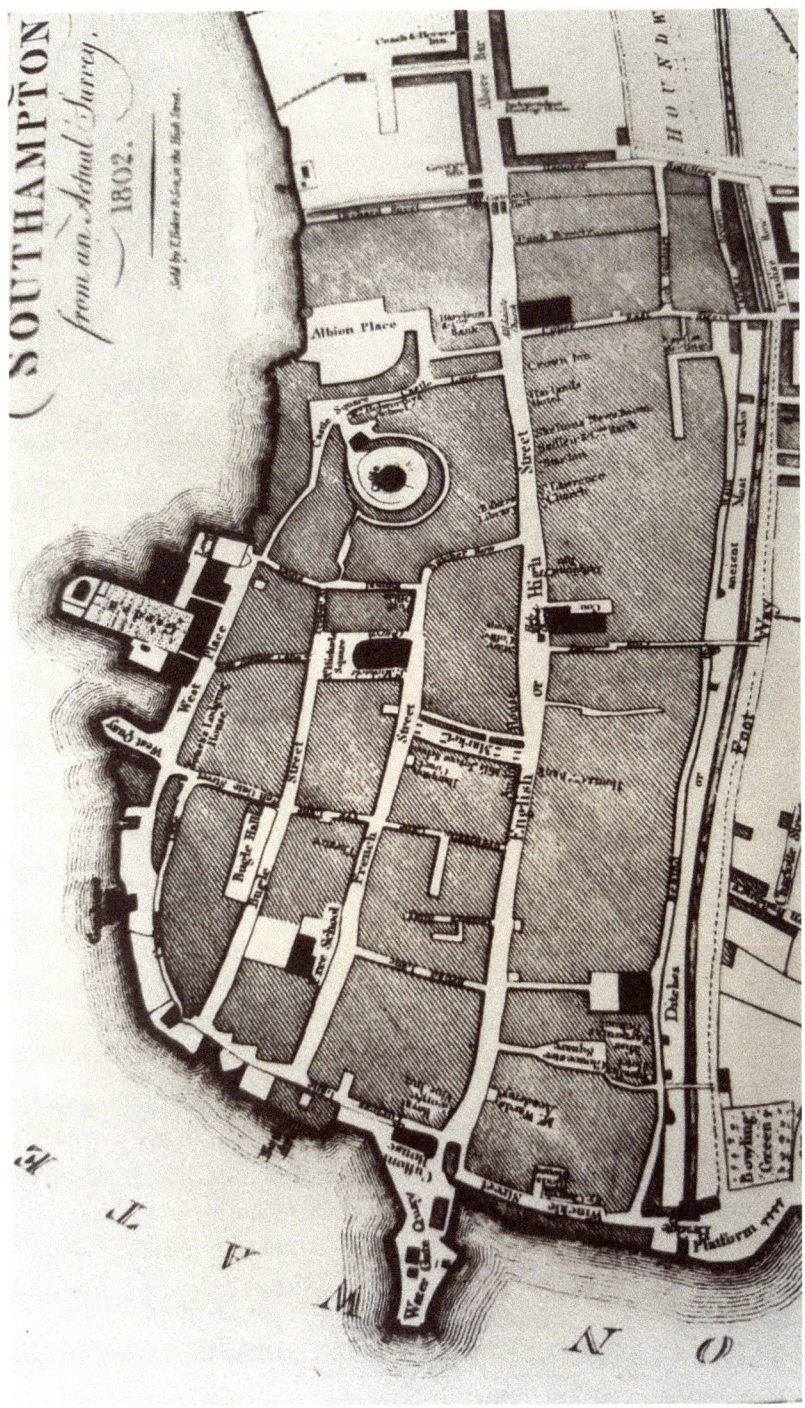

Map of Southampton 1802

View of Southampton West Walls, by unknown artist

pleasing; but as it was about the time of low-water on a warm day when we were there, the smell was somewhat disagreeable.[1]

Being on the south coast the town had an equitable climate, if on occasion, it was buffeted by the wind. As the guides later pronounced: 'When other watering places are deserted on account of their bleakness, this still offers the advantages of the sea coast, combined with the warmth of an inland town.'

The town could claim to have the royal patronage of the heir to the throne when Frederick Prince of Wales and his children made a visit in 1750. The royal party were made honorary burgesses and even Frederick's death the next year did nothing to dampen the enthusiasm of royal dukes and aristocrats from returning to Southampton. Other visitors flocked to the town following the lead given by the royal family which soon put pressure on the limited number of lodgings available. The *Universal British Directory* reported that: 'The inhabitants vie with each other in fitting up their houses in the best and most genteel manner to accommodate the company; and the shopkeepers are

1 SA D/S 19/1/1 pp. 168-191. The *Lady's Magazine* was first published in 1770.

equally strenuous to excel in the elegance of their shops and display of their goods.'

This shortage saw an increase in rents as well as availability:

> The people of Southampton undergo many inconveniences, through the scarcity of houses of this description; being under the necessity of either residing in disagreeably confined houses with scarcely any outlet, and the rents often unreasonably high.[1]

Or, as the visiting poet Thomas Gray quipped in 1764, 'lodgings very dear, and fish very cheap'.[2] Gray also complained that at this point there were no coffee houses, booksellers or pastrycooks.[3] The lack of coffee houses was soon rectified with coffee rooms available at the George Inn in Above Bar and the Sun Inn near town quay. Even as late as 1811, however, the *Hampshire Chronicle* reported 'a great number of visitors are daily resorting here, many of whom are obliged, however, again to leave it, without alighting from their carriage, in consequence of the want of room to accommodate them'.

The Bar, Southampton

Southampton as a destination became much more accessible in the late eighteenth century due to both improvements in the road system and the

---

1 Baker's Guide 1818 p. 46n. *Universal British Directory* 1792-8 p. 458.
2 *Visitors' Description* p. 15.
3 The *Hampshire Chronicle* 2 September 1811.

increase in coach traffic. In the early 1770s diligences were popular being fast but they could only accommodate four people. The arrival of the mail coaches meant the provision of spaces for up to 25 passengers on the double coaches, although these were much slower. By the early nineteenth century journey times were falling.

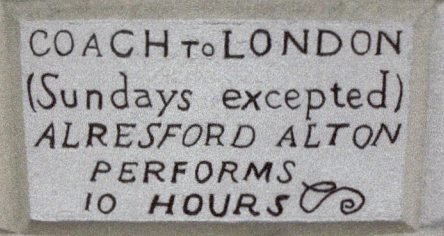

Coaching Plaque, & The Star Hotel

The journey from London to Southampton was cut from fourteen and a half hours in the 1770s to just eight hours in the 1820s. Average passenger numbers went up from 6.7 in the winter to 13.3 in the summer in the period 1772-99 and up to 9.7 in the winter and 14 in the summer in the period 1800-1820. There is a surviving plaque on The Star coaching inn on the High Street which proclaims 'Coach to London (Sundays excepted) Alresford Alton performs ten hours'. There were races between coaches coming down Above Bar to make the narrow entrance to the High Street via the Bargate first so they could claim to offer the fastest service. The importance of Southampton as a destination and the number of journeys did rise but then plateaued but this had more to do with the shortage of horses and the rising cost of provender due to the Revolutionary and Napoleonic Wars.[1]

In 1774, when Southampton's popularity as a resort was at its height, the number of houses in the town was around 705, all but 120 within the old

---

1 M J Freeman 'Stagecoach system of South Hampshire 1775-1851' in *Journal of Historical Geography I, 3* 1975 pp. 264, 266, 278-9.

medieval walls. By 1810 this had doubled to 1505 and the local population had also risen from around 3000 to 7629 souls.[1] This increase was not always appreciated by wealthy residents such as Lady Lansdowne who had wanted to demolish a hundred houses around the family's Southampton home, Lansdowne's Castle, to improve the view.[2] A newspaper article in the *Basingstoke Gazette* of 1809 and the *Gentleman's Magazine* remarked that the castle 'has no

Southampton High Street, by G F Sargent

ground, and the base is entirely blocked up with small houses of the poorer inhabitants, and it is with difficulty that any door of entrance can be discovered'. Moy Thomas visiting in 1810 thought it 'situated in the worst part of the Town, very confined and surrounded with mean little hovels occupied by the lowest description of poor people'.[3] In the meantime, the town fathers wanted to provide additional facilities in the town to encourage more visitors and to give them a better experience. An act of parliament instigated the Pavement Commission which was designed not only to improve the pavements around the main streets in the town but also support the development of new facilities

1   Guide 1810 pp. 55-57. The Census records the population growth 1801: 7913, 1811: 9617, 1821: 13,353. F J G Hearnshaw & F Clarke *A Short History of Southampton* Oxford 1910 pp. 114, 119.
2   R A Austen-Leigh *Jane Austen and Southampton* London 1949 p. 19.
3   *Visitors' Description* p. 23.

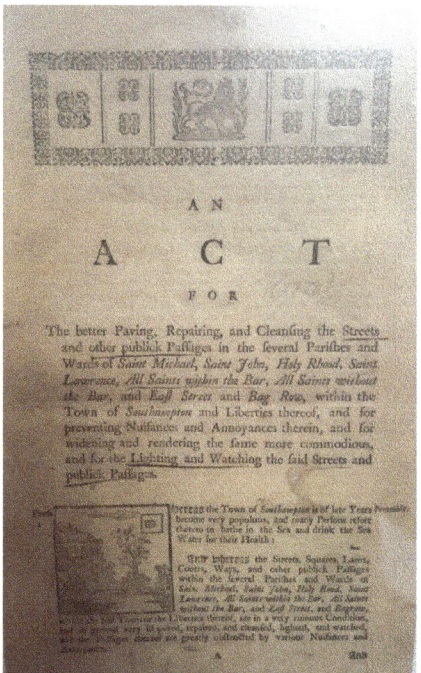

Act for Paving

and to control some of the improvements which residents had added to their properties, such as bow windows. George Lipscombe who visited the town in 1799 remarked that: 'The High-Street is very broad and well paved, but the houses would look much better if the custom of building circular fronts and throwing out immense bow-windows was less prevalent.'[1] The commissioners ordered street signs and numbering be introduced, and oversaw the taking down of some of the medieval towers and gates to facilitate the laying down of pavements, pebbles and horse flatners.[2] They also improved the collection and disposal of dirt and night soil, made repairs to dripping gutters and pipes, removed hog sties and instigated better street lighting. They even paid money to prevent the foreman of the pavement builders from being impressed into the navy. As one observer commented: 'Southampton has always been remarked as a very neat town; and it is now much improved by the London method of paving'.[3]

The entrance to the town, known as The Avenue, was laid out in 1745 and as William Gilpin noted 'the beauty of the avenue' leading out of Southampton and 'the idea of an avenue as a connecting thread between a town and a country is a good one'.[4] The Beach was 'beautified' in 1769

---

1   In 1796 when John Butler Harrison was president of the commissioners, he received a request from Mr Green and Mr Elkins to bring their storehouse closer to their property on the High Street. On 21 September 1808 the Marquis of Lansdowne gave permission for a bow window on Mr Suckett's house at the corner of Castle Square. SA SC/AP 1/2. George Lipscomb *A Journey into Cornwall through the Counties of Southampton, Wilts, Dorset, Somerset and Devon* London 1799 p. 15.
2   Larger stones used to give a stronger base and smoother ride. J Stovold *The Minute Book of the Pavement Commissioner for Southampton 1770-1789* Southampton Records Series 1966 p. vii. The East gate was demolished in 1776 and the Water Gate in 1806.
3   'A Sentimental Journey by a Lady' in *Lady's Magazine* 1773.
4   William Gilpin *Observations of the western parts of England, relative chiefly to*

as a walk for the benefit of visitors and ran from the Platform down to the Cross House, a covered space where people waited to take the ferry across the River Itchen. The repairs and work undertaken to the walkway in 1769 cost £40 and Robert Ballard Jnr. was given the role of treasurer. The town's first Directory, Cunningham's Directory of Southampton for 1803, had observed that: 'Loungers will find above bar, the polygon, the beach, and the quays, very healthy walks'.

The Beach

Despite the restrictions in the topography of the town, opportunities for socialising were maximized. To the aristocratic visitors, were added the emerging middle classes with their disposable incomes, and the classes began to mix in social settings, as R H Sweet commented:

> In many towns tradesmen had been excluded from participation in assemblies, but in a number of places such as Derby, Stamford, Bury St Edmunds, Southampton or Hull, the tradesmen themselves established their own assembly rooms with room and rituals to match those of the gentry.[1]

Soon coffee shops, public libraries, a theatre and new shops began to appear. New warehouses took over older buildings such as the old stables on

picturesque beauty London 1798 p. 352.
1   R H Sweet 'Topographies of Politeness' *Transactions of the Royal Historical Society*, Vol 12: 355-374.

All Saints Church

Winkle Street, which became the silk shop and carpet weavers.[1] Churches were enlarged and even rebuilt and some new developments were proposed to increase the accommodations.[2] Branches of London shops were persuaded to locate in the town during the season and prompted local shopkeepers in 1805 to improve their offer:

> Many of the shops rival those of the metropolis ... the shopkeepers are equally strenuous to excel in the elegance of their shops and displays of their goods. Strangers in general are exceedingly struck at the size and the very superior appearance of the shops has in this town nor are they less so on viewing the abundant stocks of goods with which they are stocked.[3]

Shopkeepers were brought before the authorities for transgressing onto the highway, for example, in 1810 James Hawkins a linendraper obstructed the High Street by hanging 3 shawls and four pieces of muslin on a cord in front of his bow window.[4] Some local shopkeepers did overreach themselves. In 1784 John Kunnison was declared bankrupt at a hearing held at the Star Coaching Inn (a medieval inn that had been given a make-over and new frontage of stucco and sash windows). Kunnison was by trade a wine merchant and leather

1 SA D/PM 64 /1.
2 SA SC9/4/654.
3 Baker's Guide 1805. See also *Patterson* p. 58.
4 SA SC9/4/654.

manufacturer but expanded to develop a fabric warehouse and shop on St Michael's Square. In 1775 he was boasting, 'an elegant assortment of half-ell and three-quarter Lustring and Ducapes, Tobined and brocaded silks, etc.' but in 1784 his establishment was forced to close and to sell off stock at a 15% reduction to save the expense of returning it to London.[1] In 1788 Andrew Nance, a hatter, hosier, dealer and chapman, went bankrupt owing suppliers from Bristol, London, Nottingham, Salisbury, and Southwark.[2]

Shortage of accommodation led to a great expansion in building, by gentlemen builders as well as local entrepreneurs. Walter Taylor, who made his fortune in making blocks for naval ships and carriages for cannon, branched out into the building of new houses named Hanover Buildings on the old Lammas lands at Hoglands. The architect John Plaw developed the area around the old castle walls as Albion Place. Wealthy East India Company General

The Polygon

John Carnac planned a magnificent hotel on the outskirts of Southampton with fifty good bedchambers and stabling for 500 horses, ballroom, eating rooms and twelve grand houses built in an octogen around a central square.[3] It

1 *London Gazette* 12 October 1784, Salisbury Journal 12th October 1772. Tambour was material stretched on a tabour frame on which patterns were then embroidered Lustring was a glossy silk fabric and ducape a stouter silk material.
2 SA D/PM 14/ 1 & 2.
3 Baker's Guide 1795 pp. 135-6. The General also offered the town a loan of two thousand pounds in 1771 – without interest – in aid of the poor, which was refused as £500 had been offered each by Lord Palmerston and Mr Stanley. Jan Stovold *The Minute Book of The Pavement Commissioners for Southampton 1770-*

was designed by Jacob Leroux, the architect of Great Russell Street in London, and each villa had a garden of one acre with views across the countryside and river and also had a central lake lying at the back of the houses.[1]

> Tuesday morning we went to Southampton to see the new building called the Polygon: 'tis a fine thing, and every house has a most beautiful view of the sea and town of Southampton - *Mrs James Harris 1771*.[2]

Not all of these speculations were successful. Plaw never completed his Albion Place project and moved to America and The Polygon was considered to be too far out of town and not able to attract and sustain the right level of tenant to enable the scheme to be completed. Mrs James Harris's letter on the subject reported that 'some make exceptions to the distance' and that three coaches were to be laid on at 3d a head to convey people to the weekly balls.[3] In the event only three houses were built, two of which were occupied by the developers Isaac Mallortie and Carnac. Mrs Lybbe Powys believed if completed it 'would have been one of the first places in the kingdom, perhaps the world, regarded in the view of modern architecture'. The hotel was later converted to provide two more houses. Isaac Mallortie along with Carnac, as the two backers of the scheme, were financially ruined. The remains of the hotel were demolished by 1775.[4]

By 1781, however, the guide books trumpeted:

> There is no neighbourhood in Great Britain where politeness, good breeding, harmony and friendship reign so universally, and are so productive of undisguised confidence and undisturbed tranquillity .... Most gentlemen of the neighbourhood are men of fortune, independence and generosity.

The town soon became encircled with gentlemen's seats and country houses, many paid for from the fortunes made in the East India Company, men such as David Lance of Chessel House, his compatriot William Fitzhugh of Bannisters, Thomas Lewin at Ridgeway Castle and Nathaniel Middleton at Town Hill Park. Many of the houses were built in the classic Palladian style

1789 Southampton Records Series 1900 p. 33.
1. Jan Stovold 'Building Developments in Southampton 1750-1830: The Impact of the Spa' Unpublished Thesis, University of Southampton 1984, pp. 50-53.
2. *Visitors' Descriptions* p. 16,
3. *Visitors' Description* p. 16.
4. Mrs Philip Lybbe Powys of Hardwick House *Passages from the Diaries* ed Emily Climenson London 1899 p. 273.

favoured by the period's architects, but others took their inspiration from the gothic, from the small houses such as the Lewin's Ridgeway Castle to the fantasy built on the site of the medieval Southampton castle, the inspiration of the Marquis of Lansdowne, the premier resident of Southampton:

> This stands near the middle of the south part of the town. From the High-street, the approach to it is up Castle-lane. The area of the castle seems to be of a semi-circular form, of which the town wall to the sea, formed the diameter. The keep stood on a very high artificial mount, and from its ruins a small round tower has been constructed, from the leads of which there is a delightful bird's-eye view of Southampton, and of the environs, lying like a map before the eye of the spectator[1]

The new castle included a banqueting room with imitation bronzes, a kitchen with Saxon architecture and a gothic dining room with a glass painted portrait of George III by a Mr Pearson.[2] This led into a chapel dedicated to St Peter. The drawing room was dominated by a picture of the French Revolutionary leader Marat. The whole building was surmounted by a small turret with a 36ft flag pole.[3] The Marquis, however, seems to have built his castle without much concern for design or sensible building methods:

> The noble owner was accustomed to treat with great good humour the strictures which he occasionally happened to overhear, on his placing so costly a mansion in a situation to which there was no convenient approach in any direction, by pleading the privilege of a 'hobby'. The fact is the building was originally begun without a definite plan, and was intended to be on a small scale, till his lordship found too much amusement in extending it, that it gradually became what it finally was.[4]

1 John Feltham *A Guide to all the Watering and Seabathing Places for 1813 Vol 2* London1813 p. 381.
2 There is a stained-glass window panel of George III seated on a throne painted by James Pearson in the Royal Collection. It was sold in 1795 and auctioned again in 1805, it is not known how it ended up in the Royal Collection but was probably sold by the Marchioness.
3 Skelton's Guide 1816, pp. 124-5. A fuller description of the interior of the castle can be found in the sale catalogue of 1816, Wiltshire and Swindon Archives 451/226.
4 Sir Henry Englefield *A Walk Through Southampton* London new edition 1841 p. 48.

View of Southampton 1819

As Lady Bessborough described Lansdowne's creation:

> a room erected at Southampton Castle after the manner of the Moorish architecture at Granada, the castle is built with brick, covered in white composition. The round tower and upper apartments command a fine view of the Southampton estuary, the river Itchen and the surrounding country but it has no ground and the base is entirely blocked up with small houses belonging to the poorer inhabitants. It is a marine villa, in which, from dining hall and private bower to kitchen and scullery all was pure Gothic [1]

The popularity of the town as a resort for both visitors and for new more permanent inhabitants was enhanced after the 'discovery' of a chalybeate spring and thereafter Southampton could promote itself not only as a sea bathing resort but also as a spa town.[2] The Universal British Directory locates the spring at the bottom of Orchard Street near to the shore and reports that it has remarkable cures and not only in disorders peculiar to chalybeates including scurvies, leprosies and scrofula. The water had a corrugating taste, turned vegetable astringent tinctures black and contracted and hardened all the vascular and soft fibrous parts of the body. North east from the Bargate, in Houndwell, were two further springs, one a spring of fresh water, the other

1   Recorded in *The Times* 1 February 1863.
2   Baker's Guide 1815 pp. 53-54.

suitable for curing disorders of the eyes. There was also another spring in the same field, Friar's Spring, which after repairs paid for by George Vincent, Esq, was now providing clear, drinkable water.[1]

It was however sea bathing that was the big draw for visitors, inspiring poetry that was included in the promotional guides.

> See! to the Baths what frequent Crowds resort
> Groaning beneath the varied Rod of Pain,
> (Tyrannic, dire, inexorable Fiend]
> And wash their ills away. *from Dr Cosens, Essay of Economy & Beauty, 1770*

The promotion and adverts worked drawing in visitors from all classes.

> Miss Ingram is a great deal better & is now gone to Southampton to bathe in the sea, which will I hope soon restore her to perfect health – *Barbara Johnson to George Johnson September 1777*[2]

The aristocratic visitors being very happy to socialise with local merchants such as Robert Ballard:

> The Duke of Chandos,[3] & your Cousin Penton came to dine, his Grace told your Uncle, that the Dutchess is to spend a week here, for change of air, as she has been very ill – *Melicent Ballard, 1781*

Sea bathing all around the coast was popular, but some sites were more informal than Southampton, places such as Babbacombe visited by the Lewins in 1800:[4]

> We not unfrequently spent the summer's afternoon en famille at Babbicomb, a romantic little bay to the north of Torbay, where only a few poor fisher-folk then lived, and a few labourers in the limestone quarries there, out of

---

1 *Universal British Directory* p. 459. The Directory was the work of Peter Barfoot a gentleman resident at Droxford near Winchester and John Wilkes proprietor of the *Hampshire Chronicle* in 1778-83 and 1791-95.
2 Bodleian Library Ms.Don.c193 23 Johnson Family.
3 James Brydges, third Duke of Chandos, his second wife Anna Gamon an heiress of the Hope sugar plantation, was declared a lunatic in 1791. In 1789 her husband had died from injuries he received when his wife inadvertently moved the chair he was about to sit in. The Chandos main estate was at Avington near Winchester.
4 *Lewin Letters* Vol II p. 126.

which very pretty marble was dug. We children used to be sent into the water, although we were never taught to swim. We wore no bathing dresses; every one at that time, both men and women, bathed naked in separate bathing coves, and there were no bathing machines – *Harriet Lewin 1800*

Even towns like Weymouth, popularized by George III, persisted in nude bathing until the press of visitors led to a petition for modesty clothing. In Southampton bathing was more formal with long green flannel gowns and oil silk fillets, for the ladies, to hold in their curls and flannel shirts and breeches for the men.[1] The numbers of bath houses in the town grew, offering both warm and cold baths. Dean's Baths at West Quay promised the availability

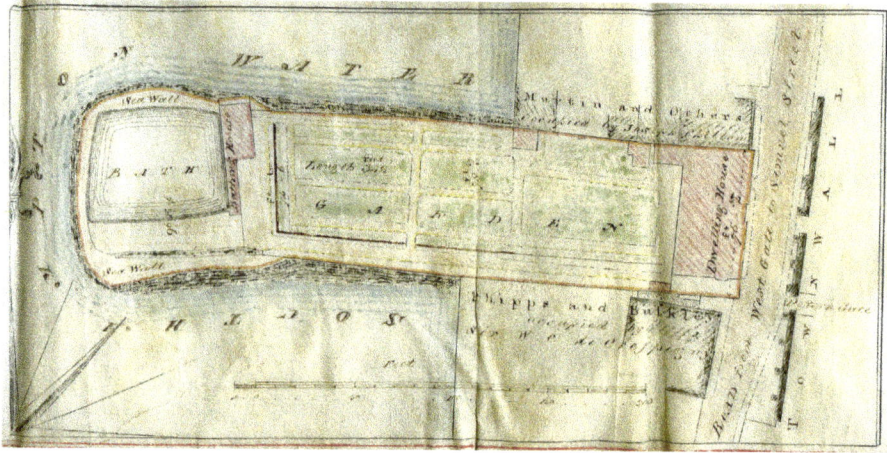

Plan of the Bathing House & Long Room, Southampton Archives

of five hours of cold baths a day with each tide. Webb's baths also on the old west quay had hot and cold baths. There were baths at the back of Portland Street and in 1802 new bathing machines were established on the marsh. There were also baths across the other side of the river Itchen at Itchen Ferry village established in 1816 and, towards the end of the popularity of sea bathing, the new Gloucester Baths were constructed near The Beach.[2] Sea bathing was encouraged for its medicinal benefits. As the guides proclaimed:

Cold Bathing or Sea Bathing is more effectual than medicine, helping with semi-paralysis, rheumatism, gout. The waters should be applied as a dry douche. It is absolutely essential to maintain a quiescent posture whilst undergoing treatment, to fatigue the body by undue movement during treatment will

1 *Visitors' Descriptions* p. 16.
2 Arthur Freeling *Picturesque Excursions* London 1839 pp. 48, 51-52.

greatly mitigate against good results.

People who wet their bodies with sea water and then put their clothes onto their wet bodies will not catch cold! If you allow salt water to dry on your skin, leaving behind a soft crust, this will prevent all manner of feverish conditions.

Sea bathing is very useful in Corpulency. Fat persons should evacuate their bowels properly to benefit fully from the bathing, because their fibres have a tendency to fluffiness. Cold bathing both breaks down solids and invigorates, vibrates and sets the blood in motion.

Thomas Gray thought it enough just to be in the proximity of the water as he wrote to a friend:

So I proceed to tell you, that my health is much improved by the sea; not that I drank it, or bathed in it, as the common people do: no! I only walk'd by it, & look'd upon it.[1]

The baths even attracted international visitors. In 1785 Benjamin Franklin stayed at the Star Inn in Southampton for three days with his friends the Shipleys from Twyford and he recorded: 'I took a hot sea-water bath, and floating on my back fell asleep'.[2] Jonas Hanway felt that in the 'reign of Saltwater' great numbers of people preferred Southampton for bathing, although he personally thought Portsmouth was better as Southampton had to rely on the vagaries of the tides.[3]

The waters of Southampton were famed for the curing of rabies; the *Hampshire Chronicle* of 1773 had reported that as there were so many mad dogs in the county, many people were having to travel to Southampton to be dipped in the sea.[4] Some not only dipped themselves but also brought animals, not only dogs but hogs and a cat were brought by a visitor from Reading. There were those who were tardy in taking a treatment. In 1761 one Saul Jones having been bitten by a gentleman's dog died 'mad' having refused to be dipped, despite the urging of his friends. By the time he did take to the waters it was too late to save him.[5] Ladies like Elizabeth Butler Harrison

---

1 *Visitors' Descriptions* p. 15.
2 Christopher Murrey *Benjamin Franklin: Biographical Overview and Bibliography* New York 2002 p. 10.
3 *Visitors' Descriptions* p. 14.
4 In 1808 tempest and snow did not dampen visitors being dipped 'the dipping in the salt water for the bite of mad dogs …. And returned home in better spirits'. *Hampshire Telegraph & Sussex Chronicle* 15 Feb 1808.
5 Jan Stovold *Bygone Southampton* Chichester 1984 item 48.

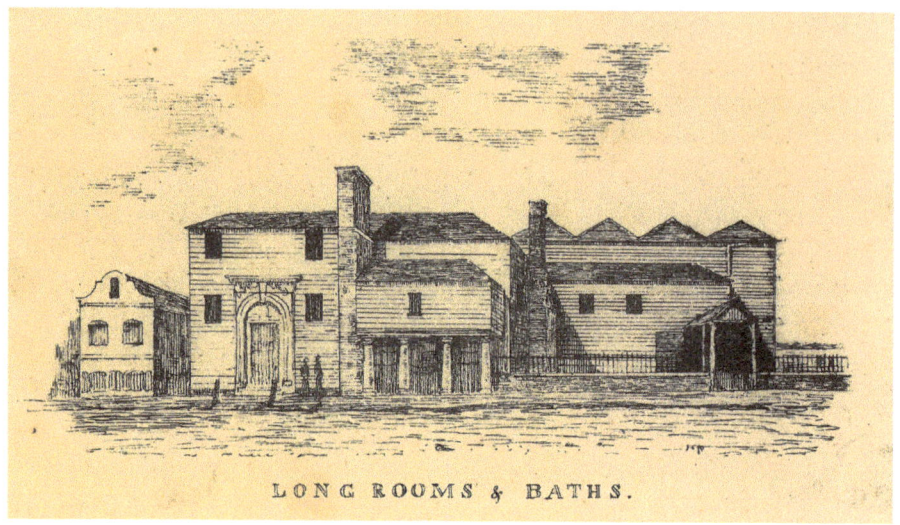

Exterior Long Rooms & Baths

would copy cures for the bite of a mad dog into their personal household books:

> Take leaves of rue, heads of garlic, London treacle, shavings of Pewter of each four ounces. Bruise and Boile them in 2 quarts of strong ale in a close vessel in kettle of boiling water. 2 hours strain these ingredients and keep them. Give of this liquor 9 spoonfulls in the morning fasting for 9 days together, more or less to Man or Beast. If the patient be wounded lay the ingredients to the wounded Part and it shall cure – From Mr Owen the Elder but taken out of a dispensatory proved by Physicians.

It was recommended that visitors combined drinking the sea water alongside sea bathing. As one visitor remarked: 'Being myself ordered to Drink Sea Water two Days before I bathed, did not begin till the Saturday after our Arrival'.[1] Local physician, Dr John Speed, thought the sea water was beneficial in the treatment of scurvy, palsy, epilepsy, rickets, relaxed nerves and gravel – that is to say kidney stones.[2] It must have been a relief to have the option to drink from the town's chalybeate spring instead, it was just as efficacious being:

> an effective deobstrurent, which successfully opens all manner of obstructions; and has done astonishing service in tedious and obstinate agues, black and

---

1 Mrs Constantia Orlebar in *Visitors' Description* p. 17. Constantia Orlebar (1739-1808) is remembered for her *Weather book 1786-1808* which records the daily weather. *Quarterly Journal of the Royal Meteorological Society*, 81 (350) pp. 622-35.
2 Baker's Guide 1775 pp. 29-30.

yellow jaundice, scirrus of the spleen, as well as in the scurvy, green sickness, and even paralytic disorders.[1]

If neither served there were several physicians who had set up in practice in the town attracted by the potential new cliental.

> No place in England can be better calculated than this, for the resort of such Invalids as are unable to join in all the bustle of life, but who are not incapable of enjoying the occasional relaxations of society – *George Lipscomb*[2]

Some of the medics were highly regarded such as Dr John Mackie who was renowned for his knowledge on the treatment of consumption or celebrities like Dr Graham 'The Hygienist' infamous for his 'celestial bed' and dirt bathing.[3] Alongside the doctors were the apothecaries and chemists, in Cunningham's Directory of 1811 the medical establishment were listed as: physicians, John Mackie in Above Bar, Perse Hackett at 25 Above Bar, Robert Wightman at York Buildings and John Middleton also in Above Bar;[4] surgeons,

Dr Graham's Earth Bathing

1 Baker's Guide 1787 p. 47.
2 George Lipscomb *A Journey into Cornwall through the Counties of Southampton, Wilts, Dorset, Somerset and Devon* London 1799 p. 16.
3 Matthew Conolly *Dictionary of Eminent People of Fife 1866* p. 312. Roy Porter *Quacks, Fakers & Charlatans in English Medicine* Stroud 2000 pp. 140-57.
4 Middleton also ran the asylum in the old manor house, Grove Place, Nursling on the outskirts of the town. Eric Raffo *Half a Loaf, The Care of the Sick and Poor of*

apothecaries and men mid-wives, Bernard & Maul 168 High St, Keele & Son 37 Above Bar, G R Corfe 5 Gloucester Square, Storer Ready 66 High St, and John Bond at Canal Place; Chemists and Druggist, William Randall[1] 146 High St, John Smith 61 High St, J P Gilmore 149 High St. Margaret Ridding and her sister Mary were in receipt of several prescriptions for embrocation for the throat and to relieve spasms, the receipts kept by their father Thomas Ridding, town clerk.[2] Acacia,[3] ammon acetate,[4] annamonie,[5] camphor,[6] castor,[7] vitriol[8] being some of the more legible ingredients. Elizabeth Butler Harrison's household book had recipes for 'The Virtues' a cure for breast cancer, Dr James's prescription for slow fever, treatments for broken shins, rheumatism and The Props.[9]

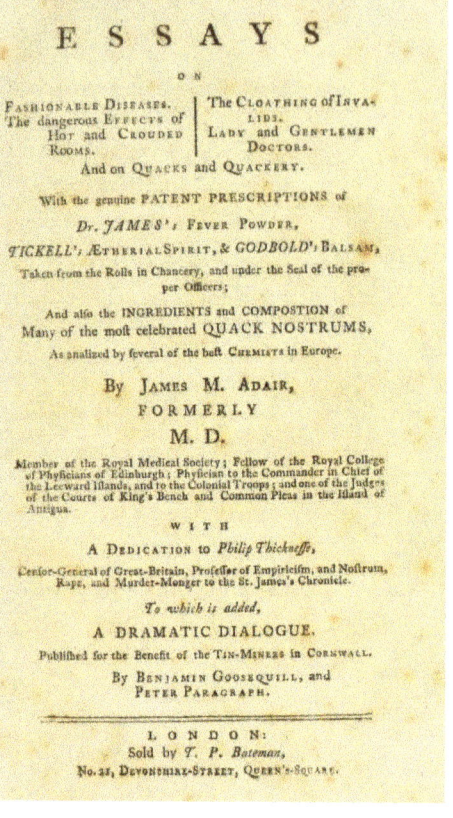

Advertisement for Dr James's Fever Powder

South Stoneham 1664-1948 IOW 2000 p. 11.

1. William Randall was entered in the Medical Register in 1779 as an apothecary at Salisbury where he remains until 1790. P J Pead, *Benjamin Jesty, the Grandfather of Vaccination* Cambridge 2020 p. 174.
2. SA D/PM Box 42 5/10, 5/15, 5/17, 5/18.
3. Treats eye pain, toothache, jaundice, diarrhoea.
4. Spirt of Mindererus used as diuretic.
5. Probably Anemone chinensis for diarrhoea.
6. Used to relieve chest congestion and inflammatory conditions.
7. Castor oil was used as a purgative.
8. Elixir of vitriol was a staple of medicine cabinets and used to treat coughs. The navy would use it as an ingredient to combat scurvy.
9. Dr James's Fever Powders contained antimony, which was toxic, as a febrifuge. Over a period of twenty years some 1,612,800 doses of James's Powders were sold, they were expensive 2s 6d for two. Roy Porter *Quacks* Stroud 2000 pp. 33, 54, 60. William Hawes an apothecary writing in 1774 says of James's Powder 'The Medicine is in such general vogue that almost every Apothecary is obliged to keep

The increase in the number of invalids in the town must have inspired the entrepreneurial Henrietta Caroline Bentley, described as a spinster of Southampton, to apply for patent in 1794. Her invention was a bed for invalids which could be made up and the linens changed with a minimum of effort and with little inconvenience to the patient. The patent was granted in August 1794 and in parliamentary accounts drawn up on the death of George III it was recorded that Henrietta was receiving a state pension of £300.[1]

There were quack cures and medicines such as Dr Norris's Fever Drops regularly advertised in the local newspapers, or Mrs Mary Remacle who promoted Beaume de Vie which could be purchased from her coffee house adjacent to Holy Rood church.[2] It was a pick-me-up for settling down the stomach and bowels of those who had overindulged. It did not help Mrs Remacle however and in the outbreak of smallpox that hit the town in 1778 she fled to her daughter's home Millbrook, leaving her daughter-in-law in Ann Remacle in charge of the coffee house. Mary Remacle died shortly after arriving in Millbrook on 3 March 1778.[3] The libraries and book sellers sold guides which promoted a range of remedies such as Parrs Life Pills, recommended for invalids as they invariably restored the stomach to a healthy longing for food, while its sedative quality gave sound and refreshing sleep as well as acting as 'a most agreeable purgative'.[4] The advert also warned that: 'The Spring has been always remarked as a period when disease, if it be lurking in the system, is sure to show itself', a Mr F Mattheisz of Jaffra, Ceylon the advert reported ordered 1000 boxes. Fletchers the bookseller was a vendor of patent medicines as well as books. Many people self-medicated with patent cures, one of the most popular preferred remedies calomel was cure-all for illnesses and disease from malaria and yellow fever, mumps, typhoid, constipation dysentery, syphilis and vomiting. It worked as purge and was popular from the sixteenth century through to the twentieth.[5] In 1804 Thomas Lewin wrote to a friend 'Thanks

it.' P S Brown The Venders of Medicines Advertised in Eighteenth-Century Bath Newspapers' in *Medical History* Cambridge 1975 p. 363.
1   Parliamentary Papers Vol II *Estimate & Accounts 21 April – 23 November 1820* p. 231. Bennet Woodcraft *Patents of Invention Part II* London 1854 p. 837.
2   Hampshire Chronicle 12 October 1772. Dr J A Paris exposed Beaume de Vie in 1804. W A Campbell *The analytical chemist in nineteenth century English Social History* PhD Thesis Durham 1971 p. 51.
3   Mary L South *The Inoculation Book 1774-1783* Southampton Records Series 2014 p. 96.
4   SA D/PM 42 3/37 Newspaper Paragraphs.
5   Lydia Kang *Quackery: A Brief History of the Worst Ways to Cure Everything* New York 2017.

for your recommendation to " Dr. Calomel." He is indeed a noted Leech, and may be called in, some future day.'[1] Some invalids even had special clothes they wore at times of illness, as James Mylles recorded in his will of 1779 in a bequest to his servant Mary Lambell:

> My Camblet cloak and also my white swan skin cloak which I wear when I am sick and my green worsted Damask night gown and half a dozen of my worst shirts. And also £10 (over and above wages) providing she be living with me at the time of my death.[2]

As Dr Granville commented on Southampton: 'It is singularly free from endemic causes of disease of an irremedial character: and it will be a remarkably healthy town when proper sanitary regulations are established.'[3]

---

1 *Lewin Letters* p. 100.
2 TNA PROB 11/1061/301 Will James Mylles.
3 Edwin Wing for *Southampton Considered as a Resort for Invalids*. London 1848, pp. 19-22.

BALLS, ASSEMBLIES AND OTHER ENTERTAINMENTS

The lofty, ample doors unfold
Harmonious turning as on hinge of gold
The Train pours in, the young, the grave advance,
Nor age itself denies to lead the dance,
All gay and glorious![1]

To keep the visitors amused when they were not at the baths there were viewing areas so that those not partaking could watch the bathers whilst enjoying refreshments such as tea and coffee. In the evenings there were assembly balls. The old assembly rooms at the Royal George in the High Street were found to be too small by 1761 and Mr Martin constructed an assembly room as part of his bathing establishment.[2] Martin's rooms were known as The Long Rooms, they were lit with five glass chandeliers, had pretty pale stucco walls and looking-glasses with papier-mâché decorations.[3] Originally there were 'dressed' balls on a Tuesday and 'undressed' on Thursday. For women 'undress' meant that you could wear a day dress to the ball, whereas for 'dress' balls a formal ball gown, which would have short sleeves and a lower bodice, needed to be worn. Some of the balls were costumed such as the masked ball which took place in 1774:

> Last Friday night there was a very brilliant Masked Ball at Martin's rooms at Southampton; the characters were numerous and well supported. The Duke and Duchess of Cumberland were there in dominos. The Duchess left the room

---

1 Elsie Sandell 'Georgian Southampton: a Watering-Place and Spa' in *Collected Essays on Southampton* Southampton 1958 p. 81.
2 Ladies Pocket Guide SA D/PM 42 3/33.
3 The pavement commissioners in 1775 allowed Mr Martin to take down two of the medieval town towers facing the Long Rooms at West Quay. Jan Stovold *Minute Book of the Pavement Commissioners for Southampton 1770-1789* Southampton Records Series 1990, p. 73.

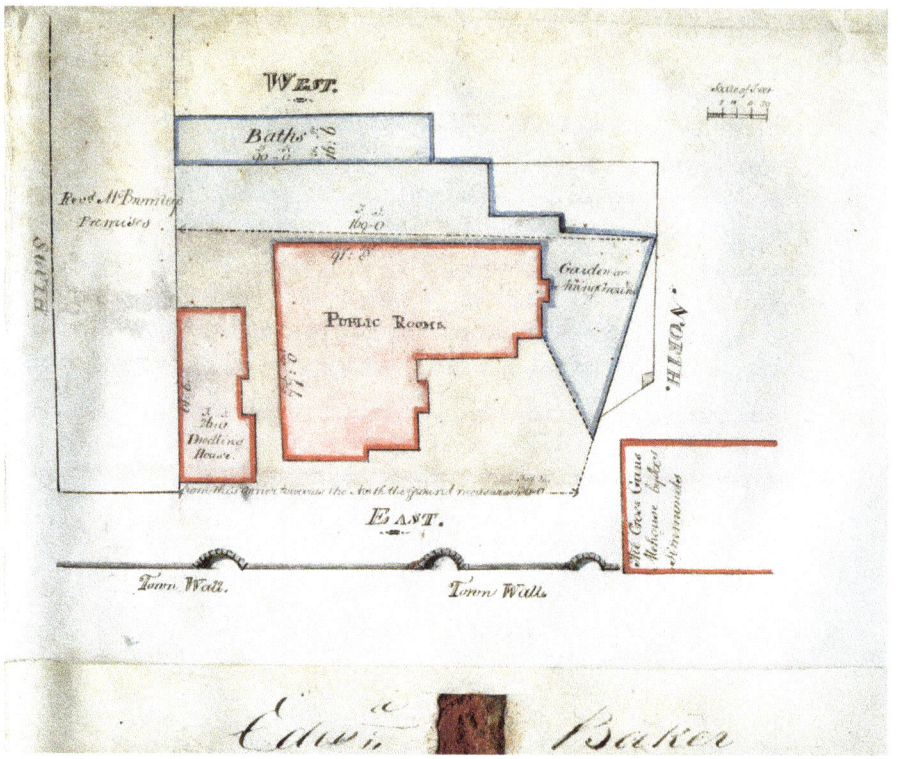
Plan of the Long Rooms, Southampton Archives

about twelve o'clock, but the Duke staid supper. The whole company did not break up till between three and four o'clock. There was a Tancred, A Cyrus, a very good Jew Broker, a Major Sturgeon, a Watchman, an excellent Sailor, who sung Rule Britannia exceedingly well on the Duke's coming into the room, as he did many other songs; several Indian Chiefs, a Harlequin, a Cricket Player, Mother Shipton, Nuns, Friars, etc, out of number - *Atherley Papers*[1]

There was also a card room which was papered with Crimson and was on the right-hand side as you entered the building. The music gallery was considered superior to that at the Polygon, being on a better level with the company. The dancers paid a shilling a piece to the musicians. The Long Room season was focused on the summer months. Although the Rooms did stay open because of their situation they were at the mercy of weather, especially the wind. The assemblies continued every fortnight as did the concert programme. The latter looked to local performers or the local militia for their music:

---

1   SA Atherley Papers SA D/S 19/1/2 p. 5.

Lord Rivers[1] & several gentlemen play upon different instruments Goss & Sibly both from Salisbury with Martin are the vocal performers. The Dorsetshire are a very genteel corps, you cannot have forgot their excellent band of music, ... Burgat attends the concert as a gentleman performer, he is reckon'd a good fiddle, & as he comes to town Friday, to teach Saturday, its no inconvenience to him to oblige by performing.- *Melicent Ballard*

In the off or winter season assemblies could still be had at the ancient Dolphin Inn which had been modernised by Nathaniel St Andre, formerly court anatomist to George II, with large bow windows on the first-floor assembly rooms, with a programme that began at 7pm and ended at midnight:

Southampton Assembly, Long Rooms interior

Hampshire Telegraph 16th December 1816 One of the most brilliant assemblies we have witnessed for some time was held on Tuesday evening at the Dolphin Hotel. It was the first subscription ball of the season and was graced by all the beauty, rank and fashion of the surrounding country. The display of beauty was unparalleled and many gentlemen who had just returned from a Continental trip were loud in the admiration it excited. English country dances served only as a prelude to the more elegant French quadrilles, waltzes, and Spanish dances. Nothing could exceed the grace with which the former were danced by the accomplished Mrs E., the Miss M. S., Miss T and Miss H and in the mazy

1 George Pitt, Lord Rivers. Mr Goss was a distinguished counter-tenor Bath Chronicle 2 May 1782. Rev Sibley was rector of Walcot where he put on musical concerts. *Bath Chronicle* 29th November 1787.

windings of the waltz the lovely Miss C. T. shone eminently conspicuous. The tunes of the Spanish dances caused every eye to sparkle with delight and nearly 20 couples circled through those intricate but beautiful figures. Quadrilles and waltzes were resumed and grey eyed morn had already topped the East ere many could be brought to tear themselves from so enchanting a scene.

Southampton Assembly, Long Rooms external

Balls were also held at the Polygon which were at times quite lively: 'Lady Pinch & her Mama were again at the Ball, & the Mob wanted to get a jack ass into the room, for my lady to ride on but the obstinate beast would not walk up stairs.'

This was apparently not unusual:

In September 1773 there was a grand Masked Ball in the great room at the Polygon, which was attended we are told by a very polite and genteel company. The politeness and gentility seems to have been chiefly inside, for the mob without sent some stones through the window, one of which narrowly missed the Duchess of Gloucester's[1] temple; and a gentleman, who was walking to his lodgings in the dress of a shepherd, was seized by the sportive populace, who made a football of him. But for timely rescue he would probably have been kicked to death. - *Hampshire Chronicle* 27th September 1773, and 5th September 1774.

There were other venues for balls as the same newspaper reported: *Hampshire Telegraph* 6 Jan 1817 'A ball in Bugle Street. The floor of the ballroom was chalked in a very masterly style which did great credit to Mr Young, the artist.' Chalking the ballroom floor was undertaken on special occasions, the designs to charm the guests but also to prevent the dancers from slipping.[2] Tobias Young was a popular and successful artist who made his living

1 Maria Waldegrave was married to George III's brother William Henry Duke of Gloucester. They had married in secret against the wishes of the king.
2 In 1813 Harriet Lewin chalked a design at a ball for her friend Emma Chamier who had just got married, it was the initials of the bride and groom surrounded by cupids. The Travel Journal of Ann Sophy Mackie, Chawton House Library.

by painting many views of Southampton and the surrounding area which were commissioned by local families like the Lewins, who employed him to paint a picture of their villa. Young lived at Walter Taylor's new development at 1 Hanover Buildings: his purchase of the property in 1819 was facilitated by a loan from Harriet Austen, the sister of Elizabeth Butler Harrison, who was lodging with the Youngs. Young could not afford to buy the property when Walter Taylor's widow want to sell it and Austen stepped in with £200 to make the purchase.[1] Tobias Young's obituary of December 1st 1824 described him as a painter of great merit, who began his career working for the well-known rake Lord Barrymore, painting scenery for his private theatre.[2]

There were also private balls and, perhaps, the grandest ball given was by Lady Lansdowne, as reported in the Hampshire Telegraph on 24th August 1807, whose husband had recently completed the building of the gothic castle, his principal residence in the centre of the town:

> The Marchioness of Lansdowne gave a ball and supper on Thursday for more than 300 nobility and gentry. The Gothic Castle which is built on a commanding eminence was most splendidly illuminated and exhibited a very grand appearance; more than 7000 variegated lamps adorned the outside while the interior was decorated in the same manner and with the most elegant and superb chandeliers. So brilliant a spectacle had never been seen in Southampton and to describe it by words would give but a faint impression of its effect. The flagstaff was entirely covered by lamps; the edges of the towering minarets, the arches of the windows were adorned in the same elegant style; over the grand window was a superb illuminated star which had a striking effect; a beehive also attracted general admiration; indeed the whole seemed to partake of the nature of those enchanted castles which we have read of in fairy romance than any possible reality. The dancing began about half past ten and continued until one when the company retired to the supper room and the tables were set out in the most finished taste and were sumptuously covered with the choicest viands and wines. Sir Joseph York gave the most noble toasts which was honoured with three times three

As with all aspects of life there were rules overseen by the Master of Ceremonies. The visitor John Swete commented that the master: 'is absolute

---

1 SA D/PM/4/9/1-14.
2 Michael Bryan *Dictionary of Painters and Engravers, Biographical and Critical* London 1889 Vol II p. 73. Lord Barrymore had died in 1793, aged just twenty-three, which might have accounted for Young's move to Southampton.

in determining causes that fall under his Arbitration, and in adjusting the Etiquettes of Precedency':[1]

THE RULES OF THE BALL 1774[2]

There will be a ball every Tuesday night during the Season

Ladies and Gentlemen to subscribe 10s 6d for the Season or pay 2s 6d each night. Children not excepted.

The Balls shall begin at 7 o'clock and Country Dances at eleven

Ladies and gentlemen who intend to dance minuets, must send their name to the box appointed for the purpose before six o'clock every Ball night

In Country dances, ladies are to draw for places; those excepted whose rank entitles them to precedency

Ladies & gentlemen who dance down a Country Dance shall not quit their places 'til the dance is finished, unless they intend to dance no more that night. Yet the Master of the Ceremonies may, in particular circumstances, dispense with that rule

That no lady will be permitted to dance in an apron, black mittens or black gloves

That the time for tea drinking be determined by the Master of Ceremonies. Each person who drinks tea, or a dish of chocolate, is to pay sixpence, except ladies that dance, as it is customary for their partners to pay for them

It is expected that gentlemen will not place themselves before the ladies or prevent them seeing the minuets danced, or to continue to sit on the benches when ladies want seats

That no gentleman or lady takes offence that another dances before them and that ladies who do not dance minuets and children be content with the back seats

Gentlemen and ladies are desired to order their servants not to crowd the stairs leading to the room, but to remain in the place appointed for them

Gentlemen are also desired not to come to the rooms any evening in boots

In 1770 John Marsh, not yet eighteen, and Master of Ceremonies at Romsey thought that the people of Romsey: 'were not so proud & did not hold up their heads quite so high as at Southton', where tradesmen were not being admitted to balls in the town.[3] There was a subscription for the Southampton

---

1 *Visitors' Description* p. 19. John Swete was a clergyman, artist and antiquary and wrote *Travel Journals*.
2 Ladies Pocket Guide; Baker's Guide 1775 pp. 25-26.
3 Brian Robins 'An Introduction to the Journals of John Marsh' *Huntington Library*

BALLS, ASSEMBLIES AND OTHER ENTERTAINMENTS

William Dawson, master of ceremonies, by Thomas Hickey, Victoria Art Gallery

season which varied according to the time of year but could be as high as a guinea.

Key to the success of any assembly room was the post of Master of Ceremonies who would call on all new-comers to the town to ascertain if they be suitable to be admitted into polite society and: 'that all improper company should be kept from these Rooms'.[1] The post was keenly fought over and when Mr William Dawson, master for seven years, was rumoured to be contemplating a move to Bath in 1777 Mr Andrew Haynes put himself forward as a suitable replacement. Dawson, however, maintained he had no notion of giving up his Southampton position, in fact he planned to serve in both Bath and Southampton whose seasons did not coincide. The Southampton season ran from mid-June until mid-October, although balls and concerts were kept up in winter. The subscribers to the assembly room balls were put out that Dawson was contemplating splitting his loyalties, for a salary of £800, and turned to Haynes who declared: 'it shall be my constant study and endeavour to give all the satisfaction in my power, by a diligent and assiduous attention to the duties'. Dawson stood his ground and in May 1778 declared 'The Season will begin at this place, with a Ball, at Martin's Rooms on Thursday the 4th of June next, it being the anniversary of His Majesty's birthday'. Haynes admitted defeat and stood down in order to preserve the peace and so not to be responsible for

> the dread of involving the inhabitants of Southampton in one general scene of disorder and confusions ..... the dissentions and difference of opinion strongly prevailing amongst the inhabitants I could not hesitate to sacrifice my own

Quarterly Vol 59 No 1 (1996) University of Pennsylvania Press.
1   Elsie Sandell 'Georgian Southampton: a Watering-Place and Spa' in *Collected Essays on Southampton* Southampton 1958 p. 81.

claim and advantages, to preserve the peace, harmonies and privileges of the town[1]

Mr Haynes was still trying to improve his prospects in 1783 when Melicent Ballard reported in a letter to her nephew:

> We hear Major Haynes[2] is in hopes of being Master of the ceremonies at Manchester, which is about four hundred a year. I hope he will succeed, for he has entirely spent his fortune, which was very genteel, & I doubt more, now the Militia is discharged he has nothing to depend on, & a wife & four children to provide for. He is one among a thousand proofs, of the sad effects, an early & imprudent marriage must produce – remember this my Child & be not in haste to do, what death only can free you from.

In the event Mr Dawson presided in Bath in the winter and Southampton in the summer till 1785. Meanwhile, Mr Haynes became Master of Ceremonies for Winchester until January 1786 when, as the paper reported, he was elected to succeed Mr Dawson[3]: 'that the Balls have been numerous and brilliant, which they attribute chiefly to the subscription, and to the great politeness and attention paid to the company by the new Master of Ceremonies'.

Assemblies at the Long Rooms were a finite activity, held during The Season and even then, not every evening so there had to be a range of other activities to entertain the visitors as well as the long-term residents. Melicent Ballard enjoyed concerts, balls and horse racing on the marsh or the common, details of which pepper her letters, though some events were under subscribed:

> 1781 - Friday ye 15th. – I am just return'd from Days Concert which was

---

1 *Hampshire Chronicle* 3 November 1777, 1, 8 ,15, 22, 29, December 1777, 5 Jan 1778, 18 & 25 May 1778, 6 November 1785. George Lipscomb *A Journey into Cornwall through the Counties of Southampton, Wilts, Dorset, Somerset and Devon* London 1799 p. 17.
2 Andrew Goater Haynes was born in 1744 and went to Winchester as a scholar in 1757 but left three years later having succeeded to some property. He was a commissioned officer in the South Hampshire Militia and was Master of Ceremonies in the local directory for 1796. He remained in post until 1797. In 1791 Haynes had to obtain a bond of £600 to repay a loan of £300 in connection with a life assurance policy for S G Haynes. Haynes was in debt due to this bond in 1793 SA D/PM/45/3/77. He had insured a property in French Street in 1788 and another in Above Bar in 1791. London Metropolitan Archives MS11936/356/547737 & 378/589023.
3 *Hampshire Chronicle* 1 March 1784, 23 January 1786, 17 July 1786.

not very full of company. Alexander's Feast, with a Miscellaneous Act, & the Coronation Anthem, with God save the King was the entertainment chosen – in the morning, the Oratorio of the Messiah, was performed at the Church, I am told not more than a hundred people were present & I doubt Day[1] will not be much in pocket.

This was not only the poorly supported concert in Southampton at a time when the town had become fashionable:

Mr Storace[2] a native of Naples announces a public breakfast at ten o'clock, to be followed by a concert at half-past eleven: principal vocalist, Miss Storace, aged seven years. Between the parts of the concert the spirits of the audience to be recruited with lemonade, orgeat[3], and capillaire.[4] Tickets, including breakfast, concert, and refreshments, 3s. 6d. A lady wrote subsequently to say she was sorry to see such a small audience and she hoped that more would be present when the concert was repeated, as Miss Storace was a very fine singer.[5]

Many of the great and good of the town entered horses in races such as the Give-And-Take Plate, which started at the Guildhall and also included a Pony Race. During the event no publicans were permitted to sell liquor, without leave, on pain of forfeiting his licence:[6]

16th August 1806 our races commenced on Thursday. They were attended by much fashion and beauty amongst who appeared the Marquis of Lansdowne in a landau drawn by 4 Shetland ponies who looked extremely well in harness and drew the attention of the public as much as the races. The beautiful daughters of the Marchioness appeared on the ground in a coach and four.[7] The servants had most elegant new liveries trimmed with silver and Italian shoulder knots

1 The only Day in the 1783 Directory of Hampshire was John Day, shoemaker on the High Street p. 147.
2 Stephen Storace was actually born in London to an Italian father and English mother. His sister Nancy was an opera singer and this was her first professional public performance in 1773.
3 Drink made from orange flower water and either barley or almonds.
4 A syrup flavoured with orange flowers or maidenhair fern.
5 Quoted in *Hampshire Field Club* Vol VI 1910 in an article on extracts from the *Hampshire Chronicle* by Rev. T L O Davies.
6 SA Atherley Papers D/S2/2/6, horse owners included Atherley, Jackson, Rose, and Amyatt.
7 The Marchioness's three youngest daughters were still living with their mother and often seen around the town.

The stewards of the races also acted as patrons for vocal concerts, such as one that took place on 17th August 1807 at the Long Rooms, headlined by Messrs Elliotts, Harrington and Mr and Mrs Goss. The programme of songs, duets and glees having been performed by them at the: *Nobility's Concerts in London.*[1] Racing also encouraged gambling and card-playing was another popular distraction. The Long Rooms had a card room and in the winter months residents could enjoy the Whist Club at the Star Hotel. Card tables in the assembly rooms were provided with two packs of cards for a fee of 7s 6d, a single pack for a round table at 5s, with any other games being 4s. Melicent Ballard did not like to play for high stakes and wrote in April 1783: 'a low stake being one where losing could occur with good humour, either wise it ceased to be an amusement.'

There was even the opportunity to gamble on the Lottery and those who wished could gamble on the Irish State Lottery too and, it was possible to buy half and a quarter share of lottery tickets.[2] Resident of Southampton, Lady Betty Craven, had once been given a lottery ticket by her husband shortly before their marriage crumbled. She won two thousand pounds and purchased land by the side of the Thames between Hammersmith and Fulham upon which her husband erected a villa known as Craven Cottage. Gambling was something of a disease of the age which contributed to the increase in the number of debtors in the town and so a debtor's prison was established in the tower of God's House prison. Charlotte Braxton, a spinster from the Isle of Wight, was imprisoned in God's House gaol for debt in 1795. She owed money to Mr John Arnold a hairdresser and perfumer, to Mr Jonathan Wavell a mercer and draper a sum of £3 13s and ten guineas to Alexander Leeth.[3] The number of debtor prisoners was usually low, 4 in 1802, 1 in 1803 and 1 in 1807.

Lottery Ticket, Southampton Archives

1   SA D/PM 40/37/2.
2   Details contained as part of a bankruptcy case showed a complainant trying to secure their share of half a share of the 1787 lottery ticket number 16 in 236 and a quarter of the 1788 lottery ticket number 14 in 328, total value two pounds and ten shillings. SA D/PM 95/16/1-2.
3   SA D/PM/ 82/8/1-3.

BALLS, ASSEMBLIES AND OTHER ENTERTAINMENTS

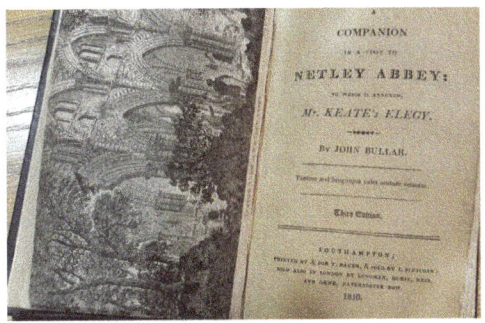

Visitor Guide to Netley Abbey

As a magnet for visitors, Southampton also promoted the surrounding area for days out and water parties. The New Forest and Isle of Wight were popular places for excursions, but the 'Lion of The Neighbourhood' according to the guides was the medieval ruins of Netley Abbey.[1] Appealing to the devotees of the picturesque and the gothic it attracted not only the casual visitor but also a stream of artists, from the highly talented such as Turner and Constable, to the jobbing artists, Francis Towne, William Shayer, and Michael Rooker, among others who produced views as souvenirs. In addition, the Abbey was the inspiration for writers Horace Walpole and Thomas Gray and for an opera (William Pearce), a gothic Novel (Richard Warner), piano music (William Sheppard), and poetry (George Keate, David Richardson, William Sotheby, William Bowles). There were many, many more including female poets such as the rather melancholic writer of sonnets Susan Evance[2] and the talented but little-known artist Miss

Netley Abbey, by Richard Harriden

1   Arthur Freeling *Picturesque Excursions* 1839 p. 59.
2   Evance published two collections one in 1808 and the other in 1818 prompted by

Selby. The Abbey featured as an engraving on maps and even on a souvenir penny produced in 1797 by Thomas Gorton, a merchant of Gloucester. It was the scene of masques, dances, parades as well as picnics such as the one enjoyed by Jane Austen and her family.[1] People arrived either by a lengthy coach journey or more usually by water taking boats from town quay and the cross house or, if they were well off like the Lewins and Lances, by their own yachts.

The growth in yacht ownership also led to an increase in yacht races which were often held off of town quay and were augmented by rowing competitions including races for women as the *Hampshire Advertiser* reported:

> Last match of all to end the day's amusement was the Female Rowers in their varied ribbons two in a boat, who went round the course – if not 'swift as an arrow from a Tartar's bow' much faster than expected and arrived thus: the Rose, scarlet ribbons; Maria, green; Ariel, white; Paul Pry, blue; Eliza, yellow and Sting, pink. Ann Diaper in her boat Anna Maria and Maria Diaper in her boat May Flower had great success.

In 1828 the reporter was so carried away with the race he likened the ladies to:

> Cleopatra sailing down the Cydnus with their oars moving to the sound of breathing music rowing with natural dignity and returning in precisely the order they started which is proof of the harmony and decorum of the proceeding. In addition to their monetary rewards the ladies also won tickets to a play.

Many of the villa-owning families like the Lances, the Marquis of Lansdowne[2] and the Lewins had accidents and even naval officers experienced

---

the death of Princess Charlotte. Her poems have a focus on female suffering.
1 See Cheryl Butler *Jane Austen & Southampton Spa* Southampton 2017. Walpole visited in 1755 'We walked long by moonlight on the terrace above the beach. The town is crowded, sea baths have been established there.' Elsie Sandell 'Georgian Southampton: a Watering-Place and Spa' in *Collected Essays on Southampton* Southampton 1958 p. 79.
2 The Marquis was experimenting with a design for a double-bottomed boat without ballast. It overturned within the sight of Lady Betty Craven, who happened to glance out of the window of her house, sending her servants to rescue the Marquis. After the rescue she provided wine *to refresh the drenched experimentalists. The Beautiful Lady Betty Craven* Vol II 1826 p. 142.

BALLS, ASSEMBLIES AND OTHER ENTERTAINMENTS

A Fresh Breeze, Thomas Rowlandson

problems.[1] On December 25th 1811, Lieutenant Dumaresque, of the '*Hawke* sloop, came to Southampton being rowed up the river from the ship by six men to dine with Admiral John Fergusson'.[2] After he had taken his dinner, he re-embarked the same boat to return to the *Hawke*. 'With a breeze springing up they found it necessary to set the sail but in doing so it caused the mast to fall', overpowering the sailors and upsetting the boat. The whole party including John Sherlock a local musician, whom Lt Dumaresque had taken into the boat at the request of the men to amuse them during the holidays on board, was plunged into the river. Lt Dumaresque, the musician and five sailors out of the six were drowned.[3]

Circulating libraries were another new innovation fed by the growth of the novel, periodicals and newspapers, the town's first newspaper being the

---

1   There was a story that circulated that when John Wesley was crossing to Southampton from the Isle of Wight in 1790 the boat was upset and passengers were left in the water for an hour until picked up by the passing Ryde packet. *Southern Daily Echo* 13 May 2008.
2   The memorial to the Fergusson family, including the Admiral, can be found in St Michael's church, Southampton. The Admiral lived at 3 Bugle Street. The Atherley Papers SA D/S2/2/6.
3   All but Dumeresque were buried at Peartree church., he was buried at St Marys. SA Peartree Burial Records. PR6/1/2.

Public Library

Above Bar Southampton, showing Skeltons Printers

Hampshire Chronicle launched in 1772.¹ Baker's Library in the High Street

1 Thomas Cooper, a saddler, was in trouble in 1762 for stealing a volume of magazines, in 1764 he stole a book valued at 10d, and a cheese valued at 10d and was sentenced to transportation to the West Indies for seven years. SA SC9/4/607, 608 and 626.

had 7000 volumes as well as a printing office 'that would do no discredit to the London presses'[1] and there are forty known books printed by Baker; Skelton's Library, also on the High Street, ran a subscription service and a news room which opened from nine in the morning until nine at night. Skelton's eventually boasted 30,000 volumes in its circulating library but their reading room, however, was restricted to men. When Thomas Skelton died in 1816 his business was carried on by his second wife Elizabeth and two of her step-daughters Mary Mabella and Elizabeth. They also were agents for the Royal Exchange Assurance and Lottery Agents and publishers of the *Southampton Herald*.[2] Also on the same street were Fords, Byles[3] and Mrs Street's establishment which combined library, stationers and registry office for servants. The Marquis of Lansdowne had a large library in his residence and there was also a growth in non-aristocratic libraries in the homes of wealthy merchants, like the Middletons whose library had mahogany bookcases and an Italian marble chimney; William Gunthorpe had a spacious library at Bull Hall;[4] Nathaniel St André of Bellevue House had 1100 books which he left to George and William Pill, the children of his former maidservant, in 1776 and they bequeathed the library to the corporation; John Bullar's library was eventually bequeathed to the Hartley Institute, the forerunner of the University of Southampton. The Hartley name, which is still the name of the University library, refers to Henry Robinson Hartley whose family fortune, made from the wine trade, funded the Institute to which he bequeathed his books and papers; family collections were passed down the generations, Harriet Austen gifted her collection of books to her nieces and nephews in her will.[5] Elizabeth Goring Butler Harrison gave books on history to her young Goring relations: '(Charles) is particularly interested in the Jewish history and immediately begged to have their wars with the Romans read to him for he has

1 John Feltham *A Guide to all the Watering and Sea-Bathing Places* London 1803 p. 321.
2 Richard Preston 'A Precarious Business: the Skelton family of stationers, printers, publishers, booksellers and circulating library owners in Southampton and Havant, c.1781- c.1865' in *Southampton Local History Forum Journal No 21*, 2013, pp. 6-8. Thomas Skelton's son William also set up a bookshop in the High Street, also taken over by his widow Elizabeth. Both Skelton businesses eventually foundered and went bankrupt.
3 This was probably the George Byles who ended up in debtor's prison. In the 1803 Cunningham Directory he was listed at 15 High Street as an auctioneer, stationer and agency office.
4 Gunthorpe's library was lost in a fire in 1791 which gutted Bull/Bugle Hall. SA D/2 191/2 p. 7. Patterson *Corporation Journal* pp. 50-51.
5 SA D/PM 30/2 will of Miss H L Austen 1808.

not patience to bear the interruption which the hard names occasion him on reading to himself.'[1] Local wine merchant and entrepreneur Robert Ballard was encouraged enough to agree a performance of agreement bond of £5000 for a new publication *The Royal Engagement Pocket Atlas*[2] so that discerning visitors could be kept up to date with important events and anniversaries. Ballard was to compile and compose the atlas annually and it was to be printed in Baker's name but to the proper use and behalf of Ballard to cover costs. Baker would get 3d for every book sold until the outlay of £100 was reached and on demand to give up any copies of plates, prints and other material. If Ballard sold the copyright Baker was to receive £100 for every year of the agreed term. Baker's Guide for 1779 advertised the atlas with '365 commodious pages'. The *Atlas* had a long life running until 1826, it had twenty-four diary pages, two for each month, gave information on society events, members of the royal family and had the innovation of illustrations. Journal writing, keeping day books and diaries were also other popular past times.

Newspapers were not only full of advertisements but also gossip with thinly disguised references to scandalous liaisons such as that of Letitia Powlett, wife of Col Powlett. As Jane Austen recorded:

> This is a sad story about Mrs Powlett. I should not have suspected her of such a thing. – She staid the Sacrament I remember, the last time that you & I did – A hint of it, with Initials was in yesterday's Courier; & Mr Moore guessed it to be Ld Sackville, believing there was no other Viscount S in the peerage, & so it proved – 22nd June 1808.[1]

Letitia had a liaison with Lord Sackville and the pair were discovered in the bedchamber of a Winchester inn. After a high-profile court case Col Powlett was awarded £3000 damages but failed in his attempt to attain a divorce. The affair did not survive, but it was not until the colonel had died that his wife could remarry to Thomas Lisle Follett and regain something of her reputation.[4] The cases of criminal conversation even involved the Marquis

---

1 Jane Goring, Joyce Sleight, Jill Turner, Janet Pennington & Janine Harvey *Lives, Loves and Letters, The Goring Family of Wiston, Sussex 1743-1905* p. 18.
2 Draft agreement for the printing of the *Royal Engagement Pocket Atlas* in 1778 between Robert Ballard and Thomas Baker, printer and bookseller SA D/PM Box 97/10. Sandro Jung 'Thomas Stothard's Illustrations for The Royal Engagement Pocket Atlas 1779-1826' *The Library* 7th series vol 12 no 1 March 2011 pp. 5-11.
1 *Jane Austen's Letters* p. 131.
4 Stephen Mahony 'What became of Mrs Powlett' in the *Jane Austen Society Report* 2019, Cheryl Butler 'What became of Col Powlett: This Wonderous Affair' in the

BALLS, ASSEMBLIES AND OTHER ENTERTAINMENTS

Laetitia Powlett Memorial

of Lansdowne then Lord Wycombe before he inherited the title, who had had a liaison with the wife of William Wyndham, the British ambassador in Florence. He was also linked to Adelaide, Countess of Flahault, and is said to have rescued her and her son from the French Revolution, allowing her to stay at his seat at High Wycombe, where she later gave birth. *The Times* in 1793 reported:

> An Evening Paper has announced Madame Flahault's being brought to bed at High Wycombe! We conceive that this intelligence must be untrue; as if we mistake not, her unfortunate husband was guillotined in France, more than a year since; and we have never heard of her being married again.

For women lower in the social scale having liaisons outside marriage could have a serious effect on their standing in society. Amelay Mash had an affair with Col Powlett, after his estrangement from his wife, and accused him of being the father of her unborn child. She was desperate for money having been thrown out of her lodgings and abandoned by her parents. Only her brother stood by her and he was under pressure from his new wife to expel Amelay from the family home. In the end she gave birth in the poor house and it was discovered the father was not Powlett but another married man. Powlett wrote to his lawyer: 'The Lady I understand is brought to Bed not before her time but it seems considerably before mine and the child is sworn to some married man; but whom, I know not, thus ends this wonderful affair'.[1]

Sarah Truss, the daughter of Jeffery John Truss, gaoler of the town prison, also was a victim of seduction. Her father had particular responsibility for the debtors in the prison which included, for a period of nearly three years, John Geagan heir to a plantation in St Kitts. Geagan had run up £1000 in debts and was trying to persuade his mother to sell some of his property in order to pay

Jane Austen Society Report 2020. Hampshire Chronicle 6th August 1808.
1   SA D/PM/79/14.

off those debts. This turned out to be a long-drawn-out process and to ensure some income to improve his stay in prison Geagan agreed to the suggestion from gaoler Truss that he took on the education of his daughter Sarah. That education covered more than just lessons in reading and writing and Sarah found herself pregnant. This caused an uproar in the Truss household and Geagan complained about his treatment in prison after the affair was discovered. Sarah gave birth to a daughter, Maria, the name of John Geagan's mother. This affair did end more happily, when Geagan's debts were eventually paid off and he was released, he and Sarah were married by special licence in St Mary's church and she travelled with him back to St Kitts.[1]

The Truss family home at God's House Prison

As Ann Eliot remarks in *Persuasion* this was also a golden age for poetry and Jane Austen was not the only young woman with a devotion of William Cowper, the poet himself being another visitor to Southampton in 1752.[2] Harriet Lewin was presented with a copy of his verse by her aunt. Southampton did have the distinction of being home to the Poet Laureate, Henry Pye, who lived at Little Testwood House. Unfortunately, even his peers did not have a high opinion of his verse. The Lives of the Poets Laureate dismissed poor Henry with faint praise:

> although the slightest knowledge of his voluminous writings will show that his intellect had been highly cultivated and that he possessed erudition, judgment and sense ... we are afraid that, with all our reverence for Mr Pye as a man

1 Cheryl Butler *Powder, Prisoners & Paintings: The History of God's House Tower* Southampton 2019 pp. 82-90.
2 William Hayley *The Works of William Cowper his Life and Letters* London 1835 p. 66.

Henry Pye, by Samuel James Arnold

of ancient family, unimpeachable character and high position, we must admit that as a poet, his Muse's chief attributes are Mediocrity and Morality.[1]

The Ridding sisters cut and kept poems out of periodicals such as the Ladies Pocket Directory and Jane Austen transcribed the poetry of Byron.[2] Local poets commissioned the printing of their collected works, as William Andrew's attorney at law did in 1793, covering the cost by

Portswood House

subscriptions. His subscribers included Valentine and William Fitzhugh, Thomas Lewin, Mrs Middleton, Robert Ballard, Bland Wollstonecraft, Tobias Young and the writer of books on the migration of birds and effects of inoculation, John Legg. Andrew's poetry had local interest including a poem called *The Modern Mansion* which praised the Portswood home of East India Company

1 A G K Leonard 'A Forgotten Poet Laureate Recalled. Southampton Connections of Henry James Pye' in *Local Heritage Forum Journal* Spring 1997. Lord Byron said of Pye *a man eminently respectable in everything but his poetry.*
2 *Lines of Lord Byron, The Character of Buonaparte* Hartley Library, University of Southampton special collections AO 174.

man General Stibbert.[1] In 1804 George Byles a prisoner in the Debtor's Ward with a debt of £33 wrote a poem *Reveries in Confinement* which was printed and sold by Skelton the book sellers in the High Street for 2s 6d a copy to raise funds towards his release. It was so popular it went into a second edition.[2] On his release Byles recommenced his profession as Writing Master attending on families and ladies boarding schools in town or country: 'He purposes to instruct his Pupils to mend and make that most useful Instrument the Pen, which he trusts will be found of the greatest Utility in their future Pursuits'.

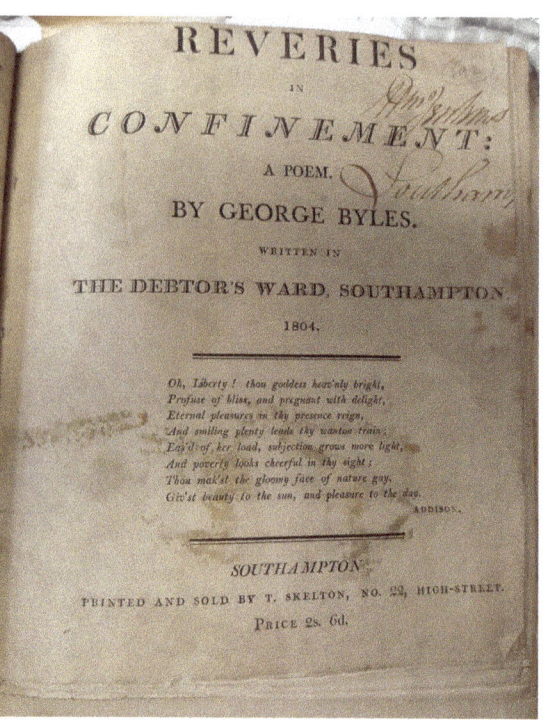

Reveries in Confinement by George Byles, Southampton Archives

1 *The First Volume of the Poetical Works of William Andrews, Attorney at Law, Southampton* Cunningham Printers 1793.
2 Senior subscribers included the mayor Frederick Breton, the MP James Amyatt who took two copies, Arthur Atherley, Thomas Durell, Arthur Hammond, John Butler Harrison, Sir Yelverton Peyton, John Rowcliffe, Admiral Scott and Samuel Silver Taylor plus 144 other subscribers, including a Samuel Jackson Pratt Esq who added he was Author of the *Gleanings, Family Secrets* etc. The Atherley Papers SA D/S 19/1/1 pp. 192-209. *Reveries in Confinement: A Poem by George Byles written in the Debtors' Ward, Southampton* Skelton 1804. Byles had lost a leg in an accident which may have contributed to his distressed state.

WAR

Politicks I never meddle with, but I love my Country & wish it's prosperity, tho I cannot wish; me, or those Dear to me, should draw ye sword, & possibly spill innocent blood, to defend our Cause – Melicent Ballard, 1781

SOUTHAMPTON FOUND ITSELF on the front line at the time of the Revolutionary and Napoleonic Wars and references to potential invasion pepper local letters and newspapers. The streets of the town often saw the local militias and regulars parading and there was also an influx of Royalist French refugees. Generals, admirals and officers made Southampton their home. The last line of defence rested on the companies of militia, made up of local men aged between seventeen and fifty, who were liable to be called on to serve, the number required determined by an annual ballot. Those selected were called up for twenty-eight days training each year, usually ending with manoeuvres which were often social occasions. The Hampshire Militia had two regiments, the North based at Winchester and the South based at Southampton. The Southern battalions held a grand field day on the marsh in 1773 with tents provided for a large number of spectators to whom the officers gave a public breakfast. The various armies that were from time to time assembled around the town had to be fed, clothed and entertained and although seen at times as an imposition also created employment and even supported the visitor economy with military displays, banquets, and opportunities to visit ships and even prisoner of war camps.

1779 was a time when fear of French invasion was raised, following from France and Spain giving their support to the American War of Independence. It was thought that the French would land on the Isle of Wight and invade the naval centre at Portsmouth. On 5th September a parson on the Isle of Wight lit the warning beacon having been told the French were coming. A physician staying in Southampton, Messenger Monsey, wrote: 'I fear that the Southampton Governor was as much, if not more, alarmed than the rest of the inhabitants, which is not very clever.' The French and Spanish fleets, however, were struggling with sailors dying from smallpox and typhus so that

Militia at the Bargate, by Stephen Taylor

an invasion was not practicable. Bodies were thrown overboard causing a local fear that fish had been poisoned.[1]

There were also visits to Southampton from other militias like the Dorsetshire that were stationed in the town and over-wintered there in

---

1 A Patterson *The Other Armada* Manchester 1960 pp. 37-58. C Haydon, 'A Letter from Southampton, September 1779' *Proceedings of the Hampshire Field Club and Archaeological Society* Vol 41 1985 pp. 284-7.

November 1780 and provided more than just military entertainments:

> We have had two exceeding good Winter Balls. the Dorsetshire Militia are quarter'd here till they encamp, they are a very genteel corps, & their Music you know is very fine the Sugar House is making into Barracks for them, to ease the publicans, who are at present very much crouded – *Melicent Ballard*

It was up to the navy to prevent any potential invasion by the French and the port of Southampton often had naval ships stationed there which was another attraction for locals and visitors and gave opportunities for social occasions. In 1780 Melicent Ballard wrote about visiting the *Royal George*:

> all the rest of the party were perfectly well. we went on board the Royal George, Capt Beaumaster, a Brother of Mr Brown's who is Chaplin to the Victory; on board which, we intended to have gone, but Mr Brown was on shore, the Royal George is a fine ship, carries a hundred brass Guns, & near nine Hundred men. we cast Anchor, & dined in the Harbour, upon cold Roast Beef, tongue, biscuit's, & cheese, very heartily. while we were in Harbour twelve men of War sail'd to St Hellens; you cannot conceive a finer sight, than so many noble ships under sail.

Captain Beaumaster was John Bourmaster, who was captain of the *Royal George* until 1781, which may have been lucky for him as the ship foundered at Spithead in 1782 with a loss of around 800 men.[1] Naval ships were also being built on the river Itchen at Northam:

The sinking of the Royal George

1   *Skelton's Visitor's Guide to Southampton, the surrounding area and Netley Abbey* 1843 p. 48.

Ship Building at Northam, Southampton Maritime and Local Heritage Collection

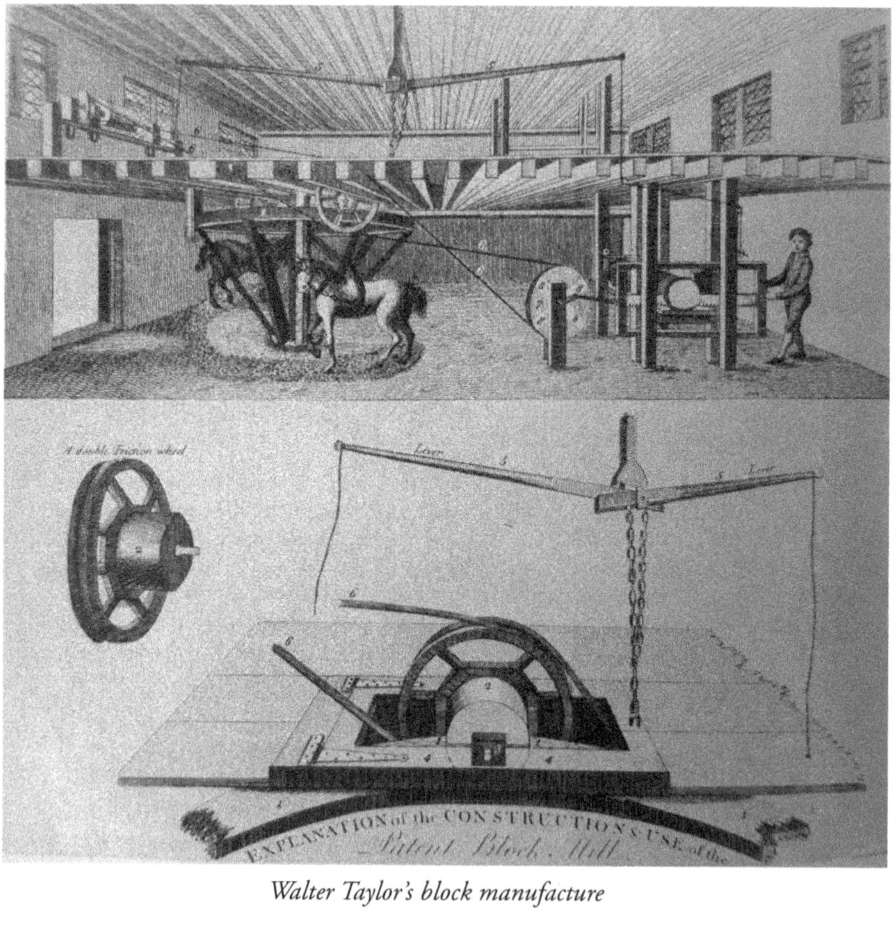

Walter Taylor's block manufacture

The ship at Northam was launched last spring tide, & went off very well, two more are in building, one of 64, & the other of 36 guns. - *Melicent Ballard* 1780

The entrepreneurial Taylor family of Southampton, a dynasty of builders and inventors, made a fortune developing products for the Royal Navy. These included a system of pulley blocks used to hoist and take down sails.¹ A single first-rate ship alone required around two thousand blocks and in the five years before Trafalgar the Taylor factories produced near half a million blocks. Walter Taylor II secured a patent from the crown for the security of his invention and other naval contracts followed, and his son Walter Taylor III refined his father's invention and also designed ship's pumps operated by valves.² In 1806, however, there was fire at the family block shop at West Quay which required the services of the Queens Regiment of Foot to help contain the blaze but the premises were burnt along with the workmen's tools. With so many young men serving in the navy and the army many people had relations and friends that died or were injured in the almost unbroken period of war:

Walter Taylor III, attributed to Gainsborough Dupont, Southampton City Council, Arts & Heritage

It is much fear'd the Thunderer Man of War is lost, as she has not been heard of, since that dreadful storm in Octbr. our valuable friend Robt Boyle Nicholas was Captain, see the effect of ambition, with a Paternal estate of seven hundred a year, he was not content, but would tempt the Sea, to add to his fortune, & has doubtless found it, his grave. - *Melicent Ballard* 1781

1   R A Pelham *The Old Mills of Southampton* Southampton Papers Number Three 1963 p. 19
2   Joseph Townsend *A Journey Through Spain* London 1791: 'The imperfection of sucking pumps is prevented by a late improvement, which bids fair for universal approbation. Mr Taylor of Southampton, the same gentleman to whom not only England but all Europe are indebted for blocks, which by long experience, have been found perfect both in point of strength and of prompt obedience: applied himself to the consideration of this matter and soon found a remedy.'

The *Thunderer* was wrecked in the Great Hurricane of the West Indies in 1780, all 617 on board were lost. Captain Robert Boyle-Walsingham was the younger son of the earl of Shannon.

The Dorsetshire Militia were still in town in 1781 having over-wintered in Southampton:

> The Dorsetshire Militia march'd Thursday for camp – they fired exceedingly well the King's birthday & there was a very genteel Ball in the Evening. I think I wrote since ye corps gave a very elegant breakfast & a dance after – Ld Rivers has petitioned to be quarter'd here again this Winter, as they all like the Town, & the Town was pleased with them. - *Melicent Ballard* 1781

The militias were often stood down if there was no immediate threat. As Melicent Ballard commented in 1783 'the Militias are all disembodied'.[1] Although the town was temporarily without the delights of local militias, Southampton was a popular place of residence for admirals and officers of the navy who were perhaps even more glamorous and many a younger son looked to make a career in the senior service with its opportunity for making a fortune by taking prizes:

> Mr McCombe is here in Lodgings. I believe you heard of his Wife's death - his son Jack is with him for a few days. he is grown a polite lad for a sailor, & is very soon to go to Newfoundland, he has been on one or two voyages already & taken a prize his share of which is about twenty pound – he tells me he smokes very well, but cannot learn to chew, he drinks his pint of Port with pleasure & begins to be very polite to Ladys – Roger Mears is well spoken of by his Captain, not so Tom Sherer, who has been with Sir Richd. Hughes, but is turn'd over to another ship, call'd the Nymph.[2] - *Melicent Ballard* 1783

Not everyone did as well at supplying the navy as Walter Taylor. Christopher Potter had a steam mill with ten ovens at his premises at Chapel Mill in Southampton, established in 1781 and he also had premises at

---

1 The Militia was put back onto a wartime footing in 1803
2 *Nymph* was originally a French Ship captured in 1780 by Captain John Ford. Roger Mears was drowned in 1783. *Steel's Original and Correct list of the Royal Navy* London 1799 p. 43. Sir Richard Hughes was on the *Leander* in 1783 stationed in the West Indies. Robert Beatson *Naval and Military Memoirs of Great Britain from 1727-1783* London 1804 p. 485.

Rotherhithe. He was contracted by the Navy to provide 1000 bags of biscuit a week from 23ʳᵈ June 1781 until further notice.[1] In the second half of 1781 he delivered 18,937 cwt to Portsmouth, however two years later he was bankrupt:

> Sunday morning ye 20, 1783 - have I ever mention'd a capital bake house built by Mr Potter at Chapell, he had a contract with Government for Sea Biscuits, & has laid out seven thousand pounds in Mills Bake-house & houses for his principal workmen. it really looks like a little parish – he himself rented 'Belle-Vue', kept two carriages drove six horses & was quite the fine Gentleman. but this day his name is in the Gazette a Bankrupt, & we hear he owes thirty thousand pounds in this County. in all probability many familys will be ruin'd by him. such a man deserves worse, than a common highwayman, who only takes the triffle you have in your pockett, while these fine folks by artful tales grasp every thing - your Uncle has no concern with him, but Ward Kellow Bernard & some others in this Town, are taken in pretty deep. the gentleman is gone to France, & has left his wife & children in great distress. Mrs Potter brought him a good fortune, but was not prudent enough to have it secured.
> – *Melicent Ballard*

In June 1789 George III and Queen Charlotte visited Southampton, on the eve of the French Revolution, where they were taken down to the Quay and the Platform to admire the promenade. In 1790 the Hampshire Chronicle recorded the arrival of the hated press gang in Southampton but on this occasion a warning had been received and eligible seamen had fled and it was the unfortunate Itchen fishermen who were taken, despite official protests. Back in 1781 the Ballard's wine business was affected by the loss of men to the press gang:

> - we have had very stormy weather ever since ... & the Wind is very little cull'd yet – several . drove up to Platform last night ...& a Port(uguese) ... with wines on board was bulged , & some of the wine was mostly for Hull the like accident never happen'd in our River before, & was now occasion'd, by having so many men press'd, that they had not hands enough to secure her properly. it is thought Government must pay the loss - *Melicent Ballard*, February 1781

In 1793 when war with France broke out again after the execution of Louis XVI, the Southampton corporation tried to encourage volunteers for

---

1   R A Pelham *The Old Mills of Southampton* Southampton Papers Number Three 1963 pp. 24-30.

Embarkation of the army at Southampton 1794, Thomas Rowlandson

the Royal Navy by the establishment of a fund to bestow a bounty of three guineas to every able seaman and two guineas to every landsman in addition to the royal bounty. There were still not enough ordinary sailors willing to take the King's shilling and so press gangs operated around the port which also disrupted the local economy. The voluntary corps of Sea Fencibles was set up in 1793 and given the responsibility for guarding the coastline of Britain. They were commanded by officers of the Royal Navy and had to learn to use pikes and cannon. The men had to be living and have families in the local district which they guarded. They trained on one day a month for the wage of one shilling, a rate which they also received in the event that they were needed to provide extra service. Unless the enemy invaded it was understood that they would not have to leave their locality but had permission to leave their location to go fishing or to the fish markets.[1]

In June 1793 the town publicans lobbied for the erection of barracks because of the numbers of soldiers quartered at their houses which was

---

1 Jennifer Killick (ed) *Sea Fencibles 1805 Vol 3 – Hampshire Coast* Hythe 2000.

causing suffering to their families.¹ In 1794 military troops were sent to the town in transport ships but, after having been at sea for several weeks in cramped conditions, many were sick with typhus. The men were transferred to temporary hospitals about the town, including the old Sugar House which had hastily been turned into a barracks for upto 1000 men² whilst tobacco was used to fumigate the ships. This just had the effect of spreading the infection to the local population. Later the remaining troops, along with French émigré soldiers, departed leaving sheets, blankets and other things from the temporary hospital in storage. Unfortunately, this storage was broken into and the infected linen was stolen further spreading the typhus epidemic around the town.³

1   *Hampshire Chronicle* 29 April, 17 June 1793.
2   The Sugar House got its name from being a sugar refinery built earlier in the century by John Brissault for the refining of sugar that came from the family's Jamaican plantations. When Brissault went bankrupt, the building was requisitioned for the army. SA D/PM/1-34 and D/PM/ 23/10/1 Bankruptcy of John Brissault 1774. John Oldfield 'From spa to garrison town: Southampton during the French Revolutionary and Napoleonic Wars, 1793-1815 in Miles Taylor (ed.) *Southampton Gateway to the British Empire* London 2007 p. 3.
3   M South 'Epidemic Disease, Soldiers and Prisoners of War in Southampton 1550-

The Woolhouse, with graffiti from French prisoners

The town also had to respond when French prisoners of war were brought to England. In 1793 there were around a thousand prisoners that needed secure accommodation. Henry Austen, brother of Jane Austen, was sent to the town with the Oxfordshire Militias Southampton unit to help escort the prisoners to Stapleton Prison near Bristol.[1]

As well as prisoners there were also refugees and Thomas Rowlandson caught the landing of escaping Royalists at the town quay in 1794.[2] One the 'Comte de Castries', took up residence not far from Ridgeway in a little cottage on the heath where the Lewins and the Lance families lived. A French Revolutionary refugee, Comte Toussaint-Ambroise Talour de la Cartrie de la Villeniere, had been involved in the abortive Royalist revolt at Le Vendee. After a series of adventures, he managed to escape to England and took part in the assault on Brittany by Royalist soldiers. Again he escaped to Jersey; he was 53 at the time. The French were ordered to leave Jersey and go to

1800' *Proceedings of the Hampshire Field Club and Archaeological Society* Vol 43 1987 pp. 185-96.
1   Clive Caplan 'Jane Austen's Soldier Brother' in *JASNA Persuasions* 18 1996 p. 125.
2   *The Disembarkation of the Royalists of Toulon at Southampton in 1794*, V&A accession number P.113-1931. *The Hampshire Chronicle* reported that in 1796 1,000 French priests and refugees arrived via Jersey, 6 August 1796. See also *Patterson* chapter on Southampton and the French Wars.

Disembarkation of French Royalists at Southampton, Thomas Rowlandson

Southampton. The Comte was destitute and forced to look for work and found himself as a labourer on the estate of the former East India Company man, Mr Dott at Bitterne Grove, working for ten hours a day. He then after a period of illness through gout, moved to Itchen Ferry living on a government allowance of a shilling a day. His luck changed in 1798 when the Act of Amnesty in France meant he was able to take possession again of his chateau. He had to raise £50 from friends to secure his return to France. On his return home he was still impoverished but lived on till his eighties.[1] Another escapee was the talented amateur artist Henri Roland Lancelot Turpin de Crissé who took time to draw the sights of the town, Netley Abbey and Woodmill.[2]

There is also a legend recounted in Gerald Mornington's book on Peartree Green, *Southampton's Marquis and other mariners,* that whilst a schoolboy in 1793, a young Corsican travelled to Southampton on the *Havre de Grace* where he was befriended by Captain James Bryer of Peartree who had him lodge at his house on the Green during his stay. He made such an impact on the family that several of the boys of the family were christened with his name: Napoleon.

A barracks was eventually established on the outskirts of the town in

---

1 Cheryl Butler *Jane Austen & Southampton Spa* Southampton 2017 p. 88.
2 Collection held at the Musées d'Angers. De Crissé emigrated to America in 1794.

Woodmill by Henri Turpin de Crisse, Musees d'Angers

Shirley called the Toulouse Barracks[1], although some of the people kept there were also suspect:

> Me Lord Duke
> In Consequence of your Grace's Letter I have seen Monsieur John Dairens & delivered him the Copy of his Majesty's Letter to quit the Kingdom. He is at present close confined at the Toulouse Barrack at Shirley, as they are afraid of his doing them mischief which he threatens if he is at large. I have there fore desired Mr [blank] the Lieutenant to confine him in Custody till I have your Grace's Directions what should be done with him.
> [In the margin was a brief description of the prisoner: The Description of John Dariens Person – aged 40 five feet five ... Face flat also stout made.][2]

In 1794 the Duke of York's Military School was built on the Avenue leading into Southampton, designed by John Plaw, which was used up until 1806.[3] Also, in 1794, an army was encamped near Netley destined for Ostend.

1 The camp appears to have been on Shirley Common. Prior to this period troops were usually billeted in inns and houses but garrisons and barracks increased greatly particularly on the south coast where 70% of barrack accommodation was located. This was driven by the threat of invasion. Kevin Linch 'Garrisons and the South of England in the late eighteenth and early nineteenth centuries' paper Southern History Society Conference November 2023.
2 SA DPM 93/11/113.
3 It became the Royal Military Asylum in 1816 and in 1841 it became the

Soon the numbers of troops in the town were raised again prior to the planned attack on Quiberon in 1795:

> We passed through a forest of transports, which were partly waiting for troops, and were partly laden with horses for Lord Moira's expedition. As soon as we got into the town, nothing but red coats and military were to be seen on all sides. *J H Manners.*[1]

As Manners observed, six regiments had just sailed and a further nine were camped at Nursling Common with another arriving from Jersey, he continues:

> Col Stewart son of Lord Galloway and Deputy-Adjutant General on Lord Moira's staff .... Told us that notwithstanding the disastrous defeat of the Emigrants in Quiberon Bay, the preparations for Lord Moira's armament, wherever it might be destined, were carried on with the greatest alacrity... Col Stewart also told us that Lord Moira's staff was suitable to an army of 50,000 men. One regiment had just arrived from Jersey, where they had buried 250 men of a fever. Some of them did not muster above 340 men.

The military expedition in 1795 was a disaster and again the surviving troops were sent back to Southampton. Eventually this force sailed for the West Indies where most perished from disease. The numbers of troops in the town caused suffering for the inhabitants. John Butler Harrison wrote to the government on 4 August 1795 explaining that though the magistrates had tried to procure bread, corn and flour and to reduce consumption, the demands of the large military force in the town and the need to supply the Channel Isles, had nearly exhausted the local stock. Harrison appealed to the government for relief.[2] In 1796 barracks were being fitted up in the town and surrounding area to receive 10,000 French emigrants and other foreign troops and stables were being made ready for 500 horses. A Half-Way Barn, that had been established between Southampton Quay and Calshot Castle fitted up for the French emigrant artillery and for the reception of the troops and stores, was consumed by fire. There was some suspicion that the fire was not an accident.[3]

headquarters of the Ordnance Survey. F J G Hearnshaw & F A Clarke *A Short History of Southampton* Oxford 1910 p. 118.
1   *Visitors' Description* pp. 20-22.
2   TNA HO 42-35-146.
3   Newpaper cutting March 1st 1796 The Atherley Papers.

The long-running war was in constant need of new troops. Ann Newell's near neighbour, Col Powlett of Albion Place, had begun his army career in the 95th Regiment of Foot in 1793 and after the regiment was disbanded in 1796 Powlett took on a new role as a Field Officer for the Recruiting District of Southampton. His area covered Hampshire, Dorset and Sussex co-ordinating the Parish Officers who, as part of the country's Defence Act, had to drum up recruits for the army.[1]

The soldiers did make a dashing sight as visitor J H Manners, 5th Duke of Rutland, recorded:[2]

> The 42nd the oldest Highland regiment, and which is reckoned the best in the service was there. One of the prettiest corps on the ground was a regiment of light dragoons, commanded by Colonel Gwyn and consisting of 300 men. Their dress is exactly similar to that of the French Hussars, so much so indeed, that they are going to have red clothing to put over it, in order that when they are in actual service, they may not be mistaken for the latter, from which fatal consequences might ensue. There were also about 800 French Royalists encamped by themselves, dressed in the habit of Chouans, in grey, turned up with red

Not to be outdone many of the local gentry formed Loyal Volunteer troops. They had written an open letter on 2nd April 1796 to the mayor Arthur Atherley:

> Sir
> The undersigned request that you will call a Meeting of the Inhabitants of the Town and county for the purpose of taking into consideration the propriety of forming a Corps of Infantry by voluntary Enrolment to serve in this Town and neighbourhood at this moment of National Danger
> Fred Breton, John Keele, William Lomer, J. Robbins, George Hookey, Val. Fitzhugh, J A Mant, John Thomas North, J H Brohier, John Colson, Thomas Pipon, W. Tinling[3]

In 1797 England lived in fear of a French invasion and in this year the Southampton Volunteer Cavalry was formed by Major William Smith,

---

1 John Philippart ed *The Royal Military Calendar Vol 3* London 1820 p. 341. See also Eleventh Report of the Commission of Military Enquiry Parliamentary Papers 1809 Appendix 9 p. 72 and Parliamentary Reports 1808 Vol 4 pp 47-64.
2 *Visitors' Description* p. 21.
3 SA Atherley Papers D/S 19/1/2 p. 52.

the Collector of customs. In addition, three volunteer infantry corps were also raised: The Southampton Volunteers under Captain William Tinling, the Portswood Green Volunteers led by Walter Taylor, and the Associated Householders under Sir Yelverton Peyton.[1] Their petition sent to the mayor was agreed and on the 13th of August 1798 the Corps of Associated Householders received their colours stitched by Miss Barnouin a local headmistress and daughter of a former minister of the French Church, Isaac Barnouin. The event was celebrated in a song by the poet laureate Henry Pye.[2] Not everyone was so enthusiastic, John Hawkins a ropemaker in St Mary's parish complained that his apprentice John Miller aged sixteen had enlisted with the Southampton Volunteers.[3] Another apprentice, Robert Hill had a warrant put out for his arrest for leaving his master James Newlyn, a women's shoemaker, to enlist as a soldier.[4]

The Volunteer Regiment of Horse exercised on the estates of the local gentry, Thomas Lewin served with them and in 1797 they could be found going through their paces at the home of Nathaniel Middleton at Townhill. Walter Taylor trained his band of local militia at his business headquarters at Woodmill where they were commanded by his son Samuel. The men were inspected by General Cowell who expressed himself as highly satisfied with *the corps of Walter Taylor*. Invasion by Napoleon's armies however was thought to be imminent: '1798 April Our reports from London say that he and his 'army of England' are confidently expected.' – *Thomas Lewin*[5]

The amount of dashing young men in the town offered opportunities for romance and in 1798 Mary Lewin's sister, Charlotte Hale, found herself much admired by the officers of a Dragoon Regiment quartered at Southampton with Col Affleck[6] and Major Moore being her foremost

1 Hampshire Chronicle 28 April, 30 June, 18 August, 3September 1798. *The Hampshire Repository* Winchester 1798 Vol I p. 49.
2 The poet laureate Henry Pye resided in Southampton. The Atherley Papers D/S 19/1/2 p. 55.
3 SA SC9/4/807, John Hawkins was later accused of assaulting his apprentice, SC9/4/836.
4 SA SC9/4/850.
5 *Lewin Letters* p. 55. There was a French force which attempted to support the Irish Rebellion of 1798 and did reach the Irish mainland but was eventually defeated. 'Here come the French, sure enough. They have taken Killalla, and are in this house at the moment I am writing to you.' Letter from the Bishop of Killalla to his brother Stephen Stock August 1798. HRO 9M73/G1964.
6 There is a picture in the Royal Collection of Colonel James Affleck of the 16th Light Dragoons made by Robert Dighton showing his blue uniform with its scarlet facings, silver lace and braid, crimson sash, black boots and belt with a black turban

admirers. In 1799 troops were gathered at Shirley pending an assault on the Helder in the Netherlands. In May 1800 there was a camp on Netley Common commanded by Lord Moira whose troops were destined for a descent on the coast of Holland. The Lewin family governess took three of her charges to visit the camp where they observed a military band and women in pits dug out of the ground cooking and washing linen. It was said that traces of the holes remained visible on the common as late as 1839. The troops at Netley were also destined for Egypt.[1]

Also, in 1800, Mary Lewin's brother George visited Southampton. He was of the 2nd Queen's Regiment of the Line and sadly he died shortly afterwards of fever in Minorca aged twenty-five.[2] Mary Lewin's twelve-year-old son, John Dick, was shipwrecked as he started his naval career in 1800 but luckily survived.

The greatest naval hero was the iconic Horatio Nelson, who used Southampton as a port of embarkation in 1801 when he was enroute for the Baltic. Whilst in the town Nelson called at George Rose's house but unfortunately the gentleman was not at home. Nelson then suffered a fit of malaria before he could travel on to Honiton. The *Hampshire Chronicle* reported that whilst at the Dolphin in Southampton Lord Nelson: was 'about to be employed on a secret mission... his instructions will not be opened until he arrives in a certain latitude.'[3]

Civilians found themselves caught up in the conflict, such as in June 1801 when Stephen Buckle, a local ferryman, returned to Southampton after being a prisoner in France. He and his boat had been hijacked by three Frenchmen and forced to go to Cherbourg where he ended up in prison with the three hijackers who were escaped prisoners. Another Sotonian who lived in Cherbourg managed to facilitate his release and on his return to England it was reported that the Southampton resident had also negotiated the release of other English captives.[4]

    topped by a white and red plume. RCIN 990807. There was a Major Henry Moore of the 4th Dragoon Guards who died in Cornwall in 1810.
1 F J G Hearnshaw & F A Clarke F *A Short History of Southampton* Oxford 1910 p. 118. For information on 18th-century camp layouts and dugouts see Richard Osgood and Paul McCulloch. 'The Hessians of Barton Farm: Uncovering when a German army defended Britain' in *Current Archaeology* 345 November 1 2018
2 *Lewin Letters* p. 137.
3 Nelson's flagship in 1801 at the battle of Copenhagen was *HMS Elephant* which was built in 1786 at Hamble by George Parsons.
4 *Mottley's Naval and Military Journal* 18 July 1801. Francis Abell *Prisoners of War in Britain 1765-1815* Oxford 1914 p. 102.

In October 1801 Thomas Lewin wrote to his Parisian contact John Frederick Perregaux:

> The blessing of peace having been once more restored to us, and the means of corresponding opened again after an interruption of almost nine years, I embrace with eagerness the first opportunity of paying my respect to you and renewing those habits of friendly intercourse which I have for many years had the pleasure in cultivating with you.[1]

Other locals travelling in France could find themselves unable to leave the country as happened to Meselina Trench who lived just outside Southampton at Bursledon. Trench was an heiress and author, poet, travel writer and lady of letters. She supported many causes including the abolition of slavery, child labour laws, prison conditions, and taxation on salt. Meselina had married her second husband Richard Trench in Paris in 1803 and in her letters, she complained that she was 'ill lodged, ill fed and ill served' in Paris. The couple were detained in France after the peace of Amiens was revoked. Meselina spent the next four years confined in Orleans and trying to obtain the release of her husband. Meselina eventually appealed, in person, to Napoleon himself to secure his release.[2]

The Militia was put back onto a wartime footing in 1803 and the various bands were joined together to form the Loyal Southampton Fusiliers under the command of the plantation owner Josias Jackson of Bellevue House. In 1805 the Volunteer corps exercised on Woolston Lawn, the property of Mr Chamberlayne who was then captain of the corps, Mr Thomas Lewin being the lieutenant.

John Sturdy,[3] a local auctioneer, cabinet maker and appraiser of Canal Place, kept a journal of his time in the Yeoman Cavalry between 1803 and 1809. He presented this journal to his officer John Butler Harrison who was captain of the 1st Troop. Sturdy records the uniform that he wore which included a jacket, white breeches, blue overalls, a pair of spurs, boots, cloak, helmet,

---

1 *Lewin Letters* p. 86. Perregaux had been managing property Lewin had in France. Perregaux was a Swiss banker with offices in Paris.
2 Several of Trench's works were published by her son Richard *The Remains of the Late Mrs Richard Trench* London 1862. HRO 23M93/1-49.
3 He was the same John Sturdy who offered his workshop in his house later renamed The Pineapple Inn, St Michael's Square, to a group of Roman Catholics for a place of worship. *Patterson* p. 113. A John Sturdy, cabinet maker, was arrested by order of the Sheriff in regard to a bail bond of £88 on 23 August 1808. SA D/PM/ Box 83/4/7/1.

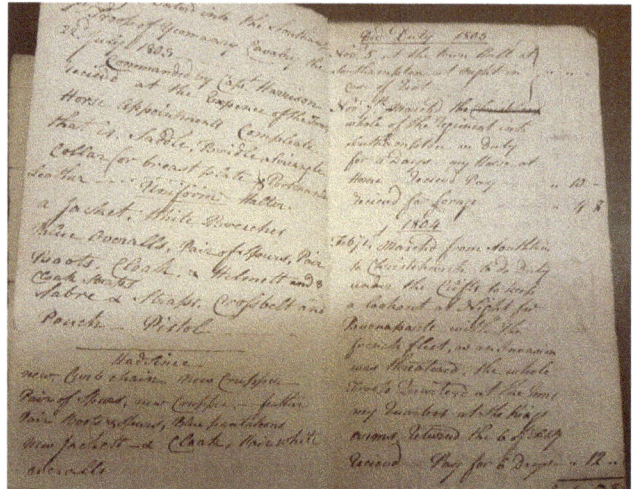 

John Sturdy, and his journal, private collection

sabre, straps, crossbelt and a pouch and pistol. The troop mainly saw service around the local area and provided other services as well as being defenders of the coast. On November the 5th they were on duty at the town hall overnight in case of riot and then on 7th November 1803 the whole regiment marched into Southampton and were on duty for five days.[1]

Despite all this activity the government still needed regular recruits for the army and navy. On 13th June 1803 the local paper noted:

> At Trinity Fair a vast number of horses were bought for sale, few were good and these fetched the highest prices ever remembered. Not a single showman was to be seen, occasioned, it is thought, from an apprehension of being disturbed by the Press Gang.

John Diaper of Itchen Ferry was granted a sandwalker's licence on 3rd November 1804 which was renewed annually by the mayor of Southampton up until 3rd May 1815.[2] This minor appointment as a town official was an object of desire during the Napoleonic Wars as a protection against impressment into the navy. A sandwalker had the right to search for and seize flotsam, jetsam, ligans, wrecks of the sea, goods taken by pirates and all royal fish taken within the town's precincts. This was quite a distance and included the Hamble River, over to Redbridge, down to Calshot and over to Hurst and Langstone on the Isle of Wight.

Meanwhile in the West Indies the 31st Regiment of Foot had its numbers

---

1 John Sturdy's Journal, private collection of Colin Hyde Harison.
2 SA SC8/2/15 and SC8/1/3.

so decimated by fever that they actively recruited slaves and black freemen from the islands. There were large numbers of black soldiers and sailors who served in the forces at this time. In 1800, of the 130,000 serving in the Navy, only half were British.

By 1803 when the three groups of volunteer corps had been amalgamated into one a unit of Sea Fencibles were also raised. In December 1803 almost 2,000 local volunteers were reviewed by the Duke of Cumberland[1] on Shirley Common and, as fears of invasion grew, the next spring saw an exercise in which volunteers from Southampton and other areas staged a mock attack on Pear Tree Green from the river Itchen. In February 1804, when the thought of a French invasion was increased, Sturdy's troop marched to Christchurch to do duty for six days on the cliffs to keep night lookout for Bonaparte and the French Fleet. Whilst there they were quartered at the local inns such as the Kings Arms. At the end they returned to Southampton in June and spent eleven days quartered there. In October they were in Lyndhurst and were inspected by Brigadier General Michell and were part of a corps of a thousand men being marched down to Weymouth. They drilled around South Stoneham, Redbridge, Nursling and Millbrook and were joined by the Lyndhurst Sharpshooters and the Duke of Cumberland's 15th Light Dragoons. Captain John Butler Harrison had injured his hand and his second in command, Murry, took over. The fear of invasion continued and was particularly high in 1804 and 1805:

> March 1804 What do you say of M. Bonaparte's visit? It must either be near or not at all – so at least one would suppose from the vast amount of preparatives that we hear of. What strikes one as remarkable is, that the Funds are not depressed by the near approach of the coming danger. On the contrary, they are better within these fewe days. This looks as if the public opinion was that Boney would not come, or that if he did he would be effectually and quickly repulsed. *Thomas Lewin*[2]

In November 1804 King George III came to Southampton. He had been staying at Cuffnells, Mr Rose's place, near Lyndhurst and the Lewins watched the king's arrival from a friend's house in Above Bar. The King came down

---

1 Prince Ernest Augustus fifth son of George III and later King of Hanover.
2 *Lewin Letters* p. 102. Baron Bolton, the Lord Lieutenant of Hampshire was tasked with preparations in case there was an invasion, including the evacuation of civilians and the numbers of military personnel and equipment needed. HRO 11M49/231-244.

from Moira Place at a canter, Mr Rose riding at his horse's flank, with equerries each side but a little behind. He wore a single breasted dark green hunting frock, the uniform of the New Forest Verderers, and he wore it to compliment his host Mr Rose. The rest of his outfit included gilt buttons, light kerseymere breeches, flapped waistcoat, high boots without tops, white stocking at the knee, small plain three-cornered hat with a black ribband cockade, hair powdered with a pig tail tied closely to his head. The king stopped at Colonel Nathaniel Heywood's door, on Above Bar, and was presented to Mrs Chaloner and one of her daughters as they were related to Admiral Harvey.

In 1805 on the 8th anniversary of the Yeoman Cavalry's founding, a celebratory dinner for the officers was had at the Crown Inn on the High Street. Later that year it was reported that Bonaparte had been crowned Emperor so the troops marched with a fife to St Lawrence church where Rev Mears, the troop chaplain, preached a sermon: 'Put on the whole Armour of God that ye may be able to stand against the wiles of the Devil.' Frances Harris wrote to her father the Earl of Malmesbury in October: 'Bonaparte seems destined by Providence to acquire universal dominion.'.[1]

Marching, parading and inspections continued for Sturdy and the local volunteers, though not all were as conscientious as Sturdy. On 26 May Mr

Death of Lord Nelson

1   HRO 9M73/310/26 Letter of Frances Harris.

King, a private, was voted out of the troop for non-attendance and leaving the exercise ground without leave. Sturdy recorded the strength of the local militias, the Wiltshire Yeomanry had 900 men, the Dorset 500 and Southampton 400. The companies were paid for the days that they served and for the eleven days Sturdy was in quarters in Southampton he received £1 2s. The end of 1805 saw a great victory and a great loss following on from the naval battle at Trafalgar. Sturdy recorded in his journal:

> Dec 1805 public thanks giving for the victory at Trafalgar on 21st October NB Lord Nelson was Killed on board the Victory which ship carried his Flag by a Musket Ball which Pierced his left Breast. He was Opposed by 33 sail of the line to 27 – he was 47 Years of age had fought in 120 Battles and had lost his right arm and right Eye in other Engagements in Defence of his country!

George Miller Bligh, National Maritime Museum

George Miller Bligh of Southampton was severely wounded by a musket shot through the breast and head in that same memorable battle of Trafalgar where he was serving as Flag Lieutenant of the *Victory*. He had been appointed to *Victory* at the desire of Lord Nelson, out of regard to his father's distinguished conduct in the service, his father being Admiral Sir Richard Rodney Bligh. George lived at Blighmont; an eight-bedroom house built on a 50-acre estate in Millbrook on the outskirts of Southampton. George witnessed the Admiral's death but survived his own wounds and attended Nelson's funeral.[1] Frances Harris wrote to her father Lord Malmesbury:

> Lord Nelson receives and deserves from the Nation the tribute of regret & adoration that he has earned with such glory. Had he wished for any particular kind of Death he has probably fallen in the manner he would have prayed for.[2]

1 The Atherley Papers D/S2/2/6.
2 HRO 9M73/310/ 30 Letter of Frances Harris.

Following the death of Nelson in 1805 the French Street Theatre, which had closed for the season, was reopened especially in the November by Mr Collins for a benefit concert for the widows and orphans of Trafalgar. Visitors could see the scenery and wardrobe and view a full-length portrait of Nelson before seeing a play and farce. Harriet Lewin read about the loss of Nelson in the Courier Newspaper in 1806, as she was drying the newspaper by the fire for her father:

> As I held the paper before the fire I was attracted by the sight of many lines printed in large Capital letters, and I read the lines out loud and remember the shock it gave my Father when I uttered the concluding words. The news announced was the great Naval Victory of Trafalar, and the last sentence was "Lord Nelson was killed in the actions", The neighbours all ran about to each other's houses discussing the important news and lamenting the death of our great Commander. The fear of Napoleon Buonaparte had indeed for some years past formed a standing terror to all who, like, ourselves, lived near the English Coast. Our nursemaids would tell us that "Boney" would catch us if we broke bounds, and whenever a suspicious vagrant made his appearance he was at once set down as a French spy. Every gentleman's son was encouraged to learn the manual exercise with a toy musket by his nurse, she assuring him that his duty was "to fight the French and beat Boney". The exultation caused by the victory of Trafalgar afforded a temporary encouragement to the Hampshire folks of their being able to resist Bonaparte's power. All sorts of demonstrations took place in celebration of the event, and a ball was given at Southampton to which everybody went.[1]

Rev Mears rector of St Lawrence and chaplain to the corporation preached a sermon at St Lawrence before the mayor and corporation, a service of thanksgiving with a collection made for widows, orphans and those who suffered. The sermon was printed on the 18th December by Thomas Skelton and sold for 1s. Sturdy also records a second blow, having lost the naval hero Nelson within a few months the prime minister, William Pitt the younger, also died: 'Feb 26 1806 day appointed for a General fast and Humiliation. Sermon on the good qualities of our late Minister, Mr Pitt as being the greatest statesman we ever had.'[2]

Sturdy's journal also gives a detailed description of the funeral of private

---

1 *Lewin Letters* Vol II p. 141.
2 William Pitt the younger had died in the January aged 46.

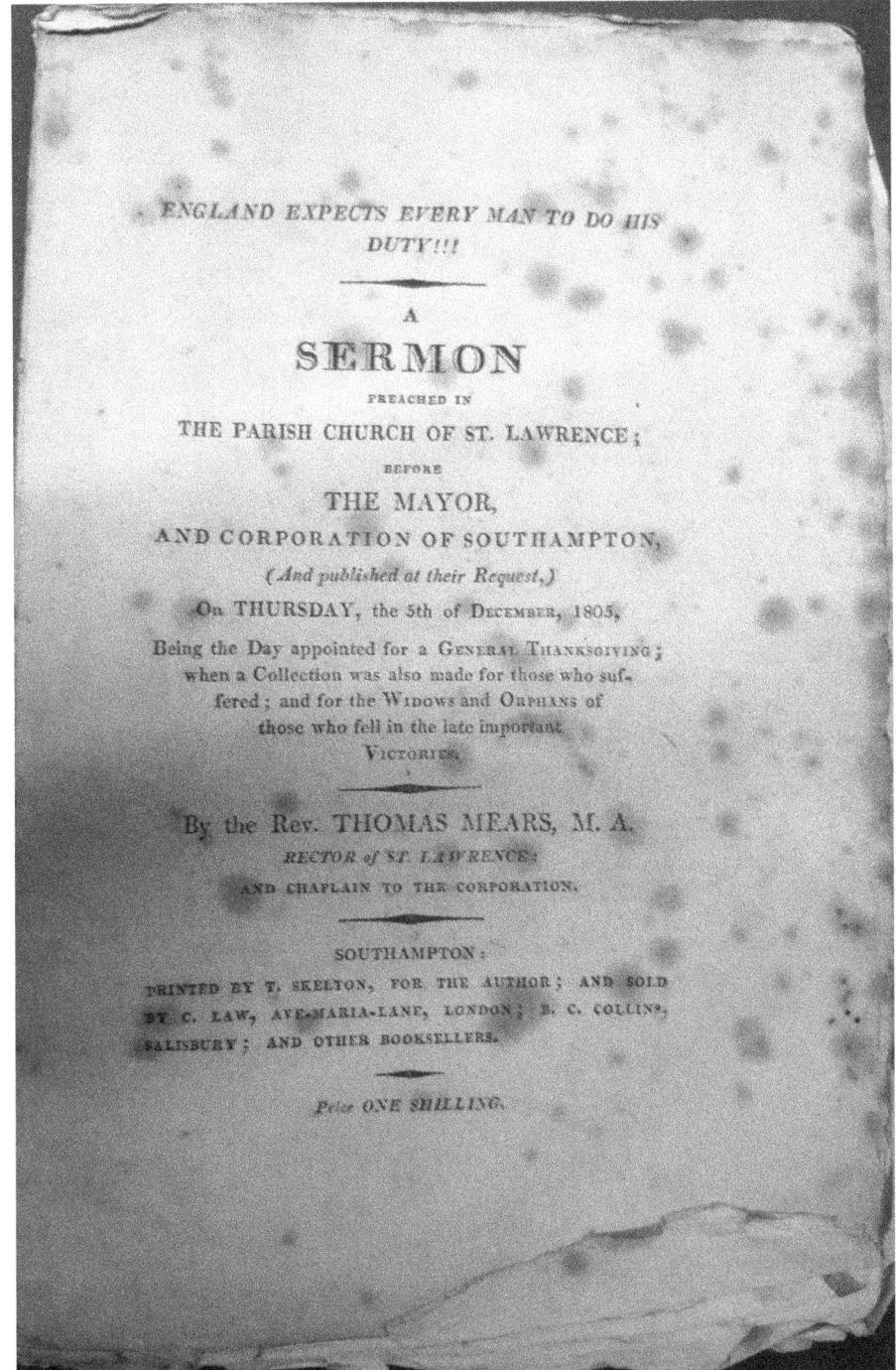

Remembrance Service for Nelson, Rev Thomas Mears, private collection

George Hills in April 1806. At the time of his death, he was not yet 21.[1] After the defeat of the French and Spanish fleet at Trafalgar there was an armistice which did not go well with everyone. Thomas Lewin wrote to his brother on 31 December 1805: What dreadful news from the Seat of War! An armistice declared and a Peace likely to follow: leaving poor old England to stand singly the whole brunt of the Corsican's vindictive fury.[2]

The volunteer forces were still on standby as Sturdy writes:

> 1806 4th June Wednesday being the anniversary of HMs birthday it was observed as usual with the banners displayed on the churches, bells ringing, a muster of the Cavalry and Infantry Volunteers who fired volleys and Feu de joies opposite the Audit House where officers commissioned and non-commissioned afterwards joined the Corporation and drank the customary healths accompanied by the different bands playing 'God Save the King' and 'Rule Britannia'. The Ball in the evening was very splendid (it rained)

On 11th August the *Hampshire Telegraph* reported that a grand rural Fete was held at Netley Abbey and the band of the 13th from Winchester and the 14th from Portsmouth were:

> engaged in the venerable ruins where upwards of 300 of the most fashionable took part of a cold collation; 40 couples danced on the turf till a later hour and broke up with extreme regret. The parties went in general by water and returned in carriages.

The *Hampshire Telegraph* reported on 25th May 1807:

> Lord Holland arrived here on Thursday with his retinue having taken the

---

1 Thirty-one Southampton people are recorded as fighting at Trafalgar, Thomas Johnson, who was pressed into service in 1803, lived at Back of the Walls and was killed in the battle aged twenty-three; his mother Elizabeth claimed his pay on 8 March 1806. Lt Andrew King went on to rise to be Post Captain in 1821.Turner places him bending over Nelson, between Hardy and Atkinson, in his depiction of the battle ; James Lenham a fifty-year-old, quarter gunner was invalided out of the navy in 1810; Joseph Painter a twenty-three- year old able bodied seaman was discharged in 1814; James Parker, 24, was a volunteer and still in service in 1814; Thomas Pickering, 22, joined the navy in 1803 and died aboard *HMS Ocean* in 1807 and John Gantlatt, 25, ordinary seamen survived and deserted in 1806 whilst his ship was in Portsmouth.
2 *Lewin Letters* p. 114.

Margravine of Anspach's mansion at West Place for 2 months. Peace is only wanting to establish this place as a fashionable resort.

Although naval officers like Frank Austen found themselves on half-pay due the lull in activities after Trafalgar which prompted him to move his family to Southampton and to join household forces with his mother and sisters, the war continued. Not everyone, however, was keen to continue the fight.

In 1807 John Jackson of the 31st Regiment of Foot, which company had provided part of the honour guard for Nelson's funeral, decided to desert and could be found drinking in the Cross Guns pub at the bottom of Simnel Street, just opposite the Long Rooms. Unfortunately for Jackson, his former sergeant, decided to use the same ale house and recognised Jackson immediately, not least of all because he was black. As a deserter Jackson had a price on his head of 20s so his sergeant took no time in taking him into custody and Jackson was probably taken down to God's House prison and clamped into irons.[1] This certainly happened to the twenty-two-year-old, Michael MacDonald in 1800, he absconded from the 13th Regiment of Foot and had been apprehended in Salisbury but was then taken back to his corps which was at that point stationed on Netley Common. His subsistence whilst in transit in Southampton prison was 4s 6d plus 3s 6d for handcuffs.[2] Jackson's company was due to be sent to Egypt and Thomas Lewin was concerned about events in that part of the world:

How culpable the Grenville Ministry rejecting the overtures of Russia in every way! Now look at the Declaration of that power, then judge, whom of our pretended Patriots we have to thank for assisting the intrigues of the Corsican to alienate the Heart of Alexander from us. O Fye! Fye upon it! They ought to be impeached.[3]

On the 10 August 1807 the Hampshire Telegraph reported the launch of the gun brig *The Pilot* from Mr Guillaume's yard at Northam. Jane Austen took her nephews on a water-party to Northam and they passed by Mr Guillaume's yard and saw a '74 gunship in October 1808, probably the *Conquistador*.[4] At sea things were going better:

1 SA SC9/4/785. A John Jackson had enlisted in the 31st Regiment of Foot on 25th April 1805. TNA WO 25/390. *findmypast.co.uk*. Information supplied by John Ellis.
2 SA D/PM 84/11/3.
3 *Lewin Letters* p. 120.
4 R A Austen-Leigh *Jane Austen and Southampton* p. 28. Guillaume eventually built thirteen ships for the Navy, most of them being brigantines.

July 1808 Cadiz and the two fleets at once in our possession! John Bull will begin to fancy that the mighty tyrant Buonaparte is already at his feet sueing for mercy. If the Spaniards do but go on as they have begun, he may be destined to fall with much greater rapidity than he rose. The moment the tide is seen to turn against him, he will have all the North and East of Europe on his back. The ways of Heaven are always inscrutable to Man; yet it may perhaps have been decreed that the present shall be the moment for wreaking upon his devoted head the Vengeance due to his crimes - *Thomas Lewin*[1]

In 1808 Frank Austen brought French prisoners back to England after the battle of Vimeiro. The old medieval warehouse, known as the Wool House, near to town quay was put into service as a temporary prison and its timbers still have graffiti scratched there by French prisoners.[2] The prisoners also eked out a living making carved bone ships that could be sold to visitors to the town. Not every battle was successful and could be felt personally in individual households, Charlotte Fitzhugh lost her twelve-year-old son Henry at the sea battle of Alvoen in 1808.

The volunteer corps were still important and to encourage the men Sturdy reported in 1808, that Captain Butler Harrison with his usual liberality made a present of *Two Guineas* to the Troop on June 1. In 1809, a loyal address to His Majesty was given in Parliament and the local mayor James Amyatt presented a copy to the corporation which included reference to: 'an impious and tyrannical usurper' that is to say Napoleon Bonaparte and a reference to the 'insidious Character of the French Consul'.[3]

In 1810, the Reverend Mant's school performed the plays *Douglas* and *Hamlet* for the French prisoners. There was a fear that English soldiers and sailors could also be captured of course and Thomas Lewin insured his son John Dick in 1804 in case he was captured and needed to be ransomed.[4] In an example of war as tourism, it was even seen suitable for some to go on a visit to view French prisoners as Harriet Lewin did in 1814 going to 'Fortin' prison, actually Forton prison. It was located near Portsmouth harbour at Alverstoke, Gosport. Originally an army hospital it had been previously used for American

1 *Lewin Letters* pp. 122-123.
2 The rate book for 1782-3 rated the French Prison at £15 and there was also a Spanish burial ground listed in St Michael's parish next to Marrett's Boarding house. SA SC/AG7/2. In 1781 Spanish prisoners were repatriated from the town to St Lucar. SA D/PM Box 97/11.
3 The Atherley Papers SA D/S2/2/6.
4 *Lewin Letters* p. 111.

prisoners during the American Revolutionary war.[1] Back in 1806 Ann Sophy Mackie had visited the *Temeraire* in Portsmouth and was delighted with a sight of that little world, though it was a melancholy thing to see the ravages made by the Enemy – 'One of the largest balls was still sticking in the side of the ship, having done much mischief in passing. We were even shown the marks of the blood on some of the beams.' In August 1810 the *Conquestadore* of 74 guns was launched from the Guillaume yard at Northam:

> Such a grand spectacle not having been seen on this water since the launching of the Saturn in 1786, it attracted a great number of persons. It is computed that more than 200 carriages and 10,000 spectators were present. ...... A sumptuous dinner on the occasion was given by Mr Guillaume at the Dolphin's Inn, to the most respectable inhabitants of this town and neighbourhood. – *Hampshire Telegraph*.

In 1810 the Sea Fencibles were finally disbanded. The war now was primarily a land one and although the main theatre of war against Napoleon would be focused on Spain and Portugal another conflict developed in North America. In 1812, Britain went to war with the former colony, the now independent, United States. Thomas Ridding, town clerk and attorney to many of the East India Company families as well as the Lewins, Ballards and Butler Harrisons, also acted for the 103rd Regiment. The Regiment was shipped out to Quebec in 1812, that town being the only permanent fortress in Canada, which had some 2,300 soldiers posted there.[2] The 103rd, however, were said to be the 'worse regiment in Canada'[3] due to the high desertion rate, the youth of their recruits and poor discipline. There are several records of courts martial that took place when the regiment was deployed.[4] For those who deserted

1 There were POW prisons across Hampshire, one of the largest at Portchester Castle which could house 7000 prisoners with others held at Petersfield and Odiham. The latter parish's bastardy register recorded that several of the fathers were French prisoners on parole between 1809-12. Claire Skinner *The French Connection, Les Relations avec la France* Hampshire p. 34
2 SA D/PM 20 1-5 letters of the 103rd.
3 Niagra 1812 Legacy Council.
4 The four degrees of a courts martial were laid out in *Standing Orders & Regulations for the 85th Light Infantry* London 1813 pp. 135-9, confinement to quarters; confinement to quarters with disgrace, coat turned and a letter C sewn on the right sleeve in a distinguishing cloth; confinement to the black hole, plus letter C, and fed only bread and water; corporal punishment. A regimental court martial needed three to five staff officers with the decision approved by the governor of the garrison, a general court martial had thirteen members and could impose capital

whilst on active duty, if captured, justice was swift. Privates Beafoot, Wilson and Carter attempted to desert to the enemy in 1813 and were sentenced to be shot.[1] The same sentence fell to Private Rufus Moon in the same year.[2] In 1814 Private William Tumulty deserted and stole a regimental horse, the general court martial with thirteen members who voted two for death, one for transportation for life as a felon and ten for eight hundred lashes. The majority vote would be the one that was carried out.[3] Private Thomas Lambert of the Royal Marines similarly had a split decision when he was apprehended whilst making his way towards enemy lines. Only one officer voted for death, five for eight hundred lashes but the majority, eight votes, was for transportation for life.[4] In 1816 privates Joseph Widdows, Williams and Smith were condemned to eight hundred lashes by six of the court, two others had voted for 999 lashes and one for 1,000.[5] Widdows survived the ordeal and was not put off from making another attempt to desert in 1817 and on this occasion received six hundred lashes. Others also had an additional punishment being marked with the letter D on their left side, two inches below the armpit, with the size of the brand being not less than half an inch long.[6] In contrast Lt Francis Small of the 41st Regiment was only given a private reprimand in 1814 for abusing his authority. Whilst trying to move sleighs to be used in a convey he had had a dispute with the local blacksmith, Josiah Proctor, over horses, he ordered the bugler to draw his sword and cut off his arm which resulted in an injury to the man's arm and hand. Small unsuccessfully tried to overturn the decision.[7]

The 103rd Regiment did improve and took part in the expedition to Plattsburg and Lake Champlain in July 1813, even earning prize money, however, the campaign took a turn for the worse and several of the company were captured and became prisoners of war. The regiment returned to Britain in 1817 and was disbanded.[8]

The Army and Naval presence in the town was felt with it being a centre for both the naval press gangs and the army recruiting office. In 1811 Cunningham's Street Directory advertised:

punishment by a 2/3rd majority.
1   SA DPM20/25.
2   SA DPM20/26.
3   SA DPM20/28.
4   SA DPM20/29.
5   SA DPM20/30/1.
6   SA DPM20/34-36.
7   SA DPM20/27.
8   SA DPM20/7/2/1 and DPM20/7/2/3.

Regulating Office for the Impress Service
Captain – J N Marshall, Lieutenant – J G Cock, Clerk - W T Morris, Two midshipmen and ten in the gang.
Recruiting Districts – West Gate Street
Inspector Lt Col Poulet, Paymaster John Hayman esq, Adjutant Capt George Gregory, Surgeon John Goosman, Sergeant Major Robert Charles, Clerks Richard Pirce, Simon Craske, J Brown
Barrack Dept
Inspector Capt Baron, Barrack Master William Alston Brandreth esq, Sergeant at the Depot Barracks Alexander Wilson, Cavalry Sergeant J Yeates

The Napoleonic War was finally drawing to a close following on from the victory over Napoleon at the battle of Waterloo in 1815.[1] The emperor had been captured before and held prisoner in Elba, the town celebrated by illuminating civic buildings including the Custom House, Audit House and Town Hall. There were also a large number of 'beautiful and appropriate transparencies' which 'surpassed any thing of the kind that has before been attempted in this town'.[2] During this brief respite many English families, like the Lances, took the opportunity of travelling to the continent where they were taken by surprise when Napoleon escaped captivity. He raised an army and was very nearly successful but this time his second exile to St Helena was permanent. In July 1815 the town clerk, Thomas Ridding, drafted a letter in regard to the Waterloo Subscription:

> The Committee for conducting the subscription for the Benefit of the Families of the slain and of the numerous seriously wounded of the British army to under the Command of the Illustrious Wellington in the signal victory of Waterloo and in the several Battles which have been or may be fought in the present Campaign having applied to the Magistrates of the Town for their assistance prompting this subscription. Notice is hereby given That Books for such subscription are now opened at the several Banks in this Town for the purpose of this just and necessary act of Liberality & Beneficence
> By order of the Mayor & Justices[3]

1 Walter Nassau, a school friend of Francis Sladen Harrison, in 1859, visited Crystal Palace and wrote to his friend to report he had seen a picture of the battle of Waterloo, there were three Frenchmen walking up and down and apparently would not look at it because 'they were beaten in it'. SA D/Z 676/5/15.
2 Oldfield *From Spa to Garrison Town* p. 11.
3 SA D/PM 93/11/227.

The Corporation itself subscribed ten guineas and also requested that Rev Thomas Mears print his sermon of public thanksgiving on the conclusion of the peace treaty which they would pay for.[1] The result of the long conflict meant not only a period of peace but a growing Empire to police and defend. In India it was the East India Company which ran the military so mothers like Mary Lewin still had sons to worry about. Mary Lewin wrote to her son William serving in the Hon Company's Artillery in March 1826:

> Your two accounts of the army are admirable. One I had put into a daily paper, and it was thought much of. Tom forwarded it, and your last of your Band playing over the hills, and made me shed tears, for there was a corresponding feeling of the soldier in your old Mother, and had I been a man the Army would have been my choice.[2]

---

1 A Temple Patterson *A Selection from The Southampton Corporation Journals, 1815-35 and Borough Minutes 1835-47* Southampton Records Series 1965 p.3, 8.
2 *Lewin Letters* p. 209.

THE FEMALE SPHERE

. . . young Rooke the clergyman is in a melancholy low way, which too much religion, (or rather mistaken Religion) has brought him into – Melicent Ballard

THE CHURCH WAS a place where women could find the opportunity to have a role and some influence. Southampton saw a rise in Protestant non-conformity. When John Wesley visited the town in 1787, he noted the

Above Bar Church

missionary zeal of the congregation who were capable of developing the Free Church without his support. They had established themselves in Above Bar in 1745 as Congregationalists and Presbyterians. The ladies of the church established a charity school in 1792 and the church was enlarged in 1802. Whilst the building work took place the congregation met in the Long Rooms. The Church was enlarged again in 1820 for up to 1500 worshippers. During the building of this church the congregation met in the Baptist Chapel in

East Street. The Quakers were also strong in the town and met in St Michael's Square, near to Jane Austen's home.[1] Elizabeth Butler Harrison's clergyman father, Henry Austen left the Anglican church and became a Unitarian. This had such a social and financial impact on the family that it probably led to Elizabeth's brother and sister moving to Southampton. Mary Lewin's daughter Charlotte also became a dissenter. The daughters of town clerk Thomas Ridding, Mary and Margaret, copied reams of sermons into their day books and journals.[2] Elizabeth Goring Butler Harrison was a subscriber to the Society for Promoting Christian Knowledge which distributed bibles, prayer books and other tracts throughout the world and from time to time she taught at The Church of England National School. The Southampton Branch of the British and Foreign Bible Society was formed in 1814 and held its meetings in the Long Rooms.

The clergy were keen on Sunday Schools and bible study and in 1810 established a school on Dr Bell's system in a new and commodious school room in St Michael's Square.[3] Twenty-Five girls who attended Sunday School were also selected to attend a School of Industry in 1795 to learn reading and needlework, etc., and were 'clothed uniformly'. Elizabeth Anne Ridding was one of the Lady Visitors for All Saints church who made it her mission to visit the poor giving out religious texts and urging them to attend church services despite the needs of their families. Elizabeth was not impressed by mothers who chose to stay at home with sick children, or with the impact of unemployment, ill-health or other reasons for not attending the church. She deplored drink and swearing or any amusements that distracted from religious devotion. She encouraged the illiterate to attend adult school and children to go to Sunday School. Olive Hebolitch was a woman who had fallen on hard times despite running a school and having a second property that took lodgers. She was a poor widow living in Goater Alley who, Elizabeth thought, deserved some sympathy. A poor milliner with very little employment, Sarah Thomas, also found favour although Elizabeth was not so sure about her eldest son who did buy books by Scott, Fletcher and Baxter, laying out every farthing he had, but not by authors Elizabeth approved of.[4] She also felt his choices were down to his living in an inn on the Isle of Wight. Elizabeth met poor

1 Rev J S Davies *A History of Southampton* Southampton 1883 pp. 428-433.
2 SA D/PM 42/2/15 Diary of Mary Ridding.
3 Sunday Schools had been established in 1786 by the corporation 'One happy tendency is already obvious, viz. that few children are to be seen idling in the public streets on the Lord's Day, a practice which was before too prevalent.' *Universal British Directory* 1792-8 p. 458.
4 SA D/PM 48/32.

people who had managed to get work, some as fishermen who supplemented their income by offering pleasure cruises and a father and son who worked for a wagon carrier. The problem for Elizabeth was that both these trades were particularly busy on a Sunday and prevented attendance at church. Many of those Elizabeth visited did not attend Anglican services but went instead to dissenting chapels and one French family were especially pulled up for being Catholic. Some were converted and a case reported in local papers in 1804 told the tale of Mary Plenty who died aged 77. Forty-three years of her life were spent, it was said, in ignorance and unbelief. She was married when young and carried on a profitable trade in smuggled goods and was much addicted to common swearing and Sabbath-breaking. Occasionally she attended divine service at her parish church and thought herself a good Christian and a sound believer. She, however, found religion after attending a Dissenters meeting.[1] When, because of her dress being not in good repair, she had gone there rather than church as she was ashamed of her appearance. She gave up smuggling and became a washerwoman. Her husband said the preacher had, 'done more in reforming that woman in a little time, than he had been able to do in many year'. It may have been her remorse that caused her, in her last years, to suffer from nervous fever and sleepless nights and to experience The Horrors.[2]

St Lawrence Church

In 1778 Hannah Gilbert took up the post of sexton for St Lawrence parish, she was a widow and her late husband had originally held the post and her election was unanimous.[3] She was not the first female sexton in the parish Sarah Blackmore held the post for a number of years from 1727, earning £1 5s per annum as her salary.[4] A

1   The Independent Meetings took place in Above Bar, the Baptists in Upper East Street, the Methodist at the Ditches and Quakers in St Michael's Square. *Cunningham Directory* 1811.
2   The Atherley Papers SA D/S2/2/6.
3   SA PR4/2/2 St Lawrence Churchwardens 1743-1830.
4   SA PR4/2/1 St Lawrence Churchwardens 1567-1743

number of the town churches began to install galleries and private boxed pews is this period. Lady Rumbold and Catherine Hale both had pews which could sit six persons at Peartree church at £1 16s each, and Lady Rumbold had a further five places in the west gallery at £1 10s.[1]

As well as her work with the poor Elizabeth Ridding was also a witness on a number of legal documents produced by her father Thomas Ridding, and her brother Thomas who were both notary publics. Her signature can be seen a number of times in the Southampton Notarial Protest Books.[2]

Lady Visitors from the dissenting sects also performed services in regard to women who found themselves in the local prison at God's House offering practical help, giving lessons in reading and writing and helping the women

Old Gaol & Debtors Prison, by W Jefferson

find employment when they completed their sentence.[3] Mrs Mary Truss lived with her husband Jeffery John Truss in the gaoler's house which abutted to the town prison at God's House Tower, as prisoners could pay money for better lodgings whilst in gaol Mrs Truss benefited from gifts from grateful inmates.

1   SA PR6/24/3 seating accommodation Peartree church.
2   Geoffrey Hampson *Southampton Notarial Protest Books 1756-1810* Southampton Records Series 1973 entries 139, 140, 141, 147, 151, 154, 157, 158, 177, 178, 179, 210, 224, 262. Her sisters Mary and Margaret also occasionally signed, entries 142 and 172.
3   Cheryl Butler *Powder, Prisoners & Paintings: The History of God's House Tower* Southampton 2019 p. 105.

She would prepare special food for generous prisoners and made her feelings felt if they were not able to afford little extras. As the debtor John Geagan wrote to his lawyer in 1810:

> As I was in the habit exclusive of what I pay for my room of making presents to those who attended me for some time I received every civility from the Jailer and his family but since I ceased to give I have experienced very different treatment. A short time since a Mr Geagan was ordered out of my room by Truss in the most abusive manner although I have repeatedly been kept up by Truss's own family until after twelve o'clock at night. During my illness Mrs Truss more than once brought her family and friends to dance in the Prison for the express purpose of disturbing me.

The Trusses allowed alcohol to be brought in to the gaol, a Mrs Bone bringing in rum for her husband, and were even accused of bringing in the alcohol themselves. They even kept the prison open for Mrs Bone when she went out to the theatre.[1]

Women's education for the middle classes was still focused on skills required to attract a husband and to run a home and there were a number of schools for young ladies which flourished in the town. As early as 1720 Elizabeth and Jane Shergold had an established boarding school. In that year they requested, and it was agreed, that Elizabeth could build a pew in St Lawrence church for the use of herself and her boarders.[2] The printer and bookseller, James Linden, even experimented with a school for both sexes at 53 The High Street, but it closed when he went bankrupt.[3] Southampton advertised six schools in 1785 and in 1803 there were 22 schoolmasters and mistresses in the town.[4] There were sixteen day or boarding schools for girls listed in Cunningham's 1811 directory.[5] There must have been temporary

---

1 SA D/PM 77/17 letters of John Geagan.
2 SA PR4/2/1 St Lawrence Churchwardens f287r. The parish of St Lawrence had female led schools from 1668 when three women were accused of running unlicenced schools, Elizabeth Wormestall, Mrs Wise, and Mrs Broomen. HRO 202M85/3/1084 Presentment 1668.
3 John Oldfield 'Private Schools and Academies in Eighteenth-Century Hampshire' in *Proceedings of the Hampshire Field Club Archaeological Society Vol 45*, 1989 p. 156.
4 Ibid p. 147.
5 Mrs & Miss Allison, 162 High St; Mrs Barnouin boarding school High St; Mrs Burdon 47 French St; Mrs Cotterell boarding school St Michael's square; Mrs Fielder, French St; Miss Holland, boarding school 133 High St; Mrs Holsworthy,

educational groups visiting the town, as happened when Jane Austen, her sister Cassandra and cousin Jane Cooper travelled here in 1783 with Mrs Cawley who was in charge of their education. Austen's unfinished novel *Sanditon* features the excitement of a school group coming to that watering place and the opportunities that engendered when one of the pupils was found to be a wealthy West Indian plantation heiress.

When Miss Barnouin sold up her school premises in Gloucester Square it was described as substantial building with an attached three-stall stable, double coach-house, garden, yard and offices. There was 'an exceeding good drawing room,' papered and dadoed, with a marble chimney, a breakfast room, good bed chamber and spacious landing. The ground floor had a dining room, parlour, back parlour, hall, staircase and china closet. Unusually it had a purposed built school room which had been added to the building and was 37 feet long and fifteen and a half feet wide, plus an adjoining room. The basement had the kitchen, pantry, wash-house, and wine, beer and coal cellars.[1] The curriculum of the schools, as advertised by Miss Easom's Boarding School for Young Ladies in the 1770s, included English and needlework with French theory and practice, writing, arithmetic, geography and drawing being added extras. Fees were an entrance fee of two guineas and then sixteen guineas a year. In addition, pupils had the opportunity to bathe and take the waters. Dancing classes were led by Mr Pierre Daigueville a principal dancer and ballet master from Drury Lane he taught the Minuet, Louvre, Cotillions, Allemande, Minuet Dauphine, and Country Dances.[2] Many young ladies would have been schooled at home by governesses. With so many French emigrees living in England at this time some found themselves employed by families is a variety of roles, as Melicent Ballard commented: 'Mrs Peers has taken a Governess for her girls who is a french woman & cannot speak a word of English, neither Mr or Mrs Peers understand a syllable of french which is very awkward'.[3]

> boarding school Above Bar; Miss S Holsworth day school French St; Mrs Hoskins Prep School,4 Bugle St; Mrs King Above Bar; Misses Lomer Red Lion square; Misses Ludlow boarding school Polygon; Misses Mant boarding school 1 High St; Misses Matthews boarding school Hamton Court, French St; Mrs Pringle boarding school East St; Miss Pullman French St.

1 SA D/PM 79 sale particulars.
2 *Drury Lane Theatre 1773-1774 Vol 4.*
3 HRO 75M91/B29/1 The 2nd Earl of Carnarvon had a French governess in 1783 and wrote verses about her 'Mam'selle draws her red cloak tight though the wind blows not and the sun shines bright'. HRO 9M73/192/183 An Englishwoman, Elizabeth Semple, owned a school in Calais which she was forced to leave owing to the Revolution. Claire Skinner *The French Connection, Les Relations avec la France*

Mary Lewin's daughters' education was also in the hands of a series of governesses, all of whom the girls disliked, and of which there seems to have been quite a turnover, including, in 1800, Miss Davies who had left to marry Mr Orgill a man of liberal education and large expectations from Jamaica.[1] Miss Horne, her successor, was thought prim, cold and formal. Miss Baggs lasted just a few months, whilst Miss Beetham was considered tyrannical and brutal for wanting to cure the girls of propensities 'unbecoming in a young lady'.[2] The girls even suffered at the hands of their Aunt Charlotte Hale when they were without a governess, who had no compunction over beating Harriet Lewin with a rod for not knowing her French dialogues. They were taught music, French, English Literature, grammar, arithmetic and drawing. They must also have been taught dance as Harriet attended a child's ball in Southampton organised by Mr Chamier, a friend from the Lewin's time in India.[3] The eldest daughter, Mary, was educated at a boarding school in Hayes, Middlesex, thought to be one of the best but Mary still ran away and had to be pursued and taken back to the school. Harriet claimed to have been educated by her father in her early years and 'she inherited from him her own brilliant powers and intelligence as well as her skills in music'.[4] As Jane Austen observed in regard to women's educational accomplishments in *Pride & Prejudice*:

> Oh! certainly," cried his faithful assistant, "no one can be really esteemed accomplished who does not greatly surpass what is usually met with. A woman must have a thorough knowledge of music, singing, drawing, dancing, all the modern languages, to deserve the word; and besides all this, she must possess a certain something in her air and manner of walking, the tone of her voice, her address and expressions, or the word will be but half deserved."
>
> "All this she must possess," added Darcy, "and to all this she must yet add something more substantial, in the improvement of her mind by extensive reading."
>
> "I am no longer surprised at your knowing only six accomplished women. I rather wonder now at your knowing any."

Hampshire.
1 *Lewin Letters* p. 143. George Richard Orgill married Harriet Davies by licence in Salisbury in 1800.
2 *Lewin Letters* Vol II p. 134.
3 A John Chamier was with the EIC from 1772 to 1805 and whose sister was married to Dr John Mackie of Southampton. *Gentleman's Magazine* Vol 151 1831. Three of his sons were also with the company, Henry, William and Edward.
4 H E Busteed *Echoes from Old Calcutta* London 1908 p. 275.

Alice Mant's novel 'Mother and Son'

Work for women of the gentle class tended to be limited but some took the opportunity to become writers. The development of the novel saw local women, such as the daughter of the Rev Mant, taking up the pen. Alicia Catherine Mant, born in Southampton in 1788, wrote at least seven novels which were moral tales for children. Two were published in Southampton - *Ellen: or the Young Godmother* in 1812 and *Caroline Lismore, or the Errors of Fashion* in 1815. Her most successful work was *The Cottage in the Chalk Pit* first published in 1822 in London and running to six editions. She also wrote religious books, *A Child's First Introduction to the Study of the Holy Scriptures, in a series of Dialogues* and *Ingenuous scruples, chiefly relating to the observance of the sabbath, answered: in 8 Letters* and the interestingly titled *The Study of the Heavens at Midnight during the winter solstice, arranged as a game of astronomy* in 1814.[1] Her 1818 novel *Margaret Melville and the soldiers daughter; or juvenile memoirs* had the interesting subtitle *interspersed with remarks on the propriety of encouraging British manufacture.*

1 C F Russell *A History of King Edward VI School Southampton* Cambridge 1940 pp. 257-8.

Another of her works was titled *A Young Naturalist* illustrating the broad range of her interests. Alicia eventually married Russell Philpott, a man fourteen years her junior, at Bath in 1835 before moving to Ireland. The sisters Susannah and Margaret Minifie of Sydney Cottage, Peartree, were novelists and several of their works were written in the form of letters as was the custom in early novels. Susannah's first novel *The Histories of Lady Frances S ... and Lady Caroline S* was written in 1763 and their creations had a tendency towards hyperbole which led Lady Harcourt to coin the work 'minific'.[1] Two other novelist sisters, Elizabeth and Jane Purbeck, authors of *Honoria Sommerville, Raynford Park* and *Matilda & Elizabeth,* among others, also lived in Southampton: 'in not very affluent circumstances but above the reach of want'.[2] Their works were: 'much read and approved, being well calculated to inculcate virtuous principles and to expose vice'.[3]

For some, who fell on hard times, options for making a living required them to take a step downwards. Mary Wollstonecraft was for a short period a companion to a Mrs Dawson who travelled to Southampton in 1779. The town was home to Mary's wealthy great uncle Edward and his family on Gloucester Square.[4] Some had to take on more obvious paid employment and Miss Perkins'[5] trouble is reminiscent of the fate of Miss Bates in *Emma*:

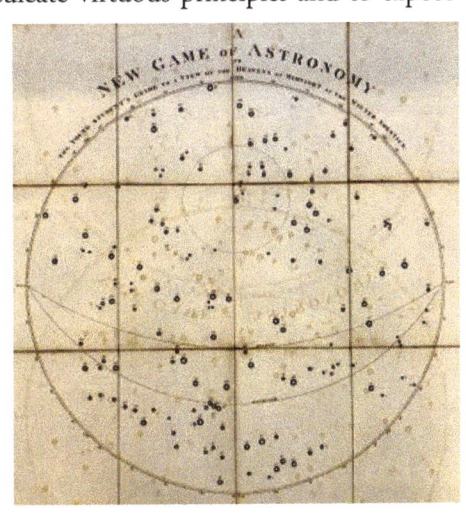

Alice Mant's astronomy game

1 Debbie McVitty 'Familiar Collaboration and Women Writers in Eighteenth Century Britain: Elizabeth Griffith, Sarah Fielding and Susannah and Margaret Minifie' Unpublished D. Phil Thesis St Hilda's College, University of Oxford 2007 p. 229.
2 The preface to *Neville Castle* praised *Camilla, The Mysteries of Udolpho* and *The Italian*. Patterson p. 115.
3 The Atherley Papers SA D/S 19/1/2.
4 Andy Russell, Peter Cottrell and Jane Ellis, *Southampton's Holy Rood: the Church of the Sailors* Southampton 2005 p. 35.
5 Possibly Miss Perkins was a daughter of Daniel Perkins vicar of Holy Rood church who died in 1773 PROB 31/592/48. It seems she made enough of a success of her business to be a subscriber in the 1783 Inoculation Book where she donated 5s. Mary L South *The Inoculation Book 1774-1783* Southampton Records Series 2014 p. 180.

you will be surprized to hear that Miss Perkins has taken Miss Carter's Shop, & meets with great encouragement, I cannot say I should have advized to that step as I think considering her former station here, it must be very mortifying to stand behind a counter. all her acquaintances make a point of taking notice of her, & she is very commendable to endeavour to improve her little fortune, but I think her own feelings would been less, had she undertaken business in any other place.   *Melicent Ballard,* 1781

Shopkeepers and warehouses proprietors strove to offer products that would appeal to fashionable women and the local newspapers were full of enticing advertisements. Mrs Short brought London fashions and had 'informed herself of all that was new and genteel in the make of all dresses relating to her business'. A coat made from prunella, a worsted fabric sometimes made with silk, could be bought for 7s 6d, from Taylor's warehouse, Persian coats were 15s, satin coats started at 44s and riding habits were advertised at the moderate price of £4 10s.

Some women who fell on hard times could look for support from charitable bequests such as the one left by Alderman Taunton who provided money to educate poor boys, and for girls a marriage portion as well as funds to support 'decayed' Aldermen and their wives. The spinster, Silena Fifield left £1300 to be used to support the poor, provide coal for God's House alms houses, and for the maintenance of her family tomb. Elizabeth Bird left £1400 in the 3% with the interest to provide for her servant Jane Cash for life and thereafter to provide six £5 annuities for poor single women.[1]

The soldiers who regularly marched into Southampton did not travel alone and often bought their wives and children with them. They were often distraught when their husbands were shipped out. When French émigrés arrived in the town they threatened them saying they would have shot them if they had their own firelocks to have prevented the need for their husbands to leave. One woman was reported to be so overcome with grief that she threw herself into the river and was drowned. They also succumbed to the diseases that were rife in the camps along with their children, St Boniface Church at Nursling recorded the burial of fifteen camp children between August and October 1795. Harriet Lewin described the wives of encamped soldiers cooking and washing linen in the temporary pits dug in the camp at Netley.[2]

There were female artisans, such as the whitesmiths Ann Carter and her business successor Catherine Morant, who specialised in pewter work

1   Patterson *Corporation Journal* p. 31
2   Olding *From Spa to Garrison Town* p.7.

Large pewter flagon by Catherine Morrant

goods. Their goods were inscribed '*a posse ad esse*' - from possibility to reality. Elizabeth Taylor, wife of Walter Taylor II the inventor of a circular saw for the navy, must have been actively involved in the business as the patent was taken out in her name in 1762.[1] In 1746 Anne Grove leased a tenement near to God's House prison which had been used as a hospital for sick and wounded soldiers and marines and set up by her father the former mayor John Grove. Anne must have assisted in the running of the hospital but the authorities, however, were not keen for Anne to continue the operation and stated that in her lease.[2] The 1811 guide listed female shopkeepers some who made and sold band boxes, straw bonnets, dresses and mantuas or were milliners, linen drapers and tailors. Some traded in china, whilst others ran lodging houses and hotels. Mrs Taylor, along with her sons, ran a stonemason's business, Mrs Bruguiere was a dancing teacher, Mrs Beare the postmistress, Mrs Brewel a plasterer, Mrs Bricknell a milkwoman and Mrs Cheffer a calenderer or textile worker. There were female bakers and laundresses. Mrs Street ran a combined stationer, library and register for servants at 141 High Street. Mrs Thompson,

1   J P M Pannell *Old Southampton Shores* Newton Abbot 1967 p. 54.
2   Mary L South *The Inoculation Book 1774-1783* p. 12.

wife of a gentleman of the same address at 73 High Street, practised dentistry. There were new roles created around the act of sea-bathing, Mrs Martin who ran several baths employed maids to assist in the dressing rooms as female bathers changed into the bathing gowns and then assistants like Mrs Tring who acted as a guide taking the women into the water to take the 'flounce'.[1]

A popular publication for young ladies was the pocket guide and Mary Ridding and her sisters the daughters of the town clerk Thomas Ridding, collected them regularly from the 1780s to the 1830s dissecting the handy almanac to retain the extracts of most interest to them. As the editor wrote to:

> The LADIES of GREAT BRITAIN
> WHOSE Virtues and Accomplishments have ever stood unrivalled, and whose generous Protection and Encouragement of our little Essay for their use, has encouraged us to continue; we respectfully present our humble Offering for the Patronage, under the Sanction of its containing necessary Rules for their Instruction and Amusement; assuring that every Care shall be taken to collect such Matters as may tend to the adorning the Female Mind; we are happy in our Thanks to our Female Correspondents who have favored us with some Pieces of Poetry, and again intreat their future Favors of such Articles as may serve to promote Virtue and Industry, connubial Happiness and domestic Felicity.
> Under these Considerations it is submitted to their Patronage and Protection.

This included brain teasers such as enigmas, charades and logogriphs;[2] songs and poetry, including poems from Lord Byron put to music by Isaac Nathan and songs made popular by actresses of the day such as Mrs Jordan; helpful essays such as *The Comparative View of the Sexes* extracted from Hannah More's strictures on female education and *Select thoughts of Matrimonial Happiness*. Household hints included recipes such as the means of extracting pitch, tar, rosin or wax out of silk or cloth:

> Take oil of turpentine, warm it a little, and apply it to the place, suffering it to soak in for the space of half an hour; and then gently rub it and you will perceive the rosin, etc loosened, and instantly to crumble away

or methods to preserve gold and silver from tarnishing

---

1 *Visitors' Descriptions* pp. 16-17.
2 Anagram puzzles.

fold them always up with fine Indian or lawn paper; and over that fine whited brown paper well aired before the fire, then fold them in a piece of green baize well dried at the fire, and in the drawer or trunk where they lie, keep some saffron papers; you buy them of the person who sell saffron; and keep them in a dry warm place; and never put any thing of gold or silver into a deal box.

Or remedies for curing the stone and gravel which the reader is assured, were never before published – wild carrot was recommended for those distempers – and were endorsed by testimonies such as Thomas Butler, esq. of Warminster who was a sufferer for 46 years despite the ministrations of physicians and apothecaries. There was also a method of recovering 'Drowned Persons', who should be stripped naked, laid in front of a good fire, rolled about, rubbed with salt and covered therewith. Apparently, many were brought to life again even having lain under water for more than half an hour. It advised on how to make an artificial turtle from a calf's head, nice ways to dress a cold fowl, how to hodge-podge a hare or make an Apple Floating Island. The trials of rearing turkeys could be overcome by following instructions translated from a Swedish Book entitled *Rural Economy*. A bill of fare for every season of the year was also helpfully included and to keep an eye on investments, the days and hours of transfer of public funds with dates of dividends was also produced.[1]

The pocket guide also gave recommendations on various spa towns, Southampton featured in 1770:

> This place has been much resorted to of late years by the nobility and gentry during the summer months, for the benefit of bathing in the salt water, for which it is very commodious, and pleasantly situated, so as to command a variety of beautiful prospects both by land and water: it has many seats and pleasant villages round it, and is extremely agreeable in all respects.

Women had no formal place in politics, that was the preserve of men, but it did not stop them becoming involved in the leading issues of the day including the drive to end the slave trade. In the middle of the eighteenth century the town politics were dominated by the 'West Indian' party, that is to say, members of wealthy plantation families. These men, when they gained power, used their influence in parliament to thwart the abolitionist

---

1 Thomas Ridding carried a Diary book which gave information useful for a lawyer and pages for noting accounts, as well as expenses, relating to his work. Ridding included costs for dyeing his pantaloons, visits to plays, attending a tea assembly, having haircuts and his losses at cards. SA DPM 88/4/1.

left: Melesina Chenevix Trench by George Romney; right: Charles Dibdin by Thomas Phillip

movement.[1] Women, like Ann Newell and Anne Middleton, of course, owed their wealth and position to revenue from their family plantations which they also at least, nominally ran. There was an active anti-slavery movement in the town often led by members of the non-conformist community such as James Bullar, schoolmaster, writer and member of the Southampton Bible Society. Meselina Trench wrote *A few words; on the subject of the slave trade addressed to English women* in 1814 which she paid to be printed and distributed herself. The Southampton actor, writer and composer Charles Dibdin created a two-act opera *The Padlock* with the central character being a black West Indian servant and slave called Mungo. Dibdin played the role of Mungo himself, using black cork or carmine to darken his face, and wearing a striped costume which became associated with depictions of slavery. In the 1780s, an abolition epilogue was added to the play which included the words: 'Comes, freedom then from colour? Blush with Shame and let strong nature's crimson mark your blame. For though no Briton, Mungo is a man.'[2] The play was performed in Southampton where the audience would have included families whose fortune came from the West Indies and who had both black servants in Southampton, and black slaves on their plantations. Towards the end of Southampton's popularity as a watering place in 1828 an actor, who was at the start of an

1 The West Indian faction, at its height, had sixty members in Parliament.
2 Felecity Nussbaum 'Mungo Here Mungo There: Charles Dibden & Racial Performance' in *Charles Dibden & Late Georgian Culture* eds Oskar Jenson, David Kennerley & Ian Newman Oxford 2018.

international career, appeared in sell out performances at the Theatre Royal, so popular were the performances that additional shows were demanded by those not able to attend the programmed shows. He was the black American actor, Ira Aldridge, who performed his two most successful roles, that of Shakespeare's *Othello* and partnered that with the character Mungo.

The Theatre Royal attracted the cream of the dramatic performers of the time including the Kembles and the most popular actress of the day Sarah Siddons. Since the end of the seventeenth century a career on the stage was another opportunity for women, although the profession was considered a little better than prostitution but by the end of the eighteenth-century actors like Mrs Siddons were becoming more respectable. Mrs Siddons even tutored the children of George III in reading.[1] George's son, the future William IV, had as his long-term mistress the actress Dorothy Jordan with whom he had ten children and the nations hero Nelson had a scandalous liaison with the one-time actress and dancer Emma Hamilton. There is a long-standing oral tradition that the Hamiltons had a house in Southampton and that Nelson made secret visits there along a path which is still called Nelson's Cut. In fact, his wife Fanny Nisbet had more experience of Southampton as she used the port to travel back and worth to the West Indies and lived in nearby Romsey.

At the pinnacle of the social scale were women who could take a prominent role as leaders of polite society. Elizabeth Austen had written, in 1783, that the town was going through a revival in its fortunes, and that aristocrats were still visiting although she was somewhat scathing about the Duchess of Devonshire and Lady Duncannon who, she said, dressed like their maids and strolled about like showmen. Southampton society was led by two permanent residents of the high aristocracy, Elizabeth Craven (the Princess Berkeley and Margravine of Anspach) and Mary Arabella Petty (the Marchioness of Lansdowne).

Elizabeth Berkeley, Margravine of Anspach by Ozias Humphry

Both ladies had something of a chequered past. The Margravine, also known as Lady Betty Craven, had been

---

1 Robyn Asleson (ed.) *A Passion for Performance: Sarah Siddons and her Portraitists* Los Angeles 1999 p. 85.

unfaithful to her husband, Lord Craven, on more than one occasion to the extent that her husband granted her an allowance of £1500 and banished her abroad. Lady Betty, aged thirty, seemed quite happy to desert her husband and seven children in 1780 and toured Europe with the man who would become her second husband, the Margrave of Anspach, posing as his 'sister' and in the company of his wife.[1] During her travels she met people like Gustavus Adolphus, King of Sweden, who told her that he regarded Bonaparte as the anti-Christ foretold in the Book of Revelation and consequently always called him The Beast. In addition, Lady Betty had been told Napoleon detested women who wore shawls as he liked to see their full shape and thought those with the shawl have something adverse to conceal. Lady Betty had met Napoleon in person in 1802 and neither had taken to one another.[2]

Lady Cravelings teapot

When both their respective partners died in the same year, 1791, Elizabeth and the Margrave, Charles Alexander, married in Lisbon and moved to England. Elizabeth's once close friend Horace Walpole commented: 'Lady Craven received the news of her Lord's death on a Friday, went into weeds on Saturday, and into white satin and many diamonds on Sunday'.[3] The

Charles Alexander Brandenburg

1   In her memoirs Lady Betty portrayed herself in a positive light. The editors of her letters, Alexander Broadley & Lewis Melville, gave, perhaps, a more balanced view in their introduction to *The Beautiful Lady Craven* published in London & New York 1914 pp. xxi, lxxx, c.
2   John Goldworth Alger *Napoleon's British Captives* London 1904 p. 239.
3   Mary L South *The Southampton Book of Days* Stroud 2012 p. 207.

Margrave had sold his lands in Germany to the King of Prussia at the time of his second marriage, for an annuity of 400,000 rix-dollars[1] and his wife tried acquire a pension for him as a relative of the British royal family, the Margrave being a great nephew of Queen Caroline, wife of George II, and great-grandson of George I.[2] Two years after the marriage the Margravine attempted to persuade Lord Glenbervie to act for her to achieve £600 a year for life for the Margrave but Glenbervie declined the honour.[3] The couple had a home on the outskirts of London, at Brandenburg House, Fulham, yet found it difficult to be accepted into the best society as even for the racy Georgian period her behaviour was thought to be outrageous.[4] It was, perhaps, for this

Brandenburgh House, Hammersmith

reason that property was acquired in Southampton and in 1806 was where she spent time after her second widowhood.[5] She herself said that she felt her London villa was being engulfed by the growth of London and thought

1 A name for small silver coins of Germany, Netherlands and Scandinavia in use up until the 19th century. *Merriam-Webster Dictionary*.
2 T Faulkner *Historical Account of Fulham* 1813 p. 420.
3 Walter Sichel *The Glenbervie Journals* London 1910 pp. 110-111.
4 The Margrave also purchased Benham Place and park in Speen from his step-son Lord Craven in 1798-1800. Berkshire Record Office D/EX 192/7.
5 The Margrave left all of his estate to his wife but there is no detail in the will TNA PROB 11-1436-168.

the local populace weak and effeminate. She felt luxury had increased in London with down beds and soft pillows whereas she preferred hard mattresses that were exposed to the open air as frequently as possible. She thought married servants were more settled and attentive to duty and that an idle and pampered bachelor 'is every species of corruption'.

In Southampton she lived near the west gate and in surviving documents is usually titled the Princess Berkeley, a title that had been granted to her in her own right by the Holy Roman Emperor in 1801. In 1810 she took out five leases with the corporation for properties around the west gate, including the Ronceval warehouse and the Linen Hall, which had originally been used by the Taylor family for their naval block manufacture, and a tenement, coach house and store lately belonging to the Martins, who had run a bathing establishment, as well as a gateway in the town wall. The buildings all surrounded the Anspach Place house. The Ronceval rent was sixty guineas and two capons, the linen house twenty-six guineas and two capons and the buildings from the Martins £168 with the old medieval west gate a mere five shillings.¹

Anspach Place

Lady Betty was a travel writer (*A Journey Through the Crimea to Constantinople*, 1789) a playwright (*The Miniature Picture and The Robbers; A Tragedy in Five Acts*, among others which were performed in the theatres she created in her London homes) and also had the distinction of writing the first recognised pantomime: *Puss in Boots*. One of her earliest works was advertised in the Hampshire Chronicle in July 1779, a Christmas tale with the unwieldly title *The Modern Anecdote of the Ancient Family of the Kinkvervankotsdarsprakengotchdems*. She performed in her own productions as well as producing her own memoirs.² She was a friend of the Lansdownes and

1 SA SC4/3/1199a, SC4/3/1203a, SC4/3/12004.
2 'The beautiful Lady Craven; the original memoirs of Elizabeth, baroness Craven, afterwards margravine of Anspach and Bayreuth and princess Berkeley of the Holy

even organised the rescue of the Marquis after his yacht overturned in view of her waterside property at West Place.

> During my residence at Southampton, where I had a house pleasantly situated near the river, the Marquis of Lansdowne, who was extremely fond of aquatic excursions, and delighted in nautical experiments, had prepared a vessel, which he had built at Southampton under the Superintendence of a skilful engineer. It was in the month of November, and Captain Hayward, of the Navy, requested permission to attend his Lordship, who wished to try how the vessel would sail without ballast, it being double-bottomed. The Captain having proved the experiment, they agreed to leave the Quay at twelve o'clock; the tide then running up, and it being nearly high water, with a gale blowing hard. In a few minutes they had proceeded from the Quay about a mile, and the vessels being schooner-rigged, by the time the head-sails were set, in running up the mainsail, she overset. Lord Lansdowne was the only person thrown out, as he was standing inattentatively on the deck; the rest of the party, seven in number, clung to the side of the vessel; fortunately his Lordship caught hold of the masthead, and thus preserved himself from destruction.

Maria Arabella, Marchioness of Lansdowne and her page, by David Wilkie, National Gallery of Ireland

Lady Betty witnessed the events from her window and ordered her servant to run up to the Marchioness and inform her what had happened. In the meantime Lady Betty ordered her own boats out to rescue the party and to 'refresh the drenched experimentalists on the beach'.

Mary Arabella had been married first to Sir Duke Gifford of Castle Jordan, Ireland in 1781, and they had five daughters: Ann, Harriet, Eliza, Louise and Maria, but their only son died young. Sir Duke died in 1801 and Mary Arabella was then linked to the unmarried John Petty, Lord Wycombe, heir of the first Marquis of Lansdowne. When

---

Roman empire (1750-1828); Craven, Elizabeth Craven, Baroness, 1750-1828' : Free Download, Borrow, and Streaming : Internet Archive

John Petty. Marquis of Lansdowne, by Francois Xavier Fabre

John's father died on 7 May 1805 the couple married on the 27 May though in a later court case between Mary Arabella, when dowager, and the third Marquis it was said they had married before his father died. The couple moved to Lansdowne House on Castle Square whilst her husband set about constructing his gothic castle nearby. Mary Arabella's unmarried daughters lived with them, which might have sometimes been a challenge for the Marquis. He wrote to Lord Holland on 17th June:

As my house is now little better than a magazine of young virgins whose minds stand more in need of cultivation than their bodies ... I have confided to Lady Lansdowne the management of my table, and to her daughters the care of my (...illegible) and my Irish Correspondence which I hope will prove of advantage to them.

The Marquis meanwhile kept adding to the castle as The Observer noted on 17th September 1809:

Lansdowne House

The Marquis of Lansdowne's Gothic Castle at Southampton, which we cannot help considering as a proof of the wealth rather than the taste of the owner, is carrying on with spirit; and yet we question whether part of the work will last until the whole is finished, another settlement having lately been discovered in the advanced South wall, and that weighty mass of masonry is prevented, by props, from burying in ruins its beggarly neighbourhood.

The Castle

Their time together and life in the castle was cut short when the Marquis died in 1809 at the age of forty-three. His obituary in the *Chronicle* said:

Though possessed of talents equal to the highest station, he wished merely to be considered as a private gentleman, and they only could estimate his talents, his instructive conversation, his powerful eloquence, who were among the number of his few and intimate friends in whom he shewed a long, a sincere, and unvaried attachment.

His title was inherited by his half-brother. Lord Glenbervie who visited the Marchioness in her widowhood in October 1813 and was received in the round room:

> I have just called on the Dowager Marchioness of Lansdowne in her castle which seems to overlook the world. It is a fine day, and the view was magnificent, both by land and water. She had not breakfasted, and had on a night-cap which I thought very knowing, but which every one of the four daughters, coming into the breakfast room one after the other, exclaimed on as frightful, which her Ladyship humbly acknowledged, adding that she scarcely ever wore anything over her hair. She certainly looked very fresh and handsome in spite, or with the aid of her nightcap, and being toward twenty years younger than Lady Hertford[1] and nearly her size. I cannot help thinking that notwithstanding her vulgarity and Irish brogue, she may prove a dangerous rival to that superb and puissant princess. That she is so already was the chronicle last winter, and the report continues to gain ground.[2]

Lady Hertford was mistress to the Prince Regent but Lady Lansdowne was considered a serious rival for that position. Glenbervie also recalled having dinner at the castle some years previously along with the Marchioness's daughter and her husband Col. Mellish and that the round room has a bust of Massena, the French military commander during the Revolutionary and Napoleonic Wars, on display. Lady Bessborough recorded Mary Arabella speaking of Lord Lansdowne's Worthies: Robespierre, Bonaparte as first Consul, Marat, Curran, and a very fine bust of Massena.[3] Lady Bessborough described seeing the Marchioness:

> who with her three daughters following her, wrapt in thin lace Veils, blue silk shoes, and bare headed, not only brav'd the wind and the rain, but the sharp stones and muddy streets of Southampton, and the astonish'd gaze of the passengers.[4]

1 Walter Sichel ed *The Glenbervie Journals* London 1910 pp. 214-215.
2 Peter James Bowman, *A Fortune Hunter: A German Prince in Regency England* Oxford 2010 p. 28. Gossip at the time linked Mary Arabella with the Prince Regent.
3 R A Austen-Leigh *Jane Austen and Southampton* London 1949 p. 19. An engraving from the Consul painting can be found in the British Museum 1917, 1208.3792 and it is believed that the painting had been commissioned by Petty during his stay in Northern Italy in 1796. The painting is in the Rosebery Collection at Dalmeny House.
4 *Jane Austen's Letters* p. 542. R A Austen-Leigh *Jane Austen and Southampton* London

Napoleon Bonaparte with the Genius of Victory by Andrea Appiani, painted in 1796 and bought in the same year by John Petty, later Marquis of Lansdowne

Jane Austen's nephew, James Edward Austen-Leigh, remembered seeing the Marchioness on a visit to his aunt who lived in the shadow of the castle:

1949 p. 18.

> At that time Castle Square was occupied by a fantastic edifice, too large for the space in which it stood, though too small to accord well with its castellated style, erected by the second Marquis of Lansdowne, half-brother to the well-known statesman, who succeeded him in the title. The Marchioness had a light phaeton, drawn by six, and sometimes by eight little ponies, each pair decreasing in size, and becoming lighter in colour, through all the grades of dark brown, light brown, bay, and chestnut, as it was placed farther away from the carriage. The two leading pairs were managed by two boyish postilions, the two pairs nearest to the carriage were driven in hand. It was a delight to me to look down from the window and see this fairy equipage put together; for the premises of this castle were so contracted that the whole process went on in the little space that remained of the open square. Like other fairy works, however, it all proved evanescent. Not only carriage and ponies, but castle itself, soon vanished away, 'like the baseless fabric of a vision'. On the death of the Marquis in 1809, the castle was pulled down. Few probably remember its existence; and anyone who might visit the place now would wonder how it ever could have stood there. – *A Memoir of Jane Austen*[1]

After the death of her husband Mary Arabella was still trying to improve the prospect of the castle, applying to the pavement commissioners in 1813 to build a wall in front of the house 'late of George Foyle Esquire' which was Lansdowne House on Castle Square. The commissioners refused as the wall actually went beyond the old foundations of the house.[2] The Marchioness built it anyway and was threatened with an indictment.

The second Marquis had made a settlement on Mary Arabella at his death leaving most of his estate to her and her daughters rather than his male heir and half-brother, but this was challenged by the third Marquis and Mary Arabella brought a case against him in 1813 to claim arrears in her payments. There was much discussion as to whether her annual jointure was to be in Irish or English currency. In the event she lost her case.[3] The Marchioness continued to live in the town for a few years after the death of her husband but, when she retired to London, Southampton's heyday as a watering place started its slow decline. The widow, meanwhile, was the subject of fortune hunters

---

1 J E Austen-Leigh *Memoir of Jane Austen* Oxford republished 1926 with notes R W Chapman p. 83.
2 SA SP AP 1/2 Pavement Commissioners 1813.
3 www.casemine.com/judgement/uk/5a8ff8c560d03e7f57eccfbb.

Silver tankard, engraved with the name of Maria Arabella

and considered remarriage to one, Prince Hermann von Puckler-Muskau.[1] He was younger than she but that did not matter as a marriage contract gave him control of her large income of £5000 per annum and her estate of artwork and furniture valued at £12,000. She had already given him a present of over two thousand pounds. In the event her daughters stepped in and the prince returned to the continent empty-handed in 1815. Despite the fortune hunters and court case, Maria Arabella retired to live comfortably at Wycombe Lodge and in her own will at her death in 1833[2] she left her five daughters a share of two thousand pounds left by their father but also divided out her diamonds, pearls, antique bracelets, gold and silver plate, rubies, emeralds, lapis, amethysts, trinkets and ornaments and onyx head of Queen Elizabeth I. It was said her diamonds alone were worth £40,000 and her silver service £6000.[3] In her obituary in the *Court Journal* she was praised as a friend of the current and former King who 'has left a numerous circle of distinguished acquaintances to deplore her loss'.[4]

1 Peter James Bowman, *A Fortune Hunter: A German Prince in Regency England* Oxford 2010 p. 29-30.
2 The auction of the content of her home took place over five days in 1833. Full text of "A catalogue of the elegant and appropriate furniture of the late Marchioness Dowager of Lansdowne, at Camden Hill, near to Kensington: consisting of a collection of pictures...antique bronzes and marbles of the finest order, splendid painted glass, including the celebrated window with the cartoons, fine Oriental china, and several plates of French glass of the largest dimensions, elegant chandeliers and lamps; splendid cabinets, of the time of Louis Quatorze; very elegant china, in table and dessert services...magnificent service of gold and silver plate, upwards of 8000 ounces...plated articles, a cellar of choice old wines" (archive.org).
3 Peter James Bowman, *A Fortune Hunter: A German Prince in Regency England* Oxford 2010 p. 30. Will of Mary Arabella Lansdowne TNA PROB-11-1817-343.
4 The Lansdowne's commissioned the statue of George III which is on the south side of the Bargate to commemorate his reigning fifty years. It was carved from coade stone, the use of which was led by the female industrialist Eleanor Coade. The artificial stone mimics fine-grained limestone but is much more durable.

Between the aristocrats and the working women underpinning the economy of the town, were another class of women, the women who were part of the network that Jane Austen joined when she visited and later moved to Southampton. They were the 'nouveaux riche' whose husbands and fathers had made their money through trade, or by adventuring to the West Indies establishing plantations for sugar and rum or by joining the East India Company in the hope of making a fortune in India or China. They lived lives that were constrained by the etiquette and social mores of Georgian society, and they followed the traditional paths of finding a husband of good fortune, of managing the home, and bearing children. Mrs Bennet boasted of dining with four and twenty families but that would be too large a circle to focus on and so Austen's advice to her niece that concentrating on the stories of three or four families in a county village as being the best thing to work on, seems much more manageable. Given the Ballards and Butlers Harrisons were related, as were the Fitzhughs and Lances, the addition of the Lewins, Middletons and Newells only increases Austen's numbers by one extra family.

GEORGIAN LADIES – BIOGRAPHIES OF ORDINARY LIVES

THE STARTING POINT in the selection of the women whose lives are being explored was their proximity to Jane Austen, using her fame, profile and her novels as an entry point to their lived experience, seeing literature as a source for local history. As much as they are connected to Austen, these women are also connected to each other. The Ballards supplied wine to the Lewin family, the Middletons made social calls on the Lewins, the Lances and Fitzhughs were part of the political orbit of the Butler Harrisons. Ann Newell and Anne Middleton were both born on sugar and rum producing Jamaican plantations. Anne Middleton and Mary Lewin were young brides in India. The Butler Harrisons used their connections to get a position in the East India Company for their son. Mary Lance's daughter shared romantic gossip about the daughters of Mary Lewin.

The women are also connected by geography and their links to Southampton, however, of the seven women who are the focus of part two of the book only one was born and bred in Southampton. Melicent Cropp Ballard was of solid merchant stock her father and husband being in the wine trade but an unexpected inheritance that came to her mother gave the family an income from land and the potential to move up the social scale. Elizabeth Austen Butler Harrison married Melicent's nephew who also was a wine merchant and local politician like his uncle and well established in the town, his property in Alton inherited from his father being given up by his trustees. Ann Launce Newell was a wealthy widow and chose to move to Southampton from her home in Jamaica, there were no obvious family links to the town so it must have been its reputation as a pleasant place to live with good amenities that drew her to the place. She would have felt part of the established West Indian clique, several of whom lived in the same part of Southampton. Anne Morse Middleton arrived in Southampton as a young married woman, via her original home in Jamaica and then a journey to India where she met her husband. The Middletons were just one of the several East India Company families who were building and occupying fine villas around the outskirts of the town. They were joined by another Company family that they knew previously in India, the Lewins, where Mary Hale Lewin had moved to join her husband. Mary Fitzhugh Lance was living in Southampton when she met and married an East India Company factor, this time from China, her being in Southampton was the choice of her parents who had been recommended it as a location by the English Ambassador in Constantinople. Her opportunity to marry was facilitated by her brother who had bought his colleague to the town with him on a trip back from China. David Lance had no particular roots elsewhere in the country so settled in his wife's location. It is not clear how William Fitzhugh met Charlotte Hamilton, although it was probably via a visit that her relations the Harrowbys made to Southampton in 1791, but it was that marriage that brought her to Southampton.[1]

None of these women were trailblazers, they followed the path laid out for them and succeeded in finding wealthy husbands and their material wealth and place in polite society was safely secured. Even in the biographies of Jane Austen they are lucky to be a subject of a footnote and even if their husband's had some fame the wives are in the shadows. One option would have been to weave their stories together and in and out of the narrative of life in Georgian Southampton, as they may not be seen as deserving their own discreet biographies but this is not the route taken. Instead, those passing references have been an entry point to follow clues from document to document and then to construct a biographical narrative of lives less ordinary than might first appear.

MELICENT CROPP BALLARD (1744-1784)

Elite society in the eighteenth century was a relatively small group of families. The Ballard and Austen families were linked via marriage networks, and came together to care for the orphaned children of Elizabeth and Frances Ballard. Jane Austen visited Southampton in 1783 with her sister and cousin in the company of the woman in charge of their education, Mrs Cawley. It is not known if they met the Ballards but is a real possibility they did. Whilst in Southampton the girls all were struck down with endemic typhus, probably the same illness that carried off Melicent Ballard.

Melicent Ballard speaks to us via a cache of letters she wrote between 1780

---

1 Charlotte was Lady Harrowby's niece. Lady Harrowby was Elizabeth Terrick, and her sister Anne had married into the Hamilton family, her husband Rev Anthony Hamilton was Charlotte's father.

and 1784 when her nephew and ward John Butler Harrison II was away in Lausanne at school. The young boy had asked to be sent news from home and to hear about what was happening to his friends and family. His Aunt Melicent obliged with chatty letters which give a flavour of life in Southampton in the early 1780s. The letters are so engaging and entertaining that they have been reproduced in full as an appendix to this book.

Early life and Marriage

MELICENT'S FATHER LENARD Cropp's family had been resident in Southampton for several generations, his immediate ancestors had earned their living as maltsters, producing malt for the brewing and distilling industry. Lenard had made his money as a trader in the wine trade along with his business partner Robert Ballard junior. Southampton had held the monopoly of the sweet wine trade from Spain and Portugal since the time of Queen Mary Tudor and her husband Philip of Spain and even by the eighteenth century, the Portuguese wine trade was a significant part of the port's economy.[1] One of the main customers of Cropp and Ballard was Winchester College and their names appear in correspondence and bills held in the college archives.[2] The college was regularly buying £40-£50 worth of wine from Cropp and Ballard through the 1780s and 1790s. The college even had a book which documented their wines. The wine was destined not only for the masters and

Melicent Ballard, private collection

---

1 For an overview of this important trade see Alexander Anderson *Hartleyana* Southampton Records Series 1987 pp. 18-37.
2 Winchester College Archives 33276-33281. In a letter in Magdalen College archives Cropp boasts of sending port wine to a customer *as good as England affords* ES/8/23 5th March 1739.

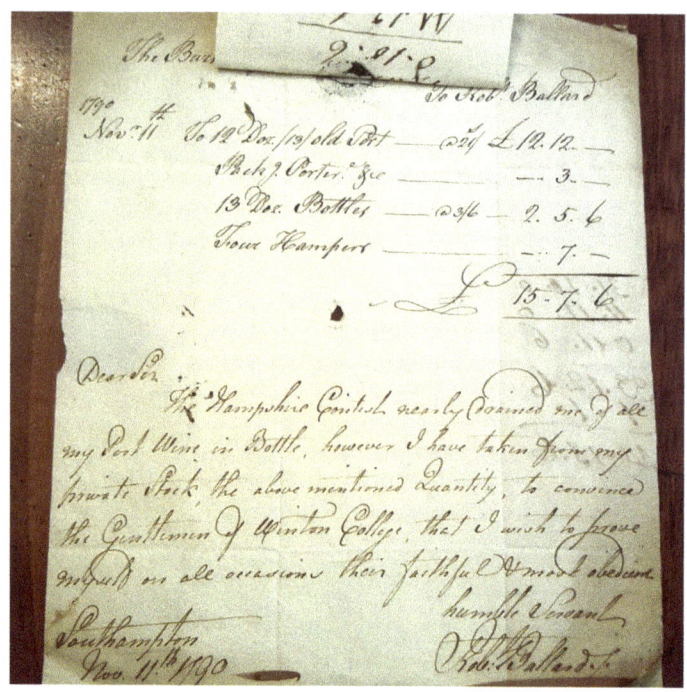

Purchase of wine from Robert Ballard by Winchester College archives

teachers but also the school children. In 1790 Robert Ballard wrote to the college to say his store of port wine had been completely depleted, thanks to the recent elections, but he did provide 12 dozen of old port from his private store. The demand for port wine was such that Ballard also had to tell his customers that it had driven up the wholesale price in Portugal. Both Cropp and Ballard entered local politics as part of the small group of oligarch families who controlled Southampton corporation. Eventually both men becoming mayors of Southampton, Cropp served three times in 1737, 1751 and 1761. Edward Gibbon, the historian who served in the Hampshire Militia, knew Lenard Cropp and described him thus:

> Crop is an honest fellow in the Tory sense; he drinks hard, rails against all ministers and keeps alive the small remains of Jacobitism at Southampton… he is most impenetrably stupid. His wife is a merry, good-natured woman but one who, in her conversation, respects altogether as little the laws of truth as the patience of her hearers[1]

1 In 1724 a peruke-maker drinking at the Dolphin Inn reported its tapster William Smith for speaking abusively of the corporation claiming *There was not any honest man in the corporation except Mr Lenard Cropp* SA SC9/4/112c.

Despite that Cropp recommended that Gibbon should become a burgess of Southampton and in thanks Gibbon entertained the corporation:

> The dinner was in the Old Assembly room and consisted of six dishes of turtle, eight of Game with jellies, Syllabubs, tarts, puddings, pineapples, in all three and twenty things besides a large piece of roast beef on the side table. The whole cost me only £13 in odd money. The company 48 in number consisted chiefly of Corporation and Corps

In 1740 Lenard had married Melicent Weekes, the merry, good-natured woman mentioned by Gibbon. Melicent Weekes had been born in 1713, in the town of Middlesex in the colony of Virginia in North America. Southampton had long-standing links with the early colonies on the eastern seaboard, particularly Virginia which colony had been promoted by the third Earl of Southampton a century before. Melicent Weekes's parents, Hobbes Weekes and Mary Parrott, moved to England in the early 1700s to Ashley in Hampshire. The village was the family's ancestral home as they were descended from Thomas Hobbes a physician to three kings, Charles II, James II and William III. It was the Weekes family who provided a large inheritance when Melicent's brother Abraham Weekes died in Boulogne in 1755. Melicent and Lenard inherited property and land in Crawley, Kings Somborne, Little Somborne, Mottisfont, Lockerley, Sherfield English, Romsey, Timsbury, Broughton, Wherewell and Stockbridge.[1]

The Cropps had four children, Melicent (born 1744) Lenard (born 1744), William (born 1746), and Frances (born 1752), however both the boys died in adolescence, Lenard after matriculating from Queen's College in 1761 and William who died also in 1761 still a schoolboy.[2] The Cropps wished to secure the future for their daughters and, in the eighteenth century, this meant making a good marriage. Frances married Dr Robert Taunton, a doctor of both divinity and law, and Melicent married her father's business partner, Robert Ballard junior in 1767. It was not an unusual practice for someone like Lenard Cropp who had a business but no male heir to follow him, to look to a favoured apprentice or business partner to marry into the family. This practice had been common since the Middle Ages; whether the marriage was a pragmatic business deal or a romance that had developed due to the close

---

1 SA D/PM 3/7/2.
2 C F Russell *A History of King Edward VI School, Southampton* Cambridge 1940 p. 244.

proximity of the two young people is speculation. Robert was thirty and Melicent twenty-three. Robert was a man of means, not only an established partner in Cropp & Ballard but Robert's father, Robert Ballard senior[1] was another former mayor serving in 1741. He was also wealthy and was, in 1782, to leave his son £1500 plus:

Robert Ballard snr

> one case of silver handled knives and forks and the case of dessert and ditto both which were my late brother John's twelve tablespoons belonging to the other case the dessert spoons the silver coffee pot the two large silver sauce boats the large silver sauce pan the two small waiters with a crest the silver tankard four silver salt sellers and four salt spoons one Silver pepper Box six silver gilt spoons one strainer one pair of silver tea tongs six silver tablespoons marked ID three glass castors with silver heads one silver cream pail and ladle with the glasses one gilt pan and marrow spoon six silver bottle labels one silver trowel one silver marrow spoon all my writings and books of account and other books and bonds and other security for money and all such things which are in the little room or counting house (except the part of the mahogany dining table) and all things which are in the bureau or bookcase in the fore parlour and all shelves cupboards locks and bolts all covers grates and other suchlike things which are fixed to the house I now live in.[2]

Young Melicent and Robert Ballard junior were married in October 1767 and they settled in to a house on the High Street close to St Lawrence church. It had a large garden with stables and an adjoining building just behind the walls called the Bottle House, doubtless for use in Robert's wine business, and he also rented a vault beneath the house of Rev Barnouin.[3]

1 Robert Ballard senior had married three times (to Mary Atherley, Margaret Jackson and Frances Cary).
2 TNA PROB-11-1089-293 Robert Ballard Senior. Ballard's property included two houses Fawley House and Salter, stock of salt, houses at Frome, a mortgage on the spa, the Black Vault and Noah's Ark Wharf D/PM/10/6.
3 SA SC/AG 8/2/2 & 3 rate book for St Lawrence Parish. It is likely the Bottle House was on the site of the Old Bond Store built by Charles Morris in 1802 on

Robert was active in parish life serving as church warden and later guardian of the poor. During one of his terms as church warden in 1780 he organised the sale of two of the church bells, and purchased a good clock to be fixed outside the church. He also had the building modernised by having the exterior stuccoed. He was entrusted with church monies purchasing £100 worth of stock in the 3%.[1] The couple had two children Melicent, known as Little Milly, was born in 1773 on the 28th August at twenty past two in the morning. She was privately baptized the same day by the Rev Dr Joseph Simpson, Rector of Weyhill and publicly christened at St Lawrence on the 26th of February 1774 by the Rev. James Scott. Their son Lenard was born at ten minutes before six on 26th May in 1778, but tragically died at just six months old on the date of his parents wedding anniversary, October 21st, 1778.[2] Apart from Little Milly the couple had no other surviving children. Robert Ballard junior, however, had responsibilities for two orphaned

Ballard Wine Store

children, Elizabeth, the child of his cousin Elizabeth Ballard, and John, the child of his sister Frances, both women having been married to the same man. The children's father, John Butler Harrison I, had married his first wife Elizabeth in 1764 but she died in childbirth in 1765. Shortly after he

> the edge of the proposed Southampton to Salisbury canal which ran along the site of the old town moated ditches. The Bond Store survives to this day.

1 PR4/2/2 St Lawrence Churchwarden's accounts
2 Lenard's sponsors were his grandfather Robert Ballard, his uncle the Rev John Ballard and his great aunt Mrs Frances Rooke.

married her cousin Frances but he never lived to see the birth of his son as he succumbed to smallpox and his wife also died of the disease only days after John's birth in May 1767.[1] Robert Ballard must have remembered his own loss as his mother, Margaret, had died of smallpox when he was just a child back in 1742.[2]

The Ballard family stepped in to support the two children.[3] It was decided that the toddler Elizabeth should be given into the care of John Butler Harrison's sister Jane. Jane had married John Hinton the vicar of Chawton and the couple took on the early upbringing of Elizabeth Goring Butler Harrison.[4] The newly married Melicent Cropp and Robert Ballard took in the baby John, at just six months old in October 1767, who became their de facto son. What Melicent thought about this arrangement at the start of her marriage is not known but the affection in which she held her nephew and ward became apparent in the correspondence that she sent him when he was a young boy which he kept and treasured all this life.

The Ballards were among the political elite and Robert was mayor in 1776 and again in 1786. This period was quite a turbulent time in local politics with two rival groups struggling for control of the town. Melicent recorded in a letter of 1781 about the parliamentary elections for Southampton:

> Fuller & Sloane[5] are chose, & poor Fleming thrown out. There was an Election ball it was an evening of joy & jollity; all sort's of people were there, servants, & every body that chose it danced. after we had done tea the second class sat down to the same tables, & they had plenty of Negus by the smell, I should

1 Ballard Family Bible private collection.
2 1742 was a particular severe smallpox year. If a pregnant woman contracted the disease there was a 75% certainty that she would die and miscarry. The virus reduced the body's blood clotting capacity which led to severe haemorrhaging following miscarriage. Robert Ballard, snr, regularly contributed to the town inoculation campaigns that took place in the 1770s. M. South 'The Southampton Inoculation Campaigns of the Eighteenth Century', unpublished PhD, University of Winchester 2010, p. 46.
3 Robert Ballard had been a friend of John Butler Harrison I before his marriage to his sister and joined him and Arthur Atherley on a tour of Europe in 1765. The children's three guardians were Rev John Hinton, Rev John Ballard and Robert Ballard jnr. SA D/PM 64/2/2.
4 Jane Hinton was the daughter of Thomas Harrison of Alton and was Hinton's second wife. She died in 1799 and was buried in Chawton Churchyard.
5 See Patterson pp. 61-66. Horace Walpole's complaint in 1761 that *West Indians, conquerors, nabobs, and admirals* were dominating parliamentary elections could have been a description of Southampton.

judge and it was pure strong & that the maids at least, must be tipsey; as they seem'd to take good sips, without fear.

The polling had taken place over two days with polling being from eight in the morning until five in the evening with Mr Rooke and Mr Missing acting for Fleming and Mr Hunter and Mr Hoarth for Fuller and Sloane. The election had been called after the death of Hans Stanley. Hans Stanley, a member of the West Indian element which dominated Southampton politics in the mid-century, committed suicide in 1780 and his nephew Hans Sloan and his brother-in-law John Fuller stood as the continuation candidates. Mrs Thrale described Fuller as *wild, gay, rich, loud*. The pair had been returned by a narrow majority, Fuller, 264, Sloane, 249, Fleming 237. They were opposed by James Amyatt of Freemantle House, a wealthy merchant from India and East India Company shareholder, and John Fleming of Stoneham House. Fuller and Sloan were supporters of Lord North's government, after the fall of the administration, they lost power and withdrew from the next election. Clarke Gervois and Mr Thistlethwaite were elected as the county members.

Robert, himself was involved with a number of civic duties such as attending the Trinity Fair at Chapel in the area around St Mary's. The fair had been established back in the Middle Ages and was still flourishing. Robert would be sat in a temporary booth in his capacity of Bailiff.

Whilst Robert contended with the political wrangling in Southampton, known locally as the 'Civil Wars', Melicent had the management of the home. This included problems with her servants. The children's former nurse had married: - 'your old Nurse & her family are well - & I tell you as a secret, is going to play the fool & marry, with her nine children, a Farmer Penny who has five.' The marriage was unhappy and if that was not enough the nurse's daughter, Nanny, who had also served in the household, had married Thomas another servant and had moved to a small property in Houndwell Lane where her husband was to join her once he could be replaced. Melicent wrote to John to inform him:

– I know you are interested about Nanny, who has attended you since your Birth, I am sorry to tell you, Thomas is her approved admirer, I say sorry because I think a lazy footman, can never maintain a family, nothing but necessity would tempt him, & then he knows not how to work haveing from eight years old, been taught only to wait at table what prospect but of beggary with such a Husband

Melicent thought it a mistake that Thomas had left his employment to then rely on work as a day labourer as she, of course, had to find a replacement. Thomas's first replacement had not worked out. In later years Melicent was even thinking of taking a foreign servant but was dissuaded because it would be expensive to bring the servant to Southampton and, if he did not speak English, he would be almost useless to the family. The Ballards were not the only family who turned to servants from overseas. David Lance had brought back a Chinese servant with him when he returned from Canton; the Lewins had at least one black servant; the Middletons and Newells relied on slaves to maintain their overseas properties and some families employed French refugees. It is difficult to know how many black, Indian or Chinese servants lived in the town or how many people of colour lived in the Southampton. With so many families having property in the West Indies it is likely that most might have had black servants, who would have been slaves on the plantations, in their homes. This was certainly the case in regard to John Fusso recorded as the black servant of William Gunthorpe of Bugle Hall in Southampton and Painters Plantation in Antigua.[1] Sometimes in church registers there is recorded the baptism of an adult such as at Holy Rood, where plantation owner Hugh Hill was vicar, 'William an African Adult (the word adult was added as an insert) was baptized August 13th 1809'. Back in 1709 one James Ocra was baptised in St Mary's and the clerk recorded he was 'belonging to Mrs James'.[2] Ten-year-old John Hampton from Antigua was baptised in 1811 also at St Mary's but there was no added information as to his status; given his age he could have been a page, as the fashion at the time was for wealthy households to have black pages. Antony de Sourze is unique in having his image recorded in a painting commissioned by the family he worked for, the Taylors, a painting that was made by a female artist, Maria Spilsbury, Taylor's daughter-in-law. The painting *Mrs Taylor's New Year's Day Feast* captures the Taylor family, their employees and children from the Taylor's charity school at Portswood, enjoying a banquet. Antony is shown as a well-dressed man, passing plum pudding to Sarah Taylor, according to a letter from Sarah's nephew. In the foreground is a young black child of an age with Antony's own

1   Fusso was baptised at All Saints in 1790 with Mr and Mrs Gunthorpe standing as his godparents.
2   In the Pear Tree Parish Records in 1735 an eighteen-year-old 'negro' was christened and in 1814 Xury George Cassimere was also baptised and was recorded as a servant from the Trinidad estate of George Dunn. SA PR5/1/2& PR6/1/1 St Mary Extra Parish Register. James Amyatt MP for the town from 1784-1806 who lived at Freemantle Hall christened his black servant George Freemantle in 1774. Elizabeth Coe *The Parish of Freemantle A History* 2nd edition Southampton 2011 p. 3.

The Taylor Family's New Year Feast, by Maria Spilsbury, Southampton Museums & Art Gallery

son. Antony had married Henrietta Forder in 1804 and the parish records at South Stoneham records the birth of their son Antony in 1805. The failure of the Taylor's business affected Antony, his daughter Charlotte was born in the South Stoneham workhouse in 1813, and the 'Black Antony' receiving poor relief in the same parish between 1812-1816 was probably Antony de Sourze.[1] The Ballards also employed people in their family business. Mr Martin from the Long Rooms worked for the Ballards as a clerk but they were in danger of losing him as Robert Ballard was trying to procure him the post of Landwaiter at the Custom House, in which position he would have the authority to examine, taste, weigh or measure any merchandise arriving in the port. Despite her misgivings Melicent still felt an obligation to long-serving staff:

> your Old Nurse continues a cripple. I know you have too good a heart to forget obligations, & tho' she has been well paid for her care of you, you are obliged, for her discharge of her Duty to you at a time when you could not complain of a want of it.

1 Cheryl Butler *Telling Other hiStories: Early Black History in Southampton c1500-1900* Southampton 2021 pp. 31, 38-40.

I love & value her daughter Nanny, for her attention nine years to our Dear Milly & every day lament her foolish marriage, which obliged us to part –

When the family felt the need for a break from the excitement of life in Southampton they had a rural retreat at Northerwood. Melicent wrote to her nephew in September 1780: 'We spent one of ye days at Northerwood, Milly was delighted with the Turkeys & fowls and wish'd for you.'

Northerwood House, the central section is the original country villa of the Ballard family

In 1781 the Southampton Guide described Northerwood as a small cottage: 'from whence the eye takes in so many objects, that one is at a loss which part of the prospect to select, and which to admire most.'

Indeed, George III was so taken with the place when he visited in June 1789, enjoying the fine views over the woods with the aid of telescopes, that he gave permission for it to be renamed 'Mount Royal'.[1] What impressed Melicent most was the excellence of the air and she made sure there was a tent erected outside so they could enjoy the setting. The land attached to the cottage was rented out to a Farmer Absolem who lived in the nearby Spencer's House. The farmer's wife, Mrs Absolem, would attend on the family when they were in residence. Melicent attempted to employ a man and a woman to manage the property for them but 'were convinced we should greatly be imposed upon'. They did have two maids and a man of work to assist in keeping the cottage up together.

1 *World*, 2nd July 1789; J S Davies, *A History of Southampton* Southampton 1883, p. 503. Baker's Guide 1795 p. 122.

None of Mary's letters survive from 1782 but those for 1783 see her irritated by her hairdressers:[1]

Southampton April ye 17th 1783
– I think hair dressers a useless set of men, were there none we should be neat clean & all alike submit to nature, but custom or fashion (if you please to call so) must in some degree be conform'd to, by those that wish to appear like the world, unless the fashion is vicious ... I have not heard our tribe of dressers have attempted more than stealing a knife or Comb. I hope they will not conceal themselves, as I am allways happy to rid the house of them as soon as possible –

When the winter balls were at an end in April along with the card parties, Melicent enjoyed her garden and even had a new greenhouse. She was looking forward to being able to enjoy the better weather as opposed to spending several hours indoors playing at cards. As more people moved to the town Melicent was obliged to visit the several families who had settled there since her nephew's departure.

Melicent's last surviving letter to her nephew was tinged with melancholy:

Wednesday ye 22d. our Company are just gone. the weather is greatly changed since I began my letter. a sharp cold wind, with a kind of cold rain, like sleet, succeeds the warm days we have enjoyed for a fortnight past. I doubt the fruit will suffer very much as it has done the last two years. I gave two shillings for a Gallon of apples this very day, therefore you may judge how scarce they are asparagus are four shillings a hundred, & all other vegetables dear in proportion – a warm rain would make all cheap -

Children

Melicent's only surviving child, Little Milly followed her private baptism with a public christening her grandfather Lenard Cropp was one of her sponsors along with Mrs Ballard, Mrs Benson, Mrs Jackson and Miss Cropp. Little

1   There were plenty of peruke-makers (wig-makers) and hairdressers listed in the Southampton section of the Hampshire Directory for 1783-4 - John Bullar, John Fursell, Joseph Light, Thomas Macklin, Joseph Turner and Thomas Warlock all on the High Street and Thomas Fisher on Butchers Row. The hairdresser John Figes had received a Thomas White loan for his business, which £25 he repaid in 1788, this was bequest which had been running since the sixteenth-century which rotated around several towns. SA D/PM 83/1/58.

Milly grew up alongside her older cousin, the orphaned John Butler Harrison II, who was adopted by her parents.

It is also through Melicent's letters to John that we hear about young Milly's education. She was taught to sing by Mr Martin, who ran the Long Rooms, and learning not only to write but to make her letters *very fine*. Initially Milly was looked after by the servant, Nanny, who had had the care of John when he was young, but as Milly got older it was decided that she needed a governess. The governess would teach her French, singing – her voice was thought good and very strong – dancing, and also letter writing and needlework. The latter Milly did not care for. Her governess was a Miss Davy who, Melicent felt, was perfectly well-educated, and thought an English woman was more than capable of teaching her charge French to a level that she would be able to converse with her cousin on his return from Lausanne. There were special balls for children to teach them to dance and Milly went to balls organised by Mr Burgat who would teach a hundred and thirty children at a time.[1] Burgat had also been dancing master at Salisbury where he was thought 'too particular & officious in enforcing the rules of country dances & also too peremptory in his manner of desiring ladies to stand up, that happen'd to sit down for a minute or two to rest'. Melicent reported that Milly was considered the best dancer, much admired, and she danced until one in the morning.

Robert Ballard jnr with his daughter Milly, private collection

Her mother commissioned a likeness of her daughter in miniature that she could wear on her watch fob. As her daughter got older Melicent found she preferred to stay at home amusing herself in writing letters to her nephew. She did hope, however, that when Milly's education was complete in eight years' time, she would be there introducing her into the world and to proper

---

1   Mr Burgat was in the retinue of Gen Clavering near Southampton. Brian Robins *An Introduction to the Journals of John Marsh* Huntington Library Quarterley Vol 59 No 1 (1996) University of Pennsylvania Press p. 13. Burgat was also a musician of violin.

acquaintances. Unfortunately, that was not to be. Melicent never saw her daughter grow up nor saw her marriage to Charles Morris.

The Ballard's ward, John, was sent to be educated in one of the best schools in the area, Winchester College, where he was a Commoner, at the age of ten and where he remained until the age of thirteen. It was not an easy existence. In 1770 a visitor noted: 'No humane parent of moderate means would allow his son to undergo rough treatment to which the lower boys were subjected in the lower chamber'.[1]

The teaching was classical, Cicero, Horace, Ovid, Virgil and was entirely in Latin. The school day began as early at 5am and, until 1838, the only place for washing was in the open air at a conduit. Meals were mostly boiled beef or mutton accompanied by bread washed down with beer. Commoners could supplement their meals by buying treats from local licensed pastrycooks. As a Commoner, John's fees were paid directly to the headmaster, a useful

Winchester College Hall

source of additional income. The boys lodged in unheated dormitories around a courtyard with a sick room and dining hall, described as a 'strange and rambling, bizarre old place'[2] and not built for comfort. Grim as the facilities sound, they were better than those for boys who attended as scholars. The Commoners also benefitted from having three servants and also three tutors to help them and who provided discipline. As there were only two masters,

1 A K Cook, R Mathew & C Johnson *About Winchester College* London 1917 p. 99.
2 Richard Foster 'Winchester College in the Age of Jane Austen' in *Jane Austen and Winchester, an Introduction* Winchester 2023 p. 14.

the Headmaster and a Second Master, the boys were also overseen by the Governors, Wardens and Fellows. John was rescued from this spartan existence at the age of thirteen when it was decided to send him to Lausanne to learn French and the manners befitting a gentleman. John Butler Harrison II had inherited £2000 from his father plus his mansion at Amery[1] (and later another £1500 from his grandfather Robert Ballard senior) so he had the means to support life as a gentleman. In 1774 his guardians managing his estate arranged for Chickenhall Farm to be leased to one William Lavington.[2] Before he left for the continent, he returned to the family home in Southampton where he had lessons in music and singing which he later said he enjoyed. The choice of Lausanne for the next phase of his education was, perhaps, to give him a wider experience which would be useful in regard to his future career. Many young foreigners went to Lausanne to finish their education, including Edward Gibbon a friend of John's father, John Butler Harrison I. As young men they had both been in the Hampshire Militia together.

It was arranged that John would board at the house of Monsieur Bugnon in Lausanne.[3] When it was time for him to leave for the continent, in August 1780, Melicent was bereft but she set herself the task of keeping him up date with all the news from home:

My dearest Boy

These are the last lines that will probably reach you in England, from a friend, that has your interest near her heart – tell me your ideas of the bustle in the busy Metropolis, tell me what pleased you most & if you like the hurry of the world better, than our quiet life – Remember I hope to hear from you very often, & if any difficulty should ever occur (to y)ou, inform your sincere friends of them, & be advised – May the Almighty direct you to the best - but remember my dear Jack, that we who are apt to err ourselves, can excuse; tho we may be concerned for your errors, therefore if you are tempted either by example, or thoughtlessness, to do any thing materially wrong; candidly confess it, to those that can & will extricate you, I do not now address myself to you, as to a Child, but as a young man of the world, take the best part of the gay world; as that is most suited to your years, but never conform to those

1 Will of John Butler Harrison I TNA PROB 11-930-154. His half-sister Elizabeth was the eldest child but John as the male heir, inherited the estate. John was born posthumously, of course, and if he had not survived the estate would have reverted to Elizabeth. She received £1500.
2 SA D/PM Box 64/2/2.
3 Burgon was another friend of Edward Gibbon. Rowland Prothero ed *Private Letters of Edward Gibbon (1753-1794)* London 1898 p. 36.

customs, that you now think wrong, for now you can judge right, & have not been corrupted, therefore abide by your own (-) of what is just & honest – I am sorry I cannot express myself better, I mean; that I hope you will continue good, amidst a world of wickedness, methinks if I could see you now & then, a gentle check would keep you in the right path, be communicative in your letters to us, & rest assured of every proper indulgence. I will add to my epistle your little Millys Love, who has told me a hundred triffling things to say, which time will not permit me to add; adieu my Dearest Boy, may every happiness this world can bestow, attend you & may you return safe to your affectionate Aunt Melicent Ballard Southampton Aug.st ye. 15th – 1780.
Milly teazes me to beg some of her pictures may be painted & some not.

A few weeks later Melicent was still missing her surrogate son:

My dearest Boy,
Your two letters gave us a great pleasure the last in particular, as you were safely landed at Ostend & write that you are well, & very merry may you long continue so we all regret your absense but flatter ourselves you will reap the advantage of our loss, continue my Boy to write every opportunity, and write freely, and without reserve every want, & every wish of your heart; you shall be indulged in every thing, that is consistent with prudence, & reason. I every post expect a letter from you, presume you now have been a week at Lausanne, you cannot so soon tell how you like the place, or customs of it, but I hope to hear you are well & happy. we flatter ourselves Mr Bugnon will delight us, by giving a good account of your behaviour, & improvement in every particular – remember my Child we have your interest so much at heart that it lies in your power to add greatly, to our happiness
you will find drawing very entertaining & if you like it, will improve very fast – don't forget your singing, you have a good Ear, & a sweet voice I was always delighted to hear you sing

Melicent was also concerned about the grooming habits of her nephew 1783:

I can chearfully allow you to be a neat Coxcomb from sixteen to eighteen, but not longer for I am convinced from observation that youth must just at that period of life, be either Coxcombs or slovens, the former, time brings us to be just agreable, but the latter grows every year worse & worse, till they become disgusting for want of cleanliness

Melicent not only kept in touch with her nephew via her correspondence but also kept up with the development of her ward's half-sister, Elizabeth. The young Elizabeth was contemplating a move to live with her late mother's brother, Dr Ballard and his family, whilst still maintaining visits to her other friends and relatives during the year: 'your sister & I correspond frequently, as I am now employ'd by her about her dress, a matter of great importance to young Ladies, & which cannot be procured at Chawton'.

Melicent's early death, and John's return to England, meant an end to the correspondence which was so useful in tracing Melicent's relations with the children in her care, giving a window into life in late eighteenth-century Southampton. Although Robert Ballard re-married he had no more children so Milly was his sole heir and executrix when he died in 1795.[1] Milly married her cousin Charles Morris that same year and the young couple moved to the Polygon.[2] In 1796 they leased a part house in the west side of High Street. Charles Morris took over Robert Ballard's place as partner in the wine business

The children of Robert Ballard Snr, by Bartholomew Dandridge, private collection

1 Robert Ballard jnr. had an estate valued at £4319 made up of his house at £850, Harris's at £515, rents £31 10s, Bathing House £150, Fawley House and Salters £400, salt stocks £234 6d, cash and notes £52 15s 6d, Donkins plate 6s 6d, houses at Frome £500, the mortgage on the spa £80 and a debt from a defaulted mortgage taken out by Edward Luttrell of £1200. Noah's Ark was sold for £410 and the chambers over the black vault for £50. Ballard's funeral expenses came to £1303 6s 8d. SA D/PM 10/6.
2 Marriage settlement SA SC4/3/832b and SC4/4/526/32, 33a-b.

with John Butler Harrison II.[1] Milly, however, as executrix of her father's will found herself embroiled in legal disputes with her relatives. Robert Ballard junior, as executor of his father's will, had not carried out the instructions properly. Ballard senior had left money to his two other surviving children from his third marriage, Edward and Lucy, as well as his grandson John Butler Harrison but he had intended that money to be invested and to grow for when the legatees reached twenty-one. Robert Ballard junior had not invested the money and Edward threatened Milly with legal action. Although John Butler Harrison was also caught up in the affair, he opted to sort the situation out along with Milly's husband Charles Morris and eventually the matter was settled amicably though not until 1816.[2] There was further problems with another branch of the family, the children of Milly's Aunt Frances Taunton, who wanted their share of the estate of Abraham Weekes, again John Butler Harrison acted for his cousin to resolve the dispute.[3]

The Morris's had five children; Melicent born 1796 and inoculated five months later, Emily born 1797 and inoculated six months later, Charles 1799 inoculated in April 1800, Elizabeth born March 1802 inoculated with cow pox in December 1802 and George baptized 5th March 1805 and inoculated the next year. Melicent, Emily, Charles and Elizabeth all had chicken pox in January 1806 but, when young Charles contracted measles whilst at school in Salisbury in 1807, sadly he did not survive. Milly died in 1809 after a lingering disease of four years and was buried in the chancel of St Lawrence church in the same vault as her parents, brother and son.[4] Her husband passed away in 1829, making John Butler Harrison his executor.[5] Melicent's surrogate son John Butler Harrison II lived a long life and married Elizabeth Austen, second cousin of Jane Austen.

Health

The scourge of the age was the disease smallpox and the Ballard family had been hit by tragedy as a result of this disease. Melicent's husband Robert had lost

1 SA D/PM 56/13 Accounts partnership of John Butler Harrison II and Charles Morris wine merchants and co-partners 1810. The Universal British Directory on 1792-8 commended Southampton on having *many opulent wine merchants* p. 455.
2 SA D/PM 96/32 and D/PM 10/6.
3 SA D/PM 3/7/2
4 Charles Morris died in 1829, his daughter Elizabeth died of a decline at Rome in 1832 and was buried there aged 30 after being ill for three years. His daughters Melicent Lenthat died in 1848 and Emily Harrison in 1872. George, who became a clergyman, died in 1880. Ballard Family Bible.
5 SA D/PM 37/2.

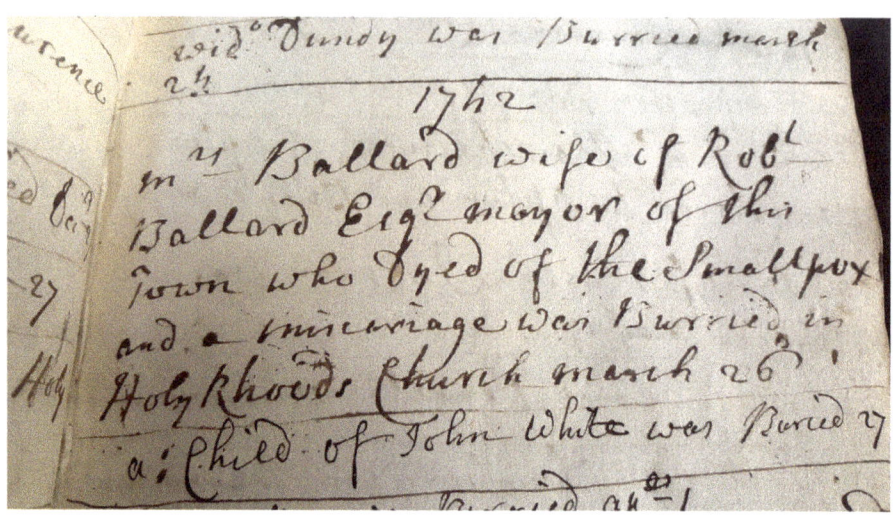

Burial Record of Mrs Ballard Snr

his mother and one of his siblings who had died during a smallpox outbreak as well as the parents and uncle of his nephew John Butler Harrison II. It was no doubt these multiple deaths, which had so decimated the family, ensured the young Ballard children were treated with the new medical breakthrough of inoculation. The health of the children was recorded in the family bible. John was inoculated by Mr Irward of Romsey on 15th December 1769 which resulted in about a hundred pustules of the 'seven-day sort'. Little Milly was inoculated by Dr Smith on 27th October prior to her public christening in February 1774 at St Lawrence Church. It was noted that she then produced ten pustules. The same year both Milly and John contracted chicken pox and Milly had a full distemper. In September 1775 young John caught measles and had 'a very light distemper' and by October Milly was seized with the same complaint.

In 1780 Melicent wrote to John to report that: 'my Dear little girl; who had eat too much fruit, and was not quite well, therefore I came home before eleven'. In the same letter she advised that Mrs Taunton, wife of the merchant and mayor Richard Taunton, was well, as were her little boys. She concludes:

> I am happy that your relation Sr. George Baker has recommended you in so particular manner to the Physician, tho I hope my Dear Boy will enjoy perfect health. our neighbour Mrs Spencer is dead,[1] after a complaint in her bowels, for a few days, which complaint is very general, every where, whether from the

---

1 Probably the wife of Ventham Spencer gent. who lived at 146 High Street. Hampshire Directory 1783-4 p. 31.

air, or from eating fruit, which is in general blighted this year; is not determined by the learn'd. our Dear little girls indisposition is of the same kind, but I hope will not be very bad, as it was taken in time, & she will have great care taken of her & is very good for taking Medicine. your Grandpapa Uncle & all their friends desire their kind Love to you & wishes for your happiness. I am sorry to tell you; Betseys eyes are much worse, than when you saw her, & Mr Hinton thought it necessary to take her to London for advice before her Hollidays were over. therefore we have no chance of seeing her here,

The Betsey referred to was John Butler Harrison II's half-sister Elizabeth. 1780 was a year when many fell ill in the town:

Nanny has had the same complaint, but is getting better, several have died of it those you know are Mrs Allison[1] Mrs Spencer & the youngest of the master Atherleys,[2] it has been more fatal among the poor, as they cannot afford proper nourishment, & the disorder requires good liveing

October ye 9th.
I have given up all thought's of going to Manningford[3] this year, as the place is very wet & dirty, & the Winter already come upon us, I am fearful it would hurt Milly, to take the journey, for her illness has render'd her rather tender both she & Nanny are much thinner, & have lost their Rosy cheeks, tho both begin to pick up again.

Your old flame Miss Rose Hughes is now on the recovery from the reigning illness, & expect's soon to see her Father; who is just made an Admiral, & must of course resign his government.

Octbr. Ye 14 – I shall now finish for the post tomorrow. Col: Vignoles[4] died last Wednesday last, of this dreadful flux. Mr Bugnon was acquainted with him. Old Rolph ye butcher is also dead of it, & that sweet little girl of the Scotts is given over. - since my last epistle, old Mrs Atherly, & Mrs Philly Carter, have paid their debt to Nature. I heard from Mrs Taunton last week

1 Probably the wife of John Allison, perfumer and elastic wigmaker of 162 High Street Hampshire Directory p. 7.
2 The Atherley Banking family lived on the High Street. Arthur Atherley and Robert Ballard had been friends since youth and had undertaken a European Tour together.
3 Manningford was in Wiltshire.
4 The Vignolles lived in Above Bar, the Colonel's daughters are shown there in the Hampshire Directory p. 34.

The records of All Saints church show that Mrs Atherley was buried on the 21st November and Mrs Philly Carter on November 24th. John's sister's health also took a turn for the worse:

> she is not to return to School, therefore direct your letter to The Rev'd Mr Hintons - poor Betsey has had so violent a fever that her life was dispair'd off for a fortnight, when she (....) was enough recover'd to bear the journey, Mrs Hinton fetch'd her from school, & she is now purely recover'd.

The deaths continued into January 1781 and Melicent herself was also taken ill:

> – perhaps a few of your acquaintance dead as Mrs Cozens, Mrs Atherly senr., Mrs White, Miss Philly Carter, & Mr Peveral - I am not certain I did not mention some of these in my last letter, but you enjoin'd me to inform you, of all deaths, and all marriages, & I endeavour to fulfill all promises that I am induced to make
> Feb. ye 4th. – this letter would have been sent a Month ago, as you may observe by the date, but that I was taken ill, & am just enough recover'd to write - . I am sorry to tell you poor Mrs Purbeck is dead, she was a worthy woman & will be a great loss to her family. we expect every post to hear, that yr friends , Mrs Rooke[1] & Mrs Cooke, are released from this painful Life, as our last accounts mention, there were little hopes of any amendment
> Doctor Speed has been very ill sometime, & is not likely to recover, the eldest Miss Halton is dead.
> Cantillo's concert was last night, not more than a hundred people favour'd him, your Uncle was one of the number, as I am obliged to attend my girl during her maid's illness, I did not go, you know I never leave her with any other servant.

Melicent's father-in-law Robert Ballard senior died in February 1782. In 1783 the town was suffering from an outbreak of typhus, sometimes referred to as putrid fever. The disease had broken out in the town amongst the army regiments stationed there. It was this same outbreak to which Jane Austen, her sister Cassandra and cousin Jane Cooper succumbed whilst they were staying in the resort in the company of Mrs Cawley who had been in charge of their education. There was also smallpox around which was also taking its toll:

---

1   Probably the wife of the Rev. Robert Rooke who lived on St Michael's Square. There was a Mrs Cooke a mantua maker who lived on Castle Lane.

1783 - my Father is but poorly. he does not take enough air & exercise to enjoy health - innoculation is over but the small pox is still in Town, & the sort very bad - Miss Davy[1] has hitherto escaped it - she is averse to being innoculated. Mr McCombe is here in Lodgings. I believe you heard of his Wife's death

It was in May of 1784 that Melicent herself became ill and died, probably of the typhus, on the 27th May and was interred in the chancel of St Lawrence Church, under the last pew on the south side. She was only forty years old. Her husband died in 1794 aged fifty-seven being buried in the family vault next to his late wife and his two sons.

Melicent's last surviving letter dates from April 1783 and it was down to her widower to communicate a *Mournful Packet* to his ward John, who after four years away was destined never to see her or receive her delightful, chatty letters again. Three years later her widower was about to remarry and on 27th October 1786 Robert Ballard wrote to his nephew:

Dear Jack
You will herewith received my Marriage Settlement with Miss Ward, suppose Saturday Morning 8 oclock you will therefor set off at 10 & dine with Dr Ballard at Wimering & get the same executed & return Sunday Time enough to forward the same to me by the Mail Coach. The Ponies will attend you on this occasion, hope the little Female For whom they were last in use is in her health.[2] Milly save a slight Cold, is perfectly well we dine together Sunday at Mr Warres. Compliments to all friends & believe me in haste sincerely your truly affection Uncle Robert Ballard

ANN LAUNCE NEWELL (1748? – 1814)

Ann Newell was the nearest neighbour of Jane Austen and her family when they moved to Castle Square in 1806. Ann does not figure in Austen's letters, though her daughter does, but as they lived in adjoining houses the families would have been well known to one another.

Ann Newell was one of several plantation owners who had chosen to make their home in Southampton. The details of her life come down to us through surviving papers held by her legal representative in Southampton - the lawyer Thomas Ridding.

1 Miss Davy was Milly's governess.
2 Elizabeth Austen, John's future wife, see letter Appendix Two.

Early Life and Marriage

Jane Austen mentions several plantation families in her letters and these include Josias Jackson who was heir to five plantations on the West Indian Island of St Vincent. By 1803 he had moved to Southampton where he became a colonel of the Local Volunteers and went on to stand for parliament in 1807. This

Small Drawings West Indian plantation slaves by William Berryman 1806-16, Library of Congress

date is significant in the story of the abolitionist movement which secured a success when the slave trade was abolished. Slavery itself, however, continued in the Empire until 1833, in particular on the sugar plantations of the West Indies. Jackson was a supporter of the West Indian planters who he said: 'in accomplishments and humanity were equal to the most polished society of England'. He attempted to attract West Indian trade into Southampton but without much success so returned to St Vincent in 1819. Another planter living in Southampton was Ballard Beckford Nembhard, who may have been connected to the Ballard family and who left a fortune of £39,000 in 1820. The MP for Southampton, between 1794-1813, was George Rose with estates

George Rose, by William Beechey

in Dominica and Antigua[1] and he had voted against the abolition of the slave trade in 1796. Jane Austen was friends with Rose's grandmother Mrs Duer and often socialized with the family in Southampton.[2] The author of *A History of Jamaica*, Bryan Edwards also resided in the town although he failed in his attempt to become its MP in 1795. He contributed money to support the University of Pennsylvania and was partner in Harrison & Maddison bank in Southampton. He was a fellow of the Royal Society and secretary of the African Association editing the travel journals of Mungo Park. He owned seven plantations and six hundred slaves and opposed the abolition of slavery. William Gunthorpe, son of William Gunthorpe of Painters plantation in Antigua and tenant of Bugle Hall in 1806, was particularly despised by Austen. On his marriage to Alicia the daughter of Josias Jackson she described him as a man who 'swears, drinks, is cross, jealous, selfish and Brutal'. The young man later became a clergyman in Antigua.

Ann Launce was the only surviving natural and legitimate child of the plantation owner James Launce of Red Hassell, but her mother's name is unknown, although there is an Anne Launce who was buried in Hackney on 12th September 1748. She is noted as a 'wife' and it could be that she was Ann's mother and died in childbirth. Red Hassell or Hazel was a sugar estate around Lower Titchfield, (later Port Antonio), in Jamaica. At the time of her father's death in 1775 she was married to another plantation owner, Joshua Newell of the Hermitage. Hermitage Estate, in the parish of Portland,[3] was situated on the west bank of Daniel's River between Hope Bay and St Margaret's Bay. It was one of the oldest estates in old St George and extended

---

1 His estates had come through his father's marriage to Theodora Duer. Rose senior was appointed, alongside Edward Jenner, to create a new institution to carry out mass vaccinations against smallpox. The National Vaccine Establishment was established in 1808. History of parliament on line.
2 *Jane Austen Letters* pp. 140, 142, 144.
3 In 1788 the population of Portland was 5,510, of which 375 were white men, women and children, 175 free coloureds and 4,960 slaves. Dr Jenny Jemmott *The Parish History Project: A History of Portland* 2019 p. 70.

Bryan Castle Plantation, owned by Bryan Edwards, by James Hakewill

over 800 acres. Its proximity to the river allowed the use of a water powered mill in manufacturing and producing sugar and rum as well as mixed crops. The couple had married in 1767 when Ann's father first drew up his will.[1] Her inheritance of plantations in Jamaica and property in Britain were conditional on her maintaining her father's tomb at the cost of £20 a year along with the maintenance of four poor families.

It is possible that Ann's husband Joshua Newell had died in 1776 when Ann is recorded as the owner of Hermitage.[2] Ann spent her marriage in Jamaica and it was where her children were born, her son Joshua and daughters Ann and Bridgett but tragedy struck, and she lost not only her husband but also her son and she re-evaluated where she wanted to spend her life. By 1789 Ann was a widow living in Southampton leaving behind the burial place of her father, to which had been joined the graves of her husband and son Joshua. As an absentee owner Ann had appointed William Sinclair and James Patterson to be her attorneys and act in her name in regard to her plantations and sugar work at Hopewell in the parish of Hanover and the other called Lances Cristine.[3] This included all the 'negroe and other male and female slaves, cattle stock,

---

1 TNA PROB-11-1013-231.
2 Dr Jenny Jemmott *The Parish History Project: A History of Portland* 2019 p. 56.
3 SA D/PM 44/41. See Hannah Young *Gender and absentee slave-ownership in late eighteenth- and early nineteenth-century Britain* Unpublished thesis UCL 2017 for an overview of female absentee ownership.

plantation utensils and stores'. They were also to oversee trade in regard to the produce in ships of Great Britain or otherwise to dispose of it as Ann Newell directed. In 1809 she is recorded as having 329 slaves, this had dropped to 151 in 1815. As mentioned, in 1807 Britain abolished the slave trade but not slavery across the Empire, so Ann continued to operate her plantations by the use of slave labour. From 1787 until 1803 the attorney acting for her estate was one William Grant, with the assistance of a number of overseers including between 1800 and 1803 James Wise, the latter being mentioned in a codicil to Ann's will.

The income from sugar and rum production paid for Ann's home in Southampton where she resided in Castle Square, making her a tenant of the Marquis of Lansdowne whose gothic castle mansion stood opposite. She was wealthy enough to keep a carriage, and applied to the pavement commissioners for permission to make a bunny over the gate so that she could more easily turn her carriage, and John Butler Harrison who was mayor that year and a commissioner, agreed.[1] In 1806 new neighbours moved in next door, Captain

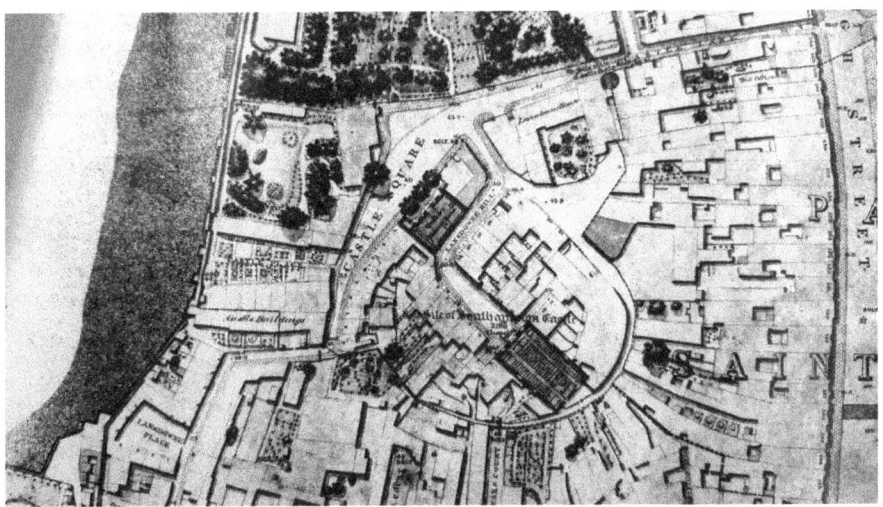

Castle Square, Southampton

Francis Austen of the Royal Navy and his wife, plus his widowed mother Mrs Cassandra Austen, his two unmarried sisters, Cassandra and Jane and a family friend Martha Lloyd. From the local rate book the Newell property was rated at a value of £50, with £9 assessment for the stable.[2] The annual rates Ann Newell paid was £3 15s for the house and 13s 6d for the stable. In 1808 Ann's

1   SA SP/AP 1/2 Pavement Commissioners 1812.
2   SA SC/AG 8/3/6 All Saints 1806.

daughter Ann Hill called on Mrs Austen and made an enquiry about a clergy family named Alford from the Austen's part of Hampshire, as an acquaintance of the Hills was looking for information and believed they lived in the vicinity of Dr Hills living. It seemed the lady in question had some work, or trimming, she was doing for the family. The Austens did not admit to the Hills that they thought the family were in fact them.[1]

Children

Ann had been joined in England by her two daughters, Bridgett and Ann, however only her daughter Ann survived to adulthood. Bridgett died on 6th December in 1790 and was buried at St Marys. Looking at Ann's marriage date it is likely Bridgett was at the most only fifteen and probably younger. Ann junior married a local clergyman called Hugh Hill at Millbrook in 1796. Hill became vicar at Holy Rood church, rector of Church Oakley near Deane, and

The Warden's House, God's House

was also the warden of the alms houses of God's House on Winkle Street a post he had held since 1792. This latter post included the accommodation known as the warden's house where he lived and had in his possession until 1824.[2] The

---

1 *Jane Austen's Letters* p. 158.
2 As warden of God's House Hill had the responsibility for the owners, Queen's College Oxford, extensive property holdings that were attached to God's House. In 1797 this bought Hill into conflict with Nathaniel Middleton of Townhill House

warden's house was not in a good state when Hill first came into the property and he did take some responsibility for putting it in repair. In 1795, he had written to the bursar of Queen's College Oxford, the owners of the property complaining that rain was: 'washing down in a very provoking manner the ceiling in my garret and my two bed-chambers... had I know the house and garden were actually so dilapidated I would never have taken possession of it at all'.[1] The Hills became involved in one of the cause célèbres of the day in regard to the marriage of Mary Cole, also known as Mary Tudor, the daughter of a butcher and publican, to the Earl of Berkeley. It was in no doubt she was his mistress and that they had twelve children, but the couple went to court to try and convince the House of Lords that they had had a secret marriage in 1785 and after the births of their first six children went through another service in 1796. This was to try and ensure their eldest son inherited the title. Both the marriage services were in doubt, particularly the first, which was said to have been undertaken by the vicar of Berkeley, Mr Hupsman. By the 1790s Hupsman was living in Southampton serving initially as curate at St Mary's Church and later as a locum to clerics such as Hugh Hill. To that end he was apt to dine with important people in the town and to regale them with his part in the nuptials of the Berkeleys. In 1811, after the earl's death the countess was still fighting for recognition for her eldest son and gathered evidence from various Southampton witnesses, particularly in regard to a dinner, held in 1793 or 1794, at the house of the East India Company man John Burdett, himself a survivor of the Black Hole of Calcutta of 1756. Also at the dinner was Hupman, Mr Henry Haynes and Hugh Hill. Burdett related Hupman telling them about performing the 1785 marriage ceremony. When Hugh Hill was interviewed, he confirmed the conversation and also said he had known the brother of Mary Cole who had been a witness to the wedding. He said he would further speak to his wife to see if she remembered more details. The next day, however, Hill recanted his testimony at the behest of his wife and his brother who had persuaded him that his memory may not have been as good as he thought. The interviewer believed he had been prevailed upon to padlock his lips. This was perhaps a contributing factor to Lady Berkeley losing her case.[2]

>   who rented a number of farms from the college. The values of the farms and the rents Middleton paid to the college were under dispute. J. M. Kaye (ed) *A God's House Miscellany* Southampton Records Series 1984 pp. 103-108.
1 J M Kaye (ed) *The Cartulary of God's House, Southampton vol I* Southampton Records Series 1976 p. lxxxvi
2 'The Occasional Review: the Countess of Berkeley's Address to the Peers in *The General Chronicle & Literary Magazine Vol IV* London 1812, pp. 186-7.

The Hills were friends with Ann Newell's physician Dr Mackie and in 1802 they, along with their four-year-old daughter Ann and their maid, shared a house with Mrs Mackie and her daughter Ann Sophy in Tunbridge Wells. The party took donkey rides to the Rocks and ate cakes along with a carriage ride to Tunbridge. In 1812 they were all in London travelling there together, Mrs Hill and Ann Sophy making part of the journey on the box.[1]

Dr John Mackie, National Galleries of Scotland

After his own marriage, Hill and his wife acted in consort with Ann Newell in the management of the West Indian properties. This included engaging English craftsmen to travel to Jamaica, several of whom, whose papers survive, came originally from Westmoreland, from where Hugh Hill originated and where his brother John still lived. Hill sent out David Milligan to work as a book keeper in 1806 and in the next year James Cushen Hall from Westmoreland followed him.[2] In 1811 William Morresby of Westmoreland travelled to Jamaica to work on the plantations at Red Hassell and the Hermitage, both in the parish of Portland, in the capacity of a carpenter for a period of three years. Morresby was to be paid £65 for his first year and £75 for his second and £80 for his third, along with subsistence, washing, lodging and doctors' bills. In 1813 another carter and wheelwright, John Thompson, and carpenter, William Blyth, also signed articles to go to Jamaica as did John Meade.[3] It is difficult to understand how Hugh Hill an Anglican minister reconciled his Christian beliefs with the receiving of income derived from slavery. This was even more of a challenge now that most of the plantation slaves would have been converted to Christianity by this period. It was at this time that the philosophical discussion about whiteness and the hierarchy of colour developed to justify what was essentially unjustifiable.

Health

There is nothing known about Ann's health, but she made her will in 1808 which may have been the result of an illness but perhaps it was written in

1 The Travel Journal of Ann Sophy Mackie, Chawton House Library.
2 SA D/PM 44/159.
3 SA D/PM 44/158, 44/159, 44/212.

response to the recent legislation around slavery. Her trustees did include Dr John Mackie, a very eminent physician, to whom she left 100 guineas and the same sum to his son John William Mackie. His biographer said he could have had a high-profile practice in London but preferred a quieter setting for his work. This did not prevent people seeking him out and, even after he had retired, he was consulted by everyone from Mrs Fitzherbert to Louis Bonaparte. During his time in Southampton, he also did charitable work by supporting the many French refugees who had fled to the town during the period of the French Revolution.[1] Dr Mackie chose to retire and leave Southampton in 1814 which was the year of Ann's death. Ann's will shows she had £7,000 in bank stock, £4,700 in 4% consuls and £4,000 in 3% consuls. In her will Ann nominates as her heirs her daughter Ann and grand-daughter Ann Newell Hill.[2] Her will also gave instruction to free her slave Kitty Fell, leaving her a £10 annuity. There were also several bequests to other family members, cousins, godchildren and friends.

A few years later, in 1813, Ann decided to add a codicil to her will adding information on another potential legatee, her former maid Eliza Clark. It seems that, close as maid and mistress had been, Eliza was actually a slave and had caught the eye of a man called James Wise who was, between 1800 and 1803, the overseer of the Newell plantations. The overseer's job was to manage the estate, to discipline workers and particularly in the case of non-resident owners, have the active management of the plantation and the slaves. An indication of the role of the overseer can be seen from *The Cotton Plantation Records and Account Book No 3* by Thomas Affleck who had that role in 1857 in an American plantation, where slavery was not yet abolished:

> On entering upon your duties, inform yourself thoroughly of the condition of the plantation, negroes, stock, implements, etc.
>
> -The health of the negroes under your charge is an important matter. Much of the usual sickness among them is the result of carelessness and mismanagement. Overwork, or unnecessary exposure to rain, insufficient clothing, improper or badly cooked food, and night rambles, are all fruitful causes of disease.

1 See Matthew Conolly Dictionary of Eminent People of Fife 1866 pp. 312-314 and his *Memoir of John Mackie MD* Atherley Papers SA D/S19/1-2 Vol III. In a case report to Dr Vaughan on a Miss Dillon's lung disorder, Mackie recommends Southampton as having a favourable climate for pulmonic patients, having the advantages of, but less rain than, Devon and Cornwall. TNA DG24/823/5.
2 Overseers were the dancing master Charles Burgat and his son William, George Harrison Cozens, a Jamaican Planter, Dr John Mackie MD and his son and clergyman John William. TNA PROB-11-1551-248.

-It is indispensable that you exercise judgment and consideration in the management of the Negroes under your charge. Be firm, and at the same time gentle in your control. Never display yourself before them in a passion; and even if inflicting the severest punishment, do so in a mild, cool manner, and it will produce a tenfold effect. When you find it necessary to use the whip – and desirable as it would be to dispense with it entirely, it is necessary at times – apply it slowly and deliberately, and to the extent you are determined in your own mind, to be needful before you began.

-You will find that an hour devoted every Sabbath morning to their moral and religious instruction, would prove a great aid to you in bringing about a better state of things amongst the negroes. The effect upon their general good behavior, their cleanliness and good conduct on the Sabbath is such as alone to recommend it to the Planter and Overseer.

-Next to the Negroes, the Stock on the place will require your constant attention. You can, however, spare yourself much trouble by your choice of a stock-minder, and by adopting and enforcing a strict system in the care of the stock. It is a part of their duty in which Overseers are generally most careless.

-The implements and tools require a good deal of looking after. By keeping a memorandum of the distribution of any set of tools, they will be much more likely to be forthcoming at the end of the month. Few instances of good management will better please an employer, than that of having all the winter clothing spun and woven on the place.

-Few plantations are so rich in soil, as not to be improved by manure. Inform yourself of the best means, suited to the location and soil of the place under your charge, of improving it in this, and in every other way.

-In conclusion,-- Bear in mind that a fine crop consists, first, in an increase in the number, and a marked improvement in the condition and value of the negroes; second, an abundance of provision of all sorts for man and beast carefully saved and properly housed; third, both summer and winter clothing made at home; also, leather tanned, and shoes and harness made when practicable; fourth, an improvement in the productive qualities of the land, and in the general condition of the plantation: fifth, the team and stock generally, with the farming implements and the buildings, in fine order at the close of the year; and young hogs more than enough for next year's killing; then-- as heavy a crop of cotton, sugar or rice, as could possibly be made under the circumstances, sent to market in good season and of prime quality.

The best-selling book by the former slave and abolitionist, *The Interesting Narrative of the Life of Olaudah Equiano or Gustavus Vassa the African* written by

Himself published in 1789 paints a grim picture of plantation life: 'It was very common in several of the islands, particularly in the St Kitts, for the slaves to be branded with the initial letters of their master's name, and a load of heavy iron hook hung around their necks ... I have seen a negro beaten till some of his bones were broken, for only letting a pot boil over.'

For female slaves they also faced sexual exploitation. It is probable that this was the case when James Wise persuaded Ann Newell to sell him Eliza Clark and that his interest was carnal. There are many examples of white overseers, who were lower class than the plantation owners and often not well-paid, leasing or buying favoured slaves to act as their housekeepers and sexual partners. Some were recognised as surrogate wives and had long term relationships but others were not so lucky and were just exploited.[1] When the sixteen-year-old William Lewin travelled to India in 1822, after the abolition of the trade, but not the practice of slavery, he observed whilst stopping off in South Africa:

> We rode the first day about 50 miles to a very pleasant village called the Paarle, and found quarters in the house of a Dutchman ... We were attended at meals by female black slaves, whose naked feet, the badge of slavery, quite offended my freeborn British feelings, and I inwardly thought 'What right has man to tyrannize thus over his fellow creatures' .... The population was scanty, while I eyed the solitary Hottentot who one met sauntering along as a creature of half savage nature. The slaves, male and female, are allowed to cohabit promiscuously for the sake of procreation, much after the manner of beasts, while the best looking among the females are prostituted to the sensual gratification of their masters' passion.[2]

Ann Newell had no qualms about selling Eliza to James Wise, although there had been an agreement that when he died James Wise would free Eliza, which was quite a usual practice, as to have freed Eliza earlier could have been seen as undermining the concept of slave ownership. It is to be assumed that Wise had died in 1813 but had not stood by his agreement. It might be thought that if Ann wanted to ensure the freedom of Eliza Clark, she could have re-purchased her and then granted her that freedom, but this is not what Ann did. Her codicil, which would only be enacted on Ann's death, looked

---

1 Cecilia A Green 'The Hierachies of Whiteness in the Geographies of Empire: Thomas Thistlewood & the Barretts of Jamaica' in *New West Indian Guide Vol 80 No 1/2* 2006 p. 23.
2 *Lewin Letters* pp. 253-4.

3

Names of Slaves belonging to Miss Sarah Theodora Foulks leased in the above written Indenture with their respective Values in Jamaica Currency

Tom Parsons	200	Boys	
Humphrey	180	Primus ⎫	
Women		Fair ⎬	110
Lauretta	180	William ⎭	
Sukey	180		1530
Nancy Cox	160		
Phœbe	180		
Iphey	160		
Cubey Judy	180		
	1420		

The value of slaves, Foukes family, Southampton Archives

to her trustees to repurchase Eliza and any children she might have had in the meantime. Ann, however, did put a cap on her generosity stating that the purchase should only take place if it could be achieved for less than £300. To give an indication of the value of individual slaves, another local family, the Foulkes drew up a lease agreement in 1803 and the three sisters Ann, Mary, and Sarah leased the slaves that they had inherited from their father, to their brother Arthur who was managing the family estates. Female slaves were valued between £120 and £180 each, presumably based on age and skills, and children were valued at a lesser price.[1] Ann Newell also included an annuity of £5 for Eliza once she had been freed. It is not known if the trustees did carry out Ann's wishes after her death in 1814 but legal papers do survive which were used to calculate legacy duty due on the estate. This document shows that Ann Newell's bank stock was valued at £16,520, the 4% consuls £3,689 10s and the 3% consuls £3,150. With other items such as cash in the house and dividend payments the value to the estate total was £24,999 10s.[2] Ann's household goods and furniture were valued at £800. In the return in regard to legacy duty it was reported Ann had £172 5s in the bank and had West Indian produce valued at £950. Her funeral costs were £155 11s 10d. It was noted that pecuniary legacies for legatees abroad stood at £210, but nothing registered against annuities. This might suggest that Eliza Clarke was not repurchased and did not receive her annuity.

In the records of runaway slaves in Jamaica there is reference to Marie, an Eboe to Mr Newell of Spanish Town. An Eboe was reference to the Igbo people an ethnic group from Nigeria. Spanish Town was the provincial capital of Middlesex County. In 1816 Marie was in the St Ann workhouse and it was recorded that she was marked on her right should with an MV and on her left shoulder with AN.[3]

When Ann Newell's daughter died a widow in 1848 (her husband Hugh Hill having died in 1824) the family still had an estate in the West Indies at the Hermitage which was managed on her behalf by James Brough. The family would have benefited from the scheme the British Government set up, in 1837, to compensate slave owners and Ann Hill received £3518 for her 258 slaves. In her own will[4] Ann Hill left £100 to her attorney James Brough,

1 SA D/PM 64/3/101 draft lease 1803 re slaves on The Lodge plantation, Jamaica.
2 This would be the equivalent of around £2.5 million in 2013. SA D/PM 70/8 settlement of Ann Hill in regard to the legacies of her mother.
3 Douglas B. Chambers (ed) *Runaway slaves in Jamaica (II): Nineteenth Century* University of Southern Missouri (Feb 2013).
4 TNA PROB 11-2082-45.

Holy Rood Church

and £500 in trust for the maintenance of the graves of her mother and sister in St Marys. Her husband was buried at Holy Rood Church, where he had been vicar, and Ann set up a charity linked to Holy Rood. This charity continued to 1955 when, after the bombing of Holy Rood church in 1940, the charity was then applied to St Michael's Church. Her own unmarried daughter and heir, Ann Newell Hill, born in 1798, left an estate of over £100,000 when she died in 1892.

ANNE MORSE MIDDLETON (1758-1823)

Through her marriage to Nathaniel Middleton, a close colleague of Warren Hastings, Anne would have known Jane's Aunt Philadelphia and her cousin Eliza Hancock. Jane Austen was interested in the trial of Warren Hastings and no doubt would have been aware of the connections when she moved to Southampton. Nathaniel Middleton's brother John was a sometime tenant of Chawton House and his daughter Charlotte recorded her memories of Jane Austen from her time living there.

Anne Middleton's story was the subject of national interest due to three court cases that took place during her lifetime, and the newspaper reports that accompanied them, alongside the content of her will. The first court case put under the microscope challenged her ethnicity and the impact of that on her rights to inherit from her father; the second was a long running case of international interest which involved her husband, the trial of Warren Hastings; and lastly a case which examined her sanity at the end of her life brought by her son who wanted control over her assets.

Anne Middleton, by Thomas Heaphy

Early life and Marriage

Anne Morse was born in Jamaica in 1758, one of five children of the wealthy plantation owner and merchant John Morse and Elizabeth Augier alias Tyndall, who was of mixed-race descent and a descendant of slaves. Anne's baptismal record records her as the 'base child of Elizabeth Tindal'.[1] Although their parents were not married John recognised his children and sent them all

1 Morse also had another daughter Frances with a different woman of colour and she eventually was sent by her father to Amsterdam to stay with her aunt Sarah van Heelen, Frances received £2000 in her father's will. Daniel Livesay *Children of Uncertain Fortune: Mixed-Race Migration from the West Indies to Britain 1750-1820* unpublished PhD thesis University of Michigan 2010 pp. 179-180. TNA PROB 11-1077-146 will of John Morse 1781. Sarah van Heelen was John Morse's sister who had married Jan Carel van Heelen in 1752.

The Morse-Cator Family, Robert Morse, Anne Morse, Sarah Cator, William Cator, Aberdeen City Council Art Gallery and Museums Collection

to England to enter English society. His son John, a Lieutenant in the Horse Guards, took on an estate, from his father, on the outskirts of Southampton at Midanbury. Robert became a lawyer and his daughter Catherine married her father's English attorney Edmund Green in 1777. In that same year Robert decided to advance his career by travelling to India and his two remaining unmarried sisters joined him on the sub-continent.[1] In that journey the sisters were following a well-travelled route for young English women in search of a wealthy husband. Anne was an heiress in her own right but for the Morse sisters there was another advantage. A marriage to a wealthy nabob of good

1   Alfred Spencer *The Memoirs of William Hickey 1782-90 Vol III* London 1923 p. 155.

family would help their assimilation into society when they returned to Britain. On 4th November 1780 Sarah married the East India Company merchant William Cator following the example of her sister Anne who had married Nathaniel Middleton the week before. Anne's husband had joined the company in his teens and arrived in Bengal just after his twentieth birthday.[1] He moved up the company ranks and became resident at the court of Shuja ud-Daula, Nawab of Oudh (Awadh), in Lucknow, working very closely with Warren Hastings. At the time of his marriage to Anne he already had an Indian family with his Indian mistress or bibi;[2] his youngest child of the relationship, Eliza, was baptised on the same day as his marriage to Anne. He had at least two other children, Charlotte and Henry George.[3] One of Anne's friends and a

Nathaniel Middleton, by Tilly Kettle

1 Nathaniel's brother John rented Chawton House from Jane Austen's brother Edward Knight in 1795 and 1808-13, although he was not successful there in the haymaking season: *but here he has had better luck than Mr Middleton ever had in the 5 years that he was tenant. Jane Austen's Letters* pp. 215, 554. He married Charlotte Beckford, of the Jamaican sugar plantation family, whose sister Maria also lived with the family. Maria Beckford and a Miss Middleton attended a party at Henry Austen's London home in 1811 *Miss M seems very happy, but has not beauty enough to figure in London. Jane Austen's Letters* p. 183.
2 Hindustani word for lady, English Ladies were also called Bibi with their surnames added. Sydney Grier (ed) *Letters of Warren Hastings to his wife* Edinburgh & London 1905 p. 63. Johanna Barr, spinster, who was mistress to Alexander Champion colonel and commander of the East India Company in Bengal was living in Southampton in 1775 and setting up a trust for her 'natural children' by Champion, Ganny Cummings and Alexander Champion. Champion had married Frances Nynd in 1759. There was no mention of his natural children in his will SA D/PM 20/17, TNA PROB 11-1231-50.
3 Daniel Livesay *Children of Uncertain Fortune: Mixed-Race Migration from the West Indies to Britain 1750-1820* unpublished PhD thesis University of Michigan 2010 p. 258. Eliza married Thomas Charles Pattle who served in the EIC in Canton

former teacher, Guiseppe Baretti, wrote of the young Mrs Middleton:

> I shall probably never see my brothers or my other relations or you or any of my friends at home again, and, above all, a dear child whom I have educated, the daughter of a worthy friend of mine. She married another worthy friend of mine two years ago, and started for the East Indies with him at once, taking a large slice of my heart with her.

Later when Baretti was in debt owing £70:

> Fortune relieved him, by bringing him an Easter present from a young lady, who had been one of those he took pleasure to instruct; who was just married to Mr Middleton in Bengal, and transmitted him, among other treasures, a diamond of fine value; the use he made of it was to lodge it in Mr Cadell's hands, till it could be sold, and the debt discharged.[1]

Shuja-ud-Daula, copy from a painting by Tilly Kettle

In the meantime, Anne's father had returned to England but he died shortly afterwards in 1781 and when the content of his will was made public it resulted in the first of the three court cases in which Anne was to become

and he died in 1815. One of his executors was Eliza's half-brother Hastings. TNA PROB 11/1582/228. He was extremely wealthy and left his wife £20,000 and his daughter £30,000 plus large bequests to his siblings. His widow moved to Princes Street, London. She also took a case against Hastings TNA C 13/198/39. Her seventeen-year-old daughter eloped with Edward Gibbon Wakefield, Mrs Pattle eventually was reconciled and moved with the couple to Turin Italy. TNA C13/718/23. When her daughter Eliza died aged twenty in childbirth her husband tried to get hold of her estate and failed as she was not to inherit until the age of twenty-one. He later abducted another heiress and ended up in prison before moving to New Zealand. Papers of Edward Wakefield London University EW.

1 Gentleman's Magazine Vol lix p. 569.

embroiled during her lifetime. It also meant that if Anne had hoped, by her move to India and her return to England as Anne Middleton, to have completed her transformation into Georgian Society she was about to be proved wrong. Anne was going to be thrust into the public gaze and have her background and ancestry spread across the press. John Morse divided his estate between his illegitimate children making them all wealthy. The law of the time, however, stated that mixed race children could only inherit up to £2000 from their white parent. In fact, this act had been brought to the statute book in 1761 because one of Anne's mixed-race relations, her great aunt Susanna Augier, had successfully sued to gain control of her father's estate and to be granted the status of a white person. John Morse had been extremely rich and his five children were due to inherit a lot more than two thousand pounds. The will was challenged by Morse's nephew, Edward, who took his case to court claiming that he was the residual and rightful heir of his uncle's estate and not his cousins. Anne's sister Catherine's husband Edmund Green took on the defence of his wife and her siblings. The story made headlines in the *Morning Herald*. Nathaniel Middleton was interviewed to see if he knew of his wife's ancestry, which he maintained he did not and declared it *an entire strangeness* and claimed that *having resided in India* he had never heard or been informed of the Morse family background. Edmund Green was able to prove that the children had been granted status as 'whites' thanks to an act applied for by their grand-mother, Mary, sister of Susannah Augier in 1747.[1] Shades of whiteness led to a huge range of classification amongst the mixed-race populations of the Caribbean and depictions thereof and shown in Casta Paintings.[2]

Edward Morse however suggested that his uncle had not been of sound mind when he made his will, and pointed to the fact that his cousins were also illegitimate. This was despite the fact that all the children had been specifically named in their father's will. It was probably Edward who sent an anonymous letter to the *Morning Herald* in 1786 targeting Anne's sister Sarah revealing her mother was a 'mulatto'. The case drifted on until 1794 along with the public's interest in the private lives of the Morse children. To give an indication

1 There was a special statute peculiar to Jamaica by which 'free coloured' could petition for special privileges which then classed them as legally white. Cecilia A Green 'The Hierachies of Whiteness in the Geographies of Empire: Thomas Thistlewood & the Barretts of Jamaica' in *New West Indian Guide Vol 80 No 1/2* 2006 p. 22.
2 The Braemore House collection of Casta paintings depicts a cycle of fourteen family portraits and portrays and catalogues the complex racial intermixtures of native, Spanish and African populations in Colonial Mexico and were commissioned from Juan Rodríguez Juárez in Mexico City c.1725 for Philip V of Spain.

of the amounts of money involved, in 1788 it was reported that at the time of Anne's Indian marriage her diamond shoe buckles were worth thirty-five thousand pounds. The case eventually ran out of steam when Edward died in 1795 although his heirs tried to continue the dispute and it was not officially closed until 1799 with Edmund Green being finally successful on behalf of the Morse siblings.[1] Although the Morse children were of mixed-race descent when they came into their inheritance, they continued to run the plantations by slavery in the same way their father had done.

While the trial ran its course Anne and her husband Nathaniel returned to England in 1784. She not only had the case to deal with but was still mourning the loss of her father. Just two years after their nuptials Anne also suffered when her infant son became severely ill. Middleton worried to a colleague that, were the child to die: 'it will be a severe blow, especially to Mrs. Middleton, whose affliction for the death of her father is yet fresh'.[2]

On the couple's return to England they also had to decide where to live. The Middletons had a London property on Wimpole Street and then purchased an estate, Townhill Park, close to Anne's brother John, at Midanbury House, on the outskirts of Southampton:

> Townhill Park a richly wooded vale bound with oak fencing entered via a gothic arch between two octagonal towers, one lived in by the porter. On the other side of the property there were wrought iron gates supported by Portland piers and with elegant brick lodges. The house faced south-east and built of white malmstock bricks, a semi-circular flight of steps led to an elegant Portland stone Portico enclosed by six tall doric columns. At the rear was a domed cupola. It was a trait of East India men to enhance their house with a dome. Architect Thomas Leverton. The interior was influenced by the Italian style, the entrance hall with Portland and black marble diamond flooring, enclosed with fluted doric columns, and with marble chimney piece. The Drawing Room had cornice, gilt mouldings, marble chimney, and Florentine sculpture. The library had mahogany bookcases, and Italian marble chimney. The Lady's Drawing Room, had a domed ceiling, and marble chimney inlaid with Verde Antique. There were dining and music rooms, a billiard Room, gentleman's dressing rooms and bedrooms. Bramah water closets were on first and attic floors.

1 Daniel Livesay *Children of Uncertain Fortune: Mixed-Race Migration from the West Indies to Britain 1750-1820* unpublished PhD thesis University of Michigan 2010 pp. 179-186. Morse's wealth was estimated at £140,000.
2 Nathaniel Middleton to Elijah Impey, May 12th, 1782, Correspondence of Sir Elijah Impey, Add. MS 16263, ff. 154-55, BL.

Townhill Park House

Servants' quarters included a kitchen, sugar closet, still room, large servant's hall, housekeeper's room, cook's bedroom, servants' bedroom, laundry and wash house. There was a kitchen garden that had lofty fruit walls, hot house, fruit house with furnaces, a tool shed, 96ft long peach and a grape house. The Pleasure Ground had stuccoed buildings and a transparent lake. It held a cold bath and dressing room with fireplace. Water for the cistern was piped from the brick engine house situated by a long and spacious sheet of water on the edge of River Itchen water meadows. A wheel was powered by a three-cylinder engine. There was also a farmyard, dairy house, brew house, stable for eight cart horses and icehouse.

The *Universal British Directory* thought it: a neat and elegant house and the furniture is rich and fashionable.[1]

The house must have been beautifully furnished not least of which with a magnificent art collection which Anne's husband had acquired whilst living in India. Nathaniel Middleton was an avid collector of Persian manuscripts, Indian paintings and miniatures and natural history drawings by Indian artists

1   Universal British Directory 1792-1798 p. 475.

Persian manuscript owned by Nathaniel Middleton

which were displayed in his home.[1] Whilst in India he had his portrait painted by Tilly Kettle, in 1773, which showed him seated with an illustrated manuscript. In addition, in 1782 Anne had inherited all the household goods, furniture and plate from her husband's aunt, Anne Lane, who lived in Saint Luke's parish in Chelsea, with Nathaniel also being his aunt's residual heir.[2]

The Middletons were important people locally and in 1790 the parish officers of South Stoneham resolved to apply to Nathaniel Middleton for eight or ten acres at Goaters Green for the purpose of building a poor house. Middleton agreed and in 1792 offered a spot in West End Common, near to the Botley Turnpike Road, on the easy terms of *five pounds per cent per annum for the money expended on the same* and the parish engaging to rent it for the term of 21 years. The old poor house was to be sold and Middleton was offered first refusal on the site. After her husband's death, Anne continued to receive monthly

1   An album once owned by Middleton was sold at Christies in 1909 and described A magnificent collection of 62 high finished drawings, illustrating the costume of India, with descriptions in Persian at the back of each drawing with richly illuminated borders. Among the drawings is a highly interesting portrait of Emperor Jehan Gir [sic] with equestrian attendants ordering a criminal to execution. Also a whole length portrait of Shuja ud-Daula, who presented this superb collection to the late Proprietor. It is sumptuously bound in red morocco with blue silk registers and a gold fringe.

2   TNA PROB 11-1096-336 will of Anne Lane. Anne Lane asked to be buried in Battersea Church (St Mary) where Nathaniel was later buried and where the Middleton memorial can be found.

disbursements related to the poor house. In her will she also left money to the institution and this was used to provide blankets at a cost of £27 1s 1d.[1]

Running in parallel to the Morse family trial Anne's husband, Nathaniel, was embroiled in an even bigger trial, himself, regarding charges against Warren Hastings, former governor general of Bengal, for high crimes and misdemeanours. The Middletons were so close to Warren Hastings that they named their eldest son after him with his father's name only being the boy's second name. It is true that Nathaniel owed much of his career to the man. The Middletons however were not the only local family who became caught up in the tribulations of Warren Hastings. In 1793 the Lewins, with whom Anne was on visiting terms, taking tea with Mary Lewin, were in correspondence with Hastings. In 1798 Richard Lewin and his son Richard, both company men, were asked by Hastings to vote for Mr John Hudlestone over another candidate, Mr Dundas, for a post on the company council in England.[2] Richard junior was in Southampton at the time staying with his aunt and uncle. Elizabeth Butler Harrison's cousin, Eliza Hancock, was Warren Hastings' god-daughter and there

Warren Hastings, by Joshua Reynolds

was even speculation that she was in fact his natural daughter. It is possible young Eliza spent some time in Southampton as there are some recipes in the Elizabeth's household book attributed to Miss Hancock. It was however Nathaniel Middleton who was most deeply embroiled in the affair.

1   Eric Raffo *Half a Loaf, The Care of the Sick and Poor of South Stoneham 1664-1948* IOW 2000 pp. 8, 11. One unfortunate young woman to find herself in the poor house was Ann Aldridge a servant of the local MP, Hans Sloane, who had had an illegitimate daughter by one William Talbot, a 2nd lieutenant on *HMS Juno*. Her monthly expenses were £2 and thereafter 10s for six weeks. Ibid p. 11. In 1813 Amelay Mash was also in the poor house having accused Col Thomas Powlett of fathering her child which was successfully refuted by the colonel. Cheryl Butler 'What became of Col Powlett: This Wonderous Affair' in The Jane Austen Society Report 2020.

2   *Lewin Letters* pp. 49-50.

In 1787 Nathaniel Middleton was called upon to give evidence, however, he was so successful in rebuffing questions over four days of questioning that he was given the nickname 'Memory Middleton'.[1] Edmund Burke in 1794 even accused Middleton of being an *active instrument* in Hastings administration in India, as oppressor of Awadh. Nathaniel did suffer the ignominy of being caricatured in a print made by William Dent and published by William Moore in 1788. A print can be found in the British Museum which describes the cartoon thus:

> A coat (left) in back view, round whose waist is a rope inscribed 'Manager's'. The wig and the legs belonging to the owner of the coat are beside it; between wig and legs are a number of sealed letters; to these objects and to a heart inscribed 'Truth' strings are attached held by Hastings, whose head and hands appear on the extreme right. He says, "But for equivocation I had been thus" (i.e. headless, like the wig to which he points). The wig is inscribed 'Frontispiece Index', the letters are 'Select Passages', the legs are 'Loose Leaves'. On the back of the coat is a placard inscribed 'M.. . .n's [Middleton's] Select Oriental Tales'. A cravat (?) showing over the left shoulder is inscribed 'False Title'. From the coat-pockets jewels are falling. Beneath the title (and included in the design) is etched:
>
> Here I must come in aid of Mr. Middleton a little; for one cannot but pity the miserable instruments that have to act under Mr. Hastings. I do not mean to apologize for Mr. Middleton, but to pity the situation of persons who, being servants of the Company, were converted, by the usurpation of this man, into his subjects and his slaves. The mind of Mr. Middleton revolts. You see him reluctant to proceed. The Nabob begs a respite. You find in the Resident a willingness to comply. Even Mr. Middleton is placable. Mr. Hastings alone is obdurate. His resolution to rob and to destroy was not to be moved, and the estates of the whole Mahometan nobility of a great kingdom were confiscated in a moment. Your Lordships will observe that his orders to Mr. Middleton allow no forbearance. Edmund Burke

The trial eventually collapsed after seven years. Anne's husband tried to put the unfortunate incident behind him and, in 1792, set up a London bank

---

1 As William Hickey noted, [Middleton] 'rendered himself famous . . . when his total want of recollection respecting any fact or circumstances which he conceived could tend to the prejudice of his patron . . . that he acquired the nickname of 'Memory Middleton,' and retained the same to the day of his death.'. Alfred Spencer *The Memoirs of William Hickey 1782-1790* London 1923 p. 155.

with Richard Johnson,[1] who had served under him in Awadh, and others: it traded from Stratford Place as the London & Middlesex Bank.[2] The senior partner was Gerard Edwards along with George Templer and John Wedgwood, the MP Samuel Smith was also briefly involved. As a business the bank did not prosper and came to be dominated by Alexander Davison who had helped to bail out the bank in 1803.[3] The bank also required large capital injections from Middleton at the end of his life and the banks financial affairs were in a state of flux when Nathaniel died in 1807. The situation was not helped by the fact that Nathaniel Middleton's will was misplaced and not found until nine years later. The bank was finally wound up, to the financial distress of its remaining investors in 1816.

Banking was seen as a good career opportunity in the eighteenth and nineteenth centuries with many of the banks established from monies made in India or in the West Indies. Robert Ballard recommended it as a possible option for his nephew John Butler Harrison. Samuel Harrison, who may have been a relative of John Butler Harrison, had an office at 173 High Street opposite All Saints Church. Harrison was in a banking partnership with Bryan Edwards the West Indian planter, John Simpson and Martin Maddison. In 1814 there were said to be four respectable banks in the town, one of which was Harrison

---

1 Johnson was known as 'Rupee Johnson'. Interestingly Warren Hastings wrote to his wife *I have been privately told that the friends of Richard Johnson are amongst my worst enemies in England. He is a sad fellow if this be true. Be on your guard both with him and Middleton.* H E Busteed *Echoes of Old Calcutta* London 1908 p. 349.

2 This private bank was established in 1792 at Stratford Place, Oxford Street, in London's West End, under the title of Edwards, Smith, Templer, Middleton, Johnson & Wedgwood and was otherwise known as London & Middlesex Bank. George Templer had amassed a fortune in India; John Wedgwood was the son of the potter Josiah Wedgwood; and the senior partner, Gerard Noel Edwards of Exton Park, Rutland, was a connection of the Earls of Gainsborough. The firm got into difficulties in 1803 and was rescued by a £100,000 advance from Alexander Davison, a British government contractor. In 1804 the business, then generally known as Davison, Noel, Templer, Middleton, Johnson & Wedgwood moved to Pall Mall. By 1806 it was formally known as Davison, Noel, Templer, Middleton & Wedgwood. The bank's financial difficulties persisted despite capital injections by Lord Barham and Josiah Wedgwood and, in 1816, the business was wound up. It was recommended to customers that they transfer their accounts to Thomas Coutts & Co. Archive holdings of NatWest bank.

3 Within nine months Davison had been arrested for corruption and conspiracy and committed to prison. Martyn Downer suggests Davison had not paid his £100k for the shares. On 19th June 1804 Middleton and George Templer came before King's Bench where they reported they were losing £2000 of their own money a day. *Nelson's Purse* London 2004 p. 270-2.

& Maddison who later amalgamated with another of the four, Smith & Sons. The bank drew on Kennington, Stigan & Adams. The bank was later renamed the Southampton Commercial Bank and survived to be taken over by Lloyds. The Southampton Register of 1811 reported that a Banker's Licence cost £20 and enabled the banks to re-issue notes.[1] Jane Austen's brother Henry also became a banker and when his bank got into financial difficulties it impacted negatively on his siblings, who had invested money in the same way that the Middletons had.[2]

Nathaniel's interest in banking passed to his eldest son, Hastings, in 1807. The bank was, by then, known as Alexander Davison & Co but this legacy led to disastrous results which saw the family lose money and status after the bank failed. Hastings bitterly regretted inheriting his place in the bank from his father: *the bitter pill was gilded ... instead of inheriting a patrimony, I embraced ruin.* Hastings blamed Alexander Davison for the disaster which he estimated had cost the Middleton family £100,000. Hastings was forced to sell the contents of his house in September 1816 and had to move to Tunbridge Wells in much reduced circumstances.[3]

Children

Nathaniel died aged fifty-seven in 1807 but there were problems caused by his will being mislaid. Anne made her own will a few years later, possibly after her husband's will had finally come to light. Nathaniel's original will, made in 1788, left ten thousand pounds each to his two illegitimate daughters, Eliza and Charlotte, and three thousand to his illegitimate son Henry George. Although these sums were large they were less than he left to his legitimate children. It was not unusual for illegitimate children, if recognised, to receive less than legitimate offspring and it may have been Nathaniel was also drawing some distinction with regard to his money and money that came to him on his marriage, in the divisions he made. It is likely these children had remained in India. Charlotte seems to have spent most of her life there but Eliza lived much of her later adult life in England. To his legitimate children, then

---

1 In 1798 Harrison had established his house, garden and offices in a new property called Archer House as his rural retreat on the grounds once used by the company of Archers. In 1794 Jane Austen was working on her early novel *Lady Susan* which has a character, Charles Vernon, who earns his living as a banker, a rather dull character of which not much is known, *when a man has once got his name in a banking-house he rolls in money.*
2 See Emma Clery *Jane Austen: The Bankers Sister* London 2017.
3 M Downer *Nelson's Purse* London pp. 357-9, other partners also lost their property included George Templer, Sir Gerard Noel and Davison himself.

living, Nathaniel left Hastings twenty thousand pounds and William, Sophie, Augusta and Emily fifteen thousand pounds each plus a similar sum to the child his wife was then carrying. In 1789 a codicil then left fifteen thousand pounds each to his latest children Henry and Charles. All his children were underage at the time of the will; Louisa was not yet born and her father never updated his will to include her inheritance. Nathaniel, however, did add a codicil in 1793 which highlighted that circumstances had arisen which might make it impossible to fulfil the financial disbursements in his will. He asked his executors to divide his estate equally between his children, male or female. It was highlighted by executors in 1824 that Louisa had not been specifically named but with the note that she should receive an inheritance.[1] As well as the mislaying of the will the partners in Nathaniel's bank wanted to make claims on the estate to cover bank losses. A second will also exists and was much shorter leaving what Nathaniel had to Anne and asking her to look after the children. In Anne's will she mentions her love and affection for her late husband and also repeated the specification in his will that he wanted both his natural and legitimate children looked after.

The Middleton's had ten children, Frances, Sophia, Augusta, Emily, Harriet, Louise, Hastings, William, Henry and Charles. A number of them were born in India and returned there in later life. Anne's first daughter Frances died aged only thirteen months in 1784 in Dacca. Two of Anne's other daughters also died young, Sophia (aged 4) in 1790 and Augusta (aged 17) in 1802. William, who had been born in Calcutta in 1783, returned to the sub-continent in 1799 to become a member of the company army. He achieved the rank of captain in 1811 but was dismissed and it seems he returned to England. He was restored in 1813 and reached the rank of major in the 16th Native Infantry and died in Kamptee in 1822.[2] Anne's younger son Henry, born in 1790, also joined the company and after studying at the East India College he joined the Bengal Civil Service in 1809. In 1817 he married into another company family; his wife Mary Ann Ochterlony was the daughter of David Ochterlony. Henry returned to England and spent his last years in Bath where he died in 1866. Anne's younger child, Charles, also spent time in India after attending the company college and graduating alongside his brother and then working

---

1 TNA PROB 11/1689/161 Will of Nathaniel Middleton. TNA PROB 11/1470/260 Will of Nathaniel Middleton.

2 William was posted as a Lieutenant in 1801, was involved in operations in Jumna Doab in 1803 and took part in the attack on Thathia fort. He served as adjutant and quartermaster and was part of the operations in Bundelkhand in 1809-11. V C P Hodson *List of the Officers of The Bengal Army 1758-1884* 1927 London p. 202.

Hastings Nathaniel Middleton, at Townhill House, by Thomas Heaph

Emily Middleton

as a writer in Bengal. He left India in 1836, the same year as his brother Henry. Charles had married Eliza Carpenter and the couple spent some time on the family estates in Jamaica where his daughter Catherine was born.

Harriet and Hastings both married into the Purling family, Harriet married John Purling and Hastings married Emily, both the children of Charles Purling of the East India Company.[1] Anne's daughter Emily married the barrister Edward Jerningham in 1804. He was the scion of a Catholic family and the couple both died in 1822 from erysipelas, a bacterial infection of the skin.[2] Louise, to whom her mother was particularly close, married Charles John Herbert of Muckross Abbey in County Kerry. The Herberts were a wealthy family making their fortune in the copper mining industry. Louisa had been born at Townhill House and after the early death of her husband Charles, in 1823, at the age of thirty-seven, Louisa and her six children moved to the Middleton's family home at Bradford Peverell in Dorset. Sadly, Louisa died just five years later.

1   The Purlings were also related to the Fitzhughs, Valentine senior's sister Nancy married John Purling MP an East India Company Director. Charles Purling was with the Bengal establishment. Alfred Spencer *The Memoirs of William Hickey 1782-1790 Vol III* London 1923 p. 352.
2   Finding aid to the Jerningham Letters: Aristocratic Women; the social, political and cultural history of rich and powerful women, A Listing & Guide to Part 2 of the Microfilm Collection, Adam Matthew Publication 1998.

The Six Children of Louise Middleton Herbert by Richard Rothwell, National Trust

Anne Middleton was for many years a widow and spent much of that time revising her own will. Her eldest son Hastings and eldest surviving daughters Emily and Harriet were financially taken care of by their father's will when they should have received their inheritances at the time of their marriages. Anne did leave them bequests but also wanted to make sure her younger sons and her then unmarried daughter Louisa were in receipt of suitable bequests. Charles was to inherit the Midanbury estate but not Townhill House, where the family had lived when young, as this was sold in 1808. Charles did return to take up residence in Midanbury Lodge in 1840. He also retained property in Jamaica and had two houses in Calcutta, India which he purchased in 1835. He died in January 1844 with the intention of the Midanbury estate passing first to his wife Eliza and then to his brother Henry, but Charles had had to mortgage the estate for £1500 in 1843 and, as there was still not enough money to pay off the loan, all his property and holdings had to be sold to service the debt although the residual of the Midanbury estate did remain with the Middleton family.[1] Charles's wife erected a memorial to him in South

1   Beavan, Charles; Langdale, Henry Bickersteth Baron; Romilly, John Romilly Baron; Chute, Chaloner William (1st January 1853). *Reports of Cases in Chancery,*

Stoneham church and she and her daughter retained a link to Southampton living at 9 Anglesea Place from 1871-1891.¹

The fallout from her husband's will involved the family in litigation that rolled on for years, long after Nathaniel's death and even after Anne's. Anne had thirty thousand pounds which was her own marriage settlement plus her inheritance from her father, and her financial affairs were complex, including a bond for three thousand pounds due from her brother-in-law William Cator who had died when his ship, on route to India, was attacked by the French.² William had been returning to India in search of replenishing his fortune. Anne directed the three thousand pounds be used to support her sister Sarah, the widow of William and her niece Ann Frances. She was also keen to make good the request in her late husband's will that his illegitimate children should be taken care of. There is a large part of Anne's will which concerned a bequest to Charlotte, who Anne calls her daughter-in-law, married to Charles Tucker. She was her husband's eldest illegitimate daughter by his Indian mistress. Charles Tucker was another East India Company officer working in the Bengal Civil Service. The couple had married in 1809 after Nathaniel's death and it was unlikely that his estate could have given Charlotte the bequest her father intended.³ Anne set up a

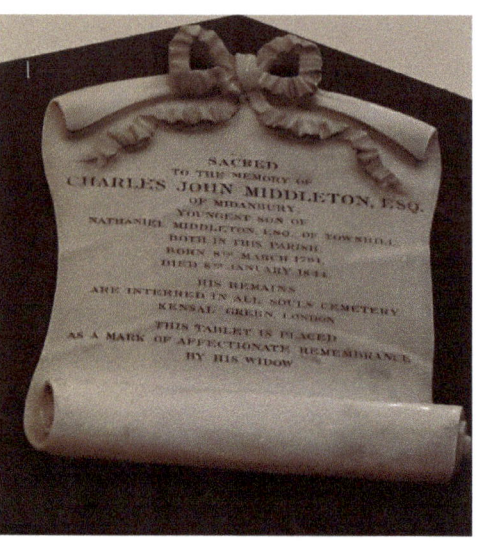

Memorial to Charles Middleton

Argued and Determined in the Rolls Court During the Time of Lord Langdale, Master of the Rolls. [1838-1866]. Saunders and Benning.

1   Paula Downer 'Nathaniel Middleton's South Stoneham Offspring' in *Westender Vol 10 no 6* 2016 pp. 8-9.
2   Daniel Livesay *Children of Uncertain Fortune: Mixed-Race Migration from the West Indies to Britain 1750-1820* unpublished PhD thesis University of Michigan p. 260. Anne had also lent Zachariah Button £5000, Robert Peter £9000, Thomas Norwood Saffery £1000, Sir George Jerningham £5000 and George Johnson £5000. TNA PROB 11/1748/87.
3   Bengal Marriages – on the 23rd Jan., Charles Tucker Esq. of the Civil Service, to Miss Middleton: Madras Courier, 15.2.1809: Government Gazette (India) 16.02.1809. The couple had at least two daughters, Marian and Henrietta Eliza.

Emma Pattle, grand-daughter of Nathaniel Middleton

trust worth £5000 for Charlotte independent of her husband which suggests she wanted her to have some financial independence being mindful of what had happened to her own husband's finances. Of Nathaniel's two other children by his Indian mistress, Eliza and George, there is no mention of them in Anne's will. Eliza, however, was well-off thanks to her marriage to East India Company merchant Thomas Pattle in Bengal in 1798, and when she was widowed in 1815, she was left £20,000 and their only child, another Eliza, £30,000.[1] Eliza later remarried to Major Alexander Robson in 1821.[2]

The relationship between mother and her eldest son Hastings was breaking down and Anne's will is littered with

Charlotte died in 1837, The Bengal Obituary - Volume 1 - Page 194 (GBO). Charles died in 1851 from gout, his obituary included the words 'We have never heard but one opinion as to his character. If not among the most able, he ranked assuredly very high among the most noble upright, the most assiduous, the most highly respected of the Service. His private worth, his kind-heartedness, his benevolence, his happy temper, his genial warmth and cordiality, were the theme of all his associates'. *The Bombay Gazette and Indian News*, 30th June 1851, p. 5.

1 TNA PROB 11/1582/228 Will of Thomas Pattle. Globe Newspaper 12th July 1834, Eliza was still involved in fall out from her father's will and was granted administration in 1824 as surviving residual heir TNA PROB 37/909. The will of her second husband Alexander Robson states she was left £10,000 by her father. TNA PROB 11/1875/157.

2 Asiatic Journal and Monthly Register for British India and its Dependencies Vol II London 1821 p. 641. Sarah Cator's income had also been affected by the downfall of the Middleton bank. Davison, Noel, Templer, Middleton & Wedgwood Papers 4864/70 – 10 Jan 1817 – Anon Re: Cator's West Indian estate: 'After paying Mrs Cator's anny there remains only £600 p ann to keep down the Int on $40,000 – 1 ½ p Cent – the proportion of Int therefore arising on Mr Middleton's £16,000 part of the above mortgage is only £240 p ann & on Mr Templer's £2000 - £30 p ann – the regular payment of the above depend upon the sale of West India produce, which is very uncertain.' 4864/61 - 9 Dec 1816 – Mr Templer's property: Mortgage on Mr Cator's Estate in the West Indies £2000; Legacy from Mr T C Pattle £1000.

codicils[1] where she cut out people she felt were against her, most particularly her eldest son. The *Law Journal* of 1828 reported that Anne had first made her will in 1814 when she left a legacy of six thousand pounds to her eldest son Hastings but afterwards made seven codicils to her will. She revoked the legacy and changed it instead to an investment of twelve thousand pounds held in trust to give her son an annuity. A hearing in 1828, after the time of Anne's death, argued that she did not mean to revoke the six thousand pounds left to her son and that the second legacy was independent and subsisting. The waters were muddied considerably because of the bequests of jewels, watches, trinkets, dress and personal ornaments to be found in two jewel boxes, one japanned and one of shagreen, at Messrs Rundell & Bridges of Ludgate Hill which were to come to Anne's daughter Louisa. By the time Anne died it was found that the jewel boxes were in fact deposited in the Bank of England under an order made by the Lord High Chancellor because Anne was now considered a lunatic. There was confusion as to which jewels were originally destined for Louisa and which jewels should be considered part of the residual estate. Another codicil desired her executors to retain in their hands her father's West Indian property that she had been bequeathed by her brother Robert, to be used to make good any legacies to her younger sons William, Henry and Charles, all now in India and to her two Purling grandchildren. The West Indian property, which had come to her directly from her father, was also to be used for the benefit of her seven surviving children. Anne had previously given one-tenth of her share to her brother, receiving from 1802, the profits thereof, her brother Robert had restored this to her in his will on his death in 1816.[2]

Health

Unfortunately, Anne Middleton's old age was one that was plagued with mental health problems and her family had to put various strategies in place to deal with the outcome. Anne had initially gone to stay in Bath with her widowed sister Sarah. In 1816 Sarah wrote to Anne's son Hastings concerned about the health of her sister: 'she sits absorbed, and seldom speaks, but raises her eyes to Heaven, in prayer, goes out daily in carriage and wheelchair, is blooded, and blistered to quell the irritability'. It shows Anne had been subjected to the common cure of bleeding to restore her health, but the family felt her mind was more diseased than her body. Anne's mental health deteriorated and her son Hastings wrote of her: 'restlessness of manner, perpetually picking, and searching as it were, for pins, around her person, biting her fingers, almost

1 TNA PROB-11-1748-87. Will of Anne Middleton.
2 TNA PROB 11/1577/513 will of Robert Morse.

to the drawing of blood, and, of late, employing her nails about her neck, to a degree provoking an appearance of rash – sitting athwart her chair, instead of straight upon it, with her head, and looks eternally down-cast'. He was also concerned about how she was using her money. Hastings, himself, was in financial difficulties due to the bank failure and was living in more reduced circumstances than he had been used to. Anne was also physically weak. Her son said: 'her countenance too, is a sad index of her perturbed condition of her mind, there is a pitiful lack-lustre in her eye, the mouth is pursed, and her whole features haggard and elongated'.

Anne moved to other spa towns in the hope of restoration of her spirits by a change of air, including Brighton where she stayed with her daughter Louisa, and did show some improvements. Hastings, however, blamed his sister Louisa's elopement as the main cause of her mother's condition along with his mother's secrecy, especially about her finances. It may have been that Hastings own financial collapse may have affected his mother more than he cared to admit. It also may have been that Anne's wish to keep her financial affairs discreet was a reaction to the court case she had endured after the death of her father and the litigation after the death of her husband. Hastings was worried that she was wasting money on useless pills and literally throwing money out of the window in an attempt to give alms to passers-by. Well-respected doctors of the day were called in to assess Anne's condition including John Latham, president of the Royal College of Physicians, Matthew Baillie FRS physician to George III and George Man Burrows an expert in insanity who ran a small asylum in Chelsea. Little Chelsea in this period had a number of private asylums for wealthy patients.[1] Hastings continued to believe his sister Louisa's marriage to be the main cause in his mother's decline. Hastings did think at one point to have his mother come live with him and his family but eventually decided against it as he was concerned about the resulting gossip and stigma of having a lunatic in the family. He imagined people whispering that: 'Mrs Middleton once so provident, and highly gifted, was under surveillance and incompetent to the management of her own affairs'.[2] In 1818 Hastings wished that his mother be placed in a discreet asylum away from the prying eyes of society and it seems he was successful in this, an inquisition of lunacy was held that year when Anne was then living in the house of Alexander Amyot in Little Chelsea.[3] Amyot was the Chevalier Alexandre Amyot, a French Royalist, who

1 See http://studymore.org.uk.
2 Akihito Suzuki *Madness at Home 1820-1860* Berkeley & Los Angeles 2006 pp. 95-103.
3 TNA C2/11/16/M107.

Memorial to Nathaniel Middleton

had been evacuated from Toulon in 1794 and went on to serve the British Government in several functions, successfully applying for denization in 1817.[1] Hastings, meanwhile, pursued an action in chancery to control his mother's affairs.[2] He died shortly after achieving that aim in 1821, whilst visiting Paris, and his mother lived on until 1823 dying at the age of sixty-five. She was, at that point, living at Milton Street, Pimlico, and she left in her final short will the disposition of her personal possessions that she wished to go to Louisa. It consisted of a few table decorations, some boxes, candlesticks, bottles of rosewater, egg cups and one ivory elephant.[3]

Anne's whole life had been dominated by legal wrangles from her mother fighting to establish the ethnicity of her children, the battle to secure her legacy from her father, the mockery of her husband during the Hastings trial, the preservation of the Middleton estate from executors and business partners and finally the controversy around her sanity. In her will Anne entreated her

1 TNA HO1/7/15.
2 Reports of Cases in Chancery 1828.
3 TNA PROB-11-1748-87 will Anne Middleton.

executors to add details to the memorial set up in St Mary's Church, Battersea. The memorial can still be seen today.

> Sacred to the Memory of NATHANIEL MIDDLETON Esq. who terminated his earthly career on the 7th November 1807 in the 57th Year of his Age. As a Memorial of departed Excellence, not less than as a Testimony of Affection this Tablet is erected by his afflicted Widow In the Vault near this Spot are deposited the Ashes of Daughters SOPHIA whom departed this life in 1790 at the Age of 4 Years & 3 Months and AUGUSTA on the 30th of April 1802 in the 17th year of her Age This grateful Tribute, sacred shade ! receive, All that a sorrowing Bosom now can give Also in the same Vault are deposited the Remains of ANNE FRANCES MIDDLETON, Relict of the above NATHANIEL MIDDLETON Esq. who departed this life on the 3rd November in the Year of our Lord 1823 Aged 65 Years In the Vault Beneath are Interred the Remains of LOUISA ANN HERBERT, youngest daughter of the above named Nathaniel and Anne Frances Middleton and Relict to CHARLES HERBERT Esq. of Mucross Ireland who died 23rd May 1828 Aged 31 years

MARY HALE LEWIN (1768-1837)

The Lewins final years in Southampton overlapped with the Austen's time in the town. They would have attended the same balls and events. Frank Austen's links with the East India Company would have made him aware of Company families in the neighbourhood.

We have a more complete picture of the life of Mary Lewin thanks to the cache of family letters and journals collected and privately printed by one of her descendants, Thomas Lewin. We see Mary in her own words especially in her early days, and then as others saw her, particularly her daughter Harriet. It feels at times her children judged her quite harshly. There are resonances of Mrs Bennet about Mary Lewin. She has a large family that she wants to see established in good professions for the boys and good marriages for the girls, however, the children often rile against her.

Early Life and Marriage

Mary Hale was the daughter of General John Hale and his wife Mary, of the Plantation in Guisborough. Her mother had given birth to twenty-two children and only one of whom had died in infancy. The size of the family had financial implications and meant that Mary's mother educated her numerous family

left: Mary Lewin, by John Smart right: Thomas Lewin as a young man, by Johann Heinrich Hunter

herself. Mary Lewin felt in later life that she was not sufficiently educated and: 'laments that she did not attend more to her own education' (Harriet 1822).[1]

Mary was one of identical twins and most people could not tell her and her sister, Anne, apart, including their prospective husband, Thomas Lewin. The poor man did not know which one to choose and in the end said the first one he led out at a dance would be the one he would marry, and that was Mary. He did admit, however, he would have been happy to marry either of them - perhaps not the best basis for a marriage. Mary later said her own mother could not support her during her marriage arrangements as she was confined with her second set of twins. Mary was only fifteen at the time of her marriage and according to the family was not even wearing adult clothing but bib and tucker. Nevertheless, her family thought the match a good one because the Hales were struggling to support their growing family. Mary said later that she married Thomas Lewin because she was told to do so and because her sisters thought it would be delightful to travel with so charming a gentleman. Her husband was around thirty years of age, considered handsome and was tall, being 6ft 8 inches in height. The couple were painted by John Smart a celebrated miniaturist with two versions of each portrait created and a set

1 *Lewin Letters* p. 199.

given to each of their parents.¹ On her marriage Mary was not only about to leave her family but also the country. Thomas Lewin was a member of the East India Company having joined the service in 1770 when he was just eighteen years old as a writer on the Madras establishment.²

In 1780 Thomas was returning to England bringing company despatches from India. The journey from the sub-continent was fraught with danger due to the French Revolutionary War and there was a further complication when the Dutch ship on which he was travelling became an enemy vessel when war broke out between England and Holland. Lewin thought it was his duty to destroy the despatches when the ship's course changed to Cadiz. Thomas's thoughts however were not all about business, a fellow-passenger, Madame Grand the wife of another EIC officer, George Grand, was also on the vessel. The Grands had separated and Catherine then began a liaison with Sir Philip Francis, a member of the Governor-General's Council in India.³ Francis returned to England in 1780 and Catherine Grand decided to follow him. On the voyage, Madame Grand and Thomas Lewin began a short but passionate affair. They lived together in Cadiz, London and Paris but their romance fizzled out and Thomas returned to England and met Mary Hale. Catherine Grand remarried and became the Princess Talleyrand but Thomas Lewin paid her an annuity until her death in 1835.⁴ She was not his only mistress prior to his marriage but was perhaps the most noteworthy.

When he did reach England Thomas initially avoided contact with the East India Company secretariat, who in frustration ordered him to be apprehended. Despite this setback to his career, in August 1784, the newly-weds took passage on the *Nottingham* bound for Madras.⁵

> I dined on the 8th at Mr D. Scott's with our fellow passengers Mr and Mrs Lewin, and a very agreeable day we passed, the whole of the cuddy passengers being invited, so that we sat down once more together, assuredly for the last time - Mrs Eliza Fay, August 1784

1 Daphne Foskett *John Smart, the man and his miniatures* London 1964 plate xiii no 47.
2 *Lewin Letters* pp. 86-88 gives an overview of Thomas Lewin's career with the East India Company. Thomas was of an East India Company family whose fortune had been established when his father joined it. His brother Richard was also with the company in China.
3 William Hickey described Francis as a *pompous, haughty coxcomb* Alfred Spencer *The Memoirs of William Hickey 1775-1782 Vol II* London 1914 p. 125.
4 H E Busteed *Echoes from Old Calcutta* 4th edition London 1908 pp. 270-7.
5 *Lewin Letters* p. 24.

Mary was very popular flirting with the younger company men such as George Sullivan Martin, a future London banker and John Ramsay aide-de-camp to Sir Archibald Campbell. Thomas wrote to Mary's father about her conduct and even planned to send her home. Meanwhile Thomas's faltering career improved and he was appointed Resident at the Negapatam in July 1786. Mary's concerns were more about the fripperies that delighted young girls and she wrote to her brother-in-law Richard:

> I must inform you what the enclosed bits are for. The large one is to give an idea of the striped Ribbon and the small one is the Stripe I wish the narrow Ribbon to be. I made a mistake when I mentioned the breadth of the Ribbon. They must both be the same breadth as the enclosed paper. Send me a box of Crackers to the extent of 6 Dollars.[1]

Mary had the first two of her surviving children in India, Mary born in 1785 and Thomas born in 1787. Her husband however was about to resign the company in March 1788, and later that year Mary and Thomas returned to England. Thomas told his employers the reason for returning to England was the state of Mary's declining health she being: 'a very young woman with 2 small children and a third likely to come soon into the world'.

She described her own temperament thus: 'My disposition as you know is very warm and where my Friendship is once fixed I cannot suffer it to be abused'. She had a falling out with her brother-in-law in 1788:

> Your letter to your Brother astonished me this Morning, and I left the Breakfast Table with a resolution to give you my mind on the subject. As to any change in my Behaviour to you I defy you to prove any, as I have always treated you and thought of you, in a manner I am now convinced you little deserved.[2]

Mary's next surviving child Richard John, known as John Dick, was born in England in 1788 and with their family growing the Lewins had to find a suitable establishment. In 1791 Ridgeway Castle on the outskirts of Southampton was decided upon. The rural situation was popular with several East India Company families with its stunning views and close to the proximity of the watering place of Southampton, yet within easy reach of company headquarters in London and the ports of Southampton and Portsmouth. Two more children were born in quick succession, Anne, who died in infancy of

1 *Lewin Letters* pp. 25-6.
2 Ibid pp. 26-7.

Ridgeway Castle

whooping cough, in 1791 and Harriet in 1792. A brief respite in the war with France in 1791, and to recover from the death of Anne, enabled the couple to visit Paris in that year.[1]

In May 1793, however, Thomas Lewin sailed again for India to resume his duties with the company. Mary remained behind at Ridgeway with her growing family and her journal for this year gives an overview of her daily life.[2] Visitors received at Ridgeway, included the wife of a senior East India Company Officer, Anne Middleton, as well as Miss Gale and Mrs Hester Munton, the wife of Antony Munton of Peartree Lodge, she being a member of a prominent plantation family who had had property in Antigua. Mary occupied her time in visits, riding and reading (*Travels of Reason; Wright's Tour through France; Maupeau's Eloisa; Pope's Homer's Iliad; Sterne's Sentimental Journal, Ireland's Hogarth, Entick's History* being among her books of choice). She went dancing, indulged in tea drinking, had her hair professionally dressed and went to plays including *The Modest Wife* and *The Hungry Footman*. Improvements to Ridgeway took place including a good deal of work on the garden. So pleasing were the results that the artist Tobias Young was commissioned to produce two oil paintings of the views from Ridgeway for which he was paid £14 14s. Mary's other purchases included a pair of pistols bought from Mrs Yeoman at a cost of £1 1s and Ballard, the wine merchant, provided £25 worth of wine to go with the tea allowance £1 1s 1d. Mary also suffered a miscarriage and

1 Ibid p. 86.
2 Ibid pp. 30-43, 401.

this may have contributed to her extended visit to friends and relations in the second half of the year.

In 1795 Mary's husband returned from India for the last time. This situation did impose some financial difficulties on the family and money he had accrued was stuck in India for some time. The family was growing apace, Charlotte was born in 1796, Frederick in 1798 and there were also miscarriages (an earlier child also called Frederick had died).

The international situation had worsened and invasion by Napoleon Bonaparte was very real in 1798. These wars had led to more imaginative ways of the government raising taxes, including window tax, and thanks to this we know that Ridgeway had twenty-eight windows.[1] Financial constraints did not stop the Lewins spending £200 in 1798 on repairs and improvements to their home. The family kept up their links and connections with India, writing to family members still in the sub-continent and with former native contacts such as Chinniah Moodilar of Madras who sent Mary a pipe of wine in 1801. Another brief respite in hostilities enabled a second trip to Paris in 1801.

Remodelling of the family home continued with further garden enlargements in 1802 and the building of a tool house,[2] but the architect John Kent was berated in a letter over how the building work was being conducted.[3] An idea of the value of the house and property survives thanks to details from an insurance policy. Insurance for the house was two thousand pounds plus £200 for the outhouses. Household goods were valued at £440; china and glass £20, printed books at £80 and wearing apparel at £100. Musical instruments accounted for £160, being £80 for an organ, £40 for two violins, £20 for a grand piano, £10 for a small piano and £10 for a violoncello making a total value of three thousand pounds.[4] Daughter Harriet described the life at Ridgeway:

> the River Itchen washed the shores of my father's grounds, the fine oak woods reaching to the river's marge. The fisher-folk were in the habit of mooring their

1 Thomas Baker's Guide of 1775 gave details of window tax duties p. 21. *Lewin Letters* p. 60.
2 *Lewin Letters* p. 93.
3 Ibid pp. 96-8. John Kent was a builder as well as architect and also worked on Chessel House for David Lance. The Lewins were not the only customers to complain about his work, the owners of Leigh Hall in Havant went to court because of the damage done by dry rot. *Hampshire Chronicle* 8th March 1819. Kent spent time in debtor's gaol at the Marshalsea following a disastrous project to develop the land around Northam. SA D/PM Box 68/3, Box 69/14/1, Box 44/171. He was declared bankrupt in 1810 though he still continued to work.
4 *Lewin Letters* p.103.

boats to the sedgy shore, and whenever we girls could espy an empty boat we seized each an oar and shoved off into the river; but it usually happened that the boat was dirty and half full of water, so that on our return our clothes gave ample evidence of our employment, for which we duly suffered. My father's yacht sometimes lay at anchor off the wood, and we would persuade the sailors to fetch us off in the yacht's boat, and my sister Charlotte manfully bore me company in these adventures... I used to be an expert climber of trees; would cross over bogs and mud-flats in mud pattens; ride horses bare backed when we could catch them, with a bit of string round the nose by way of halter ; or we would drag the child's chaise through the woods, racing down the steep descents and often getting upset at the bottom. Sometimes we would climb to the top of the faggot stack and lie in hiding there, making clay figures for hours together, while Miss Beetham would fruitlessly pursue us, screaming, through the grounds. In the wintertime we were incessantly on the ice, sliding or snowballing, for skates we could not afford to buy, or making fires in remote parts of the wood to roast potatoes which we appropriated from the garden; anything, in short, that could get us out of the neighbourhood or proximity of Miss Beetham.[1]

Mary's son William said of Ridgeway in his memoir:

A lively recollection of the delightful situation of my father's residence at Southampton and if freedom from care and the innocent gratification of the powers of enjoyment constitute a criterion of human happiness, that period was perhaps the happiest of my life.[2]

There was an expectation that the family would eventually inherit the Lewin family estate (The Hollies), from Thomas's father. This did not appeal to Mary who listed her objections to the deficiencies of that house which is also an indication of what things Ridgeway could offer:[3]

1st. The smallness of the land when divided would not admit of furnishing everything a large Family require.
2nd. The want of a Market Town near.
3rd. The disagreeable road and the distance from Town for one pair of horses.
4th. The being so near Edward Lewin. (Thomas's brother)

1 *Lewin Letters* Vol II p. 134.
2 *Lewin Letters* 243.
3 Ibid p. 131.

5th. The total want of every comfort in the present house for our large family; the want of Stables; of a Garden; of a walk in winter — would require in these times the expenditure of a large sum of Money. We should besides consider the uncertainty of human events and our limited Fortune, the demands on which are increasing with the Growth of the Children. Common prudence cannot warrant the laiding out of such sums: added to which, should anything happen to Mr. Lewin, it must come to the hammer: and every one knows how little is got for another man's plans, as a house is generally altered as soon as it is purchased.

The Hollies, private collection

The family settled down to life in Southampton. Mary wrote to her brother-in-law: 'We have formed a club here of three families and meet once a week to the number of 20 to supper; think how we shall stuff'. These networks and acquaintances included Lady Rumbold, whose husband had been a company man as well as an ambassador, another company man Mr Dott whose estate was at Midanbury and Sir John Doyley of New Park, Lymington who also owed his fortune to the EIC, the Shirreffs (an army family) the town's popular MP, William Chamberlayne, whose estate was very near the Lewin's and who was godfather to their daughter Frances, Dr Middleton who ran the local asylum at Nursling, the Tate family who lived across the water at Hythe whose patriarch was the gifted musician George Tate, and Henry Hulton of Bevis Mount.

In 1804 Mary lost her mother, and her husband was soon making enquiries as to whether his wife was due some inheritance but, with twenty-one siblings Mary could not have expected to receive much from her mother's estate. That same year Mary gave birth to another daughter, Frances. Mary's older children were growing up and as war again loomed her second son, John Dick, just twelve years old was already at sea serving as a midshipman in the Royal Navy.[1] Mary gave birth to four more sons, William in 1806, George in 1808, Edward in 1810 and her last child Emilius in 1811.

Like many women in her position Mary Lewin took up good works and made visits to organisations such as the Chelsea College and Foundling Asylum. Locally she raised money for the Poor Club, although William Cobbett, the author of *Rural Rides*, refused to give a subscription to the club in 1808:[2]

> he is, and always has been, of opinion that these sort of clubs or societies have, and necessarily must have, an effect injurious to the manners, character and welfare of the nation. He thinks that it is good that we should be daily exposed to accidents and infirmities, that we should feel that we are so; that there should be no office of insurance against them; that every individual should rely upon himself only; and that in providing against infirmities and accidents we should still be uncertain as to the sufficiency of such provision.

The next few years saw Mary saying goodbye to her children. Mary travelled to India in 1807, Thomas junior went to India in 1816, Frederick was sent to India in 1819 and William followed him in 1822.[3]

Mary's aged father-in-law, Richard Lewin, died in 1810 and the family took the decision to leave Ridgeway and eventually to move to the family estate at The Hollies. Mary was able to maintain her links to Southampton as two of her sisters, Charlotte and Catherine, had moved to the area just a short walk from Ridgeway at Little Chessel, sometimes known as Chessel Cottage, leased from David Lance.[4] Mary took the opportunity over the coming years to return to the neighbourhood of her former home through visits with Charlotte.

1 At twelve years of age John Dick was serving with Captain Robert Winthrop on *The Stag* which was driven ashore in a violent storm in 1800, the crew and provisions were removed and the ship then set on fire. Ibid p. 80.
2 *Lewin Letters* p. 123.
3 Her husband continued to use his links with the East India Company not only to benefit his family but also friends such as procuring four hundred-weight of East India rice for *A Gentleman of Southampton*, Samuel Harrison the Banker Ibid p. 93.
4 SA D/PM 54/12.

Mary's later life at the Hollies was not to be so happy. The family comment in letters that their parents felt isolated and as Mary's children set up their own establishments, she and Thomas became lonelier and the word *ennui* is frequently mentioned. In 1818 John Dick said that his mother: 'if possible less visible than before and might puzzle Dr Herschel the Astronomer to know her rising and setting, even though aided by the telescope of the Greenwich Observatory'.[1] There were also heartaches, Mary lost her elder daughter, Mary, in 1825 and her second son in 1827. There was also an estrangement between Mary and her husband who was conducting an affair in London. Charlotte wrote to her father in 1831:

> The dear old woman you love so well has a great stake in it, and you will not refuse to bind up a wound that has flowed too long and has furrowed her soft cheek with deeper wrinkles than those which Time has a right to place there without the canker of grief assisting him

She also writes to her mother:

> I write this that it may serve as a memorial when words may be forgotten. I have again stood in the gap when no one else dared speak to our Father of the pain he occasioned by forsaking his home every week.

Thomas however also relied on his wife and Charlotte observed:

> Now every one is ready to do their part in kindly and cheerfully giving attention to his amusement under the growing infirmities of his age. It is, however, chiefly to his Wife that he looks with rooted Custom and sincere love as most responsible for the solace and companionship of his sinking years, and the pleasure he expressed at the temporary improvement of her Temper and conjugal behaviour clearly shows how much he is sensible to the effect of it on his happiness, and it is impossible for the children to support a cheerful and rational society under the opposition of a contrary humour in their mother[2]

It was Harriet's opinion that her father had been a relatively faithful husband for the time, committing: 'fewer infidelities than could have been expected from a man so coldly treated by his wife'. It appears from Thomas's journal that he had a liaison as early as 1794 which lasted between one and

---

1 *Lewin Letters* p. 168.
2 *Lewin Letters* pp. 275, 281.

two years. Harriet believed this was the only time he had strayed until this later episode began in 1826. She thought her seventy-four-year-old father had been ensnared by a couple, the husband being short of money had encouraged his wife into an intimacy. In 1829 Thomas recorded in his diary that Harriet had remonstrated: 'with me on the subject of my absenting myself from home; she expressed much apprehension lest a spurious offspring should be the result but I assured her there was no fear of such a thing'.[1] This relationship continued until infirmity overtook Thomas and his ability to travel to London.[2]

Thomas junior's return from India in 1827 meant Mary and her husband had his support but her younger daughter then left for foreign climes in 1832. After Frances's marriage and departure for Sweden Mary complained about lack of society and family visits and that she and her husband were considering selling The Hollies and moving to live in London with visits to watering places now and then.

Children

Mary Lewin, like most women of her class and position, was destined to have a large family giving birth, on average every two years. Her daughter Harriet said her mother: 'testified her aversion to being kissed or fondled by her children after they reached the age of six years'.[3]

In letters written by both Mary and her husband Thomas, their children's future is a dominant subject. Thomas junior, as the eldest son, would be expected to inherit the family estate in due course and was sent off to begin his education at Harrow. The rest of the boys have to make their own way and follow a profession; the most popular choices for such families would be the navy, the church or the law. With the family connections in India there was also the opportunity for some of the boys to join the East India Company with the potential to make their own fortunes. Mary hoped her younger son Emilius would go into the church and used her influence with her more affluent relations to try to procure him a living, doing the same for her nephew George Hale.

In their youth Mary's children were looked after by a series of governesses

---

1 Ibid p. 146.
2 Harriet reported the couple benefitted by some hundred pounds in her father's will in 1840, which suggests the lady might be Ann Webster, bequests: Executors George Grote, and nephew Rev Charles Lloyd £500 each. Ann Webster widow £400, Harriet Histed annuity £20, George Tate £10 annuity, William Green released from debts, Gardener Richard Fillary £50, Richard Scudder labourer £20, Household servants a year's wages.
3 *Lewin Letters* Vol II p. 125.

The children of Mary Lewin, private collection

and the younger boys sent to local schools although they, perhaps, were not of the highest academic order. In 1813 William was placed in the school of the Rev Mr Griffiths in Southampton, King Edward VI, an establishment of 40 boys. He was 7 years of age and stayed at the school until he was 10 when the family moved to Kent – where he realized that his new school with the Rev Mr Yates: was 'in some degree superior to that of Mr Griffiths, particularly as embracing a greater number of subjects'.[1]

It was also to be hoped that the boys would make good marriages which generally meant to marry an heiress. Mary's sons, however, did not always make the best alliances. Thomas junior fell out with his parents over his infatuation with his mother's younger sister Jane Hale. Jane visited Ridgeway in the early 1800s to recover from a burst blood vessel in her lungs and described as a: 'lovely young woman, soft and winning with her delicate constitution adding to her charm'. In 1814 Tom complained that his mother's passions and prejudices were inflamed by his sister, Mary, and her husband who he felt had plotted against him and Jane Hale.[2] Tom and Jane were close in age, he being born in 1787 and Jane in 1784. Even when Jane married later that year to a Mr

1 *Lewin Letters* pp. 243-247.
2 Ibid pp. 153-160.

Budd she and Tom continued with their intrigue. His father threatened to blot out Tom's name from the *list of my children*. This unhappy relationship came to an end when Tom went to India in 1816. When he eventually returned to England in 1827, he chose never to marry.

Second son John Dick joined the Royal Navy in 1799 and in 1813 he caused some consternation having been involved in a duel.[1] The Lewins third son Frederick followed his brother Tom to India in 1819 and three years later William followed, he was just sixteen:

> Never shall I without emotion call to mind the last embrace of a mother who had tenderly watched over my juvenile years, and whom as the early age of sixteen, I was quitting, perhaps to see no more.[2]

In 1828 his mother wrote to William about her sufferings as he had been 'banished' at such an early age and she was hoping that Tom and Frederick might come back to England.[3] William, however, was soon to fallout of favour with his parents for declaring his wish to marry. His mother pleaded with him to wait as he has just begun his career with the Hon. Company's Artillery and was just eighteen. William did put off his marriage but remained faithful to Jane Laprimaudaye and by twenty-one they were married.[4]

Jane Hale, private collection

Marriage was also on the mind of John Dick. He had left the navy and had been suffering from poor health since 1817 but by 1826 he was complaining of being 'discarded' by his parents due to his marriage to a wealthy widow. The widow however was not just wealthy but elderly, the 'old widow Mrs Plumer (being a year older than his Mother)'.[5] Mary said he married for her

---

1 Ibid p. 132.
2 Ibid p. 249.
3 The Company did allow officers to take a furlough after ten years' service, for which they would receive a stipend of £500 for three years.
4 *Lewin Letters* pp. 213-215.
5 Ibid pp. 209-210, 212.

money to provide comforts for his declining health, and that he had been often 'shipwrecked in love, has had one narrow escape from beggary by imprudence, and so many pangs'. John Dick would get £3000 a year if he outlived his wife. It may have been these financial concerns that caused John Dick to write to his brother Tom in India when he recommended that, if Tom's health could bear it, he should make sure he has earned a million first.

Even Frederick, the steadiest of Mary's sons suffered from unhappy romantic entanglements. Whilst on leave to England in 1834 he confided to his sister that he had 'an Epanchement de Coeur with 'my lady''. He also felt distanced from his father. His brother William remarked that his father's character was averse to children and so he had small connection with his offspring:

> the stern judge of misdemeanours, the reprove of offences and governor of his family, we saw or felt but little of him, we feared, but could not habitually love him; indeed, it was congenial to avoid his sight, and as we considered him as the principal impediment to our amusements during the vacation, it was sufficiently evident that he felt toward his sons much in a similar way, and was by no means sorry when the time for our departure to school again arrived.[1]

When Frederick took leave of his father in November 30th 1834, he wrote: 'which I sank on my knees to receive. My brother Tom took down the words which he uttered, and sent them to me afterwards'.[2]

Frederick eventually married Augusta Diana Babington and set up home in Brighton. Tragedy struck when their second child, Augusta, then aged eight, died after falling under the wheel of a bathing machine. As the machine was being drawn up Augusta climbed up to have a ride but fell off under the wheels being instantly killed.[3] Frederick purchased the old family home at Ridgeway and moved his family there. He removed extensions and embellishments added by a previous owner and restored Ridgeway to a comfortable family home. The neighbourhood was not however as he remembered it as a child. It was, he said:

> An altered neighbourhood, snobs, villas, encroachments, insolence, trespass and no Gentleman or Magistrate to support one's order, are very great evils, compensated for in some measure by the sweetness of the place, the Position it gives, and Ability to live as we like despite appearances.[4]

1 *Lewin Letters* p. 247.
2 Ibid p. 318.
3 *Lewin Letters* Vol II p. 70.
4 Ibid p. 77.

Ridgeway, private collection

His wife had become 'serious and looks at life from an altered point of view' with her constitution patched up by Port Wine, Quinine and Sal Volatile.[1] Frederick also felt connubial bliss had eluded him 'as well it might, seeing my Indian Destiny'. Frederick and Diana suffered a second tragedy in 1850 when their baby daughter, Octavia, aged just seven months, was burnt to death in her cradle at Ridgeway. The couple often spent long periods apart and Harriet described Diana as 'rather a wreck considering she is still under 30', at which point she already had six children. Diana died in 1856 and Frederick moved away to Kent and the Lewin's link with Southampton ended, his Aunt Catherine Hale of Chessel Lodge having died of bronchitis in 1853.

Mary meanwhile developed a close relationship with William's wife Jane who often sent her mother-in-law gifts of silk, shawls, muslin, handkerchiefs and cuffs from India. Mary was desperate to scrape together enough money to enable William and his family to return permanently to England, so they would be closer to her for the sake of his health.[2]

1   Ibid p. 77.
2   *Lewin Letters* pp. 226, 231.

Other opportunities had to be found for the youngest boys Edward, George and Emilius. George was to train as a lawyer, Edward and Emilius were more academically gifted and it was thought Emilius would follow a career in the church. By 1829 George was in trouble with his employers, Amory & Coles, for failing to turn up at work, being indolent and neglectful and having an absence of energy and care. He was threatened with dismissal and knew that if this happened his father would cut him off but, by 1831, George had settled down and Amory gave an excellent character report to his father. In 1836 George married Mary Friend, the daughter of a sugar baker, a plain girl but with a fortune of £10,000.[1] George's son said his father felt being a solicitor very distasteful and the lack of success caused low spirits and finally the failure of his health and intellect. George died in 1856 aged just 47.

Edward, after leaving school near Birmingham, went to work in Sweden setting up a school which had up to 100 pupils and later going into the tanning business.[2] In 1831 Edward wrote to his sister Harriet: 'My greatest happiness, as my passions have strengthened in the development of my being, has been to love with intensity'. He finally left Sweden in 1845 and took up a position working for Rowland Hill at the Post Office. Later in life he developed a tender passion for the singer Jenny Lind which became something of a scandal but aged forty he finally married Matilda Rivaz in 1850.

In Mary's final years it was her youngest child Emilius who caused most grief. Considered to be the most talented of the children as he reached his twenties he seemed to have had a breakdown. In 1835 Harriet wrote of him: 'He is odious to look upon, dirty, unshaven, with a perpetual horse laugh ... Consults me about Suicide, which I seriously think it likely he may perpetrate'.[3]

Frances thought Emilius not mad but very odd and peculiar including his insistence on medicating himself with quack remedies.[4] By 1838 the family were discussing which doctor to bring in to consult on Emilius with Dr Bright or Dr Roots being suggested. Emilius died in 1844 unmarried and childless in the private Kensington Asylum.[5]

Mary's daughters also caused her heartache and frustration. In their turn Harriet said they never received any mark of affection from their mother,

1 *Lewin Letters* pp. 238-242, 348.
2 Ibid p. 219, 221.
3 Ibid p. 331.
4 Ibid p. 352.
5 Ibid p. 359. In 1844 it accommodated fifty-five patients. Dr Richard Bright was appointed physician extraordinary to Queen Victoria in 1837. His research led to the identification of Bright's disease which bears his name. Richard Bright | RCP Museum (rcplondon.ac.uk).

because having married young she had not had the chance to develop during the *ripening season of womanhood*. Harriet thought her ignorant of love or friendship and that she never: 'felt warmly to her husband, who, it must be owned, treated her more like a pet slave than an equal, and who never confided to her his intimate thoughts'.[1] Harriet felt that, from hints dropped by her mother that she was in love with someone else for a good many years but never pursued that love affair out of a sense of duty.

Mary Lewin hoped for good marriages for her daughters. Her eldest daughter Mary became engaged in 1803/4 to William Shirreff,[2] a lieutenant in the navy, but the match was not favoured by her father, (in echoes of *Persuasion*) as the young man's prospects did not seem promising. Mary was prevailed upon to break off the engagement and she was sent away to get her out of the way. Mary junior went on to become one of the women who joined the 'fishing fleet', where young ladies of modest fortunes would travel to India in the hope of capturing a wealthy husband.[3] It cost the Lewins £330 to send their daughter on the trip, at a time when finances were quite tight for the family. When her parents wanted to send her black female servant along as company they had to apply to the East India Company Court of Directors for permission. Thomas borrowed money from his brother and had to dispose of some of his East India stock to repay him to pay for the trip. Mary set sail in 1806 and in 1807 she married Hippesley Charles Marsh.[4] Mary Marsh joined her mother and sisters Harriet and Charlotte at a ball in 1813 where Ann Sophy Mackie thought Mary Marsh very affected, & 'is become very plain, her eyes having nearly started out of their sockets, from a fright, occasioned by a monkey whilst in India, & her complexion being almost black'. The couple returned to England but the marriage was not a happy one though it produced at least four children. Mary Marsh suffered from declining health and it was hoped that a sea cure would help the young mother:

1 *Lewin Letters* Vol II p. 125.
2 Shirreff eventually attained the position of Rear-Admiral of the Blue, he married Elizabeth Murray in 1810.
3 *Lewin Letters* pp. 115-118 and 121. Jane Austen in her early work *The Bower* has her heroine Catherine packed off the Bengal and an unhappy marriage to a man double her age and with a disposition not amiable. Jane Austen *Minor Works* ed. R W Chapman revised London 1969 p. 194
4 Marsh had practised law in Madras and on returning to Britain entered parliament as a radical MP. By 1823 he was in financial difficulties and fled to France. He was the reputed author of *The Clubs of London* in 1828.

All that care, sea air, expence, medical aid, etc, can do has been done and if their united effects are only attended with uncertain benefit what is there to rally on? Harriet Lewin 12 Aug 1818

Mary Marsh succumbed in 1825 and in a letter to her son William his mother apologises for the letter being blotched by the effect of her tears on the loss of her daughter.[1] Mary Lewin was very concerned about the fate of her two granddaughters, Mary and Lucy, and called Charles Marsh a 'wretch'. It transpires Marsh was £300 in debt and was living in Le Havre, his son Hippesley was, by this time, in India with the East India Company for which his grandmother was thankful. By 1827 Charles Marsh was rumoured to have gone to America with his younger son Danny leaving another child Isabella to starve in Le Havre. Mary and her husband paid for the abandoned child's keep, board and education at £80 per year. It was reported that the woman looking after the infant in Le Havre was also pregnant and that Charles Marsh was the father. The fate of the Marsh daughters was still uncertain in 1834 when the Lewins were proposing to bring Mary's daughter Isabella over from Le Havre. In 1837 Thomas refused to send his granddaughters to join their brother Hippesley in India but, in his will of 1840, four of daughter Mary's offspring are remembered with two thousand pounds left in trust for Mary, Isabella, Lucy and Hippesley. It seems that Lucy and Mary did travel to India and Mary certainly found a husband there and later Isabella went out to join them.[2]

Romantic tribulations followed all of Mary's daughters who thought their mother treated them too harshly. Harriet appealed to her father in 1814 saying her mother debarred her from the most innocent pleasures which caused Mr Lewin to admonish his wife. In 1815, in a scene reminiscent of *Pride & Prejudice* Harriet was proposed to by the local cleric Mr Elmsley. She turned him down and her father wrote to him to tell him not to visit for a time but her mother was furious. As Thomas recorded in his journal: 'Mrs Lewin burst out on me, in a torrent of passion on account of my having forbidden any mention of Harriet's affair with Mr Elmsley. I heard her out with calmness and then went to my room and adjusted my clothes.'[3]

Mary did however plead her daughter's cases in regard to their allowances for clothes and pocket money and managed to persuade her husband to

---

1 *Lewin Letters* p. 212.
2 Ibid pp. 212, 226, 356, 367.
3 Ibid p. 144. There was a Rev Elmsley of St Mary Clay in this period and also a Rev Peter Elmsely a Unitarian.

Harriet Grote, private collection

increase the stipend to Harriet and Charlotte by £4 in 1818 taking the total to £40.¹ Harriet, by this time, was in love with George Grote. She was now in her mid-twenties and her beau was two years younger and his parents forbade any thought of marriage. It was considered that Harriet had little fortune to recommend her and Mary Lewin was also put out as she believed George's mother had some scruples about her daughter's religious views. The couple continued their clandestine relationship for three unhappy years much to Mary's disquiet that the familiarity between them was not appropriate given the circumstances. Eventually the pair married in 1820 without the consent of either of their families, Harriet was by then twenty-eight, and her husband twenty-six.² In December that year Harriet gave birth to her only child, a boy, who died shortly after. From that time forward she supported her husband's political career as well as becoming a writer and radical thinker and hostess of salons which attracted the leading utilitarian thinkers of the day.³ Harriet was reconciled to her family who did like George and, in 1822, Harriet even designed a device for her father's earthenware for his boat *Coquette* as a commission to show the makers at Spode.⁴

The scandals involving Mary's two eldest daughters' marriages, were joined by gossip about the activities of Charlotte. In 1814, the daughter of their neighbours the Lances, another Mary was spreading rumours that Charlotte had been seen kissing a Mr Fontaine. Harriet wrote to her sister:

1   Ibid p. 144.
2   Ibid pp. 141, 145-6, 169-172.
3   Harriet was an author, supporter of artists such as Frederic Chopin, Jenny Lind and Felix Mendelssohn, founded the Society of Female Artists and was a campaigner for women's rights including the repeal of the Contagious Diseases Act and the Married Women's Property Act and supported women's suffrage Search results (exploringsurreyspast.org.uk)
4   *Lewin Letters* p. 146.

left: Charlotte Lewin, private collection   right: Frances Lewin, private collection

All she (mrs L) is distressed at is, that Fontaine told Mary Lance you were kissed by him. It is known that you were boxed up with him, and that you walked on the common alone with him. I have given Mary Lance a wipe, for she is very flippant on the affair, having picked the brains of Fortain, Sally Pye, and other myrmidons. I find myself belaboured without mercy by all those who know if it for upholding you in so preposterous a scheme; and they say it is unpardonable and "what a hash Mrs Lewin has made in the education of her daughters", meaning me, as well as you[1]

Harriet was also concerned that Charlotte might meet 'A' clandestinely. The gossip seemed to die away but in 1818 it was rumoured that Charlotte had run away with a Methodist preacher but was overtaken and brought back.[2] Charlotte's younger sister hinted in 1828 that Charlotte might be suffering from a further disappointment:

As For Charlotte, you do not know her, dread her, or love her better or more,

1   Ibid p. 151. Harriet was in Southampton staying with their friends the Tates.
2   Ibid 172.

The Hedge Figures, private collection

than I do. It is clear she will not mend yet awhile, if ever; even a strong-backed parson as folly's antidote would be a doubtful speculation

By 1832 Mary thought her daughter might be considering marriage: 'I consider her by no means happy in single life, I had rather she married.'[1] The suspected candidate as a husband was Charlotte's cousin another Thomas Lewin. That marriage did take place although it seems to have taken a toll on Charlotte as, in 1834, Harriet describes her as looking 45 whilst her husband looked a mere 33, Charlotte was only thirty-eight as was her husband.[2] Charlotte had also become a Unitarian and her family thought she had become drab and dowdy.[3] Charlotte in turn felt she had not been well-treated by her mother:

> Your behaviour to me once after the effect of Brother William's letter to you, was just what was due as to the only child who bore all the distresses attendant

---

1 Ibid pp. 288, 292.
2 Ibid p. 320.
3 Frances later reported in 1836 that her sister repented her Unitarianism, and that she had been estranged from many because of it. Ibid p. 351.

on a Father's displeasure over his sons, and supplied all that a faithful daughter and sister could to their amelioration.

Mary's youngest daughter was about to become involved in a round of romantic passions and by 1833 had at least two marriage proposals, one from a Mr Roebuck and another from William Prescott who had not asked her earlier: 'hindered by his suspicions that Roebuck was in pursuit of me, who being so poor, he was honourable enough not to traverse'. She had suffered a romantic reversal in 1830 that had left her so downcast that she travelled with her brothers Thomas and Edward on a visit to Sweden.

In 1832 Frances wrote to her brother William about her parents:

I love them and all our Family unfeignedly, but they will never suit me or forward my objects in life, and the most they can do is to frustrate them...... Attached as I am to dear Eddy, whose, fostering tenderness raised my head when bowed down by grief, and called in Tom's generous heart and purse to my assistance, I cannot contemplate with peace the idea of his leaving me in England, and going to live in that Land where I received so much pleasure and profit of Mind and Body.....I well remember the rays of hope and life you shed on the miserable days I led, during the uncertainty of my engagement with one I loved to Distraction, but who was not destined or fitted to by my husband

Frances did recover from her disappointment due to a young Swede who *I believe loved me at Stockholm*. He came to England in pursuit of Frances who had previously admired him (but not loved him) but then changed her mind and Settlement Deeds were drawn for what was her third proposal of marriage in short order. She wrote to her sister to tell her that the disappointed William Prescott showed up and also declared his love *with more passion and feeling than I thought were in him* but that she refused him. Frances soon married Nils von Koch and her mother said of the wedding: 'A more melancholy wedding I have never seen, for it was followed up by her leaving the Hollies and very soon embarking for Stockholm'. The wedding was a quiet affair due to the death of Frances's uncle Richard just prior to the planned event for which Frances was peeved: 'Uncle Richard's death gave Mama a good reason for her extraordinary perverseness, and I love her and forgive her, although this parting opposition cost me bitter tears.'[1]

In Thomas Lewin's will of 1840 he left his sons Thomas, Frederick and William five thousand pounds each, and Thomas also was left a brilliant cluster

---

1 *Lewin Letters* pp. 283-284, 295-296, 299.

ring. George and Edward each received four thousand pounds and were also discharged of monies advanced to them by their father. Emilius received his four-thousand-pound bequest via a trust. Trusts were also put in place for his daughters, six thousand for Harriet and four thousand each for Charlotte and Frances. With the residue of his estate divided between all the children linked to their pecuniary legacies.[1]

Health

The eighteenth century was the time of sea bathing and taking the waters and many echoed Mrs Bennet's view that *'a little seabathing would set me up forever'*. Mary Lewin certainly was an habitual taker of 'the flounce'. In Mary's journal of 1793 there are over thirteen visits to bathing establishments whilst Mary was visiting her family in the north including Redcar, which she notes she liked, and Scarborough. Her accounts detail £1 2s and £1 1s for charges for bathing, and even £1 11s for bathing her horse called Splash whilst at Redcar. Mary had just suffered a miscarriage as well as suffering other ailments, including not feeling well after being caught in a rain storm. During the year she suffered from colds cured by taking the Elixir Paregoric, a sore throat, a nervous cough and she and her daughter Mary were also treated by the corn doctor at a cost of 7s. Her other children also suffered from various ailments, Charlotte was ill, Tom needed a tooth drawing at a cost of 5s and Harriet's illness led to Hogarth being called. Medicine included physic, smelling salts (3s 6d), warm baths and a £2 18s bill for Mr Davison the apothecary. In the cause of the fight against smallpox the medic Sir Walter Farquhar was called in to inoculate Martha, one of the household staff, and Harriet. He was called back on four separate occasions to look after the child undoubtedly Harriet who was not yet one year old. Harriet had a bad reaction and it was told to her in later life that one of the reasons her mother removed to Yorkshire was to save her child's life. Harriet was rendered blind by the pustules and was carried around on a feather pillow in case the pressure of her own weight might cause disfigurement. Harriet's aunts commented that she was so loathsome an object at that time because of the disease that they could not bear to touch or look at her. Mary also paid a visit to her sick school but would not visit Mrs Chaloner as her youngest child had not yet had the smallpox. The effects of inoculation on Harriet did not deter Mary from having Frederick and Frances inoculated in 1799: 'Our two youngest were inoculated last Thursday, and we look for their sicking today or the next day. Thomas Lewin 5th February 1799.'[2]

1 Ibid pp. 367-369.
2 Ibid p. 67.

One of the major causes of early death was smallpox and Mary was at the forefront of the drive for inoculation. Variolation had been popularized as a preventative measure against smallpox by Lady Mary Wortley Montagu who learned the technique whilst in the Middle East.[1] The success rate was such that only one in eight of those treated died. Local doctors including Dr Monkton whose surgery was next to Holy Rood church, and Mr Corbin, who was working from a house in Gloucester Square, were leading the way in inoculation. When Corbin was seriously injured in a coaching accident and had to retire to Devon he was still in correspondence with colleagues to request his friend John Dewey send him: 'some cow pox matter on a bit of glass, small ivory or quill'.[2] Not all physicians were in agreement and Dr John Speed IV attacked his medical rival and promoter of inoculation, Dr Monkton in scurrilous verse.[3] Monkton and his compatriots Peter Bernard, Thomas Mears and Thomas Jeans advertised in the local papers that they were determined to continue their programme of inoculation. The interest in smallpox and in variolation and the later development of inoculation even became a topic for popular literature. Jane Austen and her family and friends even passed an evening entertaining themselves with readings from Edward Jenner's paper on the subject.[4] The town's vaccination programme was recorded in a series of Inoculation Books. Householders were encouraged to have their servants inoculated and the town took pride in advertising the programme to further encourage visitors to the spa.[5] In 1802 Mary Lewin took up the challenge of inoculating herself as she recorded in a letter to her brother-in-law: 'I have inoculated ten children with the greatest success with Cow pox virus myself — and no one else. Lancets now al-ways charged ready.'[6] Some years later in 1834 the gardener at Mary Lewin's sister's home at Little Chessil said he had been vaccinated by Mrs Lewin when a child.[7]

After Thomas Lewin's return from India he also often relates Mary's various illnesses:

1   Mary L. South *The Inoculation Book 1774-1783* 2014 p. 59.
2   At the time of his accident, which occurred in Winchester, Corbin's life was despaired of. He was attended at the County Hospital in Parchment Street where he survived through 'the skill and attention of his surgeons Mr Lyford and Mr Wickham'. Giles King Lydford, later, was physician to Jane Austen. Private Collection.
3   Mary L South *The Inoculation Book 1774-1783* 2014 pp. 74-5. Dr Speed also refused to allow his servant to take part in the free inoculation programme.
4   *Jane Austen's Letters* p. 62.
5   Example Hampshire Chronicle 19th February 1774.
6   *Lewin Letters* p. 95.
7   Ibid p. 322.

Mrs. Lewin has had a sharp attack of fever these four days, which for the most part has confined her to her bed — the effect probably of a violent cold caught nobody knows how, yet I suspect by paddling about in the flower garden during the late sharp Easterly winds.[1]

In 1797 Harriet had whooping cough and was sent for a change of air to her godparents at Stoke Park and in November 1799 Mary was ill again with a fever: 'Mrs Lewin has lately experienced a smart attack of fever and been three days confined to her Chamber, consequently is now very weak nor able yet to venture down stairs.'[2]

In 1804 daughter Mary had a bad cold consequent upon her tumbling herself and pony into the river Itchen at Bishopstoke.[3] Harriet was tall for her age and had a tendency to stoop. To counteract this she was forced to wear a collar which enclosed her throat with an iron spring clasped behind by a steel stud, her arm pinioned in the shoulder straps, the centre, made of sheet-iron and covered with red morocco leather, pressed against her back and was secured by a belt around the waist. She was expected to wear it all day.

In 1818 Miss Dickson, Frances's governess, was seized with fever and the house was fumigated every hour for fear of infection. Daughter Mary was taken ill again and John Dick's health was also causing concern and Dr Grey recommended he visit Ramsgate.[4] In 1826 Frances and George suffered from The Fever and it was thought that Mary senior, along with Frances, wanted a little sea bathing and Mr Lewin allowed them a fortnight for a 'full Dip in Tunbridge and Brighton'. It seems they settled on Eastbourne and Emilius wrote asking his mother if she flounched in the sea.[5] Mary's health had impacted on the family and both Emilius and Edward commented on not having had a proper Christmas celebration in nearly ten years.[6] It was also around this time that the family began to comment that Mr Lewin's memory was going and Mary also said that her own was also beginning to fail.[7] John Dick's visit to another spa resort at Bath was not successful and he died in 1827. Less seriously, in 1828, Edward was having trouble with his gums and put it down to his wisdom teeth sprouting. Mary was concerned about the

1 *Lewin Letters* p. 49.
2 Ibid p. 73.
3 Ibid p. 102.
4 Ibid pp. 166-167, 177.
5 Ibid p. 216.
6 Ibid pp. 216, 220.
7 Ibid p. 221.

failing health of her younger son William and in 1831, when he returned for a short visit to England along with his wife Jane and young daughter Lizzie, they went to take the waters: 'Does Missy have salt water sloshed over her dear little bear body? Would it not strengthen her in the Spring? I persevered throughout the winter[1] Frances Lewin'. Mary was finding it difficult to get around and in 1832 confided to her son William 'I have got a Donkey to ride because I cannot walk much'. The next year she wrote: 'The 10^{t}h of March I shall be 65 years old. Thank God I am now in good health; but the loss of Frederick is always uppermost in my mind, as he must return to India.'[2]

Sadly, Mary was entering a period of swift decline suffering with some form of dementia. In 1833 her daughter Harriet wrote:

> Mama is much improved as to temper, and is quite docile and tractable; her intellect indeed seems to be going; 'daffle' is the go and I find it not safe to attach any credence to what she may say. [3]

Mary must have been concerned when, in 1833, there was cholera outbreak in Stockholm where Edward was still living and later that year he suffered from typhus. Mary's own health began to fail in 1834 and she was much affected by the loss of her sister, Lady Dundas, to whom she was particularly close. In June 1834, Frederick, home on leave, talked to Dr Cottingham about his mother's health and Mary decided to return to Peartree to stay with her sister at Little Chessil for a change of air: 'I have had the benefit of sea water poured over me by my attentive maid porter'. Her husband was also contemplating a trip to Leamington Spa for the benefit of his wife's health. By early 1835 Harriet reported that her mother was senile and her father was growing unequal to his duties and said he had a failing memory which makes him more parsimonious in his character:

> he sits silent and seems to be dissolving partnership with the species daily more and more. Mother is all but fatuous. She knows me but cannot always remember my name. I found Aunt Smelt[4] there and Jessie a fortnight ago. Mother told me ' they were some ladies who had been staying with her on a visit, and she believed they were relations'. The next day we walked out, and she said to me of her own sister 'that is a very good sort of woman, that, and

1 Ibid p. 279.
2 Ibid pp. 288, 294.
3 *Lewin Letters* pp. 303-304
4 Anne Hale, Mary Hale's twin sister. Ibid p. 330.

I like her'. It is very depressing. She will Talk, but has not an idea that is not out of place. Poor dear! She seems in fair health[1]

By the end of the year her mother's maid, Rebecca Porter:

was harassed to a thread with her wearisome and thankless toil. Our mother, who is now more feeble than ever, causes her maid's duties to be more and more heavy, and Porter's health suffers. They ought to have a hospital nurse to help her, as mother's health declines. Pap is still hearty, although almost blind.

The family prevailed upon a former governess Mlle Caroline Wislez to visit The Hollies to consider taking up post looking after Mrs Lewin, it had been suggested back in 1832 that she might become a companion to Mary. However, Mlle Wislez wrote a scathing letter to Frederick in 1836:

There I found matters in a sad condition, and was not a little startled by the idea of spending several months between these two poor old people, for I was not long in discovering all the difficulties I should have to surmount. Your mother is completely childish. Her temper is gentle and much more manageable than it ever was when she had the use of her reason. But she is as careless of the comfort of her entourage and it is curious enough to observe how now she expresses all that she felt all her life viz: a great regard for herself, a profound respect for titled people, and an unrivalled admiration for all that belongs to her and her family. Have you ever read 'Les Palais de la Verite' a tale by la Genlis? Mrs Lewin's involuntary candour makes one think of it. She talks like a child, but still the intolerable pride and selfishness come uppermost, oozing out as it were on all sides and showing themselves without any of the disguises which in her better days she could now and then use to cloke these darling faults. She is not in a state of mind to wish for a companion. She requires a nurse, and cares for none but those who amuse her, that is to say, who make her dance and sing, who play on the Piano, go in and out – in short, make some sort of noise to break up the monotonous insipidity of the days at the Hollies..... I could sit with her to prevent her setting her petticoats or her cap on fire: I could hear her play on the piano or the flageolet (for she has taken to these accomplishments, rather late in life). But I could not play with her; it went against my heart; I could not laugh when

---

1   Ibid pp. 314, 321, 322, 333, 339, 341, 343, 344, 346.

Thomas Lewin in later life, private collection

she danced and jumped about. I do believe I rather could have cried.[1]

She also reports that Mr Lewin forgets the state of his wife's mind and when forced to remember becomes cross and angry with her as he had been used to consulting her on everything and still neither writes nor received a letter without communicating it to her. In August 1836 Frances visited her parents and could not believe the change in her mother. She reported her mother amused herself by cutting paper cards and writing Mrs Lewin of the Hollies upon them and that her vanity had become more obvious and she pinned all sorts of coloured papers and wafers on her sash to look grand:

> My Father is most afflicted of the two; having been governed by his wife all his life .... My father is wonderfully well and healthy; his frame is sounder, wonderful to say, since his fall than before, his bowels being more regular .... Ennui consumes him. His visits to London become every day more difficult and dangerous for him, as he is blind of one eye and dull sighted in the other, and easily upset off his legs[2]

Mary eventually passed away on 20th November 1837 as the Victorian Era was about to begin, she was sixty-four years old and had been married for fifty years. She was buried in Bexley Church alongside her mother and father and later her husband who died in 1843 at the age of ninety.

1 Ibid pp. 334-339.
2 *Lewin Letters* p. 347.

MARY FITZHUGH LANCE (1761-1835) AND CHARLOTTE HAMILTON FITZHUGH (1768-1855)

Mary Lance was an intimate of the Austens during their time in Southampton and is mentioned several times in Jane Austen's letters and it is likely that Charlotte Fitzhugh also attended the same events and Jane certainly knew her brother-in-law Valentine who she communicated with using sign language. As their husbands were prominent East India Company merchants associated with China they would have been known to Frank Austen.

The sisters-in-law, Mary Lance and Charlotte Fitzhugh were married to East India Company merchants, business associates and close friends, David Lance and William Fitzhugh. They lived lives of quiet wealth in the shadows of their husbands, occasionally being seen in the family memoir written by Terrick Fitzhugh. They come to life not through their own letters or journals but in the correspondence and writing of their friends. Their friends were the novelist Jane Austen and the great tragic actress Sarah Siddons. The women were both widowed at relatively early ages and more of an insight into their own characters come in their own wills.

MARY LANCE

Early life and Marriage

Mary Fitzhugh had been born in Constantinople in 1761 to Valentine Fitzhugh and his wife Elizabeth Palmentier who was of a Huguenot family whose ancestors had fled France to escape religious persecution. Mary's parents had married in 1754, a year when Constantinople was wracked by earthquakes.[1] The couple's grand-daughter Emily Fitzhugh recollected that:
'Valentine was in early life in the Levant trade & having made a small fortune, he married a Sciote Lady of exceeding beauty'.[2]

According to Lady Wortley Montagu, who travelled in that part of the world:

> poor Greek peasants, who wear the Sciote habit, the women being in short petticoats fastened by straps round their shoulders, and large smock-sleeves of

---

1 *An Account of the several Earthquakes of late felt at Constantinople* James Porter to Rev Wetstein 15th February 1755 XXIV pp 115-123. www.royalsocietypublishing.org.
2 Memorandum of Emily FitzHugh private collection.

white linen, with neat shoes and stockings, and on their heads a large piece of muslin, which falls in large folds on their shoulders.[1]

The family were well set-up, Valentine was working for the Levant Company, where he held the post of company treasurer in Constantinople but in 1762 the family lost much in the fire[2] that swept through Pera when two thirds of the Frankish residential quarter was burnt to the ground. 1761-2 had also seen an outbreak of plague in the city.[3] The fire, Valentine commented to his friend James Porter the former British Ambassador, 'has so much disquieted

View of Constantinople, by Antoine de Favray

Mrs Fitzhugh and myself that they had decided to leave the country initially making for Neufchatal, a Protestant French speaking haven for Huguenots, where Mrs Fitzhugh's ancestors were from'.[4] They had decided on Neufchatal as a destination as: 'having good society, great liberty and very cheap living,

1   Letters of the Right Honourable Lady M--y W-----y M------e: written, during her travels in Europe, Asia and Africa, to persons of distinction, men of letters. &c. in different parts of Europe: Which contain, among other curious relations, accounts of the policy and manners of the Turks; drawn from sources that have been inaccessible to other travellers. Robert Halsband (ed.) Oxford 1685 p. 173.
2   This may explain why William and Charlotte Fitzhugh had several policies with the British Fire Office for their properties at 18 Orchard Street, off Portman Square, London, Hill Farm, Bannisters Lodge and the ship *The Prince of Coburg*. Brighton & Hove Record Office SAS-ACC 6859/96.
3   *An Account of the Plague At Constantinople* Mordach Mackenzie MD to Sir James Porter April 1763 pp. 69-82 XI www.royalsocietypublishing.org.
4   *FitzHugh* p. 455. Elizabeth's father was English, Huguenot families having fled to England to flee persecution in France in the late 16th century and 17th century. Her mother Constance travelled to Southampton with them living in St Mary's parish, she died in in 1769 the parish register noted she had been born in Constantinople in 1679. SA PR5/1/2.

three points very essential. England would be very disagreeable to Mrs Fitzhugh as she does not talk the language.' Eventually, however, the couple and their daughter removed to Southampton. Again the Ambassador had made the introduction and via a mutual friend told the Fitzhughs that Southampton was very satisfactory. Mary's father felt that 'Though I had a fortune to live in London & make a figure, we should prefer the other, as we are both more inclined to be a quiet easy retreat than to noise and bustle.' In 1763 the family first chose to live on the outskirts of the town at Bitterne but then moved more centrally to 65 High Street. In 1779 George Cole, a house carpenter of Southampton, leased a new built house at Hanover Buildings to Valentine Fitzhugh for seven years. Cole had obviously branched out from carpentry into house building and had completed one property, almost finished a second and was working on a third. The almost complete house with associated cellars, solars, outhouses, paths, passages, garden and water-course were the subject of the lease. As a new build the Fitzhughs could detail finishing touches including a closet with shelves in the kitchen to provide a butler's pantry; a dresser with drawers and shelves in the kitchen; a separate area in the cellar for wine bins and another pantry with shelves and a third section for coal. The kitchen was to be made of lathe and plaster, with a paved wash house fitted with a pump, sink and drains. The back parlour was to have a closet with shelves and there were to be two closets with shelves in each bed chamber. More shelves were requested in the store room, along with a necessary near the wash house and a further necessary at the bottom of the garden for the use of the servants. The tenants had the right to lay dung at the back of the garden. Cole had to maintain the exterior of the property, except for the glass windows, whilst the Fitzhughs had to paper all the rooms at their own expense. The rent was £36 15s per annum paid quarterly.[1] In 1798 a memo from Valentine Fitzhugh, in relation to land tax charges, shows his dwelling house to be in Holy Rood parish and to be a house, garden, coach house and stables.[2] His grand-daughter Emily Fitzhugh remembered her grandparents had a servant in a green coat with a gold epaulette and they had a pair of horses and a postillion.[3] By 1803 the street directory shows Mrs Fitzhugh was back living on the High Street at number 68.

In 1788 Mary inherited money from her aunt and god-mother, Mary Rogers. She had left her house in Mile End to her brother Thomas, with the interest on £4000 going to Mary's father Valentine with the principal to her

1 SA D/PM/ 64/2/17.
2 SA D/PM/ 88/2/17.
3 Memorandum of Emily Fitzhugh, private collection.

View of Canton

niece. Mary Roger's sister, Nancy Purling, also received the interest on £5000. Mary Rogers money came from estates at Richmond Vale in the West Indies.[1] Mary had two brothers, William and Valentine, who had both followed their grandfather and uncle into service with the East India Company, Valentine initially in Madras, India and William to Canton, China. When Valentine fell ill in Madras William brought him to Canton to live with him.[2] Whilst in China they became close friends with another supercargo called David Lance. In 1789 William Fitzhugh returned to Southampton with David Lance and within six weeks David was married to the twenty-eight-year-old Mary, whose marriage settlement was a sum of £20,000. It is possible that David had met Mary in 1783 when he made a brief return to England, and the couple may have developed an understanding at that time.[3] David Lance had returned from China in 1789, aged 32, because his health had suffered badly in the heat and humidity of that country and he was left with chronic chest complaints.[4] There may have been another reason for the timeline in regard to the couple's

1 TNA PROB 11/1164/18 will of Mary Rogers.
2 Dirk FitzHugh '"I recommended him to read Corinna":an enigma?' in The Jane Austen Report Journal 2021 pp. 64-65.
3 In 1783 David Lance lent his nephew George Paton £200 to help advance his career in the East India Company. The money was not repaid and in 1802 Lance's lawyer, Townley Ward, sent a demand to George's father with a request to pay back the money immediately or to be pursued for principle plus interest, as well as other sums disbursed on George's account. Paton family archive, private collection.
4 David Lance was born in Sandwich, Kent to William Lance and his wife Mary Temple. Henry Ames Blood *The History of Temple NH* Boston 1869 p. 278.

marriage and for David's decision to return to England. At around the time David joined the East India Company his family fortunes were in dire straits. His father had little money and four children to support, David, William, Mary and Elizabeth. In 1784 William Lance senior wrote a new will in which he outlined the financial stress he was under, along with long term sickness. He also looked to David to sort out his debts and support his mother and siblings. David's father, at the time of writing his will, had been for thirty-four years in service to the crown and was, at that point, commissioner of the victualling office of the Royal Navy and living in Greenwich.

William Lance senior

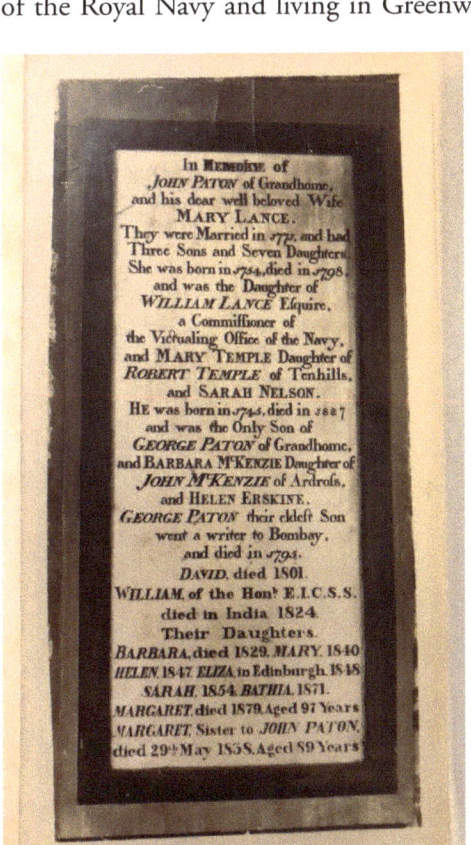

Patten family memoria

William made it clear that David understood the situation which suggests his son's return to England in 1783 may have prompted the new will. William Lance's will was probated in 1790. By that time his wife was already dead, his daughter Mary married to John Paton, son William in holy orders at St Faiths in Norfolk and his other daughter Elizabeth never married and eventually moved to Winchester. The will stipulated that, if possible, nothing was to be done until David returned so it may have been this that brought him back to England. It also meant that David could sort out his family difficulties and then focus on his own future. It is likely there was a delay between his father's death and probate as David and his brother William were summoned in person to swear an oath that the will was in fact in his father's hand and that they knew the man who had written it.[1] It may also have been an additional reason for Mary Fitzhugh's brother, William Fitzhugh, making a trip back to England to support his friend. William Fitzhugh finally returned to England for good in 1791.

Mary's father recorded his thoughts on the marriage in a letter to his wife on 30th July 1792 when he was considering the disposition of his estate. He left his wife sole mistress of his fortune: 'As Mary is now married & of course has a right to the £4000 left to her by her Aunt Rogers.'[2]

After they married Mary and David initially lived within the town of Southampton. Most of their children were born in the town, eldest child Mary's baptism was recorded at Holy Rood Church so the family were probably living near to or with Mary's parents in 1790. From 1791-1795 the family were living in Above Bar around Hanover Buildings so may have taken on the property originally leased by Valentine from George Cole; children Eliza, Emma, William and John Edwin were all baptised at All Saints.[3] The couple eventually built a new family home, Chessel House, on the east bank

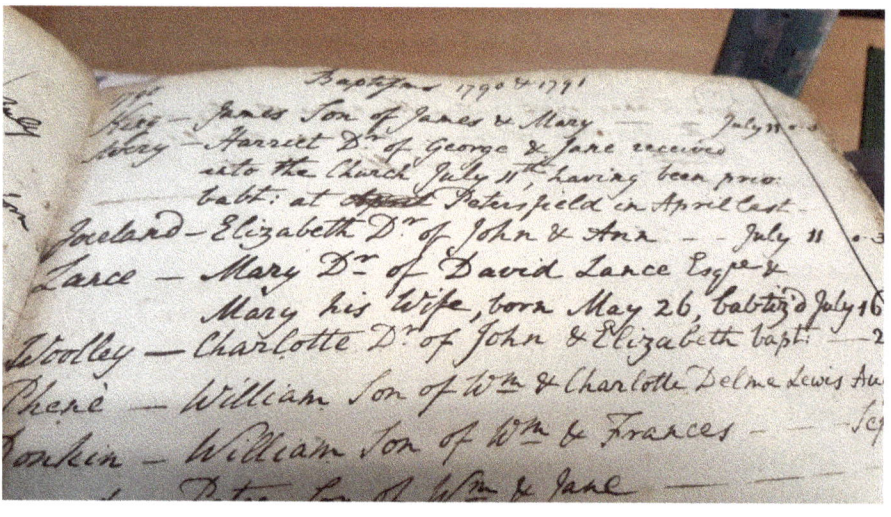

Mary Lance's baptism, Holy Rood Church

1   TNA PROB-11-1197-137 will of William Lance.
2   Family Papers of William Reginald Fitzhugh from notes by the genealogist A F Radcliffe, housemaster at Charterhouse and husband of Ernestine FitzHugh.
3   SA SC/AG8/3/5 Rate book for All Saints 1791-1795. The property was between that of Col Bayard in Above Bar and Richard Sims in Hanover Buildings. Col William Bayard was an American Loyalist at the time of the War of Independence

of the river Itchen in 1797, and in which they lived until 1817. The house was described in a *Companion in a Tour round Southampton* thus:

> the elegantly simple mansion seems to stand just where it should stand and to be exactly the building that it ought to be, for the view which it commands. Screened by a wood from the broad and busy estuary of Southampton Water, it retreats from general notice and courts the quiet inland view which it enjoys.

Chessel House, by Tobias Young, Southampton Museums & Art Gallery Collection

The house had been built and designed for the Lances by the architect John Kent in 1796. It was in the Grecian style and apparently adapted from a drawing of a Roman villa. An advertisement for a later sale of the property in 1840 suggested the grounds had been laid out in Repton's best taste.[1] The property exceeded one hundred acres with its main entrance and lodge house being on the corner of Chessel Avenue and Peartree Avenue. There were originally three lodges, one serving as the laundry for the main house. The road on which it stood, properly called Bitterne Road, is still known locally as Lance's Hill. Access from the house to Southampton was improved by the building of the Northam Bridge which had been proposed in July 1796 by

and received an annuity for *his zealous attachment and important services to the mother country*. He died in December 1804 at his Southampton home called Greenwich House and was buried at All Saints. SA The Atherley Papers & *The European Magazine & London Review Vol 45* London 1805 p. 80. The Magazine was first published in 1782. Later, after the Lances left, their property was leased to Francis Love Beckford. SC/AG8/3/6 1808.

1   Morning Herald (London) 9th June 1840.

Northam Bridge and farm, The Royal Collection

David Lance, the same year that he was building the family home at Chessel. The toll bridge was funded by shareholders, including Lance, and cost £5000 to build and eventually one of the lodges for Chessel house became the home of the toll collector for Northam Bridge.

Mary lost her father in 1800, he had reached the age of 79.[1] Valentine makes no mention of any of his children in his will, but leaving bequests to friends and relations to purchase memorial rings and the bulk of his estate to his wife Elizabeth. His other request in the letter of 1792 was that: 'His heart is to be divided into two equal parts, each put into a silver box. One to be laid on my most honoured and most dearly beloved Mother's coffin; the other, whenever my dearest Batet may die, to be placed near her heart & buried with her.'[2] Elizabeth, meanwhile, was losing her sight, and became blind at aged eighty. David also lost his sister Mary Paton in 1798.

The dangers of sailing also affected the Lances when in 1801 a boat belonging to David Lance capsized and four of his servants and his boatman were thrown into the water but they did manage to cling onto the upturned

1   Will of Valentine Fitzhugh TNA PROB-11-1347-226.
2   Family papers of William Reginald Fitzhugh. Batet was Elizabeth's pet name.

boat. The Cowes packet boat, however, ignored their cries for help and sailed on by regardless of the cries of the unfortunate sufferers. Fortunately they were rescued by Mr Langa of Hythe[1] who put out his own boat, the *Mary of Southampton*, to rescue the victims. The local newspaper reported that Mr Butter was commended for supporting the half-fainting female servant in the water throughout their ordeal.[2]

In 1802 the Treaty of Amiens ushered in a brief period of peace between Britain and France and the Lances took advantage of the situation to travel to Paris and we catch sight of them through the journal of Bertie Greatheed[3] whom they visited in the January of that year. He, in turn, attended a ball at Mrs Lances's, among a few others Mrs Cosway and Madame Le Brun were there. The family were living in the Hotel de St Far and other guests included the former governor of Bengal, Robert Clive and his wife. The journal of another English visitor Mary Berry reports on how full all the hotels were with English visitors in 1802.[4] George Jackson wrote 'all the hotels are overflowing with English; for we have an inundation of our shores since the signature of the Treaty, and the flood increases daily, and will no doubt go increasing'.[5]

Elizabeth Parmentier Fitzhugh, private collection

1. Probably John Langa who lived at 1 Shore Road in Hythe. Information provided by Hythe & Waterside Local History Society.
2. *Portsmouth Telegraph or Mottley's Naval and Military Journal*, Portsmouth 22nd June 1801, Issue 89. Mr Butter was probably Thomas Butter listed as a customs officer living in Brewhouse Lane in the Cunningham Directory of 1803.
3. Bertie Greatheed 1759-1826 was a dramatist; the actress Sarah Siddons had been maid companion to his mother Lady Mary. She later appeared in his play *The Regent*; Mrs Siddons being a close friend of Mary's sister-in-law Charlotte Fitzhugh. The Letters of Sarah and William Siddons to Hester Lynch Piozzi edited by Kalman A. Burnim www.escholar.manchester.ac.uk 1969 p. 61.
4. www.gericaultlife.com/mary-berry-1802. G
5. The Register of Passes suggests that 2598 passports were given to English migrants in 1802. Elodie Duche' *Revolutionary Ruins: The Re-imagination of French Touristic Sites during the Peace of Amiens* York 2016 p.3-4.

In 1802 the East India Company's trade was threatened by France and David Lance had to return to Chochin in China in the post of ambassador in 1803. He was accompanied on the voyage by William Kerr from Kew Gardens who was to collect plants.[1] David's nephew, William Paton of the East India Company in India, heard from an acquaintance of his uncle's return to China. William Paton intended to write to his uncle and confided in a letter to his sister: 'I have already told you his appointment in China is extremely lucrative and he has just hit the happy moment to replenish his purse while his Children are too young to require the immediate presence of the Father'.[2]

Chinese Plant bought back to England by David Lance, Kew Gardens collection

Lance, meanwhile, assisted William Kerr in his task including building a plant cabin on the East India Company ship *Henry Addington* which brought

---

1 Charles Konigh & John Sims *The Annals of Botany* London 1805 Vol I p. 399. Lance was not the only East India Company merchant bringing back exotic plants. James Drummond of Grove Place, Nursling, procured nearly 200 trees whilst in Manila on Company business and went on to create an exotic garden at Nursling. Gill Hedley and Adrian Rance (eds) *Pleasure Grounds* Horndean 1987 p. 68. David Lance's nephew, John Henry Lance, was also a keen botanist painting and recording the orchids of Surinam. Carlos Ossenbach *The Orchids of John Henry Lance (1793-1878)* in Lankesteriana Vol 20 No 1 2020 pp. 57-78.
2 Private Collection of the Paton family.

the pair back to England from the Orient in 1804.[1] The return journey was fraught with danger and the company fleet was surprised by the French. The senior captain Nathaniel Dance (a relative of neighbours of the Lances, the Dance-Hollands) bluffed the French into thinking the merchant ships were in fact ships of the line. The plants and a cargo worth six million pounds were saved. Lance's own health, however, was again badly affected by this relatively short time spent in China. It was also at this time that David Lance lost his maiden sister Elizabeth in October 1805, who died aged sixty.

Shortly after the return of her ailing husband Mary lost her mother in 1806,[2] she having reached the age of 89. Elizabeth Fitzhugh's will was much longer than her husband's and mainly included the convoluted details of the £20,000 marriage portion of her daughter. She made personal bequests to her children; William received four thousand pounds and her household goods, Valentine also had four thousand pounds and her wine and liquor, Mary received her mother's books and her husband a portrait of Mary. William, Valentine and David Lance were named as executors.

In 1806 Mary left cards with some acquaintances who had recently moved to Southampton, the naval captain Francis Austen, his mother and sisters Cassandra and Jane:

> To the Berties are to be added the Lances, with whose cards we have been endowed and whose visit Frank and I returned yesterday. They live about a mile and three quarters from S. to the right of the new road to Portsmouth, and I believe their house is one of those, which are to be seen almost anywhere among the woods on the other side of the Itchen. It is a handsome building, stands high, and in a very beautiful situation. We found only Mrs Lance at home, and whether she boasts any offspring besides a grand pianoforte did not appear, she was civil and chatty enough, and offered to introduce us to some acquaintance in Southampton, which we gratefully declined. I suppose they must be acting by the orders of Mr Lance of Netherton[3] in this civility, as there seems no other reason for their coming near us. They will not come often, I dare say. They live in a handsome style and are rich, and she seemed to like to be rich, and we gave her to understand that we were very far from

1 Lance's contribution to the study of plants included an account of the Abacá, translated from a French Manuscript, on behalf of Sir Joseph Banks. *Annals of Botany* Vol I p. 551.
2 Mrs Fitzhugh was living at 68 High Street in 1803, her son Valentine at 17 High St. *Cunningham Guide 1803*. Will of Elizabeth Fitzhugh TNA PROB-11-1453-76.
3 Rev William Lance rector of Faccombe in Hampshire, brother to David Lance.

being so: she will soon feel therefore that we are not worth her acquaintance.[1]
Jan 8th 1807

It is likely the Austens would have been offered tea during their visit and found it served in the porcelain service which had been commissioned by the Fitzhugh family.[2] The design was dominated by flowers and with objects representing the Chinese Four Treasurers or Accomplishments: a lyre-case,

The Fitzhugh Porcelain, private collection

1 *Jane Austen's Letters* p. 117.
2 David Lance advised collectors of porcelain such as Sir Joseph Bank's wife. Lady Bank's produced a Dairy Book on old china. Emma Newport *Adopting a Chinese Mantle: Designing and Appropriating Chineseness 1750-1820* Kings College London Unpublished PhD 2014.

chequers board, calligraphy and books. The design also incorporated dragons (regarded as lords of the heavens and seas) and the traditional Buddhist emblem of the pomegranate. In the early nineteenth century the pattern was taken up by the Spode factory.[1] The tea may have been hyson, David Lance was fond enough of the tea to have shipped back two chests from China in 1777.[2] This lukewarm start to the relationship with the Austens did improve and Jane made further visits to 'Chiswell', so it seems that the families became more friendly, and they attended balls together at The Dolphin Inn, and on Friday 9th December 1808 Jane wrote:

> The room was tolerably full, & there were perhaps thirty couple of Dancers:- the melancholy part was to see so many dozen young Women standing by without partners ….. We paid an additional shilling for our Tea, which we took as we chose in an adjoining, & very comfortable room. – There were only 4 dances, & it went to my heart that the Miss Lances (one of the them too named Emma!) should have partners only for two.[3]

The association with the Lance family may have had some benefits to Frank Austen who had provided services to the East India Company which resulted in him being voted a reward in 1808/9.[4] Later in the same letter Jane writes about walking with Martha to pay her duty at Chessel where they found Mrs Lance home alone. They returned to Southampton over the bridge partly financed by Mrs Lance's husband. Jane was also fond of Mary Lance's brother, Valentine, who she thought 'very much the Gentleman'. Valentine was another former East India Company merchant whose time abroad had resulted in a life changing illness. For him it meant becoming deaf but Jane Austen was able to speak to him using sign language:[5]

> Brother to Mrs Lance and very much the Gentleman. He has lived in that

1 Derek Morris *Mile End Old Town* East London Historical Society 2002 p. 46. Robert Copeland *Spodes' Willow Pattern & other designs after the Chinese* 3rd Edition London 1999, Chapter 14 'The Chinese Trophies & Fitzhugh Patterns'.
2 Hyson was a green tea from the Anhui province of China. Tea was extremely expensive until tax was reduced in 1784 thanks to the urging of tea merchants led by Richard Twining.
3 *Jane Austen's Letters* pp. 156-157. The letter suggests that Austen was perhaps already working on her novel called *Emma*.
4 Collins Hemingway 'How the 'Long War' Affected Jane Austen's Family & Her Novels' in Persuasions On line 39 No 1 2018.
5 *Jane Austen's Letters* p. 160.

house for more than twenty years, & poor Man, is so totally deaf, that they say he cd not hear a Cannon were it fired close to him; having not cannon at hand to make the experiment, I took it for granted, & talked to him with my fingers, which was funny enough – I recommended to him to read Corinna

Valentine's niece Emily Fitzhugh, rather unkindly said Valentine was 'an idle fellow & died unmarried'.[1] The Austen's final ball before they moved to Chawton in January 1809 was another occasion where they were in the company of the Lances. This time the Miss Lances did have partners and Jane: 'tucked Mrs Lance's neckerchief in behind & fastened with a pin'.[2]

Mary's husband, meanwhile, had become involved in regional politics becoming Sheriff of Hampshire in 1807. For Mary Lance tragedy was about to strike, her daughter Emma, who had elicited sympathy from Jane Austen due to her lack of dance partners because she bore the same name as a future heroine of an Austen novel, died aged just nineteen in 1810.[3] A surviving letter from her cousin Mary Paton written on 5th September 1810 records:

> We think that it is very probably that my Uncle David's family are not at home just now as Sarah had a letter from my Uncle William's daughter about two days ago saying that my Uncle David's second daughter had died in June last of a consumption[4]

Mary Lance's eldest son was also posted to Bengal in the same year. She lost her brother Valentine a year later, in 1811, from an 'atrophy', which term generally described a wasting disease.

The year 1812 saw Mary Lance and her surviving daughter in London where their paths crossed with Ann Sophy Mackie who was also making a visit. Ann Sophy saw Mary Lance junior at the Royal Institution where the poet Thomas Campbell, the author of *The Pleasures of Hope* gave a lecture on French and English Tragedy and Mrs Lance at a lecture on Vision given by Dr Roget . Mary and her daughter attended a ball at the Mackies residence where they were the first to assemble, the ball finished at 5 am. A few days later Ann

1 Memorandum by Emily Fitzhugh, a conversation with her brother at Streat Rectory private collection.
2 *Jane Austen's Letters* p. 170.
3 She was buried in Holy Rood church on 12th June 1810; however, the church was bombed in 1940 and bodies that could be identified were reburied at Hollybrook cemetery. Emma was coffin 194, ref D4 42.
4 Letter of Mary Paton private collection of William Paton.

Sophy attended an entertainment at Mrs Lances, where she heard Molieres play of *Le Tartuffe* read by French people. She considered M. Nogent a very good Tartuffe, M. La Chenay a good Orgon & Madame de Lisle de L'Orme an excellent Elmire. Miss Mary Lance was Marianne – Ann Sophy noted she had very little to say and that little was spoken low & timidly. Sophy regretted that they were all obliged to have books, as their eyes, fixed on them destroyed all the illusion, by preventing any expression of countenance while speaking. The rooms at the Lance's home opened into each other with folding doors which Ann Sophy thought were very convenient on this occasion. There were 60 people there including Mr & Mrs Fitzhugh and Mrs & Miss Lewin.

Another respite in the Napoleonic War in 1815 saw the Lances, along with their surviving daughter Mary and younger son John, in Brussels where they attended the Duchess of Richmond's Ball on the 15th June. Of the 238 people who attended the majority were aristocrats or military and only a handful were gentry including the Lances friends Mr & Mrs Greatheed. The few other non-titled attendees included Mr & Mrs Lloyd, Mr Leigh and Mr Chad so the Lances were in a very elite party. Mary's daughter, Mary, recorded the scene after the ball was disrupted by the news that Napoleon and his army were on the move. Wellington, she observed, was unconcerned and ate an excellent supper. The officers left the ballroom for the field of Waterloo two hours after the news arrived. The civilians were so close to the battle they could hear cannonading from the ramparts. The Lances were staying at a house near the city gates and so could view everything that was going and coming:

> Papa was awaked by the galloping of horses and cries of 'fermez les portes'. He got up and saw 100 Prussian Lancers galloping down the street, some with heads bound, others without eyes he was convinced the Prussians were retreating & fully expected to see the French follow, however upon enquiry he learned they were runaways, soon after, the wounded began to come in and a most dreadful sight it was. Mrs Erskine (very big with child) & whose husband was engaged, spent the day with us, and could not be prevailed upon to leave the windoe, & we remained there, to prevent her from seeing some of the most dreadful sights. Poor Captain Erskine lost one arm and two fingers of the other hand on the 18th and his life was despaired of for some days by the amazing loss of blood his arm literally streamed all the way from Waterloo to Brussels (9 miles).[1]

---

1 *Fitzhugh* p. 626. Private Letter of Mary Lance to her cousin Elizabeth Paton 29th August transcribed by a descendant of the Porcher family and deposited with the Society of Genealogists.

Everyone was convinced the French were winning the battle and would be soon at Brussels. Any English people in Brussels were advised to leave and David Lance, with some difficulty, secured horses and the family left for Ghent and then travelled onto Bruges. It was here they heard of Wellington's victory. After three weeks they returned to Brussels where they found a Prussian officer with thirteen wounds lodging in their house; he died soon afterwards. The family visited the battlefield and daughter Mary picked up a tri-coloured cockade as a souvenir and drew a picture of the cottage known as La Belle Alliance where Prince Blucher and Wellington met to signify the end of the fighting. Mary also made a plan of the engagement which she had confirmed by officers who had taken part in the battle. Brother John Edwin amused himself by showing friends arriving from England around the site. The family had originally travelled to the continent to help improve David Lance's health, which had improved and they decided to winter in Brussels rather than travel on to Switzerland.

In 1817 the family were again in Brussels and concluding the sale of Chessel House to Lord Ashtown,[1] as a new London home, South Villa, was being built for the family. It was constructed between 1819-20 as part of John Nash's grand design for Regent's Park to a design by Decimus Burton. It was the third villa to be built in the park and eventually there would be eight rather than the planned fifty-six.[2] In the interim the family travelled. David Lance's nephew William Paton did not approve of his uncle's inclination to prefer France and was sorry to hear that he: 'has taken a dislike to England and prefers the fictious manners of the French to our more solid society of his own Countrymen. False taste I think but I suppose he humours his Wife more in so doing than himself.'[3]

David Lance enjoyment of his new home was short - he died in 1820 - and Mary proved her nephew correct when she decided to move to Paris along with her surviving daughter. Mary had travelled throughout her life, born

1 SA D/RL 80 Affidavit 1817. T L O Davies the vicar of Peartree suggested that Lance had sold the property as he was disgusted at obtaining only a small portion of the common adjacent to his property when it was enclosed. Southern Daily Echo May 11th 1901. The Lance name lives on in Southampton, the hill on top of which their house sat is still known locally as Lance's Hill (rather than the official Bitterne Road). The family name can also be found in North America where David Lance had trading links, Lance Islands off Vancouver Islands. See Kenneth Cozens *East London Merchant Networks in Asia. The Fitzhugh's 1750-1800. East India Company Agents in Macao*. Paper Exeter Maritime History Conference 2007.
2 Historic England Research Records Hob Uid: 909307.
3 Private Collection of William Paton.

David Lance's pleasure grounds, Southampton Archives

in Constantinople and then moving to Southampton, living in London and visiting the continent with her husband and younger children. Her mother was a French speaker and Mary grew up in a bi-lingual household and it is likely she had some knowledge of other languages from her childhood and also relating to her husband's time in China. As a widow, however, it was to France that she was drawn for the final fifteen years of her life.

Children

Mary lived a life of luxury and duly produced a number of children, daughters Mary, born 1790 and twins Emma and Eliza born in 1791, although Eliza died shortly after birth. Her son William was born in 1792 and John in 1793. Another daughter, Frances, was born and died in 1801.

William, as the eldest son, followed his father into service with the East India Company taking advantage of the new company college at Haileybury to which he was sent in 1808. The college site had been purchased in 1805 and building work began in 1806. The aim of the facility was to train 'writers', that is to say administrators, for the company. Boys studied there from the ages of sixteen to eighteen. The curriculum embraced political economy, history, mathematics, natural philosophy, classics, law, humanity and philology as well as the study of languages such as Arabic, Bengali, Persian, Sanskrit and Urdu. The college professors were leading thinkers and academics of the day and included people like Thomas Malthus who taught political economy. By 1810 William was in India where he was beginning a career as a lawyer and about to take an examination in Calcutta in 'the Languages'. He was fortunate that he was able to stay with his cousin William Paton who was already established in India. Paton assisted the younger man in his studies:

> I hope he will be found competent. I have pledged myself with the Government to use my best effects to induce him to qualify himself. He is a fine liberal minded fellow but very extravagant and fond of pleasure. He is a great sportsman and the boldest rider I ever saw. He is very tenacious & inclined to resent the smallest affront like a military man – in short he is as unlike his Father as it is possible to be. Yet he has that good heart of the Lances and the same pleasantry & drollery about him that all the family possesses. I seldom see any traits of his Mother about him. You know she is no favourite of mine.[1]

It appears young William was somewhat estranged from his mother and according to Paton, his father had been ill again and was also *distressed* about his son. William Lance did succeed in his exams and his cousin reported in October 1810:

> William is still living here with us and is doing & likely to do very well. He has been acting Collector of the District and is intending to be deputed to another Station with higher allowances. I think he is now in a fair way of doing well &

---

1 Letter of William Paton, private collection. David Lance's sister Mary had married John Paton, when she died in 1798 he was so distraught he buried her in a cottage in the wood to await burial with him, he did not die till 1827 and was buried in London. Canmore National Record of the Historic Environment: Stoneyhill Wood NJ91SW 86 htttp://canmore.org.uk/site.136117.

I feel much satisfaction in having been able to promote his information.

William was enjoying the life and customs and was 'now a fair shot & can bring down a Partridge or Hare easily— & that from the back of an Elephant, the mode of shooting in this country'.

Paton comments, in 1820, that his cousin continued to do well and was in a position of: 'trust and respectability. I think there is no now fear of him'. In 1821 Paton also reported to his sister that he was

saddened at hearing of the death of our ever to be Commiserated Uncle David. It was the first I had heard of it and I had to communicate the melancholy event to his son William, who is still staying with us and who has felt the loss of his beloved Parent most acutely.

Paton thought it strange that no-one had contacted his cousin directly but generously put this down to the delays experienced in the transmission of letters from England to India. William Lance had further surprises in store when he found out that, in his final will, his father had distributed his fortune in a way that was unfavourable to his eldest son. The codicil to the will gave Mary Lance control of the Lance fortunes. Paton felt: 'that Mrs D L was the promoter & contriver of all this injustice that the Codicil to the Will so contrary to the Spirit of the Testament itself was all her doing'. Paton admits Mary Lance was never a favourite of his and he did not care much for John Edwin nor Mary junior either.

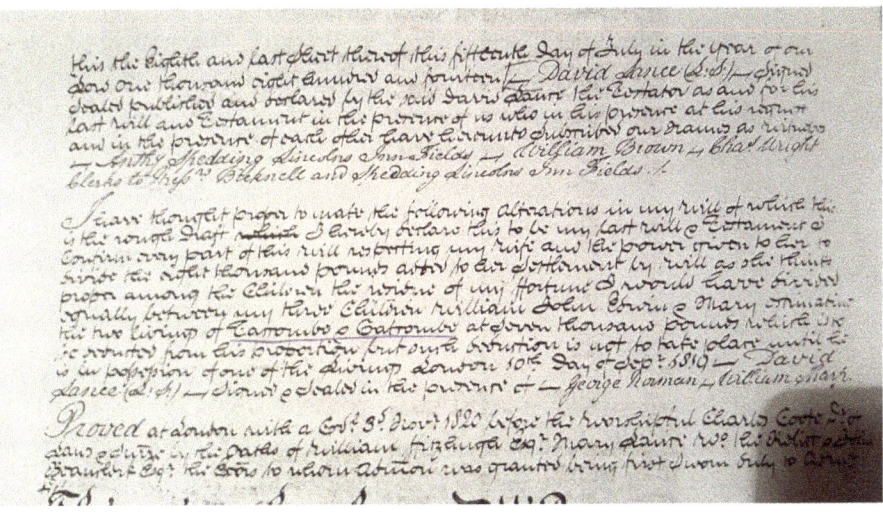

Codicil, The Will of David Lance

It was to be a little after a year from hearing of his father's death that William Lance also died. Paton wrote in September 1822 to his sister:

> but we have met with a loss, which you have probably already heard of - that has occasioned to us the deepest anguish & regret - poor William Lance our lamented Cousin is no more! He fell ill of a bilious attack the beginning of last month & on the 11th day of it breathed his last in my presence – afflicting sight. I that had witnessed his rising worth who had watched even his days of indiscretion & pushed his family to despair of his success & welfare to behold him cut off by a cruel Destine in the prime of life - with enjoyment of every earthly blessing… I am one of the trustees named in his Will, which I wrote for him five days before his Death… I followed him to the grave & saw the cold earth close over all I loved & lamented. I have written to his relations & sent them Copies of the Will.

William had died, unmarried, and in his will he left behind 'a male Elephant at Dacca unsaleable from Sickness'. William, like his grandfather before him, died in debt. After ten years' service in India he owed around £6000. His cousin, Paton, was left with the task of trying to settle his affairs. Paton noted with some bitterness that his cousin had divided what fortune he had to his brother: 'who from his splendid Marriage did not want it' and the other half to his mother and sister. 'God knows that family is rich enough' was his comment on the second bequest:

> I cannot say however that I have a great opinion of their liberality, as when I was applied to induce my poor Cousin to give up about half of what he might have gained by Law, I proposed as a fair & honourable encouragement that poor Williams Debts should be first liquidated & then an equal division made of the Estate. To this proposition no notice was given, but high praises bestowed upon poor William's liberality, which he did not live to listen to, such however is the World & it is consolatory to me to know that my poor friend had very different principles.

The only member of the family Paton had a good word for was David Lance's brother, William,

> who has the heart of a Lance & will feel the loss.[1]
> As to the rest of the family, I am so little acquainted with them -so little

---

1 The last of David Lance's siblings died in 1845. TNA PROB 11-2029-309 will of Rev William Lance.

satisfied with their conduct throughout to my poor Friend, that I feel indifferent about them. Had they acted as I suggested perhaps a better fate would have awaited William - one of the last expressions he made us of [?] was "what an ill destined man I have been." Born to the highest imputations, he lived to find himself forsaken neglected by his nearest relations. Until the death of his poor father gave him the means of attracting their attention. It then became their Interest to court him and accordingly letters flowed in apace several of which poor fellow he has not lived to peruse.

His memorial in Dacca reads:

Sacred to the memory of WILLIAM LANCE, Esq., Collector of Land Revenue at his station, who beloved and regretted by all who know his worth, departed this life on the 11th day of August A.D, 1822; aged 29 years and 8 months.[1]

It seems that Jane Austen's first impression of Mary Lance may not have been very far from the mark. As to Mary's other surviving children her younger son, John Edwin, was sent to school at Winchester, and his daughter Clara wrote of her father's early life:

My father went to Winchester in 1800, when he was 7 years old. It was very rough, and all the washing was done at the pump. He went to Cambridge (Corpus Christi) and travelled a great deal abroad with his parents, speaking French very well. [He became B.A. 1817, M.A. 1820, Deacon 1817 and Priest 1818]. On June 15th 1815 he was present at the Duchess of Richmond's Ball at Brussels, and saw the Duke of Wellington and the Guards called out.[2]

In a letter to his cousin, Elizabeth Paton, John Edwin confessed that in the week before Waterloo he had asked his father if he might join the army but was talked out of it. John Edwin's next choice of profession was the church and he was curate of Faccombe Tangley chapel in 1817 but his career did not take him to the family living at Gatcombe as John Edwin became a clergyman at Buckland St Mary. Clara Lance records:

In 1822 at St. George's, Hanover Square, he married Madelina Louisa, daughter of Mr. Josias Dupré Porcher of Winslade, Devon, and on the same day his great

---

1   C R Wilson *List of Inscriptions on tombs or Monuments in Bengal* Calcutta 1896 p. 206.
2   J A Hind & J M Colledge *Buckland and St Mary Past & Present* 1974.

friend Henry Porcher married Miss Sarah Pearse, my mother's sister. My father lived near Reading, but they must have travelled a great deal as: William was born at Rome in 1823, and James at Boulogne in 1829. In 1830, General Popham, of Littlecote, said to my father, "Go and grub at Buckland till your family living is vacant". By the time it was vacant, Buckland was much too dear to be left.

John Edwin took on the living of Buckland and went on to renovate the church with no expense spared. The church contains a monument to his first wife, Madelina, who died of smallpox along with the son she had just given birth to, in 1839, erected by her brother Henry Porcher. Despite a good second marriage to Clara Pearce, daughter of John Pearce the Director of the Bank of England, John Edwin's fortune was depleted with bequests going to his many children but on the death of his sister Mary and her husband his fortune was returned.[1] Clara continued:

My father was a very hardy man. Till he was about 61 he used to break the ice in his bath in the winter. He ate no luncheon, and in Lent ate no meat except on Sundays, and on Good Friday nothing till the evening, He rode to Honiton and back, 22 miles, the day before he died at 91. Charles is the only one of his sons like him in this respect. The reason that five of his sons went to India was that Uncle Henry was a Director of the East India Company, and gave them their appointments. If it had been a case of competitions I doubt if India would have known so many Lances.

The family's Indian connection remained strong:

My father bred horses at one time. They were all called by Indian names: Sutlej, Lahore, etc. But having to appear in a Court of Justice about some horse that he had sold, he thought it was not a nice position for a clergyman to be in, so he gave it up. John Edwin died in 1885.[2]

Mary seems to have depended on the companionship of her elder daughter Mary who remained with her mother throughout the rest of her life. Clara Lance, the daughter of John Edwin, said her aunt, Mary Lance junior,

---

1 In 1848 John Edwin sold several shares he had inherited in the Northam Bridge Company. SA D/PM 15/29 and 66/21.
2 *Buckland and St Mary Past & Present* J A Hind & J M Colledge 1974.

had married late in life, in 1837, to the Rev William Henry Turner,[1] fellow of Corpus Christi Oxford, and rector of Trent for forty years. Mary must have returned from Paris after her mother's death and took up with Turner shortly after that event. Mary was financially secure and it was probably her money than enabled Turner to spend £2000 on enlarging the church of St Andrew in 1840 as well as enlarging the rectory house and laying out pleasure grounds and Mary endowed four alms houses in 1846 and 1861. The endowment derived from about £2,131 invested in Consols which would provide an income of about £58 12s a year.[2] Mary died in 1866 and has a monument in St Andrew's church in Trent, Dorset, as does her husband, who died in 1875.

Health
Despite the rigours of childbirth Mary, unlike her husband, appears to have been in good health, outliving her husband and all but two of her children. David Lance's health had been broken by his years living in China and he died at a relatively early age at sixty-three. When David Lance died in 1820 he left shares and the livings of Gatcombe, Isle of Wight and Faccombe with Tangley (both in the County of Southampton)[3] to his three surviving children, William, John Edwin and Mary, and to his wife Mary her marriage portion, one thousand pounds and all the household goods. A codicil, which caused such pain to her eldest son, gave Mary the right to pass on eight thousand pounds as she saw fit. The livings were valued at seven thousand pounds. It was probably assumed that in due course John Edwin would take over one of the livings which would provide him with a good income and way of life. In 1821, Mary leased 95 Gloucester Place in London at an annual rent of £250 but she had plans to spend her widowhood elsewhere.[4]

Mary Lance died fifteen years after her husband, in 1835. By that time she was living in Paris with her daughter although retaining a family home in London. Her will was witnessed in Paris by the Chancellor and Consul General of the British Consulate[5] and, unlike that of her husband, was very

1 Turner's living was close to that of his wife's brother and he on occasion stood in for John Edwin when he was unavailable.
2 Dorsetshire Directory p. 215.
3 Faccombe with Tangley had been the living where his brother William was rector for many years until his death in 1848, appointed there by his brother in 1791. HRO 21M65/E2/342. William became a deacon in 1784 and priest in 1786.He married Catherine Elizabeth Elliot in 1789 and they lived at Netherton. Will of David Lance TNA PROB-11-1636.
4 Hertfordshire Archives DE/Gd/27134.
5 Will of Mary Lance TNA PROB 11-1849-331.

short. Her younger son John Edwin received two thousand pounds and her daughter Mary five thousand plus money invested in the French Funds and the Funds of the Kingdom of the Two Sicily's as well as all moveable household furniture, books, linen and carriages. Mary, though not as long-lived as her parents, did reach the age of seventy-four.

CHARLOTTE FITZHUGH

Early life and Marriage

Mary Lance's brother William Fitzhugh had married Charlotte Hamilton in 1792, another woman who lived a life of luxury thanks to her husband having made £60,000 whilst working for the East India Company.[1] Charlotte was the eldest daughter of the Rev Dr Anthony Hamilton of Hill Street, Berkley Square. He went on to become Archdeacon of Colchester and vicar of St-Martin-in-the-Fields. Charlotte met William when he returned from China in 1791 the most likely place was in Southampton which was when the Hampshire Chronicle of July 25th 1791 announced the arrival of various respectable personages in the town including Lord and Lady Harrowby, Charlotte's aunt and uncle.

Charlotte Fitzhugh, by John Smart

> The following very respectable personages have arrived here for the benefit of sea-bathing:- Earl and countess of Ailsbury, Earl and Countess of Radnor, Countess Dowager Radnor, Earl and Countess of Paulet, Lord and Lady Willoughby de Broke, Lord and Lady Harrowby, Lady Clayton, Count Bruhl, Hon. Mr Conway, Lord Folkstone, etc etc

It is probable that the master of ceremonies Andrew Haynes who was responsible for making society introductions introduced William Fitzhugh,

---

1 *Fitzhugh* p. 615.

who had arrived back in England by 6th July 1791, to his future wife's relations.¹

Although William Fitzhugh made a fortune whilst serving in China, like his brother Valentine and friend David Lance, his health was also under mined. In 1791 he had written to his employers:

Gentlemen,
I beg leave to enclose you the Surgeon's certificate that the state of my health requires I should proceed to Europe, and I request you will be so good as to permit me to go on the Hindostan.[Dr Duncan's certificate stated] The sudden change in this climate and the confinement to which Europeans are subject having affected the health of Mr William Fitzhugh, I am of opinion that a voyage to Europe will be of material service to his constitution.²

William Fitzhugh, private collection

Certificates of fictitious or exaggerated illness were traditionally accepted in the East India Company in lieu of applications for home leave – for which there seems to have been no official provision – and they could also be the first step to resignation. If this was William's aim it was successful and he returned to the family home in Southampton to marry and establish his own household. Charlotte and William were married at St George's Chapel, Hanover Square when she was 24 and he was nearly 35. Lord Harrowby ordered from Flight, chinaman, a dessert service of French clay which was intended for to Charlotte on her marriage worth £29 3s.³

Similarly to the Lances, William sought to build a new house for himself and his bride and in 1792 picked a location of 105 acres on the outskirts of

1 Hon East India Company Committee Minutes 8/113 6th July 1791 Mr Alexander Bruce, and *Mr William Fitzhugh of the Council of Supra Cargoes there, severally advising their arrival in England.*
2 Ibid p. 615 William's health had caused concern back in 1781 when Thomas Hutton felt it was an absolute necessity to take a voyage to Europe. *Fitzhugh* p. 563.
3 Letter from Lord Harrowby 6th November 1965 detailing entry from family records.

Bannister House, private collection

Southampton on part of the old Bannister Farm Estate.[1] The property was called Bannisters Court, and was described by Fanny Kemble, a frequent visitor, as: 'A house with an air of distinction, well-kept grounds, velvety turf, peacocks, swans floating on a stretch of ornamental water, a lodge where a neat woman would run out curtsying to greet the family carriage as it passed'.[2]

Paterson's Roads, a traveller's navigational guide, on its London to Southampton route, only gives mention to two properties in Southampton, Bannisters Lodge and Bevis Mount.[3] The *Baker Guide* of 1795 reported:

> A little retired from the road is Bannisters the rural seat of Wm Fitzhugh Esq, many improvements and additions made in the pleasure grounds and gardens by the gentleman since in his possession have considerably improved its beauty.

A later visitor to the estate suggested William had bought plans of his house from Italy, the grounds: 'had a good deal of statuary, and showed great taste in his building, as well as in the grounds, making the most of a narrow space & no view out of it'.[4]

1 SA D/PM 84/6/23 William Fitzhugh purchase of Bannisters Farm. Fitzhugh kept 20 Alderney cows on the property.
2 Margaret Armstrong *Fanny Kemble, a passionate Victorian* New York 1938 p. 186.
3 From Hyde Park corner to Southampton was 68 ¾ miles by the direct route.
4 A M W Stirling (ed) *The Diaries of Dummer* Thursday February 5th 1856.

William was a talented artist and painted a view of the house and grounds himself. Art seems to have been very important to the couple and William exhibited at the Royal Academy exhibition in 1799.[1] The painting reflected his time in China being entitled *Entrance to the harbor of Macao, China*. Meanwhile his wife Charlotte with time on her hands, and with interest in the dramatic arts, became acquainted with the leading actress of the day, Sarah Siddons. Charlotte's husband was already acting as agent for Sarah Siddons in 1792 along with David Lance when they were trustees in the writing of various deeds.[2] The women were already very close. In 1798 when Sarah wrote to Charlotte about the death of her daughter, Maria adding: 'oh that you were here, that I might talk to you of her death bed'.[3] Charlotte also offered Mrs Siddons sympathy when her daughter Sally was seriously ill in 1803 and the actress wrote: 'Mr dear friend, how shall I sufficiently thank you for all your kindness to me? You know my heart and I may spare my words.'[4]

Such was her devotion that Mrs Siddons was persuaded to make frequent visits to Bannisters Court and 'seldom spent a year without visiting her at Bannisters'.[5] Charlotte also sought Mrs Siddons out when she was performing in London aiming to be at the actress's side all day and to spend the evening in her dressing-room at the theatre. Sometimes Mrs Siddons was a bit overwhelmed with the attention: 'My dear Mrs Fitzhugh grudges every moment that I am not by her side'.[6]

When visiting London Charlotte had her own box at Covent Garden, on the 30th of May 1812 she invited one of her Southampton neighbours, Ann Sophy Mackie to join her. They sat in the stage box on the right hand side of the house, the theatre not being very full. The party consisted of Mde Marcet, a young Frenchman, and Mr Drummond. Ann Sophy was highly delighted with John Philip Kemble as Rolla in Pizarro and with the spectacle and music which she considered were really grand. She commented that Mrs Siddons did not like the character of Elvira but that she acted as usual admirably. Charles Kemble although a handsome Alonzo she felt appeared effeminate and she was surprized at the inferiority of all the actors excepting the Kembles and Mrs Siddons. Ann Sophy was much grieved to see Mrs Siddons on the stage for the last time, as she was not to act more than a few nights. On a previous visit in

1   The Exhibition of the Royal Academy, 31st, 1799, Ante-Room 258 p. 11.
2   SA D/Z 254/2 and D/Z 125/14.
3   R. Griffiths & G E Griffiths *The Monthly Review Vol 134 Campbell's Life of Mrs Siddons* London 1834 p. 437
4   Nina A Kennard *Mrs Siddons* Boston 1887 p. 272.
5   Thomas Campbell *Life of Mrs Siddons* London 1834 p. 215.
6   Mrs Clement Parson *The Incomparable Siddons* London & New York 1909, p. 216.

1810 Sophy had visited Charlotte Fitzhugh's London home in Orchard Street which she felt was neat but small, they had again been to Covent Garden along with Emily Fitzhugh, the box on this occasion was five from the stage on the left-hand side. Ann Sophy could see & hear very tolerable and 'were highly delighted as we saw the ever-admirable Mrs Siddons in Isabella, Kemble in Byron, Charles Kemble in Carlos. It is a very deep tragedy & her first interview with Byron is really too affecting – her acting was, as usual, incomparable – but her mad laughs are horrible. Kemble is merely a secondary character as Byron but still appears a fine actor. Charles Kemble, much improved.' On this occasion Mrs Siddons shared the bill with an Interlude and a farce starring the clown Grimaldi.

It is also from Mrs Siddons that we get a glimpse into the character of Charlotte's husband William who acted for her in some of her legal affairs including the purchase of her own property on Portland Street in Southampton.[1] Mrs Siddons described him to her nephew Horace Twiss as a:

> wise, Steady-headed man, and I should imagine him very likely to take disgust at any little flippancy or frivolity that a thousand others would overlook and excuse as the overflowing of youthful spirits.

Mrs Siddons also introduced her niece, the actress Fanny Kemble, into the Fitzhugh household and she in turn became a close friend of Charlotte's daughter Emily. Although she may have felt stifled a little by the adoration of Mrs Fitzhugh, Mrs Siddons did give her a set of four silver carasols which had been presented to her by the City of Edinburgh in the 1790s. The actress also committed her 'Remarks' on the playing of Lady Macbeth to Charlotte Fitzhugh who then passed them onto Thomas Campbell the biographer of Mrs Siddons.[2]

1   She purchased the estate for £5,750 from the property speculator Richard Evamy. SA D/Z 354/2. The property was sold back to Evamy on 24 June 1814 for £3,550, SA D/Z459/17b. Mrs Siddons continued to hold a significant financial stake in the property through a £3,000 mortgage arranged three days later. She held the mortgage until 24 February 1824. The house was demolished in early 1826 after a further series of lets, latterly to Admiral Scott, and its building materials – 800,000 bricks, several thousand feet of excellent timber and fifteen tons of lead, "all deserving the attention of gentlemen architects and builders" – were sold by private contractor. Salisbury Journal 27 February 1826.
2   Frances Kemble in *Records of a Girlhood* wrote *we drove out to Bannisters. Poor Mrs Fitzhugh was quite overcome at seeing my father, whom she has not seen since Mrs Siddon's death; we left her with him to talk over Campbell's application to her for my*

Portrait of Mrs Siddons commissioned by Charlotte Fitzhugh, by Sir Thomas Lawrence

In 1804 Charlotte Fitzhugh commissioned a portrait of the actress from Sir Thomas Lawrence which Charlotte later presented to the National Gallery in 1843. Mrs Siddons sat for Lawrence by candlelight in March and April 1804. On the 4th August, Lawrence wrote to Mrs Fitzhugh asking for permission to make two small copies before delivering the picture, one for a print to match that of Mrs Siddons's brother John Philip Kemble as Hamlet.[1] Mrs Siddons is pictured standing and dressed in a black velvet gown with her hand on a closed book. The right of the picture is labelled 'Otway', a reference to Mrs Siddons performances as Belvidera in his *Venice Preserved*, a part she had first played in 1777. The heading of the open book is given as *Paradise Lost* in an engraving made by Say. What appears to be a monument on the right is inscribed 'Shakspere', Mrs Siddons was renowned for her portrayal of Shakespeare's tragic heroines.

Mrs Siddons's niece, Fanny Kemble, felt the painting made her look like a handsome dark cow but Mrs Siddons said that it was more like her than anything that has been done.[2] The painting was exhibited at the Royal Academy in 1804 and Joseph Farington, a member of the Academy, reported that on 30th April at 12: 'the doors were opened – Mrs Siddons and Mrs Fitzhugh came, the latter was not satisfied with the likeness of the portrait of Mrs Siddons'.[3]

Despite Charlotte's disappointment the portrait was hung in the Bannisters dining room and Fanny Kemble remembered sitting under it on

aunt's letters. New York 1880 p. 413.
1 Lawrence to Charlotte Fitzhugh 4th August 1804, National Portrait Gallery Archives, London.
2 Nina A Kennard *Mrs Siddons* Boston 1887 p. 307.
3 *Fitzhugh* p. 628.

visit to: 'comical old .... Mrs F – a not very judicious person'.[1] Fanny's view of Charlotte may have been coloured by Charlotte's response to the young girl being a victim of smallpox. Fanny recalled in later life:

> I was but little over sixteen, and had returned from school a very pretty-looking girl, with fine eyes, teeth, and hair, a clear, vivid complexion, and rather good features. The small-pox did not affect my three advantages first named, but, besides marking my face very perceptibly, it rendered my complexion thick and muddy and my features heavy and coarse, leaving me so moderate a share of good looks as quite to warrant my mother's satisfaction in saying, when I went on the stage, "Well, my dear, they can't say we have brought you out to exhibit your beauty." Plain I certainly was, but I by no means always looked so; and so great was the variation in my appearance at different times, that my comical old friend, Mrs. Fitzhugh, once exclaimed, "Fanny Kemble, you are the ugliest and the handsomest woman in London!" And I am sure, if a collection were made of the numerous portraits that have been taken of me, nobody would ever guess any two of them to be likenesses of the same person.

In return for the portrait Mrs Siddons made a model of Mrs Fitzhugh in clay which Mrs Siddons was told looked: *'liker than anything that ever yet was seen of that kind'.*[2]

It was no doubt this link with Charlotte Fitzhugh which led to Mrs Siddons performing in the theatre in Southampton on more than one occasion. In October 1801 the *Hampshire Chronicle* published an advert for the penultimate night of her appearances in that season. On Monday 12th October she would perform in the tragedy of *Douglas* as Lady Randolph and on Wednesday the 14th be seen as Mrs Beverley in the Tragedy *The Gamester* positively her last performance of the season. She returned in 1809 when:

> The Managers of the Theatre ever anxious to exert themselves in the best possible way to procure novelty and amusement beg leave most respectfully to inform the public that they feel great pleasure in announcing the engagement of that great and inimitable actress Mrs SIDDONS, the unrivalled Melpomene of the British stage who will make her first appearance on Wednesday Evening next in the interesting and affecting character of Mrs Beverley, play of the Gamester. The other nights of her performance will be Friday the 6th, Monday

---

1 Frances Kemble *Records of a Girlhood* p. 10.
2 Nina A Kennard *Mrs Siddons* Boston 1887 p. 307.

the 9th and Wednesday the 11th of October in three of her favourite and most popular characters.

The actor/manager James Winston, gives this account of the history of the new theatre[1] in Southampton in the *Theatric Tourist* of 1805:

> The elegant fashionables visiting Southampton refused to patronize the theatre on consequence of its ruinous condition and most deplorable entrance; therefore as the lease was nearly out on the 12th September 1803 they commenced campaigning in another built under the regulation of Mr Slater. Collins gave 450 guineas for St John's Hospital and the ground on which it stood in French Street nearly opposite the former theatre: the charity being

The Theatre Royal, French Street

1 Subscribers to the original theatre in 1765, built on the site of an old silk-mill on the plan of the Bath Theatre, included Nathaniel St Andre, John Butler Harrison I, Arthur Atherley, Vernon Sadlier, Newe Peers, Mr Hammond, Richard Lere and Dr John Monkton. Its opening was celebrated with a fifty-line poem which was even published in the *St James's Chronicle or the British Evening Post* read by the manager Mr Samuel Johnson. According to the 1770 Ladies Pocket Guide it was said to have a company of tolerable comedians who performed there three times a week during the season. Thomas Gilliland *The Dramatic Mirror* London 1808 p. 195. The Atherley Papers SA D/S2/2/6.

discontinued this old building furnished him with ample materials for this new one. He says his theatre cost him £3000 which with due deference we should suppose an error; if we give credit for £2000 besides the purchase of the ground we think it not amiss.

The new theatre was based on the plan of the Covent Garden theatre but Winston, an actor/manager himself, thought the design of the interior of the theatre poor:

It has a bad gallery: the Pit is much too low: the Stage is short and the Boxes so near the Pit that the lower tier resemble the Orchester (sic) boxes of Drury lane the company appearing to sit below the level of the stage. The old theatre had this fault also; but we acknowledge the Green Room to be good. The house holds upwards of £100; 4 shillings admission to the lower boxes, which have a good lobby; as have also the upper tier. Charges £23. The benefit of favourite performers generally amounts to £60 or £70. The right hand entrances is to the Boxes to which there are two lobbies, lighted by the only windows in the elevation; the door on the left is to the Pit, gallery and Stage; here the old saying is verified "spoil the ship" etc., for the niche over each door, meant undoubtedly for Statues of Tragedy and Comedy; and the plinth at the top for the Royal Arms, both remain blanks.

The Fitzhughs were also friendly with Mrs Siddons's husband, the rather less successful actor William Siddons, who was somewhat estranged from his wife and chose to live in Bath, he wrote: '29 Sept 1805 did the Newspaper inform you that Mr Siddons had 'done me the honour of a visit to Bannisters'. In a letter to Mrs Piozzi, William Siddons wrote: 'Bath Oct 29 1805 Mrs & Mrs Fitzhugh dined with me in my little Oxford Cabbin yesterday. She lamented much she should leave Bath before your arrival –'

On November 10 1805 Mrs Siddons deferred her visit to Bath to: 'visit Mrs Fitzhugh at Southampton and tis convenient she should do it first as they (the Fitzhughs) are oblig'd to go to London the beginning of January, he being in Parliament'.[1] William Fitzhugh had become MP for Tiverton in 1803 - a post he held until 1819. '*Hampshire Telegraph* 17th August 1812 This town is very full of company. Mrs Siddons is on a visit to Mrs W Fitzhugh of Bannisters'.[2]

1 Letters of Sarah and William Siddons to Hester Lynch Piozzi in the John Rylands library.
2 The Letters of Sarah and William Siddons to Hester Lynch Piozzi edited by Kalman

Mrs Siddons stayed in touch with Mrs Fitzhugh even after she retired and wrote to her in her seventy-third year being anxious about her son George's children. Her son had a post in the East India Company but his children spent time with their grandmother whilst in England for their education. The great actress died in 1831 leaving a mourning ring to her friend.[1]

It seems that William Fitzhugh was in Paris in 1815 at the time of Waterloo as his nephew John Edwin Lance said his uncle had written to say that he could 'hardly resist taking a farewell leave of the Louvre'. It is not mentioned if his wife was with him.[2]

Back in England, Charlotte's husband had become very influential in regard to the development of Southampton and its transition back to a port after its spa heyday. He owned the *Prince of Coburg*, an early paddle steamer, that worked out of Southampton between 1820-66 taking passengers along

The Prince of Coburg, Southampton Cultural Services

    A. Burnim www.escholar.manchester.ac.uk 1969 pp. 83, 85.
1 The Annual Biography and Obituary for the year 1832 Vol XVI 1832 p. 171. Her son George was appointed a Writer in Bengal in 1803 and also spent time Bencoolen before returning to Calcutta as First Deputy to the Collector of Government Customs and Town Duties. James Trelawny Day *Letters from Bencoolen, 1823-28* pp.14, 114.
2 Letter of John Edwin Lance 29th August 1815 transcription held by Society of Genealogists.

the coast and over to the Isle of Wight. Fitzhugh went on to own a fleet of early steamers and daughter Emily christened the steamer *Princess Victoria* with a bottle of sherry in 1833.[1] Later that same year Charlotte, daughter Emily and William Fitzhugh attempted a crossing of the Channel to Cherbourg on the *Buccleugh* but were driven back to Swanage by bad weather.[2] William's company eventually became the Isle of Wight Steam Packet Company. In 1835 the family added a capital H into their name making it FitzHugh, such affectations had become popular during a period of gothic revival. A number of families added a 'de' to their name or returned to ancient spellings for family names inspired by the Eglinton Tournament, a re-enactment of a medieval joust and revel that had taken place in Eglinton Castle in 1839.[3]

Charlotte's husband died in 1842 although his will was first drafted in 1820 in which he recorded that Charlotte had purchased the painting of Mrs Siddons with her own money.[4] In this will as well as recording the ownership of the painting of Mrs Siddons, William also offered two paintings of his own to his wife if they were 'worthy of her acceptance' and left his drawings to his daughter Emily.[5]

Children

The Fitzhughs had four children, William, Sophia, Henry and Emily. Sophia had died young aged thirteen and in the same year, 1808, and month, that Charlotte lost her twelve-year-old son Henry. Formally a pupil at Winchester College in 1807 the boy had transferred to the Royal Navy. He was only eleven when he joined the service and should not have begun his qualifying period as a midshipman until he was thirteen. He was not the first young boy to conceal his age to go to sea. On May 16th, 1808 he was killed in action at the battle of Alvoen, whilst serving as a midshipman on *HMS Tartar*, alongside his twenty-three-year-old Captain, George Edmund Byron Bettesworth, cousin of Lord Byron. Their ship had been becalmed and was at the mercy of a schooner and five gun-boats. Lord Byron reckoned that his cousin had received four-

---

1 *Fitzhugh* p. 630.
2 Capt F T O'Brien *Early Solent Steamers A History of Local Steam Navigation* Newton Abbot 1973 p. 49.
3 *Fitzhugh* p. 631. For consistency the original spelling of the family name has been used in this book.
4 It might have been the death of his close friend, (brother-in-law and business partner) David Lance in 1820 that prompted William to compose his own will.
5 TNA PROB 11-1960-367. Mrs Siddons also sought William Fitzhugh's approval for a painting that she was attempting of her daughter Cecilia – he approved of it. Nina A Kennard *Mrs Siddons* Boston 1887 p. 332.

Henry Fitzhugh, private collection

and-twenty wounds in different places and possessed a letter from Lord Nelson which stated Bettesworth was the only naval officer who had more wounds than himself. The effect of putting himself in such danger may also have contributed to young Henry's death. Henry was stood next to his captain on the quarterdeck; they were both killed at the outbreak of the action:

> Among the first shots was one that killed Capt. Bettesworth while he was in the act of pointing a gun: and Mr Henry Fitzburgh (sic), a fine and promising young Midshipman, fell dead nearby at the same instant.[1]

HMS Tartar

The pair were the only men killed in the skirmish. A painting survives of young Henry, which was possibly painted by his father, just as he was about to embark on his naval career and Charlotte must have been glad to have had that image of her young son.

The surviving son William went first to Winchester College as a Commoner between 1806-09, then went to Christ Church, Oxford, from

---

1 William James *The Naval History of Great Britain Vol 5 1822* edited by Richard Perry reprint Mechanicsburg, Pennsylvania 2002 p. 35.

William Antony Fitzhugh, private collection

which he departed within a month having matriculated aged 17 in 1811. Three years later he reappeared as a pensioner of Trinity College Cambridge graduating with a BA in 1818.[1] He had decided on a career in the church and, in 1817, he became the curate at North Baddesley on the outskirts of Southampton.[2] William went on to take up the rectorship of Streat in West Sussex, which appointment was promoted by his mother-in-law Mary Lane, who had moved to Southampton after she was widowed in 1805.[3] He had married Mary Anne Lane in 1820 at Chevening in Kent (where her sister Harriet's husband, John Austen, was rector), she was the daughter of Thomas Lane. This marriage also linked the family to the Butler Harrisons and the Kent Austens who were connected via Mary's sister Harriet. A Henry Lane had been a business partner of William Fitzhugh and David Lance in their early days as company merchants though he does not appear to be connected to the Streat family. The living in Streat was in the gift of Henry Lane, William's brother-in-law, and had a value of £172. In 1822, William Fitzhugh also appointed William junior as his proxy when he was due to travel abroad. In the same year plans were approved for him to demolish and rebuild the Streat rectory which he also enlarged again in 1850. Streat Place was the ancestral home of the Fitzhugh relatives, the Dobells, since the 17th

---

1. Potential vicars could be offered positions as curates during their last year of study. Greg Smith 'Exploring training relationships between Training Incumbents and Curates in the Church of England and the Church in Wales: Listening to Training Incumbents in the post Hind era' PhD Thesis University of Warwick 2015 p. 4. William took his masters in 1822. There was a requirement to preach sermons as part of the degree's formal exercises which meant that a man had to be in orders before graduating. S SLinn *Ambition, Anxiety and Aspiration: the use and abuse of Cambridge University's Ten-year Divinity Statute.* University of Lincoln 2017 p. 4.
2. Ordination to priesthood HRO 21 M65 A2/4.
3. East Sussex Record Office Add Mss 11, 765 & 766, SAS-M/1/698. Her daughter Mary Ann also moved to the town.

century and the church had a Fitzhugh Chapel.[1] William and Mary went on to have seven children and, when William died in 1881, he left an estate worth £78,323 16s 1d.[2]

Emily remained at home as a companion to her mother and, like her, had celebrity friends and she appears in their letters and memoirs. These include the actress Fanny Kemble, Lady Byron, widow of the poet, and her daughter Ada Lovelace. Lady Byron was also a friend of the actress Sarah Siddons. Ada spent time in Southampton, and it was said her first experience of gambling in 1835, which eventually led her into huge debt took place at the Southampton races. Ada's son, Ralph, went to school in the town at the academy run by John Drew on Cumberland Place, which specialized in astronomy. Lady Byron sent details to Emily of Ada's last and fatal illness and also included items of gossip to be passed onto Emily's mother. Lady Byron used Emily as a prop and support in her relationship with her daughter Ada which had never been easy and at one point wrote 'you present to me dearest EF with the strongest portrait of myself as a mother'.[3] Emily's friendship with Fanny Kemble had begun in childhood:

Winchester College

1   The FitzHugh chapel was replaced with a large vestry in 1881.
2   William junior maintained interests in Southampton, in 1838 purchasing 6 Grosvenor Square and land at the Polygon from the estate of the bankrupt Charles Baker. SA D/PM 10/5.
3   Lovelace-Byron Collection Bodleian Library Letters 69 folios 118-269. The letters to Emily contain a detailed report on the treatments and the doctors who tried to help in the management of Ada's illness. This included Dr Symes who used mesmerism, Dr Locock who thought Ada was affected by *defective organisation* in her life and organised silver feeding tubes for her, Dr West founder of a hospital for

> I have alluded to a friendship which I formed soon after my appearance on the stage with Miss E F. She was the daughter of Mr F. for many years member for Tiverton, Miss F and I perpetuated a close attachment already traditional between our families, her mother having been Mrs Siddon's dearest friend, indeed for many years of her life - Fanny Kemble, *Records of a Girlhood.*

Also, Fanny recorded that Emily was revising Mrs Siddon's letters and that they had had an endless discussion of the nature of genius and creative power of the greatest actors. Emily had seen Fanny Kemble off when she left England having married the American, Pierce Butler. Whilst in America it gave Fanny a chance to write her memoirs. When Fanny returned to England somewhat destitute, after she and her husband ran into financial difficulties, she stayed with Emily at Bannisters. Fanny then travelled onto Italy and, on her return, lived in the Fitzhugh London home at 18 Portman Street for a year:[1]

> I go on very leisurely indeed with my Memoirs, and have got beyond the year 1839, the period of our return from Georgia. Yesterday I was looking over a number of Emily Fitzhugh's notes to you, written while I was staying at Banisters, after I came back from Italy, when I was obliged to resume my profession for a maintenance. They contained many details of my distressful bargainings with the London managers, about terms for my reappearance on the stage. Heaven knows, all that portion of my history is desolate and dreary enough and not worth preserving, for it can interest and amuse no one, and will never become interesting and amusing to me. (Fanny Kemble Letter March 1875)[2]

Emily was living in London at 41 Clarges Street, Piccadilly and left an estate of around £14,000 when she died in 1859. She wished her father's pictures to remain in the family but left a portrait of Fanny Kemble to her daughter Sarah Butler. In a codicil to her will she left her electro type novels to

sick children who treated her diarrhoea. Lady Byron was also tasked with finding a recipient for a £100 legacy in Ada's will. She consulted with Florence Nightingale about funding nurses for the poor and wrote she *liked her much better when I saw her engrossed by the object*. Florence's mother was one on the organising committee for the balls at The Dolphin in Southampton.

1 Deidre David *Fanny Kemble: A Performed Life* Pennsylvania 2007, p. 207.
2 University of Pennsylvania, Fanny Kemble *Further Records 1848-1883: A Series of Letters*, New York, c1891.

the museum at Southampton. This could have been a donation to the library that had been founded in the 1830s and housed in the Audit House. After a shaky start it had been expanded and a call out for donations occurred in the 1850s. By 1858 plans for a more prestigious building, the Hartley Institute, were underway and it may have been this institution Emily was intending to favour. In the event the Audit House library books were moved to the new Hartley Institute in 1863.[1] She asked to be buried in the simplest manner in the meanest cemetery or village church yard thinking, perhaps, of the family motto *In Moderation placing all my Glory*.[2]

Health

Charlotte Fitzhugh outlived her husband by fifteen years, dying in 1855, and her own will leads with the dispositions of her artwork.[3] Her son William received a picture by Carlo Dolci the subject being a daughter of Herodias (a copy of this painting is in the Royal Collection, and it is thought that there were two other copies). Five pictures painted by her husband went to her daughter Emily: a copy of a picture by Salvator Rosa, a copy of a picture by Claude Lorrain, a copy of a picture by Wilson (probably the landscape artist Richard Wilson), a picture whose subject was Knights Place and another featuring Venus in the Seas. She also left other pictures, not individually described, to her daughter. As well as her estate she also had Railway Shares. Her daughter Emily never married and died shortly after her mother in 1859 and was buried at Streat. The administration of her mother's will was passed to her only surviving child, William. Charlotte Fitzhugh was buried in the fashionable church of All Saints which had been built to resemble a Greek temple in the late eighteenth century. Unfortunately, the church was destroyed in the blitz of 1940. Charlotte's body was identified and taken for reburial in an unmarked plot at Hollybrook Cemetery. Her niece Emma Lance's body suffered the same fate.[4]

1 Richard Preston 'Pursuit of Knowledge under Difficulties': the Audit House Library, Southampton, 1831-63 and Winchester Library & Museum, 1851- 63, Local History Forum Journal pp. 1-13.
2 The motto was a quotation from Alexander Pope's *Satires of Horace*.
3 TNA PROB-11-2217-427 will of Charlotte Fitzhugh.
4 Emma Lance died 12th June 1810 aged nineteen reburied Hollybrook D4 42 Coffin 194.

ELIZABETH AUSTEN BUTLER HARRISON
(1766-1847)

Elizabeth Harrison was Jane Austen's second cousin and their fathers were very close in their youth and the families visited one another and are mentioned in family letters. Elizabeth Harrison did leave some letters; one is of particular interest as it probably describes her first encounter with her future husband (see Appendix Two) and there are also letters to her children. The other significant artefact was her household book inherited from her great- grandmother, Elizabeth Weller, filled with recipes donated by friends and family down the generations an heirloom which would pass to Elizabeth's eldest daughter, Elizabeth Matilda, and down the female family line to Sally Barton and now in the possession of her daughter Tamsyn.

Elizabeth Butler Harrison, silhouette, Southampton Archives

Early Life and Marriage

Elizabeth Austen was the eldest daughter of the Rev Henry Austen and his wife Mary Hooker whom he had married in 1763. Elizabeth had two brothers, Edgar and Henry, and a sister, Harriet. There had been one other sibling, George, who died young. Her father was the first cousin of Jane Austen's father, George, and as boys they had been educated together at Tonbridge School; twenty-two members of the extended Austen family lived at some point in Tonbridge. Henry Austen was the son of Thomas Austen, a Tonbridge apothecary, and, after leaving school, went on to Queen's College, Cambridge, being ordained at the early age of twenty-one. He was appointed perpetual curate at Shipbourne until 1754 when he was appointed curate of Chiddingstone, a village near to Tonbridge. Elizabeth's father had also been rector of Steventon from 1754-1761 which was where his cousin George followed him as vicar and where his daughter, Jane Austen, spent her early years. Henry moved to another family living at West Wickham in Kent. He spent little time himself in his Hampshire livings appointing curates to manage those whilst he stayed near to Tonbridge and the family home.[1] All of

---

1 Margaret Wilson *Jane Austen's family and Tonbridge* Jane Austen Society 2001 pp.

Henry and Mary's children were born at West Wickham. The family seemed like many Anglican households. Henry, however, had a crisis of faith whilst rector of West Wickham and he became a Unitarian and as a result had to give up the living. The family reported that the archbishop asked him to stay at his house and tried to persuade him not to give up his faith, but in vain. Henry went to live at Tonbridge near his father-in-law, John Hooker of Tonbridge Castle. Elizabeth, born in 1766, remained in the Church of England but her sister Harriet also became a Unitarian. Elizabeth was evidently sent away to school as she disclosed to her daughter, Jane, when the latter was also away being educated: 'I am much pleased you have the liberty of writing home without restraint, an indulgence I never had at school and therfor it was always irksome to me.'[1]

The two branches of the Austen family remained close. The Hampshire Austen's visited Tonbridge and, in 1786, Elizabeth visited Steventon. Elizabeth was twenty when she went on an extended visit to Hampshire. She stayed not only in Steventon but also Chawton where Jane Austen's brother was heir to the Chawton estate and then travelled on to Southampton. A surviving letter from Elizabeth to her father records her 1786 visit and her interaction with the Ballard and Butler Harrison family that she was soon to join:

July 11th. Mr Ballard arrived with his little Girl at the Hintons.
Thursday July 13th. we set off for Winchester. Mr B keeps a Phaeton and a pair

Chawton Great House

24-29.
1   SA D/Z 676/3 Letter of Elizabeth Butler Harrison.

of pretty grey poneys in which he drove Milly and myself, he also keeps a chaise like Mrs Sackville Austen only rather higher and with an head to it, which Mr Harrison makes use of and accordingly drove his sister in.[1]

Robert Ballard did move in exalted circles and, in 1788, was a member of a water party along with the Mary Temple, Viscountess Palmerston who wrote to her husband the second Viscount on 6th August 1788:

> On Monday we set off from Southampton at ten in an open boat as there was not wind enough to allow of our making use of the cutter. Our party, the Hatsells, Sloane, Stephen, Maria, Captain Southerby, Mr Ballaird and a Mr and Mrs Barton great friends of the D'Oyleys, and in truth in that consists all their merit, for I have not often seen more disagreeable people. We had a most delightful row to Governor Hornby. I think you have been there and I dare say admire the situation which is in my opinion in point of view superior to anything in this country. We went on board the yatch which lies at anchor in the Hamble River which is certainly a most complete vessel. We then row'd up to Netley where we had a most elegant dinner, Sloane having sent his cook to prepare our repast, and in the cool of the evening we repair'd to the Abby which considering every circumstance of the trees, the emannance of the ivy, the beautiful state and the situation of the ruins please me more than any I ever saw. We drank tea in the abby and came home by land. I return'd to Broadlands that night.[2]

Like many visitors to the watering place of Southampton Elizabeth enjoyed excursions to Winchester, Netley Abbey, the Isle of Wight and the New Forest: 'Mr Harrison was so kind as to conduct Milly and me to Shaysbrook (Carisbrooke) Castle. On Sunday we din'd and drunk tea with a Mr and Mrs Rogers whose neice Mr Ballard is going to be married to.' Mary Challoner Wood (1756-1829), was the niece of the Rogers whom Robert Ballard married as his second wife.[3] 'Tomorrow we spend day at Lyndhurst in the New Forrest (Thursday July 27th), a villa of Mr Ballard's.' The 1781 *Southampton Guide* describes the villa as: 'a small cottage, called Northwood, or Northenwood, from whence the eye takes in so many objects, that one is at a loss which part of the prospect to select, and admire most.' Elizabeth enjoyed her trip and wrote

1 Milly was his cousin Melicent Ballard, and his sister was his half sibling Elizabeth Goring Butler Harrison.
2 MS 62 Broadlands Archives BR 11/13/1.
3 SA D/PM 54/72 John Butler Harrison was the trustee of the marriage settlement of Robert Ballard and Mary Challenor, she went on to marry William James Le Feuvre of Southampton.

to her father: 'You see I'm always engaged & happy. I sung forth the praises of Steventon and now I sing forth the praises of Southampton.'

Her father replied with a note of caution:

> My dear Bess, We are much pleased with your truly entertaining narratives. ... don't overstay your visits to friends, but I submit to your plan as your principal adviser is Mr Hinton's and my daughter Harrison.

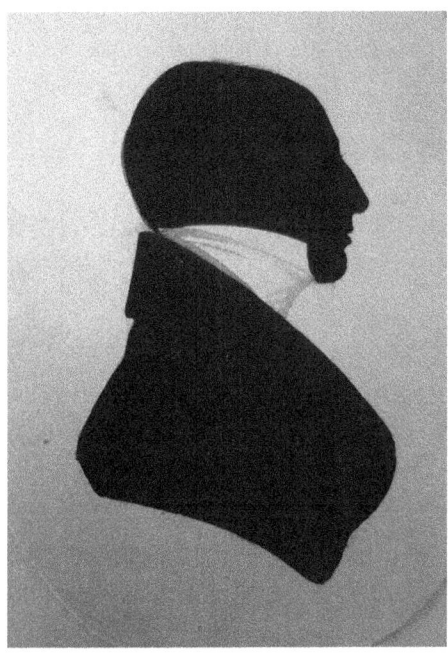

John Butler Harrison II, silhouette, Southampton Archives

The Rev John Hinton, married to John Butler Harrison II's aunt Jane Harrison, and John's orphaned half-sister, Elizabeth Goring Butler Harrison, had been brought up by the Hintons at Chawton but had also been under the guardianship of the Rev Henry Austen. It is not surprising that John Butler Harrison II and Elizabeth Austen were thrown into each other's company. John had come into his inheritances in 1788, when he reached the age of twenty-one, not only from his father but also his grandfather. Robert Ballard senior, and had already joined the civic elite of Southampton as a junior bailiff. John Butler Harrison II, on concluding his education in Lausanne in 1784, had been offered a number of career options by his uncle and guardian, Robert Ballard, including clerkships in the Treasury and the Admiralty or a secretariat post to Sir James Harris in the Hague. Robert Ballard also suggested that when his father-in-law and business partner, Lenard Cropp,[1] died John could join the firm or possibly consider banking as a career. His guardian also proposed that when he finished school, he might spend a year in France to perfect his accent in the language. John Butler Harrison had chosen to join the wine company of his guardian Robert Ballard junior. He was therefore, in 1788, prime marriage material and for Elizabeth from a well to do but not a wealthy family John was a catch.

---

[1] Lenard Cropp died in 1785 TNA PROB 11-1136-175.

On 20th February 1789, John Butler Harrison II and Elizabeth Austen were married at Chawton, the ceremony being performed by the curate Peter - John Dusautoy. The witnesses were Elizabeth Goring Harrison, her husband's half-sister, Mary Hinton (the daughter of the Rev John Hinton of Chawton, who married James Dusautoy in 1795), Elizabeth Hinton, William F Woodgate,[1] Melicent Ballard (the daughter of Robert and Melicent

John Butler Harrison I, Southampton Archives

Ballard) and Jane Hinton, John's aunt.[2] Of Elizabeth's journey to Chawton for her wedding it was written that she:

> was one of the most beautiful women in Kent & on her way to Chawton (a family place in Hants) to be married, her carriage was escorted as far as the boundaries of Kent by young men of the county on horseback.[3]

Elizabeth Goring Butler Harrison, silhouette, Southampton Archives

1   William Frank Woodgate was probably a friend of the Austen family. A recipe for his 'Plumb Pudding' written in Elizabeth Matilda's handwriting is in the household book.
2   SA D/Z 676/10/3 Helena Austen Harrison papers, extracts from Chawton Parish Register.
3   Deidre Le Faye, *Jane Austen A Family Record* 2nd Edition, Cambridge 2004 p. 86.

The couple set up house in Southampton in a new property John had acquired in 1789 having disposed of his father's property, Amery House, in Alton. Their new home was situated in the ancient parish of St Mary's on the eastern side of the town, in what was then known as Love Lane, and had a rateable value of £30 for the main house and £8 for the coach house and stables, one of the highest rateable values in the town. The property had

Amery House

a detached garden in St Mary Street and, in 1790, John acquired another two acres in the common land known as Hoglands which he leased for cultivation. John could have afforded to live further out in the country but his involvement in town affairs probably was part of the decision to live in the town. He went on to hold the post of Collector of Customs from 1803 until just before his death and was Deputy Lieutenant of the Militia, Commissioner of the Land Tax and Receiver at the Customs House for the Merchant Seaman's Hospital. He was appointed one of the first harbour commissioners for Southampton when the body was established in 1803. He was also one of the pavement commissioners which was set up by Act of Parliament with the responsibility for paving, repairing and cleansing of streets and public passages, to prevent nuisances and annoyances: 'widening and rendering the same new commodious and for the lighting and watching the said districts'.[1] He also would serve two terms as mayor in 1794 and 1811 and was a Justice of the Peace in 1815.

1 J Stovold, *Minute Book of The Pavement Commissioners for Southampton 1770-1789*, Southampton Records Series, Southampton 1990 p. 5.

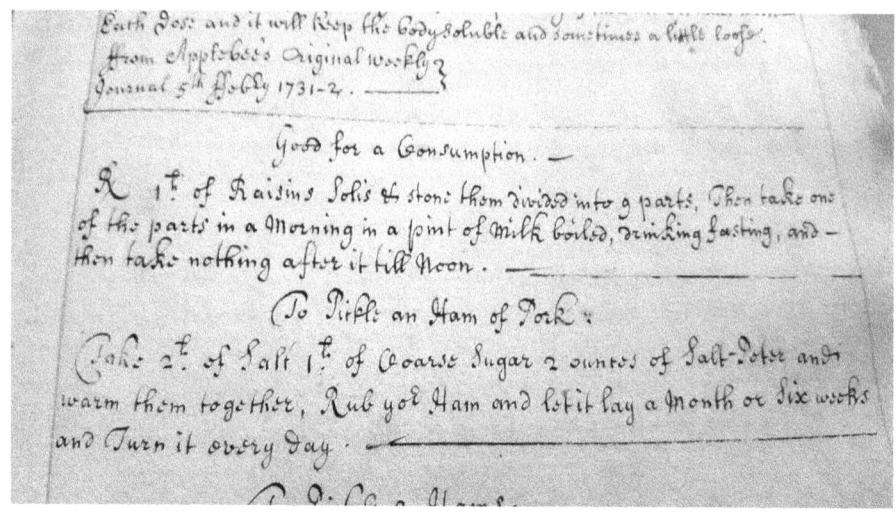
Household Book recipe, private collection

One of the gifts that Elizabeth brought with her to begin her new life was the household book begun by her great-grandmother Elizabeth Weller who had spent her widowhood as a housekeeper to a bachelor headmaster at Sevenoaks School to make ends meet.[1] The book was destined to be used by generations of the family until its last entry in 1915. The majority of recipes and household hints date from the book's inception and from the period that it was in the custody of Elizabeth Butler Harrison. There are over 205 entries and many have names attached to them of the friends and relations who donated the recipes to the book. The topics range from the culinary to the medicinal and the household items even include a cosmetic recipe for colouring red or grey hair. Many recipes are very clearly written and also show the influences of colonisation and empire. There are recipes for sugar cakes, (sugar being a major import from the West Indian plantations), Portingall cake and for wines including wine which benefited from the wine trade in which John Butler Harrison was involved. Curries and punches were made fashionable thanks to the East India Company. Medical recipes include palsey water, which you can drink or bathe in, and a recipe which does not specify its medical use but should be taken at the 'change and flush' of the moon. There are unusual ingredients such as the one which begins 'Take Dragons', and recipes for stump pye. Household hints show a liquor for boots and shoes, mahogany colouring for furniture and a cleaning product for grates, plus information on making ink, poison, and dyeing gauze. There are several recipes for the bite of a mad dog, so this must have been a bigger problem than is perhaps

1 Household book, private collection.

realized, and a cure for dog bites was a major promotion by the watering place of Southampton

Many of the ingredients required for recipes seem exotic to the modern reader. The Ladies Pocket Guide gave helpful hints as to what things should be kept in the house by small families for kitchen use.[1] Spices bought from a reputable grocer: nutmegs, cloves, mace, cinnamon, ginger, Jamaica pepper, black pepper and long pepper. Sweet herbs kept in paper bags: red sage, baum, thyme, sweet marjoram, mint, pennyroyal and not to be without shallots, onions and such like. Dried orange and lemon peel, capers, pickled walnuts, pickled cucumber, cucumbers in mango, anchovies, olives, pickled mushroom, dried and powdered mushrooms and ketchup or mushroom juice. A garden would make it possible to gather herbs at any time except the mint or sweet marjoram which were not considered good in cold weather.

In 1793 Elizabeth welcomed her cousins, Jane and Cassandra Austen, to her home probably escorted by their brother Francis. Elizabeth was joined by her sister, Harriet. Her brother, Edgar, was also part of the household and at the age of fifteen, in 1790, he had been articled by his father to the lawyer Thomas Ridding, town clerk of Southampton and thereby a near associate of Elizabeth's husband.[2] Ridding's archive shows Edgar working on a power of attorney, serving subpoenas and latitats (a writ based on the assumption the person is hiding) and, in 1793, witnessing the sealing of articles for Edmund Ludlow to become a clerk.[3] In 1794 he was coming to the end of his articles and would have been of an age with his cousin Jane and, perhaps, was a partner at the Dolphin balls she attended during her visit. Elizabeth herself was pregnant with her daughter, another Elizabeth, and her cousin Jane stayed on with the family and became god-mother to the baby. Her husband was about to be elected mayor at the age of twenty-seven, an event tinged with sadness as that same year his uncle and guardian Robert Ballard died aged 57. A year later, the second daughter, Mary, was born and her godparents were recorded as Mrs Morris, Miss Austen, Mr Mottley and Francis Austen. The Miss Austen was probably Harriet, Elizabeth's sister who had joined the Butler Harrison household. Harriet Austen was also godparent to her nephew Edward in 1799, along with her and Elizabeth's father, the Rev Henry (Harry) Austen. Harriet performed the same service for her niece Jane Butler Harrison. By this time Edgar Austen had returned to Tonbridge but changed career from lawyer to clergyman. This might have been the result of declining health. A

1   SA D/PM 42 3/20a the Ladies Useful Repository.
2   SA D/PM 45/3/54.
3   SA D/PM 45/3/74, 45/3/75, 45/3/78, 45/3/80.

letter from Francis Allnut in the Woodgate family archive of 1801 recorded this description of Edgar and his married sister Elizabeth:[1]

> I saw Mrs Harrison on Friday at Uncle John's [John Hooker], never was more shock'd in my life, she realy (sic) looks quite starved, and has not the remains of a pretty Woman. Edgar was likewise there. I have not seen him since he became a Benedict;[2] he is very much withered and looks extremely ill.

The decision of Elizabeth's father, Henry Austen, to leave the Church of England and join the Unitarian movement had a direct impact on Elizabeth and her siblings.[3] He lost his living and standing in the community and it is perhaps this reason that his two other children Edgar and Harriet spent time living with their sister in Southampton. In Southampton the younger Austens could benefit from the influence of their brother-in-law and there was a significant non-conformist movement in the town. Harriet initially joined her sister's home to help support her growing family - a role that spinster aunts often fulfilled as in evident in the lives of Harriet's cousins Jane and Cassandra Austen.

Elizabeth's husband's senior position in the Southampton corporation meant he had to host two royal visits; in July 1795 that of Prince Frederick, Duke of York and in September George, Prince of Wales. Life was not so happy for all the residents of the town and, in November, Harrison had to provide 40 or 50 tons of potatoes to be sold to the poor at a reduced price along with the corporation spending £225 on coal for the poor during the winter.

It was not long before Elizabeth suffered losses in her close family; her mother had died in 1799 and she was to lose brother Edgar who died in 1804 aged just 29 and her father in 1807. Her elder brother Henry had died as a child, aged just seven, in 1772. There was little, therefore, to keep Elizabeth's sister Harriet in Tonbridge and she moved permanently to Southampton

---

1 G Woodgate & G M G Woodgate, *The History of the Woodgates of Stonewall Park and of Summerhill in Kent,* Wisbech 1910 p. 391.
2 A 'benedict' was a newly married man who had been a long-time bachelor, although Edgar was only twenty-six at this time and had married a Miss Greenwood. SA D/Z 676/2.
3 The Act of Toleration in 1689 had granted religious freedom to a number of dissenting sects, except for Catholics and Unitarians. The latter because they did not believe in the Trinitarian doctrine. The first Unitarian congregation met in London in 1774. Although not pursued in the courts for their beliefs, Unitarians did experience social exclusion not resolved until the 1813 Doctrine of the Trinity Act which allowed people freedom to question the idea of the Trinity, God the Father, the Son and Holy Ghost.

by 1800 at the latest when Thomas Ridding drafted her will.[1] She did not however acquire her own property until 1819 when she purchased a house just north of the Bargate, and a short walk from her sister, part of a relatively new development built by the engineer Walter Taylor III (designer of blocks and pulleys for the navy). He had built on a patch of land which was on the old town moat, called the Ditches, on Houndwell Lane and renamed the area Hanover Buildings as a compliment to the frequent visits by members of the royal family to the spa town. The house was described as being around 19 feet in its frontage, with a garden, and Harriet purchased the residue of a 40-year lease valued at £407 10s.[2] Her annual payment for the lease was 3s 4d and two capon.[3] Harriet had been living in the property as a lodger with the painter Tobias Young's family, who had not been able to afford the lease when it came up for sale. Harriet stepped in to secure the property.

When the family of Jane Austen moved to Southampton in 1806 they were reacquainted with their Butler Harrison relations and they feature in her letters of the period. One of Jane Austen's letters, written from Godmersham, to Cassandra on 20th June 1808 underlines the close connections between the Harrisons and Austens during the period when they were living in Southampton: 'Happy Mrs Harrison & Miss Austen! You seem to be always calling upon them.'[4]

Jane wrote to Cassandra from Castle Square later in the year on October 1st & 2nd 1808:[5]

> About an hour and a half after your toils on Wednesday ended ours labours began; - at seven o'clock Mrs Harrison, her two daughters & two visitors, with Mr Debary & his eldest sister walked in; & our Labour was not a great deal shorter than poor Elizabeth's, for it was past eleven before we were delivered. – A second pool of Commerce; & all the longer by the addition of the two girls, who during the first had one corner of the Table & Spillikins to themselves, was the ruin of us; - it completed the prosperity of Mr Debary however, for he

1 SA D/PM 30/2 Will of Harriet Austen, bequests god-daughter Mary Saxby of Tunbridge £50, god-daughter & niece Elizabeth Harrison £100, god-son and nephew Edward Harrison £100, John Butler Harrison II £500 and silver plate. Books to be divided equally between the children of her sister Elizabeth. John & Elizabeth Butler Harrison all rents, investments, residue.
2 SA D/PM 58/3/5.
3 SA SC4/3/1425 1827.
4 This Miss Austen was Harriet Lennard Austen, sister of Elizabeth Austen. *Jane Austen's Letters* p. 131.
5 *Jane Austen's Letters* p. 140.

won them both. –

Mr Harrison came in late, & sat by the fire - for which I envied him, as we had our usual luck of having a very cold Even'g. It rained when our company came, but was dry again before they left us. – The Miss Ballards are said to be remarkably well-informed; their manners are unaffected & pleasing, but they do not talk quite freely enough to be agreeable – nor can I discover any right they had by Taste or Feeling to go their late Tour.

Mrs Harrison's two daughters would have been Elizabeth–Matilda who was fifteen and Mary–Hooker who was thirteen. Peter Debary was the recently appointed vicar of Eversley, Hampshire. The Misses Ballard may have been Mary and Frances Ballard daughters of Dr John Ballard who were born in the years 1783 and 1784, who were cousins to John Butler Harrison II.[1] A week later October 7th – 9th, Jane is writing again to her sister:

On Tuesday even'g Southampton was in a good deal of alarm for about an hour; a fire broke out soon after nine at Webbes, the Pastrycook, and burnt for some time with great fury.

The Flames were considerable, they seemed as near to us as those at Lyme, & to reach higher – happily however the night was perfectly still, the Engines were immediately put to use, & before ten the fire was nearly extinguished.- The Croud in the High St. I understand was immense; Mrs Harrison, who was drinking tea with a Lady at Millar's could not leave it til twelve o'clock.[2]

Thomas Webb's establishment was at 153 High Street.[3] Elizabeth may have been taking tea at Robert Miller, the pastrycook's, at 114 High Street. Fire was an ever-present danger at a time when candles provided light and clothes were easily flammable.[4] A fire at another local bakery in French Street meant a

1. In 1812 Mary Ballard married her distant cousin Charles Goring, she was his third wife and he was forty years her senior, John Ridding the nephew of Thomas Ridding had had some hopes in regard to Mary which his uncle showed little sympathy with SA D/PM 36/4 Letters of Thomas Ridding. Frances did not marry George Wells until she was forty-eight. Jane Goring, Joyce Sleight, Jill Turner, Janet Pennington & Janine Harvey *Lives, Loves and Letters: The Goring Family of Wiston, Sussex 1743-1905* Sussex 2017 pp. vi, 40.
2. *Jane Austen's Letters* pp. 143-144.
3. SA D/PM 54/12 lease of a dwelling house to Thomas Webb pastrycook, St Lawrence parish, west side of the High St 1813.
4. In 1795 Miss Taylor of Southampton on a visit to her uncle on the IOW stood too near the fire and was suddenly enveloped in flames and was badly burnt, dying seven days later aged just 27. In 1801 Lady Hardy, widow of Admiral Sir Charles

loss of all plum puddings baked for Christmas.¹

There were thirteen² different insurance companies operating in Southampton in 1811 whose plaques householders would affix to the exterior of their buildings to identify them for company fire engines.³ Lansdowne House, which stood between the High Street and the Austen's home on Castle Square, still retains its two plaques. A few years later, in 1816, a more serious fire took place not far from Castle Square when the house of a straw-bonnet maker caught fire and the engines of the South Hants Militia arrived on the scene, along with 200 bystanders. Lack of an effective water supply saw the fire spread to adjoining properties including one containing six sleeping children. Charles Ward, one of the militia officers, effected an heroic rescue but was then killed by falling masonry when the building collapsed. The fire destroyed four houses and a stable in a case suspected of being arson linked to an insurance claim. Ward was buried with military honours at Nursling.⁴

Later in Jane Austen's same letter there is a first mention of Elizabeth's eldest son, John Butler Harrison III then aged eighteen: *Sunday - Mr John Harrison has paid his first visit of duty & is gone*. The next letter, dated a week later, from Jane Austen to Cassandra was in answer to the sudden news that Edward Knight's wife Elizabeth had died a fortnight after the birth of their eleventh child:

> Hardy fell asleep whilst reading and her dress caught fire from a nearby candle. Though she was rolled up in a carpet by servants she died the next morning. She had had similar accidents twice before. From articles in the Hampshire Chronicle. The Atherley Papers SA D/S2/2/6.

1   September 14th 1795 a fire destroyed three baking houses in Grave's yard, the Three Tuns public house in French Street, Mrs Archer's house and 12000 faggots piled in the yard. No lives were lost but a pig and a very fine dog were victims of the flames. The Atherley Papers SA D/S 19/1/2.
2   Sun, Royal Exchange, Phoenix, Salamander, Imperial, British, Norwich Union, Hope, County, Globe, Eagle, Hampshire, Sussex & Dorset, London Corporation. The Sun Insurance Company was very popular with East India Company families, probably because its managers had links with the company and also with the Bank of England. Peter Dickson *The Sun Insurance Office, 1710-1960* Oxford 1960 pp. 270-9.
3   A town fire service was not established until c1837. A serious fire in 1825 destroyed the uninsured stock of a leading coachmaker, it was found the fire service hoses were in bad repair and not all the firemen had turned out. At a fire ten years later only 14 of 36 firemen turned up and only two of those were sober.
4   *Hampshire Telegraph & Sussex Chronicle* 9th February 1816 and the *Hampshire Chronicle* of the same date.

From Castle Square October 15th – 16th.

We are desired by Mrs Harrison & Miss Austen to say everything proper for them to Yourself and Edward on this sad occasion – especially that nothing but a wish of not giving additional trouble where so much is inevitable, prevents their writing themselves to express their Concern. – They seem truly to feel concern.[1]

The final letter in which the Harrison family are mentioned was written by Jane Austen to Cassandra from Castle Square on January 24th, 1809:

Your silence on the subject of our Ball, makes me suppose your Curiosity too great for words. The room was tolerably full, & the Ball opened by Miss Glyn; - Caroline Maitland had an officer to flirt with, & Mr John Harrison was deputed by Capt. Smith being himself absent, to ask me to dance.[2]

John Butler Harrison III, silhouette, Southampton Archives

John Butler Harrison II became mayor again in 1812 when the honorary burgesses included the Marquis of Wellington as well as Harrison's two eldest boys, John now at Magdalen College, Oxford and Henry of the Royal Navy Pay Office, Somerset House. From a letter that Elizabeth wrote in 1817 it suggests that the boys were all sent away to school as George, not ten, and William, fourteen, were both away and her daughter Jane, sixteen, was also away at school. By this time her eldest daughter Elizabeth was already married and her eldest son John had become a clergyman.

In 1839, on the occasion of their fiftieth anniversary, all the family gathered except for George and his wife who were in India. The party also

1 *Jane Austen's Letters* p. 148.
2 *Jane Austen's Letters* p. 170.

Elizabeth Butler Harrison in older age, private collection

John Butler Harrison II in older age, private collection

included Elizabeth's sister-in-law, Elizabeth Goring Butler Harrison and her grand-daughter Frances Margeritta Austen. In all, eighteen sat down for dinner. At the end a silver inkstand was presented inscribed:

presented to John Butler and Elizabeth Matilda Harrison on the Fiftieth Anniversary of their Wedding day By their ten affectionate children as a memorial of their grateful recollection of their unwearied parental love and with every feeling of devout Gratitude to Almighty God for His wonderful Mercy in preserving so large a family in health and happiness and without a visitation from Death for half a Century. 20th of Feb 1839

Following on from the celebrations Elizabeth left to spend a month with her eldest son John at his parish of Evenley. The preservation of the family however ended in 1840 when Elizabeth's younger son George died en route back to England.

Winchester College

Children

The Butler Harrison's favoured John's old school at Winchester for the education of their sons but certainly daughter Jane also was sent away to school as is shown by a surviving letter from her mother. A poem from daughter Elizabeth suggests Manniford as the site for the girl's school. Elizabeth however was also not backward in correcting her children's grammar and generally overseeing their education herself. It is likely that the girls were receiving an education similar to that of little Millie Ballard a generation earlier. Skills in the creative decorative arts are illustrated by a rare survival of a handmade letter case made by Elizabeth's eldest grand-daughter Elizabeth Matilda for her Aunt Fanny complete with a poem, the initials of the recipient garlanded with beautifully illustrated flowers and a naive illustration of a reindeer pulling a lady in a toboggan. The boys when younger also spent time with their grandfather Henry Austen who had of course been a teacher and ran a school in Tonbridge and he drilled them in Latin amongst other studies.

The Butler Harrison marriage was eventually blessed with ten children. John Butler Harrison III, born in 1790, was educated at Winchester College and Magdalen College Oxford and trained to become a member of the clergy. He was privately ordained in the chapel of St Mary College, Winchester, by

George Isaac, Bishop of Gloucester. He married Mary Anne Hyde. As a Church of England priest he subscribed to the thirty-nine articles and the three articles in the thirty sixth Canon and took the requisite oaths. He went on to become rector of Evenley in Northamptonshire, in 1832, where he remained until his death in 1871.

Henry, who entered the civil service, was born in 1791 and named for his cousin, Jane Austen's brother Henry Austen. He married Susan Standen and they had four children.[1] In 1812, when he was made a burgess of Southampton, it was recorded that he was in the Navy Pay Office. Charles, born in 1797, was also educated at Winchester College and returned to live in Southampton at the new Regency style development on the outskirts of the town, Carlton Crescent; he married Emily Morris, but had no children, and died, aged 80, in 1878.

Henry Butler Harrison, silhouette, Southampton Archives

Edward, born 1799, also established himself in Southampton at the Polygon and worked as a solicitor, like his uncle before him, in the practice of the town clerk, Thomas Ridding. Edward was also childless, though married to Caroline Courtney. Caroline was interested in Natural History and successfully bred a marmoset monkey as well as having rare specimens of feathers which she exhibited at the Hampshire Ornithological Association.[2] Edward went on to have his own firm of solicitors, Sharp, Harrison & Turner. He had as one of his clients Henry Robinson Hartley, a wealthy eccentric, who left his fortune to the corporation to be spent on an educational establishment. Edward led the case when the will was challenged and eventually after

Letter holder made by Elizabeth Matilda Austen jnr, private collection

---

1   Clive Caplan *Jane Austen's Soldier Brother* in JASNA Persuasions 18 1996 p. 125.
2   SA D/Z 676/2.

left: Charles Butler Harrison, silhouette, private collection
right: Edward Butler Harrison. Silhouette, Southampton Archive

five years, successfully upholding the will and achieving £110,000 for the town. The money was spent on establishing the Hartley Institute, the forerunner of Southampton University.[1] Another well-known client was Lady Byron, widow of the poet, who used the services of Edward Butler Harrison when she was wishing to find out what was a fair discount on a note for £100 which was held by Bernard Hewkel.[2] Edward was still living in the Polygon, aged 81. His death notice in the local press noted he was: 'The son of a gentleman holding a position in H M Customs, and who in his day was the life and soul of local musical circles.' It also noted that throughout his career Mr Harrison was a decided Liberal in politics.

Edward's brother William born in 1802, another Magdalen scholar, and in 1848 became rector of Winterborne Bassett in Wiltshire until his death. He married first Catherine Sladen and secondly to Marie Bauer, a German lady

1 Alexander Anderson, *Hartleyana Henry Robinson Hartley, Eccentric-Scholar-Naturalist, Founder of the University of Southampton,* Southampton Records Series Supplementary Volume, Southampton 1987 pp .205-13.
2 Guide to the Lady Byron Manuscript Material in the Pforzheimer Collection at the New York Public Library.

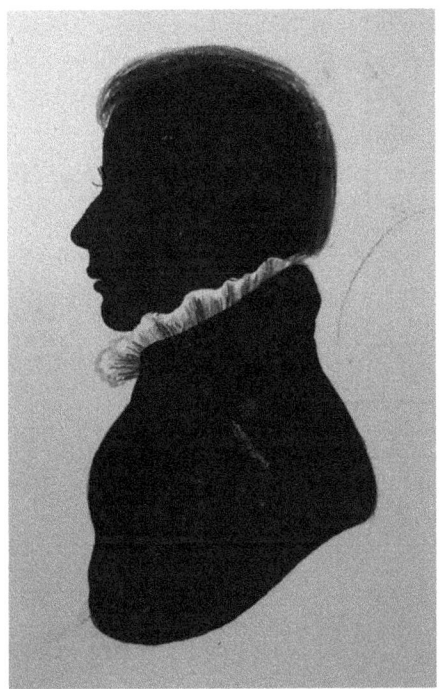 

left: William Butler Harrison, silhouette, Southampton Archives
right: George Butler Harrison, silhouette, Southampton Archives

and former governess to the Morris family. William died after being thrown from his horse in 1857. The accident was recorded in the Wiltshire Advertiser in that September, William had been out riding with his sister-in-law when his horse shied and he was thrown with great violence to the ground. His injuries were so severe he died twelve hours later without having spoken. He was buried in a vault at Winterbourne churchyard by the side of his late first wife who had died in 1854; he had recently contributed £500 towards the restoration of the church. A cross was erected on the road between Winterbourne and Broadhinton marking the spot where he was thrown. He was survived by his second wife Marie Bauer, whom he had only married the year before, and his son, from his first marriage, Frank, orphaned at just seven years of age.[1]

The youngest brother George, born in 1808, joined the Indian army. He married Sarah Shield and died young in 1840 whilst returning from

1   Frank was brought up by his maternal grandparents and his father's sisters Frances and Jane. He was sent to Twyford Prep School and then onto Harrow as it was considered that *bullying was too bad at Winchester*. SA D/Z 676/5/10. William was the grandfather of Helena Austen Harrison who donated her father Frank's archive *The Red Book* to the Southampton Archives.

India.[1] This career may have been a result of his father's connections with the many East India Company men who lived in Southampton such as Nathaniel Middleton, Valentine and William Fitzhugh and David Lance. The East India Company governed India until the 1850s and had its own army to help it maintain control, which is where George served.

John Butler Harrison III seems to have been particularly close to his sister Elizabeth Matilda to whom he wrote an ode on the occasion of her ninth birthday when he was just twelve:

> Niny to you my willing muse
> Present this humble verse
> To shew you though I sometimes teaze
> I do not love you worse
>   Consider thought not very old
> Yet you to day are nine
> And surely you will strive t'improved
> And make best use of time
>   When in good humour you are dress'd
> Then you need never fear
> For that improveth every grace
> And makes you fair appear
>   But when you look so very glum
> So sadly out of temper
> Who do you think will play with you
> Indeed I will not venture
>   And then gentility should be
> The next thing to attend to
> Or else without it you will find
> Not any one commend you
>   And learn my dearest Ninny too
> How you should take a joke
> For being very cross and glum
> Serves only to provoke
>   And now Elizabeth I hope
> From this my humble verse
> You will a little profit gain
> Instead of growing worse
>   And may you ev'ry year increase

1 SA D/Z 676/2.

In Wisdom and in health
Which you may very well obtain
Without the power of Wealth
Dec 17th 1802[1]

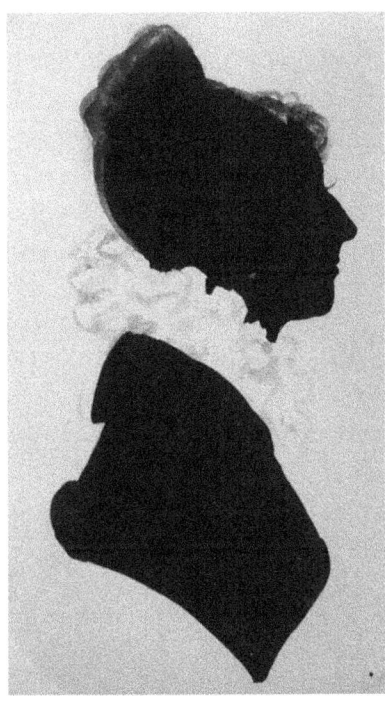

Elizabeth Matilda Butler Harrison, silhouette, Southampton Archives

The Butler Harrisons eldest daughter Elizabeth, born 1793 and god-daughter of young Jane Austen, married her cousin the Reverend William Austen. They married at St Mary's Church Southampton in 1814. The wedding was a lavish affair, as reported by Jane Austen's mother in a letter to her granddaughter, Anna Lefroy, in December 1814. It seemed the Butler Harrisons were generous in the distribution of Bride-Cake to all their relations.[2] Mrs Austen wrote that ten couples had attended the wedding ceremony after which the couple travelled into Sussex where William was the incumbent of Horsted Keynes. She was as waspish as her daughter in commenting on William's good and sweet temper whilst remarking on his lack of physical beauty. His wife however was accounted to be beautiful, like her mother but being of a livelier disposition:

> Last week I received a piece of nice Bride-Cake (just like yours) from Southampton, with Mr & Mrs William Austen's kind regards – her Wedding was a much grander affair than yours, Ten Couple walked to Church (they had not far to walk you know) entirely composed of near relations, the Brides Father, Mother, Aunts, Brothers, Sisters & Cousins Morris, and two of the Bridegroom's Brothers: Mrs Campion (his Eldest Sister) sent her Carriage to convey them into Sussex, and into Sussex they are going – his Parsonage-House is but an indifferent one, and situated in a bad Country, notwithstanding which I hope & believe they will be very happy – He is remarkable for the goodness of his principles & the sweetness of his temper, (I believe very far from handsome) – She is very amiable, inherits some share of her Mother's beauty, with a much more lively disposition; her countenance and manners remarkably pleasing

1 Private collection, Colin Hyde Harrison.
2 Ann Govas *Jane Austen's Horsted Keynes Relations* Hayward's Heath 2017 p. 35.

It is obvious from a touching letter Elizabeth Matilda wrote in January 1815 that she was missing her mother and siblings (see Appendix Two) and perhaps explains the couples later return to Southampton. The couple had three children, two daughters, another Elizabeth Matilda and Frances Margaretta who both lived to adulthood, and a son, William George who died aged just four.[1] When William retired in 1840 the couple moved to Southampton where William had previously been made a burgess of the town in 1816.[2] The 1843 directory shows them living at 74 Marland Place, later moving to Anglesea Place by 1851 along with their two unmarried daughters. William died in 1854 and his wife and eldest daughter followed him in 1855. Their younger daughter Frances Margaretta then moved in with her aunt Mrs Cary and she died in 1885. The family graves are to be found in Southampton Old Cemetery.

Elizabeth's other daughters: Mary, born in 1795, Jane, born in 1801, and Frances, born in 1805, remained as spinsters in their father's home. In the 1841 census they are recorded as being 49, 45 and 35. Their household also consisted of three servants Elizabeth and Mary Wateridge, aged 25 and 20 and Frances Lipscombe who was 25. In 1814 Frances was left £200 from her god-mother Sarah Ottley Hooker, the widow of Thomas Hooker of Tunbridge Castle.[3] Sarah was living as a widow in Testwood near Southampton and had inherited Marble Hill in Antigua from Ottley relations. Frances later married the Rev Cary, vicar of St Paul's Church in Southampton. When she was widowed, Frances came to live at Gloucester House, Brunswick Place, Southampton along with her unmarried sister Jane. Jane died in 1878 and Frances in 1892 aged 77 aged 86 respectively. Mary had died in 1868 at her home in Park Place, Southampton. Frances's obituary noted her work among the poor of St Paul's parish and as superintendent of the Sunday School. It was noted that she was daughter-in-law of

Frances Butler Harrison, silhouette, Southampton Archives

---

1 Ibid p. 41.
2 SA SC2/1/13 Council Minute Book 1816.
3 TNA PROB 11/1006/104 will William Otley.

the Rev H Cary, the translator of Dante, and a cousin of Jane Austen, the novelist. Mary, Frances and Jane are buried at the Southampton Old Cemetery along with the family of their elder sister Elizabeth and their brother Charles.

Health

When Elizabeth set up her own household armed with her mother's household book her own entries relate primarily to medicinal cures. The first were donated to her by Mrs Biddulph[1] and begin with a recipe to treat the whooping cough which could be fatal as this time. The next is for a sore throat and included ingredients such as the fat of a loin of mutton, saltless butter and beeswax and was designed to be worn, rather than eaten, spread on a rag secured around the throat. Also entered was a cure approved by one Dr Addington,[2] as well as other physicians, for putrid throat (an ailment which so concerned Mr Wodehouse in *Emma*). As a woman who was almost constantly pregnant, the next concoction was a breast salve, which might suggest Elizabeth did not use a wet-nurse. The main ingredients being beeswax and honey and diachylum armgaminis,[3] its virtue being that it was good for any pain in the breast, including cancer of the breast, and left little scarring. It was also said to cure gangrene as evidenced by Sir Robert Howard whose leg otherwise would have been amputated and also Prince Rupert's leg enabling him to walk for many years before he died.

As well as home remedies prescriptions from physicians were included such as that of Dr James's for a slow fever pill, a recipe which would make 36 pills. Garfields infallible medicine for the Rheumatism contained horseradish, buckbane[4], mustard seed, strong beer and powdered gum guaicum[5] left to soak for 24 hours before straining off the liquid. A broken shin needed finely powdered Rosin and to be covered with a rag. Ointment was made of spirit of wine camphorated old virjinica.[6] The 'Props' required sal volatile and elixir propitatis in equal measure: 'After anointing the afflicted part as hard as can be born so that the pain is pursued from limb to limb, apply hot London

1   Mrs Biddulph could have been the Butler Harrisons cook. Certainly in later years their cook Lipscombe added recipes to the book. There was a Lady Biddulph who lived at 172 High Street in 1803 *Cunningham Guide 1803*.
2   Probably Antony Addington (1713-90).
3   A diachylum was a medicament made from the juices of several plants and usually in the form of an adhesive plaster.
4   Buckbean was mainly used for digestive problems.
5   Otherwise known as lignum vitae 'wood of life' and used to treat everything from coughs to arthritis.
6   Virginica was used for soreness.

Peartree Church & Butler Harrison Memorial

brown paper, keep re-anointing and rewarming the paper and reapply.' The same concoction is then added to a pint of draught beer and drunk to promote perspiration. For a cough one drachm sweet vitre, one of elixir Vitriol, sixty drops of laundanum, three teaspoons of honey were needed and then 30 drops of the mixture was to be taken three times a day. Distilled asses milk was considered a fine restorative especially when the stomach was weak.[1] If asses

1 —*and the other is a Boarding school, a French Boarding School, is it?—No harm in that. They'll stay their six weeks.—And out of such a number, who knows but some may be consumptive and want Asses milk—Sanditon.*

were not available then mock asses milk could also be used for a cough in a recipe with comfrey, sago, rice, isinglap, spring water and seven spoonsful of milk. A plaster for a pain in the face or a headache included spreading on adhesive patent plaster rather larger than the size of a shilling added to which were twenty grains of soft extract of opium. This was to be applied to the temple for a headache or to the face for the spot most affected.

The Butler Harrison links with the East India Company may have been more distant than for many of their acquaintance but as well as opium medicinal recipes, recipes for curry and curry powder testify to the evidence of the influence of the trade of the company on the wider population.

The Butler Harrisons generally lived to a grand old age, both John and his sister Elizabeth were in their eighties.[1] Although Elizabeth Austen had lost her brothers early in life, she also lived into her eightieth decade. As inscribed on Elizabeth's golden wedding inkstand the family knew how unusual it was for parents and children all to survive into old age, thanks were not due for the medical interventions but to a higher power: 'Gratitude to Almighty God for His wonderful Mercy in preserving so large a family in health'.

Elizabeth died in 1847 and her husband three years later[2] and, along with her sister-in-law Elizabeth Goring Butler Harrison, was buried not at St Mary's Church, which was adjacent to their home, but in the associated chapel of St Mary-over-the-Water on Pear Tree Green, a more salubrious and fashionable part of the town, with its fine views over the river Itchen and back to Southampton. The area around the Harrison home had become built up by the middle of the nineteenth century, and was an area where the poor congregated. John's sons sold the property after their father's death to the Guardians of the Poor for £3000. The property became part of the workhouse which built schools, a dispensary and relieving office on the family's former 'pleasure ground' and the family home became the girls' workhouse. The plan, however, to close the public right of way known as Harrison's Cut failed and it remains to this day as reminder of the Butler Harrisons.

---

1 In 1837 Elizabeth Goring Harrison when seventy-two was *still confined to the sofa – she hopes however to be able to leave it without risk by the month of May.* Jane Goring, Joyce Sleight, Jill Turner, Janet Pennington & Janine Harvey *Lives, Loves and Letters, The Goring Family of Wiston, Sussex 1743-1905* p. 42.
2 Will of John Butler Harrison II TNA PROB-11-2111-334.

END NOTE

Southampton has, however, in my eyes an attraction independent even of its scenery, in the total absence of the vulgar hurry of business or the chilling apathy of fashion. It is, indeed, all life, all gaiety: but it has an airiness, an animation, which might become the capital of Fairyland – Mary Mitford 1812[1]

A vast number of nobility and gentry continue to arrive here daily; and there is little doubt but that the season will prove a good one – Hampshire Chronicle 17th August 1812

AFTER THE END of the Napoleonic Wars the glory days of the watering place and spa of Southampton, however, were beginning to draw to a close and by 1815 the town was not attracting the gentry and retired naval and army officers that it once had.

The corporation which had been dominated by the old established merchant families, retired naval officers, plantation owners and those with interests in the East India Company was described as 'the gentleman's party'. They had taken turns to be mayor, sheriff and aldermen, and needed to have a private income as the positions were not salaried. By the 1830s things began to change, it was resolved in 1831 than no Honorary Burgesses were to be made who were gentlemen resident in the town.[2] The old oligarchy, which had included members of the Ballard, Butler Harrison, and Fitzhugh families, was finally swept away by the Municipal Reform Act of 1835, to be replaced by thirty councillors elected by ratepaying householders.

For the next fifteen years or so after Waterloo the town drifted on and still presented itself as a watering-place but with the coming of a lasting peace with France this positioning of the town was being challenged by the lure of travel to the French Riviera and the opportunity to develop Southampton as a passenger port. The Long Rooms which had been opened in 1761 and remained in the control of the Martin family for half a century were struggling

1 *Visitors' Descriptions* p. 24.
2 Patterson *Corporation Journal* p. 56.

END NOTE

New Glocester Bath

and John Martin's widow Mary and her daughters were replaced as operators by the local MP and landowner Sir William Champion de Crespigny in 1821. The Long Rooms however were to be replaced in popularity by the New Assembly Rooms that were opened in 1830 to the north of the old town walls. There were also new baths built at the Platform opened in 1829 which offered

> hot baths of solid marble… shower baths on a new and improved principle, medicated, vapour and shampooing baths… for inveterate scrofula and skin diseases, rashes, eruptions, gouty and rheumatic afflictions, stiff joints and all those disorders dependent on a morbid circulation of the blood.[1]

Like the old Long Rooms the baths offered other amenities including London and provincial newspapers, refreshments, quadrille and card parties. These two new developments overtook the old Long Rooms as the place for entertainment and fashion, but they in turn soon found it difficult to survive as Southampton returned to its former prosperity as a trading port.

The Theatre Royal run for many years by the Collins family, John Collins being appointed manager in the 1770s, had operated a popular season during the autumn and early winter. Collins son-in-law, Mr Kelly, took over

1 Patterson *Corporation Journal* p. 38.

New Assembly Rooms

in 1807 and struggled although he managed to keep things going until he retired in 1837.¹ There were some new entertainments, in 1828 the balloonist Mr Graham was paid two guineas to offset his expenses for ascending in a Balloon from Mr Baker's saw mill yard. Graham's wife, Margaret, was of course was much more famous and celebrated than him having made her first ascent in 1826. Her husband George was in debt in 1827 due to the costs of making a balloon so his gift from the corporation must have been welcomed.²

George III died in 1820 and a public ball and supper was held at the Long Rooms attended by 400 people, the corporation dined at the Audit House and the poor were entertained on the Marsh where 6000 people took part at a cost of £475, paid for via a subscription.³ By the time that George IV expired in 1830 there were not the resources to give a public dinner and the coronation of William IV was marked with a firework display, the ringing of church bells and a gun salute on the Platform.⁴

1   Patterson *Corporation Journal* p. 30.
2   Patterson *Corporation Journal* p. 46.
3   Patterson *Corporation Journal* p. 32.
4   Patterson *Corporation Journal* p. 56.

As for our featured families, in assessing the life of the Georgian women, it does seem that life is imitating art in that so many of the story lines in Austen's novels have echoes in the lived experience of the women who resided in Southampton alongside the writer. There is many a Mrs Bennet on view trying to secure good sensible marriages for their daughters and just as many daughters determined on romance and sensibility. Many of the letters reflect the gossip that Miss Bates so enjoyed in her missives from Jane Fairfax, titbits about neighbours and acquaintances. Health is also something of an obsession, but why would it not be when children and young people were just as likely to be carried off as the elderly. Indeed, all the ladies, with the exception of Elizabeth Butler Harrison suffered the loss of children at an early age: Melicent lost her only son and had just one more child, Ann Newell also lost her son and daughter and was also left with just one surviving child. Anne Middleton and Mary Lewin left babies buried far away in India and later a son who died in service to the East India Company army. Mary Lance lost children soon after birth and her eldest son died a young man in India, having left England aged eighteen. Charlotte Fitzhugh's youngest son died in battle aged just twelve and her daughter, Sophia, in the same year aged thirteen. Mary Lance and Anne Middleton saw their daughters

Statue of George III presented to the town by the Marquis of Lansdowne on the occasion of the king's golden jubilee

die just on the point when they were becoming young women not yet out of their teens, whilst Mary Lewin was distraught over the death of her eldest daughter who left behind very young children.

There were also the double standards of the time which meant it was normal that Nathaniel Middleton would have had a long-term mistress and children right up until his marriage day and that his wife was asked to look after the future of those children. No mention, however, of what became of his native mistress. Anne Middleton's father had had a long relationship with her mother but never legitimised that relationship. Thomas Lewin had affairs both before and during his marriage, but a mild flirtation between his young wife and men of her own age saw him on the point of banishing her back to England. It is somewhat strange that there is no surviving information on Ann Newell's mother, no mention in wills and no reference to her in regards to the maintenance of the tomb of her father. Was she also a mixed-race woman like Anne Middleton's mother? Many of the marriages which appear to have had a business transaction at its heart: Melicent and Robert Ballard; The Middletons; and the Lances, seem to have been happy unions with much affection apparent in letters and wills. Perhaps the happiest of all was the Butler Harrisons. It seems to have been a romantic union, was long lasting and, at least from the perspective of their numerous children, a happy and fruitful one.

There were also a number of women who chose the unmarried life, like Jane Austen. Two of the Butler Harrison daughters were spinsters as was the daughter of Charlotte Fitzhugh although, particularly in the case of Emily Fitzhugh, they had money and position which might have attracted a match. Frances Butler Harrison, Mary Lance junior and Charlotte Lewin chose not to marry until later in life and, in the case of the first two, after their child bearing years. Sons followed well-established career paths, the clergy being particularly popular, and the church benefited from inheritances accrued from plantations and East India Company money as the benefactors built and enlarged their churches. Others chose the law and banking which may have seemed safe professions but could lead to the undermining of family finances. The link with the East India Company was strong either through direct family patronage or by making the most of networks built during social gatherings in Southampton. Elizabeth Butler Harrison, Mary Lance, Mary Lewin and Anne Middleton all lost sons in the service of the company. Their sons were also more likely to marry for money.

The war, though a constant throughout the adult lives of all the women, was so ubiquitous that it was not mentioned as much as may be thought. The Fitzhughs, Lewins and Middletons all lost close family members due to the conflict; it is also noticeable, however, that during any brief periods of peace most of the women took themselves off to France.

Ann Newell and Anne Middleton shook off their West Indian beginnings and re-invented themselves as gentlewomen in the polite society of Georgian England and if they were not mixing in the aristocratic and landowning circles of society, they were monied enough for country villas and London houses. Like Ann Newell and Anne Middleton, Mary Lance was also well-travelled and cosmopolitan having been born in Constantinople of a French mother, had Chinese servants in her house and dying in Paris. Mary Lewin had also travelled to India when still a very young girl and wife and when the war allowed visited France. If Charlotte Fitzhugh was not as well-travelled as her sister-in-law, she did make a visit to France with her family in 1802. Her husband's contacts, and interests in ceramics and art introduced her to life in China. Anne Middleton's home was decorated with exquisite Persian artifacts. Melicent Ballard and Elizabeth Butler Harrison, perhaps, led quieter lives immersed in the life of the town in which they had chosen to make their lifelong homes but they were also connected to the wider world though the trading and political exploits of their husbands.

Widowhood did make for a change in circumstances. For some, like Ann Newell, it created an opportunity and a freedom to travel and reinvent themselves in a new country. Anne Middleton, Mary Lance and Charlotte Fitzhugh had less disposable income and lived in smaller establishments after their husbands had died. One of the appeals of moving to France for Mary Lance may have been that it was a more economic place to live but still gave access to salons and gentle society. It was also the period when Paris was beginning to develop into a major cultural capital in Europe.

Compared to many women, of course, these Georgian ladies lived experience was one which had many benefits. Money gave them access to a comfortable existence with beautiful homes and servants, the ability to travel and husbands who, on the whole, treated them well. What money and position cannot buy is health and their letters show that this was an extremely important topic. The hope that sea-bathing could provide a whole gamut of cures was striking. It is easy from a modern perspective to see watering places as pleasure places but it was not for entertainment that women like Mary Lewin were regularly 'dipped' but in the hope of relief from diseases and ailments and even the prevention of death. Mary Lewin and Anne Middleton ended their lives in severe mental decay, Melicent Ballard died young in likelihood from either smallpox or typhus. Several of the ladies had long widowhoods if their partners died at a relatively young age.

Lady Betty Craven left the town a few years after Charles Alexander's death and soon after taking out her leases in 1810, spending her remaining years in Italy.[1] The Marchioness of Lansdowne was gone by 1814 and she and her daughter offered the castle site for sale, except for one messuage, in 1815 and it was eventually bought by Henry Roe for £160 for the leaseholds and £1,200 for the freehold.[2] Nathaniel Middleton died in 1807 and his wife lived her later days under medical care in London; the Lewins had inherited their estate in Kent in 1810 and moved there Ann Newell died in 1814 and the Lances moved to London in 1817. Only the Butler Harrisons and the Fitzhughs maintained their links in Southampton. The events of 1815 ushered in peace and the chance to travel abroad and by 1830 Southampton had reverted to its former existence as a premier port, helped in no small part by William Fitzhugh and his investment in steam ships and railways.

1 She relinquished several of the leases to Sir Gerard Noel Noel, of Exton Park, who became a baronet in 1814, although there was some litigation TNA C13/683/10. In a letter of 1810, the Margravine accused Philip Gell of saying she talked *bawdy* and made a complaint of it to Princes Caroline. Derbyshire Record Office D258/50/44.
2 SA SC4/4/551/4-10.

APPENDIX ONE

The surviving letters written to John Butler Harrison II, known as Jack Harrison, at Lausanne. 1780-1784. Transcribed by Malcolm Barton, husband of Melicent's descendant Sally Barton. Also included are Malcolm's comments on the letters.

M ELICENT'S LETTERS ARE a little hard to follow as she moves rapidly from one subject to another. Full stops may be no more than where she paused to think and are not followed by capital letters which were kept for words of particular importance. The 'dash' is used frequently. Although Melicent takes Jack's spelling to task, she had her own variations. Plurals of words ending in 'y' have a simple 's' added which may have been the norm then. However, Robert spells the word 'assure' with two 's' and Melicent with just one.

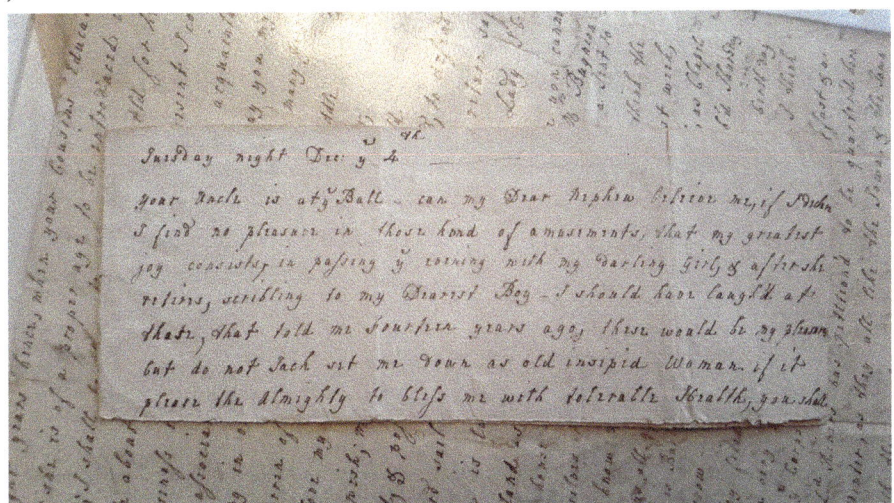

Letter of Melicent Ballard, private collection,

1. A letter addressed to Mr Harrison in London written by Melicent Ballard. No postal markings so presumably sent by hand.

My dearest Boy

These are the last lines that will probably reach you in England, from a friend, that has your interest near her heart – tell me your ideas of the bustle in the busy Metropolis, tell me what pleased you most & if you like the hurry of the world better, than our quiet life – Remember I hope to hear from you very often, & if any difficulty should ever occur (to y)ou, inform your sincere friends of them, & be advised – May the Almighty direct you to the best - but remember my dear Jack, that we who are apt to err ourselves, can excuse; tho we may be concerned for your errors, therefore if you are tempted either by example, or thoughtlessness, to do any thing materially wrong; candidly confess it, to those that can & will extricate you, I do not now address myself to you, as to a Child, but as a young man of the world, take the best part of the gay world; as that is most suited to your years, but never conform to those customs, that you now think wrong, for now you can judge right, & have not been corrupted, therefore abide by your own (-) of what is just & honest – I am sorry I cannot express myself better, I mean; that I hope you will continue good, amidst a world of wickedness, methinks if I could see you now & then, a gentle check would keep you in the right path, be communicative in your letters to us, & rest assured of every proper indulgence. I will add to my epistle your little Millys Love, who has told me a hundred triffling things to say, which time will not permit me to add; adieu my Dearest Boy, may every happiness this world can bestow, attend you & may you return safe to your affectionate
    Aunt Melicent Ballard Southampton Aug.st ye. 15th – 1780.
Milly teazes me to beg some of her pictures may be painted & some not.

2. Letter addressed to Monsieur Harrison

Chez Monsieur Bugnon, Lausanne en Suisse, Single sheet 1/3 postage paid. The letter is written by Melicent but addressed by Robert Ballard. Southampton Sunday night Sepr.ye.10 1780.

My dearest Boy,

Your two letters gave us a great pleasure the last in particular, as you were safely landed at Ostend & write that you are well, & very merry may you long continue so we all regret your absense but flatter ourselves you will reap the advantage of our loss, continue my Boy to write every opportunity, and write freely, and without reserve every want, & every wish of your heart; you shall be indulged in every thing , that is consistent with prudence, & reason. I every post expect a letter from you, presume you now have been a week at Lausanne, you cannot so soon tell how you like the place, or customs of it, but I hope to hear you are well & happy. we flatter ourselves Mr Bugnon will delight us , by giving a good account of your behaviour, & improvement in every particular – remember my Child we have your interest so much at heart that it lies in your power to add greatly, to our happiness

You desired I would write you long letters, I mean to do so, if you follow my example. if you do not , I shall think I tire you, with reading my epistles – our time has been engaged ever since you left England, otherwise a letter should have met you at Lausanne. Mr J.Ballard came to us, the day after your uncle returned from London, & stay'd till last Wednesday. we spent one of ye days at Northerwood, Milly was delighted with the Turkeys & fowls and wish'd for you. Mrs Hill & Miss Elderton, your Grand-papa, & Cousin Morris[1] were of the party. another day we went down to Spithead , to see the fleet. Mr Peers, Miss Nicholas, & Miss Moody, your Uncle Ned, & little Morris with us, it was a fine day, & very little wind; but Miss Nicholas & master Morris, are such sailors as you are. all the rest of the party were perfectly well. we went on board the Royal George, Capt Beaumaster, a Brother of Mr Brown's who is Chaplin to the Victory; on board which, we intended to have gone, but Mr Brown was on shore , the Royal George is a fine ship, carries a hundred brass Guns, & near nine Hundred men. we cast Anchor,& dined in the Harbour, upon cold Roast Beef, tongue,biscuit's , & cheese, very heartily. while we were in Harbour twelve men of War sail'd to St Hellens; you cannot conceive a finer sight, than so many noble ships under sail. I shall now wish you a good night. you must accept of long letters written by scraps & as things occur, if you wish to know what passes here.Monday & Tuesday ye 11 & 12 of this month, was our Election. Fuller & Sloane are chose, & poor Fleming thrown out. They gave a Ball Thursday ye 14th., to which I went, with the rest of the world & should have enjoy'd it exceedingly, but for my Dear little girl; who had eat too much fruit, and was not quite well, therefore I came home before eleven. it was an evening of joy & jollity; all sort's of people were there, servants, & every body that chose it danced. after we had done tea the second class sat down to the same tables, & they had plenty of Negus by the smell, I should judge and it was pure strong & that the maids at least, must be tipsey; as they seem'd to take good sips, without fear. Day's Concert being the next day, an the place erected for the musick, held a vast many people. I forgot to mention that your cousin Penton is re-elected for the City of Winchester. your uncle dined with him, the day I dined with Mr Ballard – Shepard is arrived safe & Jack Oliver

---

1 Cousin Morris was probably Charles (1759-1829) eldest son of Michael Morris and Barbara nee Ballard. He married Milly Ballard.

very much grown. Milly intends to write to you frequently, but as I think her epistles at present, will not be worth the postage, I shall keep them all back, till I can send them by a friends hands but as I would not mortify her by saying so, I wish you, every now & then, to thank her for a letter as if you had received it, for she flatters herself, a line from her, would make you vastly happy.

Friday ye 15th. – I am just return'd from Days Concert which was not very full of company. Alexander's Feast, with a Miscellaneous Act , & the Coronation Anthem, with God save the King was the entertainment chosen – in the morning , the Oratorio of the Messiah, was performed at the Church, I am told not more than a hundred people were present & I doubt Day will not be much in pockett

Mayor's Feast was to day. the dinner was at the Dolphin, the Duke of Chandos, & your Cousin Penton came to dine, his Grace told your Uncle, that the Dutchess is to spend a week here, for change of air, as she has been very ill – Mr Mears is our new Mayor, & I dare say, very glad, the Election is over, before he arrived at the honour, as it was a great fatigue. They poll'd each day from eight in the morning, till five in the evening. Mr Rooke and Mr Missing were Council for Fleming, Mr Hunter & Mr Hoarth, for Fuller & Sloane Clarke Gervois & Thistlethwaite are to be our County Members. Lady Pinch & her Mama were again at the Ball, & the Mob wanted to get a jack ass into the room, for my lady to ride on but the obstinate beast would not walk up stairs.

I have the pleasure of hearing Mrs Taunton & her little Boys are perfectly well - George Wells[1] sends his love to you. his gown was ragged & rusty & his shoes & hands not quite clean, but he is in good health. we think of going to Manningford, the first week in Octbr. please God we are all well, for a few days only – I observe by the papers the other Mr Dejean is arrived. I should suppose you might send any thing by them, & have any thing convey'd to you. I forgot to put up some of your Father's ruffles, will they be useful to you. write us, who of the Gentlemen you were recommended to, takes most notice of you, in particular if Col: Mr Moreland wrote to; has taken notice of you, as we promised to let him know. I am happy that your relation Sr. George Baker has recommended you in so particular manner to the Physician, tho I hope my Dear Boy will enjoy perfect health. our neighbour Mrs Spencer is dead, after a complaint in her bowells, for a few days, which complaint is very general, every where, whether from the air, or from eating fruit, which is in general blighted this year; is not determined by the learn'd. our Dear little girls indisposition

---

1 George Wells was a scholar at Winchester and would have known Jack there.

is of the same kind, but I hope will not be very bad, as it was taken in time, & she will have great care taken of her & is very good for taking Medicine. your Grandpapa Uncle & all their friends desire their kind Love to you & wishes for your happiness. I am sorry to tell you; Betseys eyes are much worse, than when you saw her, & Mr Hinton thought it necessary to take her to London for advice before her Hollidays were over. therefore we have no chance of seeing her here, which I rather depended on. the ship at Northam was launched last spring tide, & went off very well, two more are in building, one of 64, & the other of 36 guns. we have likewise had three days Races in the Marsh. I was not there either day therefore can give no account of the sport. I have only room to asure you that I your sincere friend & truly affectionate Aunt Melicent Ballard

Postscript in Robert Ballard's hand;-

Sunday 17th Sept. The next consideration to the care of your health is that of your Education, and in both points it has been my study to put you into the ablest hands therefore my dearest Child improve yourself in every praise worthy accomplishment and whatever Books or other articles may be condusive to this most desireable end, or to the more important regulation of your morals, Mr Bugnon has liberty to purchase for you

Believe me Dr. Jack your ever most

Affte. Uncle Robt. Ballard jun

3. Letter addressed to:-
Monsieur Harrison chez Monsieur Bugnon a Lausanneen Suisse.

Post paid in red; paid 1/3 in red ms.Red seal on reverse showing bearded man on horseback.

Southampton Octbr.ye 28th. 1780

My Dearest boy,

We were very happy to receive your letter dated ye 10th which did not reach us till Monday last the 25th – date your next the day you forward it to us, as we can then judge how long it's coming. I hope you have recvd. a very long letter from me which I sent from hence the (ultimo?) 17th. I mean my Dear, to write to you constantly once a Month, & I hope you will oblige us as often during so long an absence, frequent correspondence will keep up our affection for each other, & by my chit chat you will know every thing, that passes among your friends. I am sorry you were deceived, in regard to your mode of travelling, which we were taught to beleive, would be very commodious. I am

likewise sorry that Dejean behaved so ill, about your money, but why did my boy wish to get all changed at once, as Dejean was an entire stranger to you, would it not have been better to have kept what you did not immediately want, till you got to Lausanne, when I make no doubt but Mr Bugnon would change it full as well but you my Dear child have allways been with friends, a little knowledge of the world will teach you caution. I am very happy to find, you entertain so good an opinion, of Mr and Mrs Bugnon, recommend Yourself by a proper behaviour, & if I am not deceived you will meet with all recover'd. Nanny has had the same complaint, but is getting better, several have died of it those you know are Mrs Allison Mrs Spencer & the youngest of the master Atherleys, it has been more fatal among the poor, as they cannot afford proper nourishment, & the disorder requires good liveing – I congratulate you, on your short tail, as I suppose you have a dislike to deceit, to wear false hair. Cantillo's concert was last night, not more than a hundred people favour'd him, your Uncle was one of the number, as I am obliged to attend my girl during her maid's illness, I did not go, you know I never leave her with any other servant, this day which is St Michael Mr Mears is sworn into his office.
October ye 9th.

    I have given up all thought's of going to Manningford this year, as the place is very wet & dirty, & the Winter already come upon us, I am fearful it would hurt Milly, to take the journey, for her illness has render'd her rather tender both she & Nanny are much thinner, & have lost their Rosy cheeks, tho both begin to pick up again. your Uncle sets out the 16th. if weather permit's, which at present is very wet & windy. how is it with you – I expect you to be very descriptive in your next epistle, let me know how you like your situation &c &c. I hope to hear my Dear Boy is happy & that I shall have the unspeakable pleasure of seeing him all I wish at his return. the accomplish'd Gentleman alone, will not gratify my wishes, the just & honest man, must polish, must finish the Character, & that will not only delight your friends but add to your own happiness. I hope you go constantly to Church on Sundays – let not fashion guide you to neglect your Duty to God, never be persuaded to give up, what you was, (when a child), taught to think aright- but I must not tire you with advice – Mr Smith of the Custom House was married Saturday to his Cousin, a Miss Smith of Winchester, & brought her to his lodgings at Mr Wards to tea. our Whist Club begins Wednesday ye 18th. & is to be at the Star. the Winter assemblies are to be at the Dolphin & to begin at seven and end at twelve o'Clock – Martin's Rooms are still open, but their situation is shocking such windy weather. Your old flame Miss Rose Hughes is now on the recovery from the reigning illness, & expect's soon to see her Father; who is just made an Admiral, & must of course resign his government.[1]

Young Mr Serle is on a visit to his Father for four days, he call'd here this morning, & told me he was almost tired of the army, that he did not like the confinement, which was almost as bad as a School Boys. may not my Dear Jack after a short trial, be of the same opinion. Peter Serle was very fond of it, when he first left his Tutor. did I mention in my last that Mr James Warre has been with us a few days, he had letters from Oporto informing him, that his Brother Jack has been attack'd one night in the street & very narrowly escaped with his life. the blow was given with a broad sword across his shoulders, & cut of his fine thick hair, the stock buckle saved his pole & was very much bent by the sword. The young man that attack'd him he secured immediately, he is a Portuguese of family & fortune & its supposed will be banish'd his country, a few words had pass'd between him and a Brother of Mr Warre before, & he own'd he had watch'd every evening, to catch him alone, but as Jack was always with him, & the stoutest man, he intended to have demolish'd him first,& then have attack'd the man that had offended him. what should we think in England of such behaviour. Sheppard is going to have a few more guns to enable him to defend himself from any small thing & more men, but will not sail without Convoy.

Octbr. Ye 14 – I shall now finish for the post tomorrow. Col: Vignoles died last Wednesday last, of this dreadful flux. Mr Bugnon was acquainted with him. Old Rolph ye butcher is also dead of it, & that sweet little girl of the Scotts is given over. thank God Almighty our Dear Baby was preserved – does the Mr Bugnon to whom Mrs Daman[2] wrote, take notice of you, if he does be sure mention him, that I may tell her. Would not the Dejeans bring & carry parcels for us. I suppose you might see & ask them, if you think them trust worthy, the stage would safely bring any parcel from Town, or take them from us to their lodgings. I see by the papers one of them, is just setting out, but I shall not employ them without your instructions. I find your friend Scott has

1   Sir Richard Hughes was in command of a fleet sent to the West Indies in 1784, in which the twenty-eight-year-old Horatio Nelson was second in command. Nelson did not get on with his senior commander and had to put him right on the relevance of the Navigation Act in the Indies. 'He bows and scrapes too much for me'. It may not have helped having Lady Hughes and Rosy on board his vessel H.M.S. Boreas; he described the former as 'an eternal clack'.
2   Mrs Daman was probably the wife of William Daman, an attorney and land speculator, who developed property around the south-east of Castle Hill. J Stovold *Building Developments in Southampton 1750-1830: The Impact of the Spa* Unpublished Thesis University of Southampton 1984 pp. 68n, 137n.

wrote to you do my Love, be attentive, to both your writing & spelling in your answer to him, as I should be sorry a letter should expose you, as an ignorant young man, & you may take what time you chuse, to write his letters, & of course may be correct.

Milly longs to send her letters, to you, but the postage is more than they are worth - she speaks of you frequently, of all your little quarrels & reconciliations & says you will never disagree again as both will be older & wiser when you next meet. I already wish the time was at hand. your GrandPapa & Mr Cropp join with your Uncle Cousin & myself in the kindest Love & wishes for your welfare. this paper would not contain the names of those that enquire after – Remember you have a sister & an Uncle Harrison to whose favour recommend yourself by a well wrote epistle. Adieu my Dearest Jack beleive me your truly affectionate aunt – Melicent Ballard

4. A letter addressed to Monsieur Harrison chez Monsieur Bagnion Ministre a Lausanne en Suiss

Southampton Nov ye. 19 1780
My Dearest Jack

We have impatiently expected a letter from you for some weeks, none have yet arrived, Mr Cerjat was so kind to send a few lines to your uncle, & inform'd us you were indisposed at your first arrival, but was quite recover'd when he wrote - why does not my Dear Boy write once a Month as he promised – I hope you have received two very long letters from me, the first gave you an account of the Election, the last inform'd you among other matters of Col: Vignoles death, you have not acknowledged the receipt of either – I thank God we are all well, your Uncle goes to Alton Wednesday, to dine with your Tenants, & receive a little Cash for you - I should be very glad to see you, that I may judge of your improvement & wish you were not quite so distant from us –

We have had two exceeding good Winter Balls. the Dorsetshire Militia are quarter'd here till they encamp, they are a very genteel corps, & their Music you know is very fine the Sugar House is making into Barracks for them, to ease the publicans, who are at present very much crouded –

Novbr. Ye. 20 – we this day received your letter dated the 4th. of Octbr. for which we can by no means account, as Mr Carjats letter was dated the 16th. & came to us her a fortnight ago, enquire into this matter my Dear. I rejoice at your recovery may the Almighty bless you with health & happiness. I have already said we are all well, from which you will judge your Dear little

Cousin is quite recover'd – you used to be a fire spaniel here, how will you bear the cold. your Uncle will write to Mr Bugnion & desire him to subscribe to the Balls for you, & repay the Guinea you subscribed. we do not wish you to appear shabby on any occasion ,but hope your own prudence will keep you from extravagance, as you must hereafter feel it, if you are imprudent – direct to Giles Rooke Esqr. New Buildings Coleman Street London - & To Miss Harrisons at Mrs Stephensons School Queen Square London –

De Jean is a bad man, & you are well off to get your Money. his behaviour will not increase his business , but your Uncle will write to him & insist on his sending your things, to prevent his Characters being made publick he will gladly do it –

I wish Nanny would dress, as the maids at Lausanne , she is too fine a Lady by far - did you think the Ladies at the Ball pretty, did you dance – I will write to enquire if the Voiturier you recommend is in London, if he is a person you can depend upon, write by him, for any thing you wish to have, & I will send it immediately to him, but unless you write by him, we cannot possibly know, when he comes to England - do you think Mr. Jardain so good a master as Mr Burgat, I think that if you are tolerably taught you will be an excellent dancer. I hope you have a good writing master, I cannot compliment you on that score, there are many inaccuracys (which a little attention would get over) in your letters - , you are negligent in your spelling, but your stile is improved, & a little practice will bring you to write very agreeable familar letters – I wish my Dear Boy rather to excell, than be behind any young man of his age, in all useful accomplishments - your society is a pretty collection of Nations & Languages, I hope you will be cautious in your choice of intimates, for whether Lords or Barons, their friendships must be prejudicial; if they are not worthy honest men – you will find drawing very entertaining & if you like it , will improve very fast - don't forget your singing, you have a good Ear, & a sweet voice I was always delighted to hear you sing – Martin is teaching Milly, & I hope she will sing a ballad prettily, she comes on , amazeingly in her writing, every body that has seen her Copy book, declare they never saw such good first letters - Martin is very proud of her performance – Farmer Absolem rents all our ground at Northerwood, & is to live in Spencers House, the house they live in is to kept empty for us, whenever we chuse to go Mrs Absolem is to attend us there we were determined to keep the farm ourselves, & almost agreed with a Man & woman to manage it, but were convinced we should greatly be imposed upon – your old Nurse & her family are well - & I tell you as a secret, is going to play the fool & marry, with her nine children, a Farmer Penny who has five – I know you are interested about Nanny , who has attended you since your Birth, I am sorry to tell you, Thomas is her approved admirer, I say sorry because I think a lazy footman, can never maintain a family, nothing but necessity would tempt him, & then he knows not how to work haveing from eight years old, been taught only to wait at table what prospect but of beggary with such a Husband - since my last epistle, old Mrs Atherly, & Mrs Philly Carter, have paid their debt to Nature. I heard from Mrs Taunton last week   (parts of this letter are missing)……..are well I have been almost a fortnight late ……with this letter, according to our agreement, (to write once) a Month, but observe my Dear you sit your exa(m)……….

Friday Nov: ye 24th. your uncle return'd from ……..dinner, he left all the family well, your sister has ……..weeks, she is not to return to School, therefore dir(ect your letter to)   The Rev'd Mr Hintons - poor Betsey has had so violent a fever that her life was dispair'd off for a fortnight, when she (….) was enough recover'd to bear the journey, Mrs Hinton fetch'd her from school, & she is now purely recover'd Mr Ballard thinks the Miss Hintons are improved by their Governess, but doubts Jack wants sense, in short he is not the least mended – your Uncle will very soon write to Mr Cerjat & Mr Bugnion in the interim beg the favour of the above mention'd Gentleman , to subscribe for you at ye Balls, & reimburse you, if you want the Guinea…. . paid at the English Ball. we have received no answers from Dejean or Packe perhaps both have left London

I suppose Scotts letter was not properly directed as he sent it a fortnight before I wrote my last. I never wish you to be rude to any body, but am not desireous of your keeping up an intimacy with him. your own opinion of him was not very good, till after your friends Molesworth Buller & South left Southampton I have not heard of ye two sailors - South is in the College at Winchester and his Father & Mother spend the Winter there instead of coming to us – pray write frequently, as I am allways happy to hear from you – the family of the Andrews[1] are in distress at the unfortunate death of the Major, who I suppose you have heard was hang'd as a spy by Washington in America, he was a deserving man, 27 years of age & his Mothers darling, & he is greatly regretted by all our Army, every officer Mourn'd for him – Millys letters wait for a conveyance she joins us in the kindest Love to you & I remain your truly affectionate friend Melicent Ballard.

Mr Bugnions writing in French, deprives me of great pleasure, as I am not conversant enough in that language to understand it perfectly – Mrs Daman & family are all well Mrs Smith has been long complaining, & is rather too old to recover perfectly – end of letter missing.

1   Major John Andre.

APPENDICES

5. Letter from Melicent Ballard addressed in Robert Ballard's handwriting : To Monsieur Harrison chez Monsieur Bugnion Lausanne en Swisse

Southampton Jan: ye 3d. 1781
My Dearest Jack

  I pleased myself with the hopes of receiving the Compliments of the Season from you, but you deny me the satisfaction of frequent letters. I hoped Mr Bugnion would have reminded you of this matter, as your Uncle wrote to him on the subject. he likewise wrote to Mr Cerjat I presume both letters were received - all your relations & friends are well & desire their best wishes – your Cousin longs to see you, if I do not see her with too great partiality, I think you would already, find her improved – there has been little worthy of notice pass'd, since I last wrote last – perhaps a few of your acquaintance dead as Mrs Cozens, Mrs Atherly senr., Mrs White, Miss Philly Carter, & Mr Peveral - I am not certain I did not mention some of these in my last letter, but you enjoin'd me to inform you, of all deaths, and all marriages, & I endeavour to fulfill all promises that I am induced to make - you will be supprized to hear that Miss Perkins has taken Miss Carter's Shop, & meets with great encouragement, I cannot say I should have advized to that step as I think considering her former station here, it must be very mortifying to stand behind a counter. all her acquaintances make a point of taking notice of her, & she is very commendable to endeavour to improve her little fortune, but I think her own feelings would been less , had she undertaken business in any other place. our assemblies are kept up in great spirit once a fortnight, & a very genteel concert once a fortnight likewise – Lord Rivers & several gentlemen play upon different instruments Goss & Sibly both from Salisbury with Martin are the vocal performers. The Dorsetshire are a very genteel corps, you cannot have forgot their excellent band of music, your old master, Burgat[1] attends the concert as a gentleman performer, he is reckon'd a good fiddle, & as he comes to town Friday, to teach Saturday, its no inconvenience to him to oblige by performing.

  Feb. ye 4th. – this letter would have been sent a Month ago, as you may observe by the date, but that I was taken ill, & am just enough recover'd to write - we have not yet heard from you fie upon you my Dear, I should think you were ill did I not beleive, Mr Bugnion would in that case, write himself indeed it is unkind not to write, young Bulkely is at present here on a visit,

1 Mr Burgat appears to have lived in Winchester. He advertised in the Hampshire Chronicle from St John's House an Annual Ball on November 10th 1780, with general dancing after his scholars have performed.

he enquired after you, & I am told is a very smart young man: if he stays till I get down stairs, we hope to see him, to dinner. I am sorry to tell you poor Mrs Purbeck is dead, she was a worthy woman & will be a great loss to her family. we expect every post to hear , that yr friends , Mrs Rooke & Mrs Cooke, are released from this painful Life, as our last accounts mention, there were little hopes of any amendment – Miss Isaacson has left School, & is very much admired, I don't know whether you would not like her, as well as Miss Spriner – tho' she is a Browner Beauty – your Uncle heard at the concert Friday that Mr John Ballard is going to be married to Miss Waller of Winchester. do you know her. I am told she is a very agreeable sensible woman, very well accomplish'd, but not handsome, that she is of a suitable age, & has a good fortune. We expect soon to see Mr Ballard & perhaps may then know if there is any truth in the report. Mr & Mrs Hinton & your sister promise us a visit as soon as the weather gets warmer, I wish my Dear Jack could join the party, it would greatly add to the happiness of all, but as that cannot be, let me entreat you to soften the pain of absence by frequent letter's , I have already threaten'd only to answer yours, but it had not the desired effect, yet I must flatter myself you have some pleasure in hearing from us, & I confess I have a secret satisfaction of scribbling to you – we would not be forgot, a letter brings us to your remembrance & will serve to remind you of our affection, as a return for which I hope you will endeavour to fulfil our wishes, & be the good accomplish'd Gentleman – it is much fear'd the Thunderer Man of War is lost, as she has not been heard of, since that dreadful storm in Octbr. our valuable friend Robt Boyle Nicholas was Captain, see the effect of ambition, with a Paternal estate of seven hundred a year, he was not content, but would tempt the Sea, to add to his fortune, & has doubtless found it, his grave.

Doctor Speed has been very ill sometime, & is not likely to recover, the eldest Miss Halton is dead. Mr Watson is again Curate at Holy Roods. Mr Ward's School is much approved, & he has already forty boarders – Capt. Poole lost his ship some where abroad, but all the crew were saved. I think either Buller or Molesworth sail'd with him. Nanny & Thomas are very soon to be married, they petition to live on, & we intend to keep them some time – your Nurse has foolishly taken Jack from Sheppard, & bound him for seven years to a Capt. of a Collier, I am very angry with her for doing so –

Tuesday Febry. Ye 13 – Mr J Ballard left us this morning he desired Love to you, & says your old School fellows Wells & Goring are well – Mrs Chamier & Mrs Daman have receiv'd letters from Lausanne, & were kind enough to inform us you were well, and improved in your French very much. Mrs Vamier say, Mr Bugnion mention'd your having (more pr) udence, than your Country men in the ....

  I flatter myself you will act prudently ....do not your cheeks glow, at the reco(ognition) of your long silence, are you not willing i....... to make us happy by writing often - we have had very stormy weather ever since .... & the Wind is very little cull'd yet – several . drove up to Platform last night .....& a Port(uguese) ..... with wines on board was bulged , & some of the wine . was mostly for Hull the like accident never happen'd in our River before, & was now occasion'd, by having so many men press'd, that they had not hands enough to secure her properly. it is thought Government must pay the loss - your Grandpapa Uncle & Cousin join me in most affectionate Love & all friends kindly remember you. I am my Dr. Jack your sincere friend & affectionate aunt Melicent Ballard

6A. *Letter written by Melicent Ballard and sent by hand.*

Southampton June ye 10th 1781
Mr Burgat conveys this to Mr Bugnion's friend in London, who will be so obliging as to forward it to you with three letters from Milly, one from your sister,& one from yr Uncle, some Music, a song, Fungus, two pr of buckles of the newest fashion, & some work'd ruffles - let us hear from you often, & say when you receive the above. if the weather is fine we intend going to Northerwood for a fortnight the latter end of the week, for which purpose are furnishing the house upon the hill, which will admit two maids & a Man & ourselves; & we propose pitching a Tent to sit in - you know the place is delightful, & I think the air will do us all good. we should have gone last week, but your Uncle is Bailiffe & must attend his booth, as Chapel fair is to morrow - The Dorsetshire Militia march'd Thursday for camp – they fired exceedingly well the King's birthday & there was a very genteel Ball in the Evening. I think I wrote since ye corps gave a very elegant breakfast & a dance after – Ld Rivers has petitioned to be quarter'd here again this Winter, as they all like the Town, & the Town was pleased with them – when we return from Lindhurst Dr & Mrs Wells make us a short visit, & leave your sister who has been at Manningford some time, I presume she will stay with us, till Mr & Mrs Ballard return to Winchester, when they have promised to pass some days with us, & will possible take her back with them – your Grandpapa Mr Cropp & all your friends are well & make frequent enquiries concerning you – they also constantly complain of you for not writing so often as you ought we agreed to hear from each other once a month, & I have but three letters from you since you left England, which is ten months ago – consider this my

Dear & oblige me in future, your friend Scott is very well & lounges about the Street all day as usual, it's a sad thing for every body; young people especially to have nothing to do as idleness is the food of vice. employ your present time my Dearest Boy to improvement & when you have gained as much instruction as you wish, I think I may venture to say, you have my full leave to be negligent since I am fully convinced, that those who have been early taught to employ their time, will too well know the value, to abuse it, as they advance in life; it must be certain every moment is it flies, shortens the little space allow'd them. short at best is the longest Life – happy are those that pass it, so well, as to enjoy life eternal. may you my Dearest Boy be all the fondest hopes you can wish - may you if tempted to err reflect, the hopes of your dearest Friends are centr'd in you, & by that means give up momentary pleasures for lasting happiness, for that nothing wicked or even wrong; can afford pleasure, hourly, example proves observe this my Child, & do not think your fond Aunt misemploys that time, she endeavours to point out a safe path for you to tread – Nanny leaves me when the Governess arrives which I shall fix for the 10th. of next month, & hope your Cousin will improve as fast in French, as in other things - her voice is thought very good, & very strong, she really sings very prettily – dances tolerably, comes on amazeingly in her cyphering & of her writing you may judge by her letters; every word of which is her own inditing, except the first wrote , which is only cover'd – needle work she does not yet like, but I hope it will come in time – she is idle & as Rosy as ever. & longs to see you, tho she is thought to think, you can no more play together as you used to do – I am going to get a miniature picture of her , to hang on my watch, as we have a person now in town that takes very good likenesses, & I think her jolly face would be a pretty ornament. I dare say you are grown tall, I should be glad to hear you are likewise grown fat as your Uncle writes, I shall only add that I am Dear Jack your ever affectionate Aunt – Melicent Ballard –

6B. Letter sent under the same cover written by Robert Ballard.

Southampton June 12th 1781
My Dear Boy
I flatter myself by this time you have made a tolerable proficiency in the French language as you were so early grounded in its rudiments & pronunciation & to assured of which would give me uncommon satisfaction as it is one of the principle reasons for sending you abroad & as your expenses have greatly exceeded my apprehensions I hope your diligence in a matter I have very essentially at heart, will in some measure attone for your extraordinary

Disbursements. Whenever an Idea should seriously strike you in regard to your future situation in Life I beg to be acquainted with it, in order that your future Studies may be directed to the Plan you may adopt, and that my earnest endeavours may not be wanting to assist you with all my Interest and all my judgment on the occasion. If you knew the real pleasure your Letters give us, you could not think 12 in the whole year an unreasonable expectation, I will therefore beg of you a monthly Epistle as a small & only return to that affection which has been so long & so early shown you, my Dear Jack
Your sincerest friend
& most attentive Uncle
Robt. Ballard Jun.

7. Letter written by Melicent Ballard and addressed by Robert Ballard. To Mr Harrison At Mr Bugnion's Minister Lausanne Switzerland

Southampton Dec: ye 2 – 1781
My Dear Nephew
Your letter dated ye 8th I received last Thursday with more pleasure, than I can well express. I rejoice that you are happy, I judge the latter, as I think you write in spirits. I am glad your tedious silence was owing to Mr Bugnions neglect, rather than yours, & give me leave to say I am much pleased at your improvement in writing, both in your stile & hand - this last letter, is far better in every respect , than any other I have received - I accept your challenge & promise to answer your letters punctually. the spy Glass cost two guineas, which money, your Uncle desires you to receive, & accept of it, as a proof of his approbation. We had the happiness of hearing very pleasing accounts of your conduct, from Mr Cerjat, continue to do well my Dearest Jack. when you write next mention your Grandfather & my Father, they are both interested in you, & I may sometimes show them a letter, old people cannot like to pass unnoticed,& I would not have you lose a friend, or ever be censured by one, for neglect which, I am convinced you do not intend – Scott is appointed a Midshipman on board the Duke man of War, he has been struting about street in his Cocade, but is either gone, or will go on board, in a few days – I am glad your Cousins letters amused you, she intends to favour you with more by the first opportunity you can point out to us. I hope & think she has now a very good governess in Miss Davy, who has been perfectly well educated, & tho an English woman, will I flatter myself, teach her French enough, to converse with you in the language; if it please God, you have the happiness of meeting again, to which time, I look forward with pleasure & impatience; can

you truly say the same or shall you wish to prolong your absence - Mr Burgat had a very genteel Ball ye 2d of Nov:br - he now teaches a hundred & thirty Children here , & all the genteel people of the Town honor'd him by their presence – Milly danced a Minuet two Cottilons & two Country dances - & was generally allow'd to be his best dancer – she was so much admir'd & so very happy; that I blush to own I suffer'd her to dance till near one o'Clock. she improves very much in her singing, Miss Davy sings delightfully, & sometimes instructs her – by she will not sit down to work with pleasure – I hope you have not left off singing, you know I used to have much pleasure in hearing you – Nanny is gone to a little lodging in Hound-well Lane. Thomas continues only till we are suited in a Man, we had hired one in his place who chose to disappoint us, otherwise they would have gone together, but I beleive that he had much rather remain with us, than go to day labour, as he never liked work – Mr Martin (thro' your Uncles interest,) hopes to succeed Mr Wynne (who is lately dead) as Land - waiter at ye Custom House, so we must look out for another Clerk – your old Nurse is very unhappy, & ill used by her new Husband – I fear Nannys fate will be as hard – I every day expect your promised pacquet of letters, which will afford us much amusement. how long do Mr & Mrs Bugnion remain in England – have they been kind to you, & do they intend visiting Mrs Daman here – your sister & I correspond frequently, as I am now employ'd by her about her dress, a matter of great importance to young Ladies, & which cannot be procured at Chawton – she longs to hear from you & takes your silence unkind, she desires I would never fail to remember her to you. If I neglect to mention her lay the fault on me, she has enjoin'd me constantly to let her know when we hear from you – adieu for this night

  Tuesday night Dec: ye 4th – your Uncle is at ye Ball – can my Dear Nephew beleive me, if I declare I find no pleasure in those kind of amusements, that my greatest joy consists, in passing ye evening with my darling Girl, & after she retires, scribbling to my Dearest Boy – I should have laugh'd at those that told me Fourteen years ago, these would be my pleasures but do not Jack set me down as old insipid woman. if it please the Almighty to bless me with tolerable Health you shall see that eight years hence, when your Cousins Education is finish'd & she is of proper age to be introduced into a gay World; I shall be happy to join, that world for her sake, tho' I hobble about with my Crutch – at present I conceive my only business is to keep up a proper acquaintance for her, to associate with hereafter - & may you my Dear Boy, be happy in our innocent parlys for many many years. we are rather barren of news - Politicks I never meddle with, but I love my Country & wish it's

APPENDICES 283

prosperity, tho I cannot wish; me, or those Dear to me, should draw ye sword, & possibly spill innocent blood, to defend our Cause – Sheppard sail'd to day - & I hope will return safe. Mr James Warre is lately married to an Irish Lady – I beleive he came to England since you left us – therefore you cannot ….(conclusion of this letter is missing)

There are no letters for 1782, but fortunately one for 1783 survives and this gives a good idea of progress over the intervening months.

8. Letter of eight pages presumably sent by hand. No postal markings.

Southampton April ye 17th 1783
I had last night the pleasure of receiving a packet of letters from my Dearest Jack, I am obliged for them continue my Dear to write frequently, you have of late been very kind & good in that particular, but write of your self, you do not mention how long the fall of the table confined you, are you quite recover'd of it, & is your health perfectly good. this is a matter I am very anxious about, of a matter you seldom touch upon. yours dated March ye 15th arrived safe ye 30th remember I cannot hear from you too often – I shall be agreeable to your request scribble every thing I can recollect that can afford you the least entertainment but will first notice all that require answering in your last letters – I think hair dressers a useless set of men, were there none we should be neat clean & all alike submit to nature, but custom or fashion (if you please to call so) must in some degree be conform'd to, by those that wish to appear like the world, unless the fashion is vicious, but than I hope both you & I & all we dearly Love would dare appear particular rather than be wicked. I have not heard our tribe of dressers have attempted more than stealing a knife or Comb. I hope they will not conceal themselves, as I am allways happy to rid the house of them as soon as possible – I thank you for resuming your pen the very day you finish'd a letter to me. continue doing so both your Uncle & I find joy in complying with your every wish you have, consistent with your real good. rest asured of this truth my Dearest Jack – is Lord Inverary a clever young man - Mrs Duke is not here, nor can I learn she has been here – Mr Piper & Capt. Robertson both intimate in the Duke family (if they are of Andover) but have not heard of her being at Southampton – I did promise some mince meat next Christmas, but remember you must inform me how to send it, time enough to prepare it, & tell me if you have patty-pans to bake them in. do you wish to come home, I rather fear not but tho' I do not suppose you will return till four years are compleated, from the time of your arrival at Mr Bugnions, I consider

with joy, that little more than one is to pass, before we shall meet, I trust in happiness, & perfect health answer honestly to this question, nothing but the Idea of yr advantage would have separated us for so long a time - your sister who I dined with yesterday at Doctor Ballards , is very well & comes to us the first or second of May, she charged me to forward any letter that came from you immediately. the post this morning carried what I rec:vd last night - Mr B has lately taken his Docters degree. he has a beautiful little Boy, & expects an addition to his family in May – he has chose a prudent good woman, she is not very handsome, but by no means plain, & some years younger than himself. they are going from Winchester at midsummer & intend living at Wymering near Portsea which is a college living, & lately given him, I am told it is worth four hundred a year in time of War. your sister is at last determined to live with them & to visit us, & her other friends every year. the Dr intends keeping a coach & has already purchased Horses. I shall be glad of the Pinus Zembra[1] - how do you bear cold. the weather here is mild & pleasant, we barely keep a fire - the Gardens want rain very much, & some farmers whose lands lay high, wish for wet, that they may sow their Lent corn. do not be angry with your Uncle for supposing you a Coxcomb, you know I allways call'd you so, with the addition of dirty, when you used to steal in with the dinner, & hide your dirty shoes under the table, have you forgot my Love how it displeased you. I can chearfully allow you to be a neat Coxcomb from sixteen to eighteen, but not longer for I am convinced from observation that youth must just at that period of life, be either Coxcombs or slovens, the former, time brings us to be just agreable, but the latter grows every year worse & worse, till they become disgusting for want of cleanliness - your Old Nurse continues a cripple. I know you have too good a heart to forget obligations, & tho' she has been well paid for her care of you, you are obliged, for her discharge of her Duty to you at a time when you could not complain of a want of it. I love & value her daughter Nanny, for her attention nine years to our Dear Milly & every day lament her foolish marriage, which obliged us to part – Milly gives an account of my little God–daughter Anna - our Winter Balls are over. when I see Mr Burgat I intend to enquire if he knows the dances you mention – Milly does not like the confinement of musick but as she has an excellent ear, & her Governess is quite a proficient, she cannot help improving. she is too young to attract notice, but when the coxcomical time comes, she will take pains to appear accomplish'd some notes in her voice are very sweet – Mrs Taunton has another Boy, she frequently enquires about you & desires to be remember'd kindly to you, we intend to visit her the first week in June & shall spend a

---

1 Pinus cembra or Swiss pine

day with your Uncle Edward at Salisbury as he is now a house-keeper tho' a single man. we have been advised not to think of foreigner as a servant, as the expence of his coming would be great, & if he did not speak English, he would be almost useless in a family, as he could neither understand, or be understood, therefore we must at present drop the idea. are you fond of a garden, mine with my new Green-house affords me great amusement

    - my Father is but poorly. he does not take enough air & exercise to enjoy health - innoculation is over but the small pox is still in Town, & the sort very bad - Miss Davy has hitherto escaped it - she is averse to being innoculated. the Militias are all disembodied, Mr McCombe is here in Lodgings. I believe you heard of his Wife's death - his son Jack is with him for a few days. he is grown a polite lad for a sailor, & is very soon to go to Newfoundland, he has been on one or two voyages already & taken a prize his share of which is about twenty pound – he tells me he smokes very well, but cannot learn to chew, he drinks his pint of Port with pleasure & begins to be very polite to Ladys – Roger Mears is well spoken of by his Captain, not so Tom Sherer, who has been with Sir Richd. Hughes, but is turn'd over to another ship, call'd the Nymph.[1] I beleive young Hughes is full as idle as his friend Tom Sherer but may be better apart. as I can easily beleive they encouraged one another in idleness - our card parties are almost over. at least with us, as I now refuse going on any visit I have p'd in ye course of the Winter, for I think a mouthful of fresh air more wholesome, & much more agreable, than being confined in close crouded rooms for two or three hours – do you ever play at cards, I do not think a low stake at all amiss in a Winter evening, I call a low stake what one can lose with good humour for cards cease to be an amusement, if they cause a moments uneasiness. Jack McCombe & his Father dined with us one day last week, the former in a whisper ask'd me to indulge him with a game of Whist if I was not engaged. I desired his Father (who is lame) to make up the party, & we three, with Milly for the fourth play'd two games in two hours you may judge how much I was amused, the juniors of the party were highly entertain'd - Mrs Peers has taken a Governess for her girls who is a french woman & cannot speak a word of English, neither Mr or Mrs Peers understand a syllable of french which is very awkward. Good Night.

    Sunday morning ye 20 - have I ever mention'd a capital bake house built by Mr Potter at Chapell, he had a contract with Government for Sea Biscuits, & has laid out seven thousand pounds in Mills Bake-house & houses

---

1 Tom Sherer was presumably on board when HMS Nymph was lost, in June 1783, to a fire on board through the fault of the purser's steward.

for his principal workmen. it really looks like a little parish – he himself rented 'Belle–Vue', kept two carriages drove six horses & was quite the fine Gentleman. but this day his name is in the Gazette a Bankrupt, & we hear he owes thirty thousand pounds in this County. in all probability many familys will be ruin'd by him. such a man deserves worse, than a common highwayman, who only takes the triffle you have in your pockett, while these fine folks by artful tales grasp every thing - your Uncle has no concern with him, but Ward Kellow Bernard & some others in this Town, are taken in pretty deep. the gentleman is gone to France, & has left his wife & children in great distress. Mrs Potter brought him a good fortune, but was not prudent enough to have it secured. we hear Major Haynes is in hopes of being Master of the ceremonies at Manchester, which is about four hundred a year. I hope he will succeed, for he has entirely spent his fortune, which was very genteel, & I doubt more, now the Militia is discharged he has nothing to depend on, & a wife & four children to provide for he is one among a thousand proofs, of the sad effects, an early & imprudent marriage must produce – remember this my Child & be not in haste to do, what death only can free you from. Harry Haynes can barely see his way about, he walk'd over Platform last week. I beleive on recollection I mention'd both him & his brother in my last. You must wait for your lockett, till we hear the pocket Books are in yr possession for your Uncle will not send any thing of value, haveing trusted two parcels of several pounds value, & while triffles get safe they are delay'd. it is not easy for us to get a receipt from Packe as our parcels go by coach to him in London, to whom therefore can he give one. your Uncle means to write to him about this matter. it appears to me there is some trick in delivering trumpery things, & loseing what will yeild money. you find Mr Bugnion has his doubts by the advice he gave you in this matter, since Honesty is the best Policy, what can induce so many to be dishonest, surely it cannot give pleasure to live in fear of detection which every one must do that endeavours to deceive. no more to night as it is quite bed time to morrow I intend to finish –

Monday night - I have just eat my Bread & Cheese & shall dedicate a short time to my Dearest Nephew - who would probably be just return'd from Romsey fair, if he had been in England as young folks Love hurry & bustle. half the lower sort of our towns folk I beleive treated themselves with the jaunt - . to morrow & Thursday we are to have our last Routs. I expect about thirty each day – we must visit several familys that have settled since you left us – Miss Rookes school falls off very much, she has only four boarders which will not pay rent for the large house of Mr Monktons down the Coffee House court which she is now in - young Rooke the clergyman is in a melancholy low way, which too much religion, (or rather mistaken Religion) has brought him into – I can recollect nothing more just now – therefore adieu.

Wednesday ye 22d. our Company are just gone. the weather is greatly changed since I began my letter. a sharp cold wind, with a kind of cold rain, like sleet, succeeds the warm days we have enjoyed for a fortnight past. I doubt the fruit will suffer very much as it has done the last two years. I gave two shillings for a Gallon of apples this very day, therefore you may judge how scarce they are asparagus are four shillings a hundred, & all other vegetables dear in proportion – a warm rain would make all cheap - George Wells has fell down & cut his head a good deal – he is at the sick House – I hear him very well spoken of at College - & now my dearest Jack I conclude this long scrawl with Love from all your friends, & the sincere good wishes of yr truely affectionate friend Melicent Ballard

enclosed is some Gold-beaters skin.   yr Uncle will write to you soon by ye Mail

9. Letter written by Robert Ballard on July 1st 1784 from Southampton and sent by hand. The 'Mournful Packet' refers to Melicent's death;

My dear Boy
As long as you continue abroad I intend dedicating some part of the first of every month for your satisfaction, amusement, and instruction: & I flatter myself you will be as constant a Correspondent. I hope 'ere long this reaches you, Packe will have safely delivered the Mournful Packet together with the Locket & Waistcoat for which he gave Box the jeweller on Ludgate Hill a Receipt. I had nearly effected before the late change in the Ministry a clerkship in the Treasury for you with an £100 a year & with what your Guardians would have allowed you, you might have kept your Servant and two Horses, and provided you have been a lad of application, so as to be taken notice of by your superiors, your advancement would have been certain. I now have two other projects, one to get you into the Admiralty as a Clerk, and the other a sous secretaire to sir James Harris[1] at the Hague. Should Mr

1 Sir James Harris 1746- 1820 came from a well-known Salisbury family, and distinguished himself as Ambassador to France during the Napoleonic War and was made the first Lord Malmesbury. In 1795 he had the doubtful task of negotiating the marriage between the Prince of Wales and Caroline of Brunswick. Harris records that on being introduced Caroline knelt before the prince, who raised her (gracefully enough) and embraced her – said hardly a word, turned round, retired to a distant part of the apartment, and calling me to him said, 'Harris, I am not well; pray get me a glass of brandy'.

Cropp soon drop there wd. be an opening in my own business or if banking is your taste you may easily be placed in that situation. Now I would have you seriously weigh all these matters talk them over with Mr Cerjat & Mr Bugnion, consult your own inclinations & give me a candid answer resolving however when once fixed to give a singular attention to the Hoc Age whatever that may be. It has also been my wish to give you such a kind of Education as would fall in with most branches of genteel & at the same time industrious Society and to form & regulate your manner early in Life, the latter I would have very flattering accounts of through the means of Mr Rollestone who I find honor'd you with an Invitation. Cultivate my dear Child every useful Science, particularly Arithmatic & fine writing and habituate yourself to daily application by copying the best English and French Authors, for my earnest desire is to make you as elegant upon Paper an upon the Tapis. Should none of the foregoing schemes immediately take place & you have a mind to spend twelvemonth in France to perfect you in the pronunciation of that elegant language, I should recommend the town of Blois upon the Loire & to board you with some very genteel family & to have whatever Masters you thought proper to finish your Education, sho'd this Circumstance be agreeable to you communicate the same & I will write to Mr Bugnion on the occasion, or should you prefer remaining where you are, till you can be fixed absolutely , I have no sort of objection, but only wish my dear Boy that your time should be completely filled up by a whole train of useful and rational Improvement, & I think it would be doing you manifest injustice to send for you over before your ultimate situation is agreed on.

Mons. Talantine whom Madame Cerjal mentions and recommends meets with great Encouragment here, he is just steped over to Paris for the present holidays: je pense pour levant la tete, et pour avondir les Bras, il est beaucoup supervision a Mons. Burgat & your little cousin has edified by these particular attentions.

I think there is not much occasion for your troubling your Uncle Harrison for if he wishes for your correspondence he would most likely condescend to tell you. There is no such thing as procuring Handel's difficult music in the Country, if you are really anxious to oblige your Master in this particular I will send to London or at least order it from thence.

Miss Davy agreeable to your .... Aunt's intention leaves it until (illegible) Michaelmas & whether I shall get another Governante or send your Cousin to School is yet quite undetermined. We were rejoiced to hear by your letter of 13th ultimo that you had perfectly recovered your health & strength in which God Almighty preserve you & that you have enter'd into

Foreign correspondence with old Associates, which is a very proper and most improving Circumstance.

We all unite in kindest remembrance to you, and with my particular respects to Mr Gibbon[1] and Mr and Mrs Rolleston, not forgetting the family you are with, believe me Dear Jack
Your affectionate Uncle, and
Very sincere Friend
Robt Ballard J

APPENDIX TWO

Correspondence relating to Elizabeth Butler Harrison, courtesy of Colin Hyde Harrison, and letters left on deposit with Southampton Archives by Helena Austen Harrison, plus extracts from the household book courtesy of Malcolm and Sally Barton

Letter from Elizabeth Austen to her parents 1786

Dear Papa and Mama
As I have been favour'd with a letter from each of you, I know of no better method of expressing my thanks, than writing to you both in one and it shall be my endeavour to contribute as much to your entertainment as possible. I shall begin my narrative from the time of my quitting Chawton, as I am assured that the most trifling thing from which I receive amusement, will be a means of conferring pleasure to you both. On the eleventh of last month Mr Ballard arriv'd with his little Girl at Mrs Hintons, and on the 13th the Thursday we set off for Winchester where we were to dine and drink tea. Mr B keeps a Phaeton and a pair of pretty grey Poneys in which he drove Milly and myself, he also keeps a chaise like Mrs Sackville Austen only rather higher and with a head to it which Mr Harrison makes use of and accordingly drove his sister in. We reach'd Winton which is 15 mile from Chawton about One Oclock saw the Cathedral and the Picture I mentioned which I could have look'd at for

---

1 https://www.amazon.fr/Edward-Gibbon-Lausanne-rencontre-européennes/dp/288968038X John Butler Harrison would have been one of many young foreigners, like Gibbon himself, who came to Lausanne in order to finish their education. During the 18th century, the city was well-known for this, especially for members of the English gentry. It may have been that Harrison was a member of the Société Littéraire which had been set up by Gibbon's friend Deyverdun.

Letter of Elizabeth Butler Harrison, Southampton Archives

hours without being fatigued, it is so admirably finish'd and so very expressive from thence we proceeded to the Colledge and to many more places worth our attention, but were they to be enumerated, they would require more paper than I can well afford. At six in the afternoon we again proceeded on our journey. We had 12 mile to Southampton, the evening was mild and beautifull, and a most enchanting ride we had, the entrance to this Place is uncommonly fine, and all I have yet seen wholly out of my power to describe. On Friday we went a party on the water to Netley Abbey, an old ruinous place, but very romantic, and commands a most delightful view. Our company consisted of Mr and Mrs Waller and their son whom you know by name, Miss Letchmore and a Dr and Miss Grimwood,[1] this Gentlemans Brother married one of the Miss Cookes and is acquainted with Mr Tom Hooker. We all dined and drank tea at a farm House and return'd on the evening after having spent a very chearfull pleasant day. I must now tell you Miss Hintons are not with us our family consists only of Mr Ballard and his Daughter, Mr Miss Harrison and myself. On Saturday we receiv'd visits, which were out of number. On Sunday were at Church morning, and afternoon, and then I took a drive with Mr Ballard. Monday we return'd out visits, in the for noon, the Miss Wilsons and Miss Skinner drank tea with us, two familys we are particularly intimate with; and we enjoy'd a comfortable ramble on the beach till supper, for we all perfectly agree in our dislike of the publick walk. On Tuesday we all met again in the evening. Wednesday we breakfasted early and set off for Winchester din'd and spent the remainder of the day with Mrs Waller, where I had the pleasure of meeting Dr and Mrs Ballard, she is a most pleasing woman and I lost idea of fear as soon as I saw her, and I sincerely wish William could have got a place there as he would have had a most excellent Master and Mistress and an excellent example before him. Thursday the morning I wrote you that shameful letter, which till receiv'd you caused me many uneasy moments, in the fear that you would really think my head was turn'd and be for sending for me home at the time I thought it not proper to assign the reason which I trust you will give me credit for when I shall have informed you we were just setting out for the Ils of Wight, I had but three or four minutes to write in and that in the greatest confusion you can imagine Had I given you my reason you might I thought have been uneasy until you could hear I was return'd safe. Therefor I thought it more advisable even to risqué your displeasure the other way. Mrs Speed a very pleasing woman was of our party we went in our Habits and pack'd up Hats Gowns and ornaments, to appear at a concert and Ball there the next evening. The wind and tide were in our favour and we had a most charming passage over in about two Hours, we sang laugh'd and were merry the whole way. We din'd at Cowes the place we land at; and in the evening got six into a coach and went to Newport which was five mile. We had comfortable beds and every other convenience. Friday morning at ten we went to the Church to get good places to hear the Messiah, it was amazingly crowded and I was wonderfully pleas'd, we had between five and six hundred people and to me who never heard it at the Abbey it was particularly fine. It was over about three, we eat our dinner dresss'd ourselves to the best advantage, and made our

1   It looks as if the Leachmeres and Grimwoods are related. Dr Thomas Leachmere Grimwood hailed from Dedham in Essex and was master of the grammar school there.

appearance at the concert room about seven: that was over between nine and ten, we then adjour'n'd to tea and crakinals[1] which they are famous for at Newport. The dancing then commenc'd the room was so excessively crowded that I fond of dancing as I am refus'd every temptation of the kind, indeed one reason was, that from the heat, I was oblig'd to leave the room once on account of my nose bleeding, and I was apprehensive the exercise of dancing would perhaps increase it therefore I judg'd it prudent to be a spectator only. They had about seventy couple and they danc'd in two sets but so crouded as to have but little pleasure. We broke up at two and eat a very great supper, and did not part for bed till near four. The next morning we rose at ten, after breakfast Mr Harrison was so kind as to conduct Milly and me to Shays brooke Castle which was about a mile, and a very charming place: we return'd back about one, got into the same coach that brought us to Newport and whent back again to Cows, eat our dinner there, and in the afternoon arriv'd at Southampton after having had a most delightful expedition. Sunday we din'd and drank tea with mr and Mrs Moyes whose niece Mr Ballard is going to be married to and in the evening join'd our young Friends on the beach. Monday we did the same. Yesterday we spent the day at Mr Speeds to celebrate his birthday. And as I cannot say when I may again write, I shall finish this week as it is as plann'd. to day we drink tea with Miss Wilsons, and meet the Miss Skinners and a few more young people. To morrow we spend the day at Lyndhurst in the New forrest, a villa of Mr Ballards. Friday we go with the Skinners and Wilsons a water party and Saturday we go for the first, and I hope it will be the last time to the rooms and Ball. You see we are always engag'd and I am as happy as is possible I sung forth the praises of Steventon, and now I sing forth those of Southampton, two very different Places, and it may perhaps appear to you a paradox that I should be equally pleased with both, but so it is, not that I am the least more reconcil'd to a racketing life that I was, nor do we lead such a one, fir it is mearly a family or two that we are acquainted with (damage) most of our time and I cannot express the dislike I have of going to the rooms on Saturday but we must submit to unpleasant things now and then as they fall to the lot of every person. The season is fuller this summer and than has been known for many years, the Duchess of Devonshire[2] and Lord and Lady Duncannon have been here this ten days; I have persf'd them several times and this I am positive of, that was it not from their Rank, they never would be noticed neither as elegant or genteel women. Their walk is particularly vulgar,

1 Cracknel is a savoury biscuit
2 The famous Georgiana, Duchess of Devonshire. Lady Duncannon was her sister Henrietta, who was the mother of Lady Caroline Lamb.

for they swing both their armes more like showmen than Gentlewomen. In short the Duchess of Devonshire (damage) being taken for her maid, and for that reason she has (damage) exactly the same colour; I could send you many other anecdotes but they are too trifling to have a part in my paper. I have not yet had my Hair dres'd once, nor do I intend it, for I find many unavoidable expenses, and there is no occasion to admit unnecessary ones. My silk Gown you was so kind to give me lays by unmade up, for I aform you it is reckon'd gentiller to appear in an ordinary linen in preference to handsom silk. Pray what is your reason for asking the name of the Kentish Lady at Basingstoke Ball? The one I fancy you must mean lives at Canterbury, her name is charlotte Bridges, she is quite ador'd around Steventon and I think the young men will hardly suffer her to return by the name she came. When do you expect me home? I do not think if you will give me leave to stay that I shall see you before the middle of October, for I am to stay here till the second week in September and Mr Thortons family would be quite offended if I did not stay with them some time after my return. In about a fortnight we'll make a visit to Mrs Ballard of Wymmering for a few days. It is to be at the christening, and I am to represent Mrs Wells for her little Fanny I am then to see Portsmouth, and shall visit my cousin Frank then[1]

I do very sincerely wish Mr Hooker may succeed in his attempt after Penshurst living, as I have a very hight opinion of my Cousin tom, I know not of any young person more deserving of it. I hope soon to be favor'd with a letter from Harriet she is very near as bad a correspondant as the Bafrets. Tell Edgar I shall not let him off so easy for I shall insist upon having a few lines from him in answer to my long letter. I have not time to look over my Mothers epistle to know if I have omitted ansering any thing, but if I have it shall be inserted in my next, for I really have set writing till the very last minute and have hardly allow'd myself time to dress

Southampton July 26th 1786

You will hardly have patience to get to the end of this letter I must beg you to excuse all faults as I really have not time to read what I have written over. Remember me kindly to all friends who think me worth inquiring after. Mr Ballard and Mr Harrison desire their best respects and Miss Harrison her love and best wishes with a thousand thanks for the very high opinion you entertain of her. You will both accept my duty and believe your affectionate and dutiful Daughter EMA

---

1 In 1786 Jane Austen's brother Frank had just graduated from the naval college and joined the Royal Navy

Henry Austen's reply written from Tonbridge and dated August 8th

My dear Bess, We are much pleased with your truly entertaining narratives and are sincerely happy you are treading the paths of innocent and improving pleasures – you are now arrived at a time of life, in which it will be your own fault if you do not by observation conversation and reading lay in a stock of Ideas for future use. The happiness of all your days to come depends on the present moments. Let the fear of an Almighty God the love of your fellow creatures, and the natural duties you owe yourself be ever the leading principle of all your actions, and depend upon it, what ever evils or difficulties you may meet with in the course of things ever variable and inconstant, you will have sufficient strength given to support you under them and carry you thro them with humble submission and comfort – It is I own a very difficult task to persuade young people to believe what in a few years they will wonder at themselves for not believing – I do not mean hereby that I wish to see youth affecting the gravities and formalities that generally creep upon us as we advance in years, that is almost as bad as the reverse, to see a Grandmother painting for a ball. There are pleasures and amusements for every age, and prudence and discretion will be sure to adopt them properly as they rise. You may be certain that the best friends you have in the world are your father and mother, as they would most sincerely rejoyce to see you do well and would give you the best advice according to this knowledge, and as far as their influence reaches to teach you the right way. Never make yourself a stranger to us, but look upon us more as friends that are interested in your welfare than Parents that would exert an arbitrary authority. Perhaps you will think I have hitherto been transcribing part of a sermon, do so, I assure you it is a very good one and demands your attention – you have sit a very long time my dear girl before you think of returning home, surely you will tire out your friends, and make them more cautious for the future whom they engage on a visit to their houses. However if things are right I submit with chearfulness as your happiness is I believe concerned and your principal advisor is Mr Hinton's and my daughter Harrison. I know not with what I can fill my paper for you really deserve to have it filled in return for your very agreeable letters. You must give me leave to say in encouragement for you to go on, that I hardly know a young person whose mode of writing and art of expression pleases me better – you will hardly credit me perhaps the week before last I dined from home three days, at Ferox upon Venison, at Luttrels upon Venison and with Mrs Hassel at Lamberhurst. I am sometimes tolerable, sometimes very bad indeed, but the less of self the better. The Children and Harveys supped here last Fryday and we were all invited the next day to Mrs Harveys where we met Mrs J Harvey and her Mother. Next Thursday is the sale by Auction of the late Sir Richard Ryecroft at Penshurst. By the catalogue there are many valuable articles – yesterday Mrs Motley carried her daughter Jane to Whitelands. She is a very sensible child but wants I think a good deal of management. Ann Woodgate has been with us a fortnight. I wish she and her sisters had been permitted in a good school to unlearn what they have learnt at home, that by and by they might be able to make a good appearance and speak a good language. Fanny can't read yet, nor indeed any of them fit to be heard. I am sorry but my sorrow won't improve them. A confirmation was held here last Thursday. The Bishop did me the honour of a call and kindly asked after you. – your cosen J. Hooker has had an offer of going abroad for three years as Tutor and companion to a young gentleman of about eighteen and five thousand a year. I advised him much to accept it, particularly as it would tend to his own improvement. His Father and he go to Town to- morrow on the occasion. A letter from your Uncle John supposes you are yet in Hampshire and kindly invites you, and your friends in your return to Kent to make his house your home. – Write to him and let your letter be amusing. Is it not very extraordinary? Soon after her sister Illingworth came here Miss Harvey set of for London and after a months stay there is now gone into Cambridgeshire. – Miss de Papon we think has lost her spirits. I do not wonder at it. Miss Swayne has been some time in London. Last Saturday we were much surprized by the very unexpected arrival with Mr & Mrs Burges Comp. of a fine haunch of Venison. We dress it tomorrow, the Swaynes, Mrs Ann Woodgate, Miss Jordans and by a blunder Mr Miller partake of it. Mr Children engaged and the Hookers absent. Edgar desires you may be acquainted he is removed into a superior class. I have lately put him into Greek and he advances more that I could expect. Harriet is still with Mrs Pickard, and is to return the la (damage) this month. In her last letter she says she had written (damage). Pray notice it it may induce her to write again. I wish she would accustom herself more to it. You will be sure to pay our best respects and acknowledgments to Mr Ballard for his great civilities to you. I have often thought of writing to him myself as well as to Mr Hinton but am fearful I should give them more trouble than all I could say would pay for, and I am afraid if I live much longer I shall tumble into that very fashion which I am always abusing. – My Neice of (damage) grows I think worse and worse, in your absence I think we have had more of her company than usual. Mr Miller Aunt lag & Miss Scoones are her chief companions. Rare coalition for improvement. Poor Miss Fanny Scoones is not like to be long in this world. She swells now all over. Could you now have expected all this nonsense from me? Your Mother wished me to write, and as an address to you I own I have some pleasure in it. O my dear girl I shall joy to receive you at Tunbridge and your friends with you, but they must not expect in this dull place in the winter a return for the pleasures they have heaped on you in the summer. Continue your narratives and remember you add to our pleasures. Your Aunt Woodgate has been dangerously ill, I believe in a miscarrying way, but is now perfectly recovered – With best wishes for all your healths I am

    Your most affectionate Father HA
    Aug 8 1786

You always take care I hope to pay immediately your little debts as letters etc or they may be forgotten and you maybe the subject of foolish conversation.

Letter from John Butler Harrison III to his sisters Elizabeth and Mary

Buriton[1] October 14th
Dear Elizabeth
I was very much pleased at your kind remembrance of me, and shall take this opportunity of answering your letter. My reason for not using my sealing wax is that though not quite it is almost gone. Mrs Blunt drank tea here last night and I say down to play commerce you may guess what a figure I cut, I do not know what I should have done if I had not had Mrs Mant next me and Mr Blunt next to her who threw down many cards to mend my hand. Both Mr & Mrs Blunt are uncommon pleasant people. Tell Papa (for I shall not be able to write to him now) that I am much obliged to him for the gaters and papers and quills and that I hear from Miss Frances Mant[2] that his cavalry are going to quarter at Winchester. I dare say you will have no objection to go to Maningford and be put under the tuition of Nanny Perrot. We have for some time taken to fires. You must soon write me word whether you go or not. I am glad to hear that Aunt Harrison is well for as it is near as month since I heard from her and began to fear that something not quite pleasant was the cause of her silence. As I must write Mary believe me yours etc J B Harrison

My dear Mary
You have I hear been a long time at Winton and I hope brought back a good character with you. Tell Mama I have begun a letter to Mr Filmer. I suppose when your grand party come Charles will keep a secret. Robert Ballard told me that he was afraid William would not be able walk by the time I come back,

1   Buriton is a village in Hampshire.
2   Frances Mant 1784-1871 was the daughter of the Rev Richard Mant of All Saints church, Southampton and headmaster of King Edward VI School.

believe me dear Mary your affectionate brother J B Harrison

Letter from Rev Henry Austen to his daughter Elizabeth Butler Harrison, with news of her sons who had been staying with him. Her father had also run a school as well as being a clergyman.

My dear Bess
I cannot let the dear boys leave not without indulging a propensity of a line or two under my own hand. I have little indeed to say and for a little only am I fit. Your correspondence with Harriet precludes the necessity of entertaining you with the news and proceedings of this place which I cannot wonder at your wishing to be acquainted with. The perusal of your letters which is always permitted me is one of my greatest pleasures and I think would be increased by now and then an address to me. I will not promise to reply but think I may for Harriet. I am truly happy to tell you John advances apace in comprehension and knowledge. The Latin language begins to open on him, for a little while past I have persuaded him to attempt the first Eclogue in Virgil. He has really succeeded better than I could have believed and far better than I expected. The first entrance upon construction is a trying time for his age, however it must be gone through and will grow easier daily. He seems to delight in improvement and if that happy turn of mind continues banish all your fears for future increases I have not the least doubt of Henry's proper advances in time, he wants not by any means abilities necessary for learning but they are checked by a too great volatility which sometimes demands reprehension John loves play and his book too. Henry loves play and not his book. Consider the age of both and you will find the singularity on the side of John. While they are with you don't drive John too hard and work upon Henry with the English Grammars for in that he has sometimes almost put me past my patience knowledge of his own language makes the construction of a foreign one easy for grammar in all languages is nearly the same. Harriet manages the boys expences coach and all to Uncle Johns but is my intention after they are gone to pay her the amount that it may be my treat and no expence to you. She knows nothing of it nor will till to morrow. If Mr Harrison would have me discharge Mr Jefferies bill I can easily contrive to do it. I now regret the distance between us more than ever, as I wish now more than ever to see some of you. What with inconvenience and the expence of travelling I can have no hopes of Mr Harrison's attending the boys on their return to school. And now my dear Bess I refer you to the more agreeable entertainment of your sister's letter having no pleasures either to enjoy myself or to communicate to others. Remember me in the kindest and most affectionate manner to Mr

Harrison and let not those dear children I have known forget their Grandpapa. I intended but I had almost forgotten to tell you that I have finished about ten yards of netting, how much further I shall proceed depends on life and inclination. Now God bless you and yours prays your affectionate Father
HA Thursday 5th June 1800

Letter from Elizabeth Harrison Austen entitled the Picture of an evening party dedicated to the happiest family in England by an absent member dated Jan 13th 1815, a few months after her marriage to William Austen and her move to Kent.

Whilst alone in my cottage far, far from each friend
 The long winter nights I in solitude spend
My thoughts from my book still unbidden will roam
And fancy transports me in one instant home
There unseen by each inmate the parlour I view
And little suspected am present with you.
The tea being over the work is renewed
such a parcel of patches not mortal e'er viewed
Old shirts and old sheets are produced for repair
And my Mother in thorough enjoyment is there
 Can rags make her happy the Critic may ask
No fool it is duty that sweetens the task,
On her husband and children the labour's bestowed
And though heavy, that thought still can lighten the load.
My excellent Mother – but though I were fain
Her praises to sing still my muse must refrain
For paper would fail me were I to rehearse
In order each virture and grace that one hers
And her modesty one of the first in the train
Might the picture as fulsome reject with disdain
"Master George see there's Hannah" "Good night then Mama, Aunt, Mary, Charles, Edward, Jane, William, Papa"
"Why grizzle come here let ma stroke his white head. Good night little oak apple, make haste to bed."
Come I'll walk round the room and attempt to rehearse
your various amusements or business in verse
For though quick of sensation my Mother can find
That by pacing the room I excite a cold wind
still my shadow can surely produce no alarm

It will ne'er cause rheumatics or pains in the arm
There's Mary employed with her needle and thread
In preparing a cap for some little childs head
For who its intended I'm sure I cant guess
But I think I ne'er saw e'en a baby cap less.
"Mama you and I now the candle divide
"Now Elizabeths gone I come close to your side
But still though I'm happy to think on her joy
I must own it is happiness mixed with alloy
Perhaps it is selfish I try to refrain
But how often I wish she was with us again"
"No my dear your not selfish the Mother replies
"In affectionate hearts such desires must arise
Tis nature suggest them ne'er envy that soul
Which proudly asserts its above their control
Perhaps my dear Mary such feelings were given
to induce us to place our affections in Heaven
Wher no separations shall call forth a tear
Or pleasure be mingled with sorrow as here"
Aunt Goring comes next I well know her old place
And there is another old friend the red case
"Well Betsy?? The total just guess the amount
"You know this last three years I've kept an account
"You may laugh but should fortune still smile on my pains
I' will be difficult soon to compute all my gains
Should the harvest prove good I mean yield a fine straw
And government fail to forbid it by law
I shall furnish all Paris with bonnets of plat
And the ladies there luckily love a large hat
But my views extend further you'll think me romantic
But I hope that my straw will soon cross the Atlantic
Where the dames who the fashions of Washington rule
shall praise Nanny Perrot and Manningford school"
Little Fanny meanwhile has with books made a house
And has drawn up her paper dolls mute as a mouse
When a terrible gust oversets the whole row
"Charles do mind your summing and not teaze me so"
Says Charles "I won't do it again [Nanny hag?]
For I see I have stirred up the little black [dog?]

Who asked for some paper, come here's a spare leaf
"Oh Fanny how sadly your eyes want relief
Come here we will try what Mama's combe can do
Oh bless us pray take that nail out of your shoe"
Then come Jenny and William with paper and pen
Attempting to represent houses and men;
"Ah what are you doing come here dolly Pink
I protest she is painting a house with red ink
Yes Papa the red paint is such terrible stuff
That the water won't make it dissolve fast enough
My dearest d'not bubble, nay why such a flurry
For nothing is gained Jane believe me by hurry
"Charles your pencil wants cutting do look for a knife
For that scrooping quite worries me out of my life"
"There I've only this line now I've done with the slate"
"Why surely my dears it begins to grow late."
"Where's Edward" "Ah dozing full three hours ago."
"What a story Papa now how can you say so"
Says Papa "by your stretching I'm sure master Ned
you've been wishing some time you were snug in your bed"
Then with many good nights all the children retire
And the circle contracted just meets round the fire
And happy were Henry, Betty and John
If they Fortunatias cap might slip on
Were it left to their option which worn they would roam
I think I could answer they'd all meet at home
Then hast to that home where such parents are found
All hast to the hearth were such pleasures abound
I know first of all blessings vouchsafed are below
Whose sweets erring mortals for trifles forego
Hast family love may thy beams brightly shine
To the end of our journey on me and on mine
Can death brake thy bands or dissolve thy firm ties?
Ah no cries the Charmer and points to the skies.

SA D/Z 676/3 Letter from Elizabeth Butler Harrison to her daughter Jane 1817 and letter from her son William.

My dear Jane

We are all extremely pleased with your long letter and rejoice you are so comfortable and happy: I feel satisfied you will court your utmost ability and gratify us by your improvements at midsummer. I am much pleased you have the liberty of writing home without restraint, an indulgence I never had at school and therfor it was always irksome to me. I shall notice all your deficiencies in grammar and spelling as I did in my first correspondence with (with) Henry or the favor confered on me would be a disadvantage to you. It is probably you may have heard of the death of Mrs Austen[1] at Rippington, she was an excellent good woman and in her very infirm state it is a most happy release. She died on Sunday last very suddenly Elizabeth had just finished reading the Psalms and lessons to her and had not been out of the room three minutes when she was seized with an apoplectic fit and continued insensible till the evening when she expired. It is a great satisfaction to us all your sister was at Rippington and will be a lasting comfort to herself. As it is not likely you will see any of the Family and the mourning is short we shall not be at the trouble and expense of sending you any change of dress.

To day is Mary's birthday which very possibly you may recal to mind in which case you will wish her many happy returns of it; she has this morning received the congratulations of her Friend Anna Maria. I have had a most gratifying letter from William, which I cannot send you as John has written in the same sheet but I will presently transcribe it word for word and I assure you it is without fault and John speaks very satisfactorily of him. Fanny goes on very pleasantly she missed you very much but is naturally fond of employment and never seems tired of herself. We get up at seven and she says her lessons before breakfast and I have never turned her in one. I have not seen George since his return to school but hear his eye is quite well and we do not intend to invite him home till Easter. Your Aunt Harrison for the last day or two has been sole Mistress at the National school[2] Mrs Hort being indisposed. She is quite in her element and I really think she will be kept in the employment for some time. Your Aunt Harriet it pretty well she has been at Church to day but would not dine with us. Mr Rushworth Rule is married and returned home again last Friday; we must make out visit to form next week. All your

1 Elizabeth Matilda's mother-in-law, another Elizabeth Austen, died in February 1817. Ann Govas *Jane Austen's Horsted Keynes Relations* Hayward's Heath 2017 p. 42
2 National Schools were founded in 1811 based on teaching of the Church of England and providing elementary education. Southampton's was opened in St Michael's Square in that year, in two converted houses. By July 1819 it had 150 boys and 160 girls undergoing education. Rev J S Davies *A History of Southampton* Southampton 1883 p. 325.

Southampton friends are much as when you left them poor Miss Biddulph has not yet been off the sofa. Pray write whenever you feel disposed every thing that relates to yourself will be interesting. As I shall be much engaged tomorrow I must hasten to transcribe this promised letter but must first tell you you should always write she has - not she as for has is the verb which you may without difficulty known by the pronown Personal (tu) coming before it. Our united love and best wishes and believe my dear Jane
Your truly Affectionate Mother E M Harrison
Sunday February 23rd 1817

Monday February 7th 1816
My dear Mama
As John has furnished me with pen and paper I shall take the opportunity of writing to you as you desired me, I had not been above ten minutes at the Pelican Inn before John came, who shewed me all that was to be seen in the Town of Newbury. We went then to Boxford and the next day we went on the Pony to Uffington which I enjoyed very much. I take a walk with John and the dog every day, and I have been twice at the top of the White Horse hill where we see the country to great perfection. I was very sorry that I could not see my Aunt Harrison before I went. John says that I am very good boy and that he has great hopes of me. I hope when I come home in the Summer that you will see me quite upright and that I hold my hands properly, for John whenever he sees me stoop hollows out up-up. John went to Wantage last Friday and when he was gone I took a walk with the dog but to my great surprize when I came home little Peter Beaver came and told me that he had bought his Pony for me to ride to Mr Beaver's and that John as soon as he came from Wantage was to meet me there. Upon this news I made as much haste as I could and we both of us set off together, he upon the donkey and I on the Pony and both of us arrived there very safely, After Tea Mr Beaver read to us and Peter and Kitty Beaver and myself drew; you must not think that I did nothing while I was there for Mr Beaver heard me all my lessons. The next day after one OClock I took a walk with Peter and then we came home and saddled two donkeys and went out for a ride and then came home and got ready for dinner the next day being Sunday I went to Church, which I do not think near so pretty as Uffington I then came home and looked at all the Poultry mind you tell Fanny that I saw one of her friends among the Poultry, I came home to day after having spent a very pleasant time there, give my love to Papa and both my Aunts and to all at home and believe me your affectionate Son William Harrison.

Two undated notes to Margaret Ridding from Elizabeth and Mary Harrison, Miss Margaret Ridding a religious zealot used any scrap of paper including letters to make religious notes on, which is the only reason the notes survive.

My dear Miss Margaret
Mrs Goring Harrison having little time at her own disposal and some necessary preparations to make for her intended Tour has declined joining our Party to day so we all hope you will favor us with your Company at ten am? And with kind regards to Miss Ridding believe me truly yours E M Harrison
    My beloved departed Girl when very young asked several questions respecting the different Marys in the Gospels as she wished to be quite clear about them. Besides the Virgin Mary there are 3 particularly mentioned. Mary the sister of Lazarus Mary Magdalene out of whome Christ cast 7 Devils and Mary to whom the title of a sinner was applied, who should not be identified with either of the others see Deylings controversy on this history[1]

My dear Miss Margaret
We are very much obliged to yourself and Brother for your kind invitation and much regret we are engaged to a party at Mrs Petersons this evening. With our united kind regards to your circle not forgetting compliments to Miss Swanton believe me My dear Miss Margaret, yours very truly Mary Hooker Harrison
Jesus forgave the Samaritans, papists massacred the Hugenots, Jesus died for sinners, the Pope cause the innocent to be put to death. Jesus poor & humble went about doing good, they rich, haughty, & powerful sow every where hatred, anethemas & faggots [2]

Letter from Elizabeth Butler Harrison in 1839 (on the occasion of her 50th Wedding anniversary) to Mrs Goring of Wiston Park, Steyning, Sussex, her husband's cousin the former Mary Ballard.

My dear mrs goring
We hope you an all returned home safe and well after the grand and splendid entertainment at Goodwood. Mr and Mrs Biddulph I hear are to be there and after you are perfectly recovered and have leisure we shall like much to receive some account of it. We have had in our little way a very gratifying inviting at St Mary's on the 20th of Feb our fiftieth wedding day. It is now about three

1   SA D/PM Box 42 5/23.
2   SA D/PM Box 42 5/22.

months since that we were first informed it was the wish and intention of every absent member of the family to be present that Day to celebrate what they called the Jubilee we entered into the genial feeling and made our little arrangement with quat pleasure and it was in every sense of the word a truly gratifying meeting. John and Mary Ann arrived by the Oxford coach Thursday, Henry and Susan at ten o'clock that same evening by the Salisbury coach, that He might attend the office that morning, and it is some what remarkable that Mr Cary, Ash Wednesday, should for the first time have signified his intention of having the Prayers and a Sermon every successive Wednesday in lent, which gave us all (the Austens accompanying us) an opportunity of attending Divine service in our own Parish Church. Great indeed have been the mercies and blessings vouchsafed us through life May they ever be with thankfulness as deeply engraven on our Hearts. It was the request of every absent member that on the 20th our own immediate family were alone to be present and we sat down at Dinner eighteen and you will be pleased to hear Mr William Austen joined us, which we feared he would not feel equal to do but He had set his heart upon it and I am happy to say was very cheerful and has not suffered. Thursday we dined twelve the rest of our Family with a few Friends added, joining us in the Evening. Friday the same again. Mrs GH spending the first and last day, and resting at Home the day between. On Saturday by the Oxford Coach the John Harrisons left us, I am accompanying them for a month to Evenley. The Henry Harrison's arranged to return by the Sunday night mail. One circumstance I shall mention which tho very gratifying was so intirely unexpected as to be very affecting. After the desert was placed on the table I observed one of the servants to come in and remove a cake from the centre and put down a something that was silver, but what it was at that distance I could not discern. Immediately that the door was shut, John who was seated at my right hand stood up and expressed for all the assembled party their grateful feelings on this memorable and happy day presenting a very pretty silver ink stand for our drawing Room Table, on the reverse side of which was engraved the following Inscription which he read and I shall transcribe for your Perusal presented to John Butler and Elizabeth Matilda Harrison on the Fiftieth Anniversary of their Wedding day By their ten affectionate children as a memorial of their grateful recollection of their unwearied parental love and with every feeling of devout Gratitude to Almighty God for His wonderful Mercy in preserving so large a family in health and happiness and without a visitation from Death for half a Century. 20th of Feb 1839

  I need scarcely add that the whole assembled Party very much enjoyed themselves. We had but one disappointment in our expectations. We had all hoped to see Robert with his Family John and Henry were much mortified He was not there Johnny's visit unexpected or not are always pleasurable to us I did right we had nothing but half cold mutton to give him, but He is so easy, friendly and cheerful it is a treat to us All when He walks in. I thank you for a Ham which he did not mention or I hear of till the next day – we are very glad to hear Mr Wells continues better and as I cannot write a second letter to the same Place on the same subject I shall be quietly obliged when opportunity offers if you will relate the particulars of our Family meeting.

Your proposed excursion up the Rhine amused us Emily reminding us of old times Mr H saying Mary Ballard was ever a schemer and never met with a difficulty in her life[1]

You cannot think how much He enjoys his liberty He went with me to call on lady Thomas yesterday. My sister has not been so well the last week or two, no doubt she feels the unsettled weather and poor thing her melancholy situation more when we are altogether at St Marys. My quiet consolation she so entirely approves her nurse Mrs J Harrison extremely enjoyed her excursion she was very cheerful and expect to add to her Family in the middle of May. John was quite well Both [word illegible] kind accumbracing?

We are expecting Mr and Mrs Payne by the Hyde Packet to spend a few days with us and Fanny Griffith in her way from London Home in the course of next week. William Austen has looked very ill and suffered acutely with his Head. He has just seen Lyford again and is to try a change of system. I saw a very cheerful letter from Milicent to Emily last week, the Baby takes notice and is daily improving. The Boys are returning to school when she hopes to get down stairs, she still suffers in many ways

Mrs Walter Murray is still Here I wonder Robert rests quietly without some decision Pray accept and present to your Family our kindest regards and believe me Dear Mrs Goring your sincere and affectionate E M H
We had had most satisfactory accounts from India

I have just opened my letter to say Mr H has met Robert who has taken a House in Cumberland Place in days of your Polligon lane I think it a most desirable situation.

I have heard nothing more.

Extracts from the household book

1 Mrs Goring was Mary Ballard before her marriage, daughter of John Butler Harrison's uncle Rev John Ballard. Jane Goring, Joyce Sleigh, Jill Turner, Janet Pennington & Jane Harvey (eds) *Lives, Loves and Letters, The Goring Family of Wiston, Sussex 1743-1905* Sussex 2017 p. vi.

Recipes from the period of Elizabeth Butler Harrison's ownership were provided by: Mrs Hinton, probably the aunt of her husband John Butler Harrison

Stewing of cucumber – Put a slice of Butter into your frying pan slice your Onion and Put in with them a bit of Beef which will make Gravy enough – then pare one quarter your Cucumber take out the inside and put them into the Onions let them be floard and fryed at a high brown – Add some boiling Water but not so much as to make it thin. Put all into the stewpan and let it do gently If you think them too thick inducing all a little more boiling Water season to your taste and add a little Cayan NB the Onions are sent to table with the Cucumbers

Mrs Woodgate, the Woodgate family of Summerhill in Kent were related to the Butler Harrisons and Austens

Fish sauce – take Walnuts proper for pickling ground them, squeeze them through a course clothe, let the liquor stand a day or two to settle then pour off the clear. To every pint of liquor put a pound of Anchovies half a quarter of an ounce of Mace ditto of Cloves ditto of black Pepper laid all there together till the Anchoves are reasonably dissolved then strain it through a Hair sieve and with the back of a spoon force as much of the thick through as you can. To every quart just half a Pint of Vinegar sixteen sharlots and some Garlick boil them to gether till the sharlots are tender, let it stand till cold then stir it well and Bottle it for use.

Mrs Motley Austen
Francis Motley Austen was the cousin of Elizabeth's father and Jane Austen's father George. His wife was Elizabeth Wilson. Jane Austen refers to the connection in a letter to her niece Caroline in 1817 following Mrs Motley Austen's death, 'living here we thought it necessary to array ourselves in our black gowns, because there is a line of connection with the family through the Prowtings & Harrisons of Southampton'.[1]

Ginger wine – Take 24 gallons of Water and 24 ground of lump sugar 2 ounces of Ginger well bruised, boil it one hour, then add the whites of eight eggs well

---

1 *Jane Austen Letters* p. 331. Dirk Fitzhugh '"Such ill-gotten wealth can never prosper": the nineteenth century Austens of Broadford and Capel Manor, Kent' in The Jane Austen Report Journal 2020 pp. 96-102.

beat, take of the foam as it rises strain it into a clear dry tub and let it stand till it is cold then put it into a cask with the juice of 14 lemons and the Peals cut very thin, about half a spoonful of Ale yeast on the top, stop the cask close for a fortnight it may then be bottled and in another fortnight it is fit for Drinking.

Miss Hancock
This was possibly Eliza Hancock, daughter of Jane Austen's Aunt Philadelphia, who married as her second husband Jane Austen's brother Henry.

Lobster sauce – Pick the meats of two boild lobsters pound it in a mortar put half an ounce of mace quarter of an ounce of cloves twenty Anchovies and a handful of salt all mixed well together in a mortar with a quart of white Wine and some Lemon Peel – Bottle it and well secure the cork – this will keep years if made every year half the quantity will do
Custard pudding – To a pint and half of new milk add three Eggs the yolks and whites beated separately a table spoonful of brandy, sugar, lemon peel and nutmeg to your taste. The crust to be partly baked before the custard is poured into it and then to be baked half an hour and five minutes

Mrs Swayne

Ground rice pudding – I beat a quart of Milk with half a pound of ground Rice then stir into it half a pound of Butter half a pound of sugar and half an nutmeg, when near cool add the yolkes of twelve eggs, and a glass of Brandy – Bake it an hour

These recipes above were not in Elizabeth's own handwriting, probably being entered by the compilers of the recipes, but the next set are mostly written by her and include donations by

Mrs Porteus

Ginger beer – 9 Gallons of water 12lb of firm moist sugar 9 whites of Eggs well Beaten put them on the fire and when near boiling skim it very clear and add 8 oz Ginger well bruised let this liquor boil half an hour Pour the liquor boiling hot on the thin rind and juice of six firm lemons and when cool enough put all into your Caske with a little fresh yeast close your Caske the next day and bottle it at the end of ten days not longer and it is fit to drink in a week – a nine Gallon cask fills ten dozen soda water Bottles.

Mrs Biddulph, the Biddulphs are mentioned in EBH letter above about the Goodwood party in 1839.

For the Hooping cough – Take one oz of sena two drams of Rhubarb of Tartar of vitriol of Coriander seeds and aniseeds one dram of each half an oz of liquorish root and one oz ligman Gunaicum Boil the above ingredients in a pint of water to half the quantity strain it clear and put them in six oz of loaf sugar then simmer it up and when cold preserve in a dry bottle.
Give the child one table spoonful every morning and night going to bed bathing the back with warm rum before the fire if it should work very much give a lesser quantity or miss a dose the age of the Child should be considered a large spoonful for one of five years old, the same ingredients will make half the quantity by adding them to half a pint of water and proceding as above mentioned.
For sore throat – Take four oz of the fat of a loin of mutton put it into a new glazed pipkin with it on the fire when melted strain the fat put it in the pipkin again with two oz of butter without salt when melted again add two oz of Rosin when that is melted put to it one oz and half of Bee's wax and when all are duly melted together put in into a gallipot till wanted. Spread it then upon a rag and put quick round the neck, Rub at the plaister till the inward swelling is gone approved by Dr Addington and other doctors for all sore throats even when putrid but sovereign in a Quinsy
To clean tables – Scour them with hot vinegar and soft soap to clean them thoroughly from grease using a scrubbing brush for this purpose then to be well rubbed with a linen cloth dipped in the following varnish – no flannel must be used – ½ an oz of Alkenut root, ½ an oz of rose pink, ½ oz of black rosin one pint of cold drawn linseed oil to be well mixed together and kept for use
To distill milk – Put a Gallon of the best Cows Milk into a jar that will bear the Fire or a cast iron pot fasten the top of a still very firmly to the top of the jar or the spirit will force it up, great care must be taken that it does not burn; take only one Quart of liquor from the Gallon of Milk – The Dose is a quarter of a pint Morning and Evening – but if the patient is very weak it is better to begin with a smaller quantity NB it is a fine restorative and will frequently agree where the stomach is to week to bear asses milk

Mrs Austen of Tonbridge, Elizabeth's mother

Mince pies ¾ lb of the under part of a sirloin of beef par boiled ½ lb of Beef suet (Kidney) cut very fine 1/2lb of currrants good weight when picked and

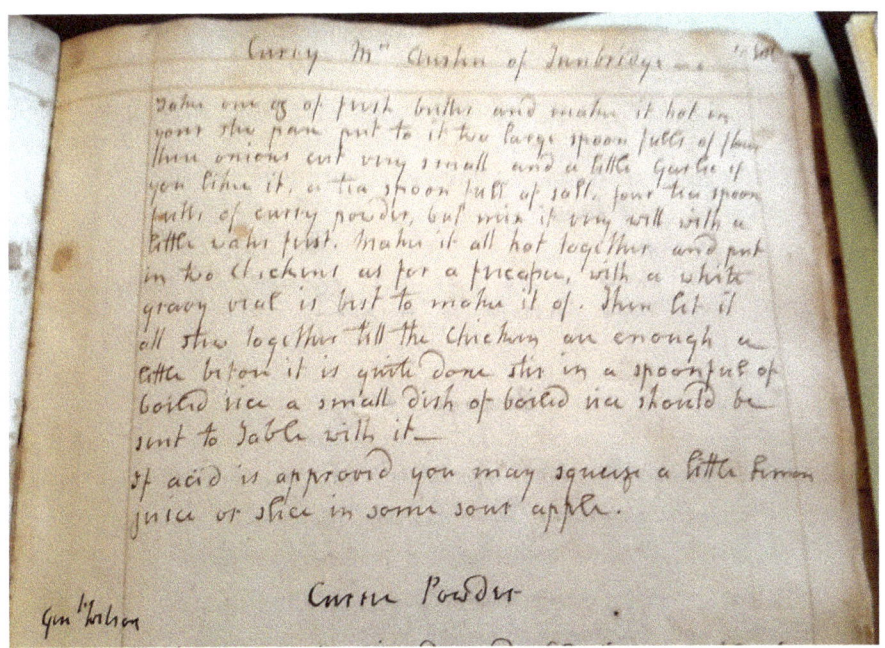

Recipe from Household Book, private collection

dried ½ lb lump sugar pounded 6 Golden Pippins or the best apples you have The crumb of one penny roll The peel of two lemons chopped very firm without a particle of the white ½ an oz of Mace and a large nutmeg a small handful of salt the juice of three lemons half a pint of port wine ditto of sweet white wine All mixed well together and put down in a Jar and covered with a brandy paper Add a very small tea spoonful of brandy to each Pie

Curry – Take one oz of fresh butter and make it hot in your stew pan put to it two large spoon fulls of flour three onions cut very small and a little Garlic if you like it, a tea spoon full of salt, four tee spoon fuls of curry powder but mix it very well with a little water first. Make it all hot together and put in tow chickens as for a fricassee with a white gravy veal is best to make it of. Then let it all stew together till the chickens are enough a little before it is quite done stir in a spoonful of boiled rice a small dish of boiled rice should be sent to table with it – if acid is approved you may squeeze a little lemon juice or slice in some sour apple

Mrs E G H, Elizabeth Goring Butler Harrison, Elizabeth's sister-in-law,

Lemon pudding – Grate a quarter of a pound of bread and the peel of two large lemon, add a quarter of a pound of lump sugar pounded, boil a pint of

milk and pour over the above ingredients and when cold add the juice of two lemon and three Eggs Bake it with puff paste in the dish or boil it if preferred
Orange jelly - squeeze the juice of eight China and four seville oranges then grate the rind of one orange and one lemon, dissolve two oz of isinglass[1] in a quart of boiling water strain it into the juice with half a pound of fine sugar stir it often and when cold pour it into your moulds. You may add the juice of one lemon if you like it. Wine may be added for company

Gen. Wilson, possibly Robert Wilson or Samuel Wilson, of the EIC army

Curry powder – To thirteen oz of coriander seed, add five oz of black pepper one oz cayenne pepper, three oz of cumin seeds, two oz of kumqick seeds and six oz of pale coloured Turmwrick. Pound these altogether very firm, then set them in a Dutch oven before the fire to dry well, and keep turning it often, when cold put it into a dry bottle corked and kept in a dry Place it will be good many years.

Mrs Barrow

Pickled beef – Rub a round of Beef with 2 oz of salt Petre finely powdered let it stand all night, then rub it well with one oz of black pepper one and half oz All spice one pound of salt half a pound of brown sugar let it remain in the pickle 12 or 14 days turning it every day. Lay some Beef suet at the top and bottom. Cover it with a coarse paste and Bake it six hours when it comes out of the Oven pour off the Gravy – this is for 20 pound of Beef
To make vinegar – to carry Gallon of water a pound of coarse sugar to be boiled till the scum is interily gone. A pound of treacle to be added to carry nine Gallons when it is nearly boiled, it is then to be put into an open vessel, and when nearly cold a slice of toasted bread, spread on each side with yeast is to be put in, and when quite Cold to be put into the Barrel with the toast which is not to be slopped down. It must stand six months at least before fit for use
Blacking for shoes – Half pound of Ivory Black 2 penny worth of oil of vitriol a spoonful of salad oil a small tea cup of brown sugar mixed with a proportion of Beer to make it sufficiently liquid

Mrs Austen

Recipe for stewing carp – scale and clean your carp thoroughly then fry them for about five minutes and take particular care that the fat boils before you put

1   A kind of gelatine made from fish, especially sturgeon and used in making jellies.

them into the toping pan when they have been fryed a nice brown put them in a stewing pan with the following ingredients. One pint and half of Port wine the same quantity of water, six anchovies, a dozen cloves a glass of mushroom catchup two sticks of horse raddish, and pepper and salt to your taste, when they have stewed an hour and half, take them out, and thicken the sauce with a piece of butter the size of a walnut rolled in flour, then boil the sauce keeping it stirring all the while, and strain it over the fish. Wash the roe perfectly clean and roll it up in a wet cloth as tight as possible in the shape of a Bologna sausage, it will require two hours boiling, when done it must be cut into slices an inch thick and laid on and round the dish with horse radish and cut lemon

Miss Morris, one of the daughters of her husband's cousin Milly who married Charles Morris

Spring pudding – 6 oz of Flour 4 oz of Butter 5 oz of sugar 6 eggs The whites of two beat well together the flour well dried previous to mixing

Mrs M Ottley

Orange pudding – six Seville oranges pare them very thin cut them in half take out the seeds carefully and put the pulp and juice into a Bason with three quarters of a pound of loaf sugar The white parts to be put into warm water and gently boiled over the fire till the bitterness is extracted then cut them in small slices an inch long the peels likewise put altogether in a Dish with a puff paste under it and bake it about half an hour

Mrs King

Orange marmalade – chuse the deepest coloured seveille oranges as free from spots as possible Wash them & brush them well in cold water. Then weight the Oranges & sugar to twelve pounds of oranges put 14 pounds of sugar. Next pare the rinds not very thin & put them into a Linen bag & boil them in soft water (putting them on with cold water) until you can pierce them with a straw. Let the sauce pan be without a cover as the steam is apt to insure the color of the rinds, while they are boiling squeeze the Oranges gently through a fine sieve which will keep back all the seeds. Then pulp the remainder of the Oranges & add the juice and pulp to the sugar which should be broken into small piece. Then cut the rind into very thin slices the thinner they are cut the nicer the Marmalade will look. Boil the juice and sugar five minutes then add the slice of rinds and boil the whole about thirty minutes. A brass preserving pan makes it the best color.

Miss Biddulph Birbury

Preserved oranges or ripe citron – Cut a hole in a seville Orange at the stalk and as big as a sixpence and scoop out the Pulp in them separately in muslin and lay them two days in spring water changing the water twice every day, then boil them in the muslin over a slow tin till they are thicker as the water wastes put more hot water into the Pan and keep them covered weigh the Oranges before you scoop them and to every pound put two pound of double refined sugar and a pint of water. Boil the sugar and water with the juice of the Oranges to a syrup drain it and let it stand till cold then put in the oranges and let them stand for half an hour if they are not clear boil them once a day for two or three days cover them when finished with brandy papers and close up with Bladder put them into jars the size of an Orange
Venison pastry – Bone a Ham take all the fleshy parts with some fat from a breast of Mutton season it well with peppers last and a very few cloves put a layer of ham and a layer of fat alternately in your dish with a little good gravy made from the bones of the Ham cover it with paste and bake it as any other meat pye

Mrs Wemsley

Risoles – Take a pound of veal which has been roasted a little suet shred very firm a quarter of a pound of Butter, a little lemon peel and onion, but altogether very firm in a marble Mortar, add a little lemon pickle to your taste and a little cyam Fry the risoles in mutton suet any shape you please

Mrs William Austen aka Elizabeth's eldest daughter

Palatable soup – Four large Onions sliced thin, put them in a saucepan with a bit of Butter, the size of a walnut whole peppers and salt put in over a slow fire, let it stand twenty minutes continually stirred. Slice twelve large Potatoes put them to the onions, and two quarts of stock stir it well let it do gently one hour and half then strain it off through a firm sieve before it is put in the turine add two table spoon fuls of cream and the yolks of two Eggs will beaten stir it well
Rissoles – take a pound of beef which has been roasted a little suet a quarter of a pound of Butter, a little lemon Peel and Onion beat altogether very firm in a

marble mortar add a little lemon pickle to your taste and a little cyam Fry the risoles in mutton suet any shape you like

Mrs H A Harrison, presumably the wife of Henry Harrison.

For cleaning tins – 1 pound Rotten Stone[1] 2 Pound soft soap 2 penny worth Camphor boiled in a little water half an hour

Mrs Pearson

Westphalia Ham – of common salt and coarse sugar each one pound. Bay salt and salt Petre of each two oz Junipur Berries one oz Infuse these ingredients in one quart of strong Beer and pour it boiling hot on the Ham turning it twice a day. Let it remain three weeks or a month then hang it up to dry. To the Ham of a Hog weighing twelve stone add to the above quantity one oz of salt Petre and half an oz of Bay salt.

Frank Woodgate

The Woodgates were a prominent Tonbridge family who married into the Hooker family. Francis Woodgate (1781-1843) lived at Ferox Hall in Tonbridge.

Plum Pudding – ¾ pound Irish Beef suet firmly stired 5 oz of Flour 5 oz of table Raisins cut in half and stoned 5 oz of little black Currants 5 oz of good brown sugar. Half a large nutmeg grated a very little salt Beat three Eggs and mix the whole together with a fork not spoon the night before wanted then well butter a shape and boil it six hours you may add a table spoonful of Brandy and a little sweet [left blank] if required

Mrs Lipscombe, the family cook

Cure of Ringworm – Twenty Grains of marieated Quick silver in an ounce of Lavander water To be applied lightly on the part affected with a feather
Excellent plum cake – Take three pints of Dough ½ lb of fresh butter ½ lb of lard ½ lb moist sugar 2 ounces candied lemon peel 4 Eggs, 1 nutmeg, grated, and a little Allspice – Add to this 1 and ½ lbs of Currants mix it all well together in a deep pan then put it in a tine & bake it

1   Rotten stone or tripoli is fine powdered porous rock used as a polishing abrasive for metal.

Taken from a newspaper

The Cottage Pudding taken from the News Paper July 12th 1785 – 2 pd of Potatoes boiled, peeled and mashed, a pint of Milk 3 eggs 2 ounces of moist sugar Mix it well together and bake it ¾ of an hour

APPENDIX THREE, FAMILY TREES

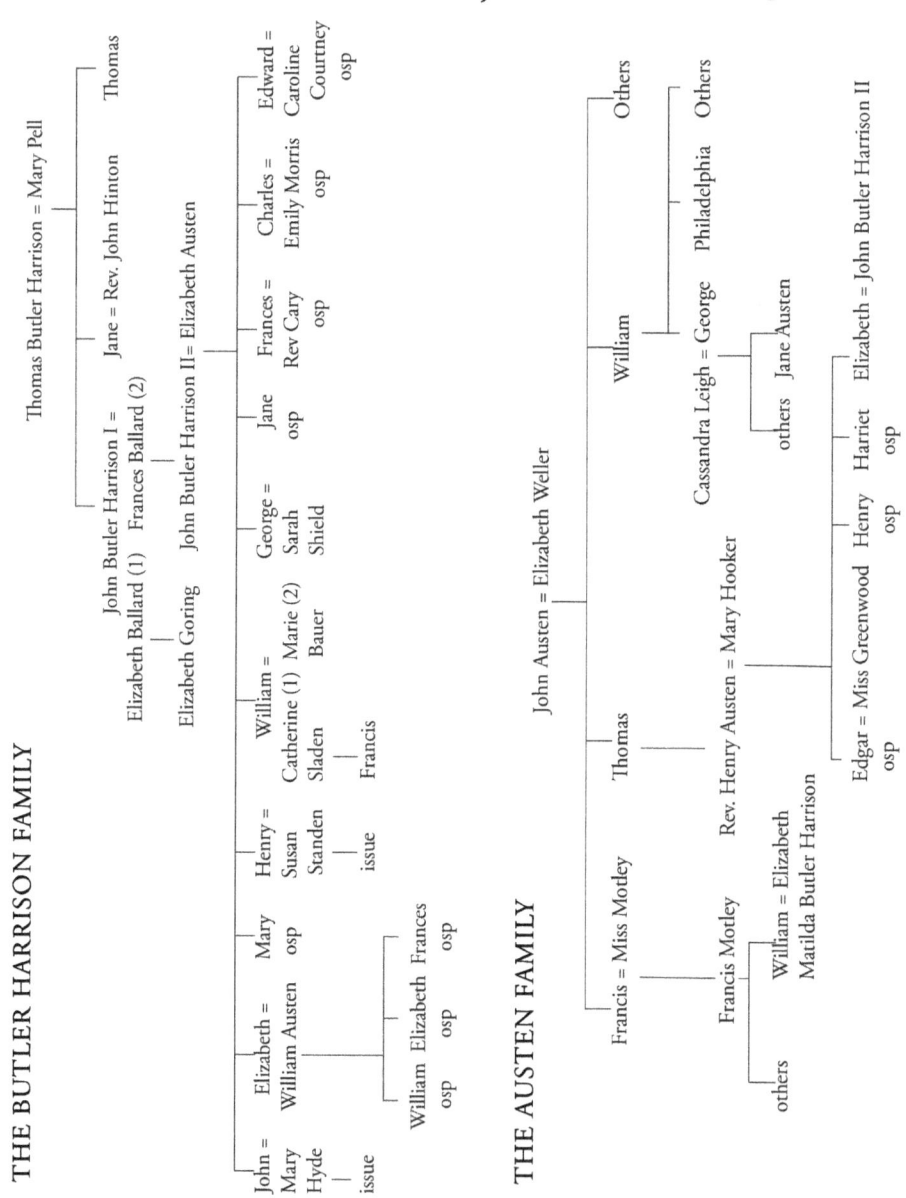

APPENDICES

THE MIDDLETON FAMILY

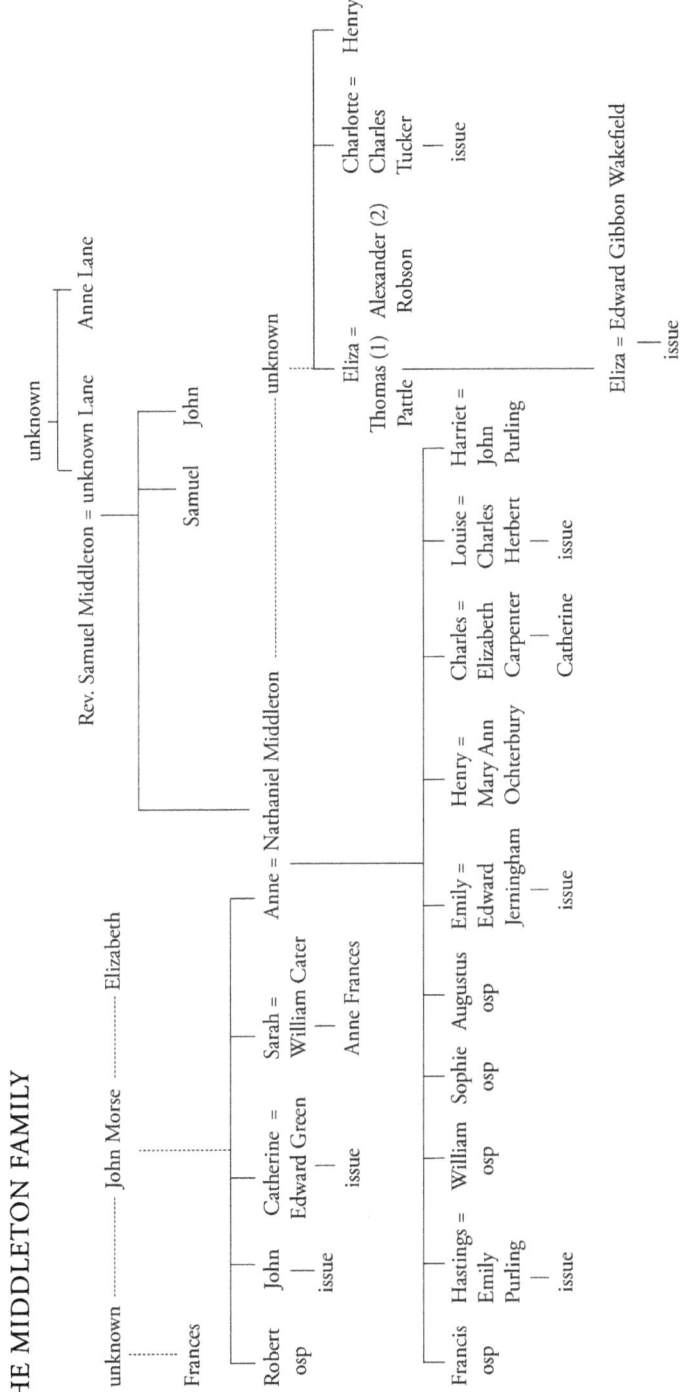

THE LEWIN FAMILY

THE BALLARD FAMILY

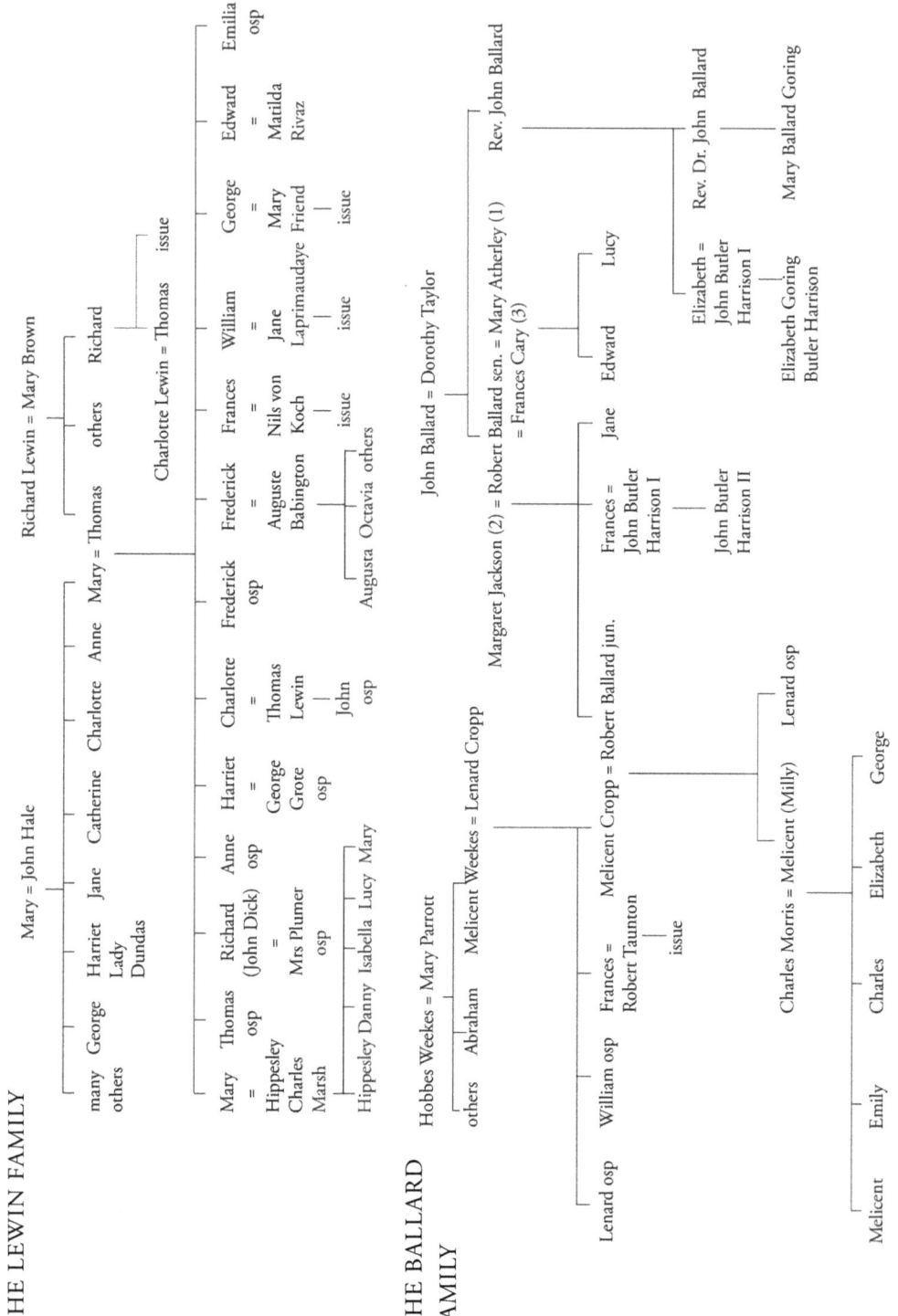

APPENDICES 317

THE NEWELL FAMILY THE LANCE AND FITZHUGH FAMILIES

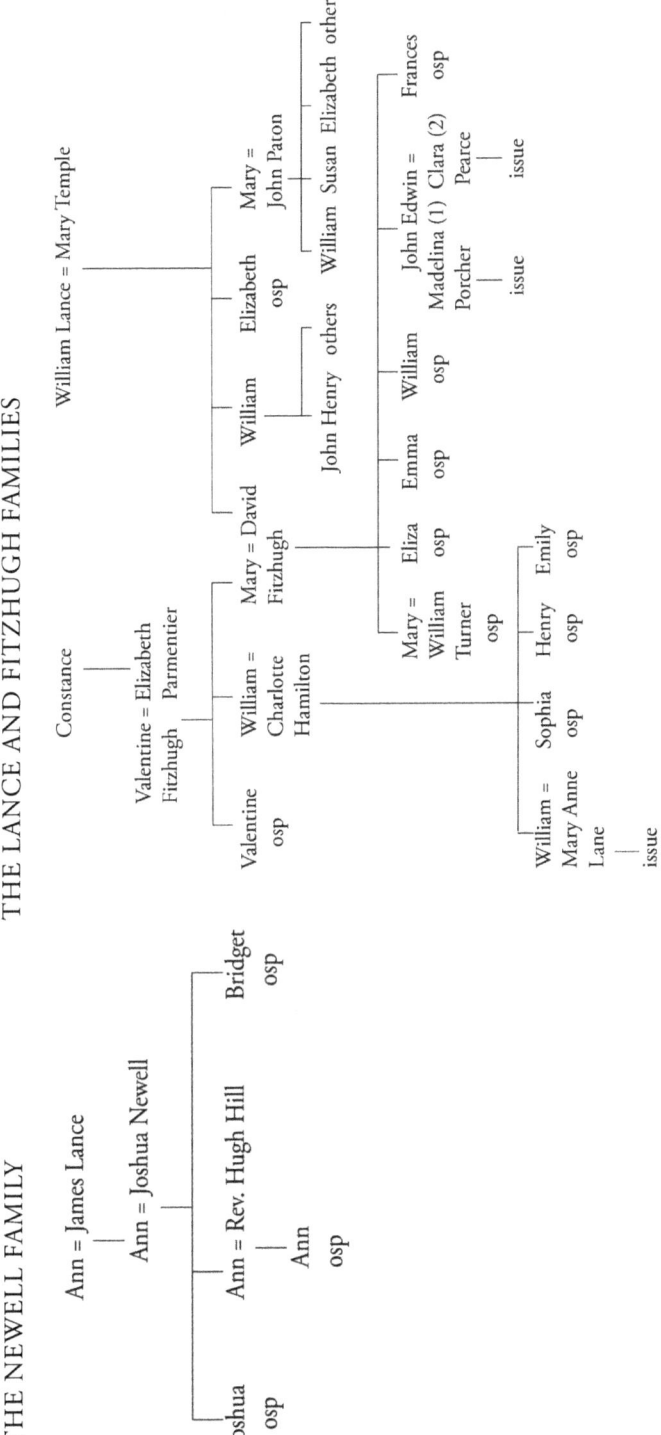

BIBLIOGRAPHY

Primary Sources

Affleck Thomas *The Cotton Plantation Records and Account Book No 3 1857*
Andrews, William *The First Volume of the Poetical Works of William Andrews, Attorney at Law* Southampton 1809.
Asiatic Journal and Monthly Register for British India and its Dependencies Vol II London 1821
Austen J *Persuasion*
Pride & Prejudice
Austen J *Minor Works* ed. R W Chapman London 1969
Ballard Family Bible transcriptions, private collection Colin Hyde Harrison
Bodleian Library Lovelace-Byron Collection Letter 69
Bodleian Library Johnson Family Letters Ms.Don. c193 23
British Library MS 16263 Correspondence of Sir Elijah Impey
Broadlands Archives BR 11/13/1 MS 62 Letter of Mary Temple
Byles, George *Reveries in Confinement: A Poem by George Byles written in the Debtor's Ward, Southampton* Southampton 1804.
John Butler Harrison I Journal Tour of Europe 1765 private collection Malcolm & Sally Barton
Cosens Dr *Essay of Economy & Beauty* 1770
Craven Elizabeth *The beautiful Lady Craven: the original memoirs of Elizabeth, baroness Craven, afterwards margravine of Anspach and Bayreuth and princess Berkeley of the Holy Roman Empire (1750-1828)*
Davison, Noel, Templer, Middleton & Wedgewood Papers 1794-1816 NatWest Archive
Day, James Trelawny *Letters from Bencoolen, 1823-1828, Thomas Day and William Day* Kilkerran 2008
Drury Lane Theatre Theatrical Season 1773-1774
Equiano Olaudah *The Interesting Narrative of the Life of Olaudah Equiano or Gustavus Vassa the African written by Himself* 1789
Finding aid to the Jerningham Letters: Aristocratic Women; the social, political and cultural history of rich and powerful women, A Listing & Guide to Part 2 of the Microfilm Collection, Adam Matthew Publication 1998
Letters of Melicent Ballard private collection Malcolm & Sally Barton
Lipscomb G *A Journey into Cornwall through the Counties of Southampton, Wilts, Dorset, Somerset and Devon* London 1799

Gilpin W *Observations of the western parts of England, relative chiefly to picturesque beauty* London 1798
Hartley Library Special Collections AO 174 Lines of Lord Byron, The Character of Buonaparte
Household Book of Elizabeth Butler Harrison private collection Malcolm & Sally Barton
Kemble F *Records of a Girlhood* New York 1880
Letters & Documents of the Butler Harrison Family private collection Colin Hyde Harrison
Lewin T H *The Lewin Letters Vol I & II* London 1909
Mackenzie M *An Account of the Plague at Constantinople* Letter to Sir James Porter 1762
Mottley's Naval and Military Journal 1808
New York Public Library Lady Byron Manuscript Material, Pforzheimer Collection
Parliament Papers Vol II Estimates & Account 21 April – 23 November 1820
Porter J *An Account of the several Earthquakes of late felt in Constantinople* letter to Rev Wetstein 1755
Philippart J (ed) *The Royal Military Calendar Vol 3* London 1820
Reports of Cases in Chancery 1828
Reports of Cases in Chancery, Argued and Determined in the Rolls Court during the Time of Lord Langdale, Master of the Rolls 1838-1866
Spencer A (ed.) *The Memoirs of William Hickey 1775-1782* London 1914
The Memoirs of William Hickey 1782-1790 Vol III London 1923
Standing Orders & Regulations for the 85th Light Infantry London 1813
Steel's *Original and Correct list of the Royal Navy* London 1799
Stirling A M W (ed) *The Diaries of Dummer: The Diaries of Stephen Terry Esq 1774-1867* London 1934
Sykes Mrs *Stories of Four Nations* London 1813
The Annual Biography and Obituary for the year 1832 Vol XVI 1832
The Exhibition of the Royal Academy 31st 1799
The Journal of John Sturdy private collection Colin Hyde Harrison
The Travel Journal of Ann Sophy Mackie, Chawton House Library
University of Pennsylvania *Fanny Kemble Further Records 1848-1883* New York 1891

Southampton Archives
SC/AG7/2 Rate Book All Saints
SC/AG7/3 Rate Book St Lawrence
SC/AG8/2/2 Rate Book St Lawrence
SC/AG8/5 & 6 Rate Book 1791-1795 & 1806-1808 All Saints
SC/AP /1/2 Pavement Commissioners
SC2/1/13 Council Minute Book
SC8 /2/25 & SC8/1/3 Sandwalkers Licence
SC4/3/832b & SC4/4/526/32, 33a-b Marriage Settlement Melicent Ballard & Charles Morris
SC4 /4/551/4-10 sale of Lansdowne Castle
SC4/3/1199a, SC4/3/1203a. SC4/3/12004 property leases Princess Berkeley

SA4/3/1425 lease of Harriet Austen
SC9/4/112c William Smith examination
SC9/4/607, 608, 626 transportation of Thomas Cooper
SC9/4/785 arrest of John Jackson
SC9/4/807 & 836 Apprentice of John Hawkins
SC9/4/850 Robert Hill apprentice
SC9/4/654 James Hawkins linendraper
D/MC/10/8-11 Shergold boarding school
D/PM 1-34 Bankruptcy of John Brissault
D/PM 3/7/2 estate of Abraham Weekes
D/PM 3/7/3 details of the property of Robert Ballard on the High Street.
D/PM 4/9/1-4 Correspondence re sale of 1 Hanover Buildings
D/PM 10/5 estate of Charles Baker
D/PM 10/6 property of Robert Ballard senior, including details in relation to dispositions in his will
D/PM 14/1 & 2 The bankruptcy of Andrew Nance
D/PM 15/29 & 66/21 sale of Northam Bridge Company shares
D/PM 20/ 1-5 Letters of the 103rd Regiment
D/PM 20/7/2/1 & 3 103rd Regiment
D/PM 21/17 trust for the children of Johanna Barr
D/PM 23/10/1 bankruptcy of John Brissault
D/PM 30/2 draft will of Harriet Austen
D/PM 36/4 Letters of Thomas Ridding
D/PM 37/2 John Butler Harrison executor to the will of Charles Morris
D/PM 40/37/2 music concert handbill
D/PM 42 5/10, 15, 17, 18 Letters of Thomas Ridding
D/PM 42/2/15 Diary of Mary Ridding
D/PM 42/3/20a Ladies Useful Repository
D/PM 42 3/37 Newspaper Paragraphs
D/PM 42/5/22, 23 letters of Margaret Ridding
D/PM 44/41 attorneys of Ann Newell
D/PM 44/158, 44/159, 44/212 plantation workers of Ann Newell
D/PM 44/159 contract James Cushen Hall
D/PM 45/3/54 Edgar Austen articles
D/PM 45/3/74, 75, 78, 70 Edgar Austen legal documents
D/PM 45/3/77 bond Andrew Goater Haynes
D/PM 54/12 Lease of Chessel Cottage
D/PM 54/72 marriage settlement of Robert Ballard
D/PM 56/13 partnership accounts John Butler Harrison II & Charles Morris
D/PM 58/3/5 Harriet Austen property Hanover Buildings
D/PM 63/3/101 draft lease re slaves on The Lodge plantation
D/PM 64/1 lease of warehouse
D/PM 64/2/2 guardians of John and Elizabeth Butler Harrison
D/PM 64/2/17 lease of Hanover Buildings to Valentine Fitzhugh
D/PM 68/3, 69/14/1, 44/171 Bankruptcy John Kent
D/PM 70/8 settlement of Ann Hill re legacies of her mother

D/PM 77/17 Correspondence of John Geagan
D/PM/79 sale particulars for Miss Barnouin's Boarding School
D/PM/ 79/14 Correspondence of Thomas Powlett
D/PM 82/8/1-3 Charlotte Braxton debtor
D/PM 83/1/58 John Figes loan
D/PM 83 /4/7/1 arrest of John Sturdy
D/PM 84/6/23 purchase of Banisters Farm
D/PM 84/11/3 Michael MacDonald deserter
D/PM 88/4/1 Diary Book of Thomas Ridding
D/PM 88/2/17 Memo of Valentine Fitzhugh re his dwelling house in Holy Rood parish
D/PM 93/11/113 Toulouse Barracks
D/PM 93/11/227 Waterloo Subscription
D/PM 96/32 legal papers relating to the dispute between Edward Ballard and Melicent Morris
D/PM 97/10 Agreement for printing of the Royal Engagement Pocket Atlas
D/PM 97/11 repatriation of Spanish Prisoners
D/PM 95/16/1-2 Lottery Ticket
D/RL 80 Affidavit 1817
D/S 19/1/1 Atherley Papers *Lady's Magazine*
D/S 19/1/2 Atherley Papers *Memoir of John Mackie*
D/S 2/2/6 Atherley Papers
D/Z 254/2 & D/Z 125/14 trustees of Sarah Siddons
D/Z459/17b sale of Mrs Siddons property
D/Z 676/2 papers of Helena Austen Harrison family tree
D/Z 676/3 Letter of Elizabeth Butler Harrison
D/Z 676/5/10 Frank Sladen Harrison
D/Z 676/10/3 papers of Helena Austen Harrison
D/Z 676/5/15 letter of Walter Nassau
PR5/1/2 St Mary's Parish Register
PR4/2/1 St Lawrence Churchwardens 1567-1743
PR4/2/2 St Lawrence Churchwardens 1743-1830
PR6/1/2 Peartree Burial Records
PR6/24/3 seating accommodation Peartree Church

Hampshire Record Office
HRO 9M73/G1964 Proceedings at Killalla, during the French Invasions
HRO 9M73/310/26 & 30 Letters of Frances Harris.
HRO 21 M65 A2/4 ordination of William Lance as priest
HRO 21M65/E2/342 presentation of Faccombe Rectory of William Lance 1791, patron David Lance.
HRO 202M85/3/1084 Presentment St Lawrence Parish 1668
HRO 23M91/1-49 Papers of Melesina Trench
HRO 11M49/231-244 Letter books and papers of 1st Baron Bolton.

The National Archives
PROB 11/930-154 Will of John Butler Harrison I
PROB 11/1013/231 Will of James Launce
PROB 11/1061/301 Will of James Mylles
PROB 11/1077/146 Will of John Morse
PROB 11/1089.293 Will of Robert Ballard senior
PROB 11/1096/226 Will of Anne Lane
PROB 11/1136/175 Will of Lenard Cropp
PROB 11/1164/18 Will of Mary Rogers
PROB 11/1197/137 Will of William Lance
PROB 11/1231/50 Will of Alexander Champion
PROB 11/1347/226 Will of Valentine Fitzhugh
PROB 11/1436/168 Will of Margrave of Anspach
PROB 11/1453/76 Will of Elizabeth Fitzhugh
PROB 11/1470/260 Will of Nathaniel Middleton
PROB 11/1582/228 Will of Thomas Pattle
PROB 11/1551/248 Will of Ann Newell
PROB 11/1577/513 Will of Robert Morse
PROB 11/1636 Will of David Lance
PROB 11/1689/161 Will of Nathaniel Middleton
PROB 11/1748/87 Will of Anne Middleton
PROB 11/1817/343 Will of Mary Arabella Lansdowne
PROB 11/1849/331 Will of Mary Lance
PROB 11/1875/157 Will of Alexander Robson
PROB 11/1960/367 Will of William Fitzhugh
PROB 11/2069/309 Will of Rev William Lance
PROB 11/2082/45 Will of Ann Hill
PROB 11/2111/334 Will of John Butler Harrison II
PROB 11/2217/427 Will of Charlotte Fitzhugh
PROB 31/592/48 Will Daniel Perkins
PROB 37/909 administration of will of Nathaniel Middleton
C2/11/16/M107 Inquisition of lunacy Anne Middleton
C 13/198/39 Litigation Eliza Pattle v George Templer & Hastings Nathaniel Middleton
C 13/718/23 Litigation Wakefield v Pattle
C13/683/10 Litigation Lansdowne v Noel Noel
HO1/7/15 Denization Alexandre Amyot
HO 42/35/146 Petition for relief
WO 25/390 31st Regiment of Foot

Berkshire Record Office
D/EX 192/7 purchase of Benham Place

Brighton & Hove Record Office
SAS-ACC 6859/96 Fitzhugh Insurance Policies

BIBLIOGRAPHY

City of Westminster Archives
0796 Letter books of Hastings Nathaniel Middleton 1816-1821

Derbyshire Record Office
D258/50/44 Letter of Margravine of Anspach

East Sussex & Brighton & Hove Record Office
Add Mss 11, 76 & 766 Conveyance
SAS-M/1/698 Deed of Covenant
SAS-M/2/6/311 discharge of Mary Anne Lane of Southampton to her mother Mary Lane widow of Southampton 10th August 1820

Hertfordshire Archives
DE/Gd/27134 lease of 95 Gloucester Place

Leicestershire Record Office
DG24/823/5 Letter re Miss Dillon

London Metropolitan Archives
MS11936/356/547737 & 378/589023 Insurance policies Andrew Goater Haynes

London University: Queen Mary University of London
EW papers of Edward Gibbon Wakefield

Magdalen College Oxford Archives
ES/8/2/23 5 March 1739 Letter of Lenard Cropp

Wiltshire & Swindon Archives
451/226 Sale Catalogue for Southampton Castle

Guides
Baker's Guide 1775, 1779, 1787, 1795, 1805, 1810, 1815,1818
Cunningham's Directory 1803, 1811
Directory of Hampshire 1783
Englefield, Sir Henry *A Walk Through Southampton* London 1841
Faulkner Thomas *Historical Account of Fulham* 1813
Feltham John *A Guide to all the Watering and Seabathing Places* London 1803
Feltham John *A Guide to all the Watering and Seabathing Places for 1813 Vol 2* London 1813
Freeling A *Picturesque Excursions* London 1839
Hampshire Repository Vol I 1798
Ladies Pocket Guide 1770
Skelton's *New Edition of the Guide to Southampton; being a description of the Ancient & Present State of that Town & Neighbourhood* 1816
Skelton's Guide, 1843
Wing E *Southampton Considered as a Resort of Invalids* London 1848

Universal British Directory 1792-8, Peter Barfoot & John Wilkes (eds)

Newspapers
Basingstoke Gazette 1809
Bath Chronicle 1782, 1787
The European Magazine & London Review Vol 47 1805
Gentleman's Magazine Vol lix
Gentleman's Magazine Vol 151 1831
Government Gazette (India) 1809
Hampshire Chronicle 1772, 1774, 1777, 1778-1783, 1785, 1791-5, 1796, 1809, 1811, 1812, 1816, 1819
Hampshire Telegraph & Sussex Chronicle 1807, 1808, 1816
Ladies Magazine 1772
London Gazette 1784
London Morning Herald 1840
Madras Courier 1809
Observer 1809
Portsmouth Telegraph 1801
Salisbury Journal 1772
Salisbury Journal 1826
Southern Daily Echo 1901, 2008
The Bengal Obituary Vol I
The Bombary Gazette and Indian News 1851
The General Chronicle & Literary Magazine Vol IV 1812
The Times February 2 1863

Secondary Sources

Abell F *Prisoners of War in Britain 1765-1815* Oxford 1914
Alger J G *Napoleon's British Captives* London 1904
Anderson A *Hartleyana, Henry Robinson Hartley, Eccentric-Scholar-Naturalist, Founder of the University of Southampton* Southampton Records Series Supplementary Volume 1987
Armstrong M *Fanny Kemble, a passionate Victorian* New York 1938
Aubrey E R (ed.) *Speed's History of Southampton* Southampton Record Society 1909
Auerbach E *Searching for Jane Austen* University of Wisconsin 2004
Austen-Leigh J E *Memoir of Jane Austen* Oxford 1926
Austen-Leigh R A *Jane Austen and Southampton* London 1949
Austen-Leigh W A & Knight M G *Chawton Manor and its Owners* London 1911
Asleson R (ed.) *A Passion for Performance, Sarah Siddons and her Portraitists* Los Angeles 1999
Beatson R *Naval and Military Memoirs of Great Britain from 1727-1783* London 1804.
Bond, H A *The History of Temple NH* Boston 1860
Bowman P J *A Fortune Hunter: A German Prince in Regency England* Oxford 2010
Broadley A & Melville L (eds) *The Beautiful lady Craven* London & New York 1914

BIBLIOGRAPHY

Brown P S 'The Venders of Medicines Advertised in Eighteenth-Century Bath Newspapers' in *Medical History* Cambridge 1975

Burnim K A (ed.) *The Letters of Sarah and William Siddons to Hester Lynch Piozzi* Manchester 1969

Busteed H E *Echoes of Old Calcutta* 4th edition London 1908

Butler, C B *Jane Austen & Southampton Spa* Southampton 2017

Butler C B *Powder, Prisoners & Paintings: The History of God's House Tower* Southampton 2019

Butler C B *Telling Other hiStories: Early Black History in Southampton c1500-1900* Southampton 2021

Butler C B 'Southampton to Sanditon: Invalids, Fashionable Cures, and Patent Medicines as Inspiration and Source Material for Jane Austen's Final Novel' in *JASNA Persuasions* The Jane Austen Journal no 42 2020

Butler C B 'What became of Col Powlett: This Wonderous Affair' in The Jane Austen Society Report 2020

Bryan M *Dictionary of Painters and Engravers, Biographical and Critical Vol II* London 1889

Caplan C 'Jane Austen's Soldier Brother' in *JASNA Persuasions* No 18 1996

Chambers D B *Runaway slaves in Jamaica (ii): Nineteenth Century* University of Southern Missouri 2013

Clery E *Jane Austen: The Banker's Sister* London 2017

Climenson E (ed.) *Passages from the Diaries of Mrs Philip Lybbe Powys of Hardwick House* London 1899

Coe E *The Parish of Freemantle A History* 2nd edition Southampton 2011

Collins Irene *Jane Austen: The Parson's Daughter* London 1998

Conolly M *Dictionary of Eminent People of Fife* 1866

Cook A K Mathew R & Johnson C *About Winchester College* London 1917

Copeland R *Spodes' Willow Pattern & other designs after the Chinese* 3rd edition London 1999

David D *Fanny Kemble: A Performed Life* Pennsylvania 2007

Davies J S *A History of Southampton* Southampton 1883

Davies T L O *Extracts from the Hampshire Chronicle* Hampshire Field Club Vol VI 1910

Douch R *Visitors' Descriptions, Southampton 1540-1956* Southampton Papers Number Two rpr 1978

Downer Martyn *Nelson's Purse* London 2004

Dickson P *The Sun Insurance Office 1710-1960* Oxford 1960

Downer P 'Nathaniel Middleton's South Stoneham Offspring' in *Westender Vol 10 no 6* 2016

FitzHugh D '"Such ill-gotten wealth can never prosper": the nineteenth century Austens of Broadford and Capel Manor, Kent' in *The Jane Austen Society Report* 2020

FitzHugh D '"I recommended him to read Corrina": an enigma?' in *The Jane Austen Report* 2021

FitzHugh T *FitzHugh, The Story of a Family Through Six Centuries* Ottershaw 2001

Foskett D *John Smart, the man and his miniatures* London 1964

Foster R 'Winchester College in the Age of Jane Austen' in *Jane Austen and Winchester an Introduction* Winchester 2023

Freeman M J 'Stagecoach system of South Hampshire 1775-1851' in *The Journal of Historical Geography I, 3* 1975 pp. 259-281

Gilliland T *The Dramatic Mirror* London 1808

Goring J, Sleigh J, Turner J, Pennington J & Harvey J (eds) *Lives, Loves and Letters, The Goring Family of Wiston, Sussex 1743-1905* Sussex 2017

Govas A *Jane Austen's Horsted Keynes Relations* Haywards Heath 2017

Green C A 'The Hierachies of Whiteness in the Geographies of Empire: Thomas Thistlewood & the Barretts of Jamaica' in *New West Indian Guide Vol 80 No1/2* 2006

Griffiths R & Griffiths G E *The Monthly Review Vol 134 Campbell's Life of Mrs Siddons* London 1834

Grosvenor Myer V *Jane Austen, Obstinate Heart: A Biography* New York 1997

Grier S C (ed.) *The Letters of Warren Hastings to his Wife* Edinburgh & London 1905

Hampson G *Southampton Notarial Protest Books 1756-1810* Southampton Records Series 1973

Haydon, C 'A Letter from Southampton September 1779' in *Proceeding of the Hampshire Field Club and Archaeological Society Vol 41* 1985

Hayley W (ed.) *The Works of William Cowper his Life and Letters* London 1835

Hearnshaw F J G & Clarke F *A Short History of Southampton* Oxford 1910

Hedley G & Rance A (eds) *Pleasure Grounds* Horndean 1987

Hemingway C 'How the Long War Affected Jane Austen's Family & Her Novels' in *Persuasions On-line* 39 No 1 2018

Hind J A & Colledge J M *Buckland and St Mary Past & Present* 1974

James W & Perry R *The Naval History of Great Britain Vol 5 1822* Mechanicsburg, Pennsylvania 2002

Jemmott J *The Parish History Project: A History of Portland* 2019

Jung S 'Thomas Stothard's Illustrations for The Royal Engagement Pocket Atlas, 1779-1826' in *The Library 7th series Vol 12 no 1* March 2011

Kang L *Quakery: A Brief History of the Worst Ways to Cure Everything* New York 2017

Kaye J M (ed) *The Cartulary of God's House, Southampton Vol I* Southampton Records Series 1976

Kaye J M (ed) *A God's House Miscellany* Southampton Records Series 1984

Kennard N A *Mrs Siddons* Boston 1887

Killick J (ed) *Sea Fencibles 1805 Vol 3 – Hampshire Coast* Hythe 2000

Konig C & Sims J *The Annals of Botany Vol I* London 1805

Le Faye D (ed) *Jane Austen's Letters* Oxford 2011

Leonard A G K 'A Forgotten Poet Laureate Recalled. Southampton Connections of Henry James Pye' in *Local History Forum Journal* Spring 1997

Mahony S 'What became of Mrs Powlett' in The Jane Austen Society Report 2019

Morris D *Mile End Old Town* East London Historical Society 2002

Murray C *Benjamin Franklin: Biographical overview and Bibliography* New York 2002

Nussbaum F 'Mungo Here Mungo There: Charles Dibden & Racial Performance' in *Charles Dibden & Late Georgian Culture* eds Oskare Jenson, David Kennerley & Ian Newman Oxford 2018

Oldfield J R 'Private Schools and Academies in Eighteenth-Century Hampshire' in *Proceedings of the Hampshire Field Club Archaeological Society Vol 45* 1989 pp. 147-156

Oldfield J 'From spa to garrison town: Southampton during the French Revolutionary and Napoleonic Wars, 1793-1815' in Miles Taylor (ed.) *Southampton Gateway to the British Empire* London 2007

O'Brien Capt F T *Early Solent Steamers A History of Local Steam Navigation* Newton Abbot 1973

Ossenbach C 'The Orchids of John Henry Lance (1793-1878)' in Lankesteriana Vol 20 No 1 2020

Osgood R and McCullock P 'The Hessians of Barton Farm: Uncovering when a German army defended Britian' in Current Archaeology 345 Nov 1 2018

Paget V C P *List of the Officers of the Bengal Army, 1758-1834* London 1927

Pannell J P M *Old Southampton Shores* Newton Abbot 1967

Parson C *The Incomparable Siddons* London & New York 1909

Patterson A *The Other Armada* Manchester 1960

Pelham R A *The Old Mills of Southampton* Southampton Papers Number Three 1963

Porter R *Quacks: Fakers & Charlatans in English Medicine* Stroud 2000

Preston, R 'Pursuit of Knowledge under Difficulties': the Audit House Library, Southampton 1831-63 and Winchester Library & museum, 1851-83 in *Southampton Local History Forum Journal No 14* 2008

Preston, R 'A Precarious Business: the Skelton family of stationers, printers, publishers, booksellers and circulating library owners in Southampton and Havant, c.1781-c.1865' in *Southampton Local History Forum Journal No 21* 2013

Prothero R (ed.) *Private Letters of Edward Gibbon (1753-1794)* London 1898

Raff E *Half a Loaf, The Care of the Sick and Poor of South Stoneham 1664-1948* IOW 2000

Read P J *Benjamin Jesty, the Grandfather of Vaccination* Cambridge 2020

Robins, B *An Introduction to the Journals of John Marsh* Huntington Library Quarterley Vol 59 No 1 University of Pennsylvania 1996

Robinson Walker L 'Jane Austen's Death: The Long Reach of Typhus?' Persuasions On Line 2010

Russell A, Cottrell P, Ellis J *Southampton's Holy Rood: The Church of the Sailors* Southampton 2005

Russell C F *A History of King Edward VI School Southampton* Cambridge 1940

Sandell E 'Georgian Southampton: a Watering-Place and Spa' in *Collected Essays on Southampton* Southampton 1958.

Sichel W (ed) *The Glenbervie Journals* London 1910

Skinner C *The French Connection, Les Relations avec la France* Hampshire County Council Publication

Slinn S *Ambition, Anxiety and Aspiration: the use and abuse of Cambridge University's Ten-year Divinity Statute.* University of Lincoln 2017

South M 'Epidemic Disease, Soldiers and Prisoners of War in Southampton 1550-1800' in *Proceedings of the Hampshire Field Club and Archaeological Society Vol 43* 1787

South M L *The Inoculation Book 1774-1783* Southampton Records Series 2014

South M L *The Southampton Book of Days* Stroud 2012
Stovold J *Bygone Southampton* Chichester 1984
Stovold J *The Minute Book of the Pavement Commissioners for Southampton 1770-1789* Southampton Records Series 1990
Suzuki A *Madness at Home 1820-1860* Berkeley & Los Angeles 2006
Sweet R H 'Topographies of Politeness' *Transactions of the Royal Historical Society* Vol 12
Temple Patterson A *A Selection from The Southampton Corporation Journals, 1815-35 and Borough Council Minutes 1835-47* Southampton Records Series 1965
Temple Patterson A *A History of Southampton 1700-1914 Vol I An Oligarchy in Decline 1700-1835* Southampton Records Series 1966
Temple Patterson A *Southampton a Biography* London 1970
Tomalin C *Jane Austen a Life* London 2000
Townsend J *A Journey through Spain* London 1791
Trench R *The Remains of the Late Mrs Richard Trench* London 1862
Wilson C R (ed.) *List of Inscriptions on Tombs or Monuments in Bengal* Calcutta 1896
Wilson M *Jane Austen's family and Tonbridge* Jane Austen Society 2001
Woodgate G & Woodgate G M G *The History of the Woodgates of Stonewall Park and of Summerhill in Kent* Wisbech 1910

Unpublished Theses

Cambell W A The analytical chemist in nineteenth century English social history University of Durham 1971
Livesay D Children of Uncertain Fortune: Mixed-Race Migration from the West Indies to Britain 1750-1820 University of Michigan 2010
McVitty D Familiar Collaboration and Women Writers in Eighteenth Century Britain: Elizabeth Griffith, Sarah Fielding and Susannah and Margaret Minifie St Hilda's College, University of Oxford 2007
Newport E H H Adopting a Chinese Mantle: Designing and Appropriating Chineseness 1750-1820 Kings College London 2014
South M The Southampton Inoculation Campaigns of the Eighteenth Century University of Winchester 2010
Smith G Exploring training relationships between Training Incumbents and Curates in the Church of England and the Church in Wales: Listening to Training Incumbents in the post Hind era University of Warwick 2015
Stanley A Mothers & Daughters of Invention New Brunswick, New Jersey 1993
Stovold J Building Developments in Southampton 1750-1830: The Impact of the Spa University of Southampton 1984
Woodcraft B Patents of Invention Part II London 1854
Young H L Gender and absentee slave-ownership in late eighteenth- and early nineteenth-century Britain UCL 2017

Web sites

www.romantic-circles.org/editions/southey_letters
www.casemine.com/judgement/uk/5a8ff8c560d03e7f57eccfbb Lansdowne v Lansdowne
Full text of "A catalogue of the elegant and appropriate furniture of the late Marchioness Dowager of Lansdowne, at Camden Hill, near to Kensington: consisting of a collection of pictures...antique bronzes and marbles of the finest order, splendid painted glass, including the celebrated window with the cartoons, fine Oriental china, and several plates of French glass of the largest dimensions, elegant chandeliers and lamps; splendid cabinets, of the time of Louis Quatorze; very elegant china, in table and dessert services... magnificent service of gold and silver plate, upwards of 8000 ounces... plated articles, a cellar of choice old wines" (archive.org)
www.studymore.org.uk Asylums
https://www.amazon.fr/Edward-Gibbon-Lausanne-rencontre-européennes/dp/288968038X
www.royalsocietypublishing.org XI & XXIV

INDEX

Absolem Farmer 124, 275
Absolem Mrs 124, 275
Addington Dr Antony 257, 308
Admiralty 239, 287
Affleck Colonel James 71
Affleck Thomas 143
Africa 122, 137, 144-145, 153, 198
Ailsbury earl of 220
Ailsbury countess of 220
Aldrige Ann 157
Aldridge Ira 101
Alexander Tsar of Russia 81
Allison Mrs 91, 133, 272
Allison John 133
Allison Miss 91
Allnut Francis 244
Almanac 98
Alresford 20
Alton 20, 113, 120, 241, 274
Alverstoke 82
Alvoen 82, 230
Ambassador 53, 114, 176, 198-199, 206, 289
America 26, 57, 67, 82, 83, 101, 117, 143, 186, 202, 212, 234, 276
Amery 128
Amery House 241
Amiens 73, 205
Amory Mr 184
Amyatt James 45, 56, 82, 121, 122
Amyot Alexander 167
Andre Major John 176
Andrews William 56
Anspach Charles Alexander Margrave of 102-103, 266
Anspach Margravine of see Lady Betty Craven
Antigua 122, 137, 173, 256
Archer Mrs 246
Architecture 16, 25-28, 154, 174, 203, 224
Arnold John 46
Artist 40, 42, 47, 67, 122, 155, 173, 187, 223, 235
Asia 165, 198, 212
Ashley 117

Ashtown Frederick Trench Lord 212
Atherley Arthur 45, 56, 70, 120, 133, 227
Atherley Mary aka Mary Ballard 118
Atherley Master 133
Atherley Mrs 134
Atkinson 80
Atlantic 299
Attorney 55-56, 83, 138-139, 147, 150, 243, 273
Augier Elizabeth aka Elizabeth Tyndall 149
Augier Mary 153
Augier Susannah 153
Austen Caroline 11, 306
Austen Cassandra 4, 5, 11, 139-140, 207, 255
Austen Cassandra jnr 2, 92, 139, 207, 243-245, 247-248
Austen Charles 8
Austen Edgar 3, 88, 236, 243-244
Austen Edward see Edward Knight
Austen Elizabeth of Horsted 301
Austen Elizabeth see Elizabeth Butler Harrison
Austen Elizabeth Matilda 250, 255-6, 297, 312
Austen Mrs Elizabeth Motley aka Elizabeth Wilson 306

Austen Frances Margaretta 249, 256
Austen Francis Motley 306
Austen Frank aka Francis 4, 7, 12, 81- 82, 139, 169, 197, 207, 209, 243, 293
Austen Reverand George 4, 7, 236, 306
Austen George jnr 236
Austen Harriet 3, 41, 51, 88, 243-245, 248
Austen Harriet aka Harriet Lane 232, 236-237, 244, 248
Austen Henry 4, 66, 88, 151, 160, 251, 307
Austen Henry jnr 236, 244
Austen Rev Henry 236-237, 239, 244, 250, 296-297
Austen Jane 1-15, 48, 52, 54-55, 66, 81, 88, 92-93, 109, 112-114, 131, 134-137, 139, 149, 151, 160, 185, 192, 197, 207,

INDEX

209, 210, 217, 236, 237, 243-245, 247, 251, 257, 264, 306
Austen John 232
Austen Mary aka Mary Hooker 236-237, 308, 310
Austen Mrs Sackville 238, 289
Austen Thomas 236
Austen Reverend William 255-256, 298, 304-305
Austen William George 256
Austen-Leigh James 109
Avington 29

Babbacombe 29
Babington Augusta Diana *see Diana Lewin*
Baggs Miss 93
Baillie Dr Matthew 167
Baker Charles 233
Baker Sir George 132, 270
Baker Thomas 52, 174
Ballard Mrs 125
Ballard Mrs of Wymmering 293
Ballard Barbara aka Barbara Morris 269
Ballard Edward 131
Ballard Elizabeth aka Elizabeth Butler Harrison 119
Ballard Frances aka Frances Taunton 115, 119, 131
Ballard Frances aka Frances Cary 118
Ballard Frances aka Frances Butler Harrison 119-120
Ballard Frances jnr aka Frances Wells 246
Ballard Reverand Dr John 119-120, 130, 246, 269, 276, 278-279, 284, 291, 305
Ballard John snr 118
Ballard John 278
Ballard Lenard 119, 263
Ballard Lucy 131
Ballard Margaret aka Margaret Jackson 118, 120, 132
Ballard Mary *see Mary Atherley*
Ballard Mary aka Mary Goring 246, 303, 305
Ballard Mary aka Mary Challoner Wood aka Miss Ward 135, 238
Ballard Melicent 29, 39, 44, 46, 57, 59, 61-64, 87, 92, 96, 113, 114-135, 240, 264-265, 267-289
Ballard Milly aka Melicent Morris 119, 124-127, 129-135, 238, 240, 243, 250, 255, 268-269, 270, 272, 274, 276, 279, 282, 284-285, 289, 292, 311
Ballard Robert jnr 23, 29, 52, 55, 63- 64, 113, 115-120, 123, 126, 130-131, 133, 135, 159, 173, 238- 240, 243, 263,

268, 271, 281, 287, 289, 291-293
Ballard Robert snr 118-119, 120, 128, 131, 133-134, 237, 239, 274, 275, 279
Ballard Robert 296
Balls 16, 26, 37, 40- 44, 59, 125-126, 169, 209, 234, 243, 274, 276, 284
Baltic 72
Banking 133, 159, 160, 239, 264, 288
Bankruptcy 46, 65
Banks Sir Joseph 207
Banks Lady 208
Baretti Guiseppe 152
Barfoot Peter 29
Barham Charles Lord Middleton 159
Barnouin Isaac 71, 118
Barnouin Miss 71, 91-92
Baron Captain 85
Barracks 59, 64- 65, 67-69, 85, 274
Barrow Mrs 310
Barrymore Lord 41
Barton Mr 238
Barton Mrs 238
Barton Farm 72
Barton Malcolm 267, 289
Barton Sally 236, 267, 289
Basingstoke 21, 293
Bates Miss 95, 263
Bath 1-2, 4, 6, 10, 35, 39, 43-44, 95, 161, 166, 193, 227, 228
Baths & Bathing 4-5, 12, 14, 16, 27-33, 37, 48, 51, 89, 92, 94, 98-99, 104, 130, 155, 182, 191, 193, 218, 220, 242, 261, 265, 308
Battersea 156, 169
Bauer Marie aka Marie Butler Harrison 252-253
Bayard Colonel William 202-203
Beafoot Private 84
Beare Mrs 97
Beaumaster Captain John aka John Bourmaster 59, 269
Beavan Charles 163
Beaver Mr 302
Beaver Kitty 302
Beaver Peter 302
Beckford Charlotte *see Charlotte Middleton*
Beckford Francis 203
Beckford Maria 151
Beetham Miss 93, 175
Bell Dr 88
Bengal 151-152, 157, 161-162, 164-165, 185, 205, 210, 214, 217, 229
Benham Place 103
Bennet Mrs 114, 169, 191, 263
Benson Mrs 125

Berkeley 141
Berkeley earl of 141
Berkeley Lady *see Mary Cole*
Berkeley, Princess *see Lady Betty Craven*
Berkley Square 220
Bernard Mr 34, 63, 286
Bernard Dr Peter 192
Berry Mary 205
Bertie Admiral 8
Bertram Tom 2
Bessborough Lady *see Lady Duncannon*
Bettesworth Captain George Edmund Byron 230-231
Bexley 196
Bibi 151
Biddulph Lady 257
Biddulph Mr 303
Biddulph Mrs 257, 303, 307
Biddulph Miss 301
Birbury Miss Biddulph 312
Birmingham 184
Bishopstoke 193
Bligh George Miller 77
Bligh Richard Rodney 77
Blois 288
Blucher Prince 212
Blunt Mr 296
Blunt Mrs 296
Blyth William 142
Bolton Baron 75
Bonaparte Louis 143
Bonaparte Napolean 75-76, 78, 82, 102, 108-109, 143, 174
Bond John 34
Books 26, 32, 35, 51-52, 55, 85, 88, 90, 94, 118, 173-174, 192, 207, 209, 211, 220, 235, 245, 271, 286, 299
Botany 206, 207
Boulogne 117, 218
Bowles William Lisle 11, 47
Boxford 302
Braemore House 153
Brandenburg House 103
Brandreth William Alston 85
Brasenose College 1
Braxton Charlotte 46
Breton Frederick 56, 70
Brewel Mrs 97
Bricknell Mrs 97
Bridges Charlotte 293
Bright Dr Richard 184
Brighton 167, 182, 193
Brissault John 65
Bristol 25, 66
Brittany 66

Broadford 306
Brohier J H 70
Brooklands 9-10
Broomen Mrs
Brough James 147
Broughton 117
Brown J 85
Brown Mr 59, 269
Browne Edward Walpole 10
Bruges 212
Bruguiere Mrs 97
Bruhl Count 220
Brussels 211, 212, 217
Bryer James 67
Buckland St Mary 217-218
Buckle Stephen 72
Budd Mr 181
Bugnon Monsieur
Bugnon Mrs
Bulkely Mr 277
Bullar, James 100
Bullar John 11, 51, 125
Bundelkhand 161
Burdet John 141
Burdon Mrs 91
Burgat Charles 39, 126, 143, 275, 277, 279, 282, 284, 288
Burgat William 143
Buriton 296
Burke Edmund 158
Burrows George Man 167
Burton Decimus 212
Bury St Edmunds 23
Butler Pierce 234
Butler Sarah 234
Butler Thomas 99
Butler Harrison Caroline aka Caroline Courtney 251, 261
Butler Harrison Catherine aka Catherine Sladen 252
Butler Harrison Charles 251, 257
Butler Harrison Edward 243, 251-252
Butler Harrison Elizabeth aka Elizabeth Austen 3, 31, 34, 41, 56, 69, 88, 101, 113, 131, 135, 157, 236-259, 263-264, 265, 289-314
Butler Harrison Elizabeth *see Elizabeth Ballard*
Butler Harrison Elizabeth Goring 51, 88, 120, 130, 133-134, 238-240, 249, 259, 309
Butler Harrison Elizabeth Matilda 243, 245-246, 248, 250, 254-257, 296, 303
Butler Harrison Emily aka Emily Morris 251
Butler Harrison Frances aka France Cary

INDEX

250, 253, 256-257
Butler Harrison Frances *see Frances Ballard*
Butler Harrison Frank 253
Butler Harrison George 248, 250, 253
Butler Harrison Henry 248, 251
Butler Harrison Jane 237, 243, 248, 250, 253, 256-257, 264, 300
Butler Harrison I John 119-120, 128, 227, 240
Butler Harrison II John 3, 22, 69, 73, 75, 82, 115, 126-128, 131-133, 139, 159, 238-242, 245- 246, 248, 250, 252, 259, 267-289, 305-306
Butler Harrison III John 247-248, 250, 254, 296
Butler Harrison Mary Ann aka Mary Ann Hyde 243, 251, 304
Butler Harrison Mary Hooker 245-246, 256-257, 264, 296, 303
Butler Harrison Susan aka Susan Standen 251
Butler Harrison William 248, 252-253, 300
Butter Thomas 205
Button Zachariah 164
Byles George 51, 56
Byron Anne Lady 233-234, 252
Byron George Lord 55, 98, 230

Cadell Mr 152
Cadiz 82, 171
Calais 92
Calcutta 93, 141, 159, 161, 163, 171, 214, 217, 229
Calshot 74
Calshot Castle 69
Cambridge 217, 236
Camden 111
Campbell Sir Archibald 172
Campbell Thomas 210, 224
Campion Mrs 255
Canada 83
Canterbury 1, 4, 293
Cantillo 134, 272
Canton 122, 151, 200
Capel Manor 306
Cards 46, 99, 125, 196, 207, 285, 296
Carisbrooke Castle aka Shaysbrooke 238, 292
Carnac General John 8, 25-26
Carnarvon earl of 92
Caroline, Queen 103
Caroline of Brunswick, Princess of Wales 266, 287
Carpenter Eliza *see Eliza Middleton*
Carpets 24, 247
Carter Private 84

Carter Miss 96, 277
Carter Ann 96
Carter Philly 133-134, 276, 277
Cary Frances *see Frances Ballard*
Cary Frances *see Frances Butler Harrison*
Cary Reverand 256-257, 304
Cary Reverand H 257
Cassimere Xury George 122
Casta paintings 153
Castle Jordan 105
Catholics 73, 89, 162, 244
Cator Ann Frances 164
Cator Sarah *see Sarah Morse*
Cator William 150-151, 164-165
Cawley Mrs 1, 92, 114, 134
Cerjat Mr 274, 276, 277, 281
Ceylon 35
Chad Mr 211
Chaloner Mrs 76, 191
Chamberlayne William 73, 176
Chamier Mrs 278
Chamier Edward 93
Chamier Emma 40
Chamier Henry 93
Chamier John 93
Chamier William 93
Chandos Duchess of, Anna Gamon 29
Chandos Duke of, James Brydges 29, 270
Channel Isles 69
Charles II 117
Charles Sgt Major Robert 85
Charlotte, Princess 48
Charlotte, Queen 63
Charterhouse 202
Chawton 10, 13-14, 120, 130, 149, 151, 210, 237, 239, 240, 282, 289
Cheffer Mrs 97
Chelsea 156, 167, 177
Chelsea College 177
Cheltenham 11
Cherbourg 72, 230
Chevening 232
Chickenhall Farm 128
Chiddingstone 236
China 7, 114, 171, 197, 200, 206-207, 209, 213, 219, 220-221, 223, 265, 310
China & Porcelain 92, 97, 111, 174, 208, 221
Chochin 206
Chopin Frederic 187
Christchurch 75
Church Oakley 140
Chute Chaloner 163
Clarges Street 234
Clark Eliza 143, 145-147

Clavering General 126
Clayton countess of 220
Climate 18, 143, 221
Clive Margaret Mrs 8
Clive Robert 8, 205
Clothes 31, 36, 175, 186, 246
Coaches 20, 26
Coade Eleanor 111
Cobbett William 177
Cock Lieutenant J G 85
Coffee Houses 19, 23, 35, 37, 286
Colchester 220
Cole George 199, 202
Cole Mary aka Mary Tudor aka Lady Berkeley 141
Collins John 78, 227, 261
Colson J 70
Concert 38-39, 43-46, 78, 134, 269, 270, 272, 277-278, 291-292
Constable John 47
Constantinople 104, 114, 197-198, 213, 265
Conway Hon Mr 220
Cooke Miss 291
Cooke Mrs 134, 278
Cooper Reverand Edward 1
Cooper Jane 2
Cooper Jane jnr aka Jane Williams 1, 9, 92
Cooper Thomas 50
Corbin Mr 192
Corfe G 34
Cornwall 22, 33, 44, 134, 143
Cosens Dr 29
Cosway Mrs 205
Cotterell Mrs 91
Cottingham Dr 194
Court Case 52, 106, 111, 149, 152, 167
Courtney Caroline *see Caroline Butler Harrison*
Coutts Thomas 159
Cowell General 71
Cowes 205, 291
Cowper William 54
Coxcomb 129, 171, 284
Cozens Mrs 134, 277
Cozens George Harrison 143
Craske Simon 85
Craven Cottage 46
Craven William Lord 46, 102
Craven, Lord 103
Craven Lady Betty, Margravine of Anspach, Princess Berkeley 46, 48, 81, 101, 104-105, 266
Crissé Henri Roland Lancelot Turpin de 67-68
Cropp Frances aka Frances Taunton 117, 125

Cropp Lenard 115-118, 125, 135, 239, 274, 279, 288
Cropp Lenard jnr 117
Cropp Melicent aka Melicent Weekes 117
Cropp Melicent *see Melicent Ballard*
Cropp William 117
Crystal Palace 85
Cuffnells 75
Cumberland Anne, Duchess of 37
Cumberland Ernest, Duke of 37
Cumberland Henry, Duke of 75
Curran 108

Dacca 161, 216-217
Daigueville Pierre 92
Dairens John 68
Daman Mrs 273
Daman William 273
Dance Nathaniel 207
Dance 3, 13, 37-40, 42, 48, 62, 80, 91-93, 101, 120, 126, 170, 195-196, 209-210, 248, 269, 275, 279, 280-282, 284
Dance-Hollands 207
Daniel's River 137
Darcy Mr 93
Dashwood Marianne 2
Daula Shuja ud 151
Davies Harriet aka Harriet Orgill 93
Davies T L O 212
Davison Mr 191
Davison Alexander 159-160, 165
Davy Miss 126, 135, 281-282, 285, 288
Dawson Mrs 95
Dawson William 43-44
Deane 140
Debary Peter 245-246
Debary Miss 245
Debtors 46, 53, 56, 90
Defoe Daniel 16
Dejean Mr 270, 272-273, 276
Dent William 158
Derby 23
Deserter 80-81, 83-84
Devon 143, 192, 217
Devonshire Georgina duchess of 101, 292-293
Dewey John 192
Deyverdun Monsieur 289
Diaper Ann 48
Diaper John 74
Diaper Maria 48
Dickson Miss 193
Dibden Charles 100
Dighton Robert 71
Diligences 20

INDEX

Dillon Miss 143
Dolci Carlo 235
Dominica 137
Dott Mr 67, 176
Doyley Sir John 176
Drew John 233
Drowning 49, 62, 96, 99
Droxford 29
Drummond James 206, 223
Drury Lane 92, 228
Duer Theodora 137
Duke Mrs 283
Dumaresque Lieutenant 49
Duncan Dr 92, 228
Duncannon Lord Frederick 292
Duncannon Lady Henrietta aka Lady Bessborough 28, 101, 108, 292
Dundas Mr 157
Dundas Lady 194
Dunn George 122
Durell Thomas 56
Dusautoy James 240
Dusautoy Peter John 240
Dutch 145, 171, 310

Earthquake 197
Easom Miss 92
East India College *see Haileybury*
East India Company 3, 7-8, 15, 25-26, 55, 67, 83, 86, 112-114, 121, 141, 151, 162, 164-165, 169, 171- 173, 177, 179, 185-186, 197, 200-201, 206, 209, 214, 218, 220-221, 229, 242, 247, 254, 259-260, 263-264
Eastbourne 193
Edinburgh 224
Education 1, 54, 91-93, 98, 114, 126, 128, 134, 170, 179, 186, 188, 229, 239, 250-251, 271, 282, 288-289, 301
Edwards Bryan 137-138, 159
Edwards Gerard 159
Eglinton Castle 230
Egypt 72, 81
Elba 85
Elderton Miss 269
Elephant 168, 215-216, 257
Elkins Mr 22
Elliott Mr 46
Elliot Catherine *aka Catherine Lance* 219
Eliot Ann 54
Elmsley Reverand 186
Emma 2, 6, 95, 209-210
Entertainment 45, 59, 211, 261-262, 265, 270, 283, 289, 297, 303
Equiano Olaudah 144

Erskine Captain 211
Erskine Mrs 211
Evance Susan 47
Evenley 250-251, 304
Eversley 246
Exton Park 159, 266

Faccombe Tangley 207, 217, 219
Fairfax Jane 263
Farquhar Sir Walter 191
Farington Joseph 225
Fawley House 118, 130
Fay Eliza 171
Fell Kitty 143
Fergusson Admiral John 49
Ferox Hall 313
Fielder Mrs 91
Fifield, Silena 96
Figes John 125
Fillary Richard 179
Filmer Mr 296
Fire 51, 61, 69, 78, 99, 175, 177, 195, 198, 246-247, 284-285, 296, 300, 307-308, 310-312
Fisher Thomas 125
Fishermen 29, 63, 89, 174
Fitzherbert Mrs 143
Fitzhugh Charlotte aka Charlotte Hamilton 82, 114, 197-198, 205, 211, 220-235, 263-265
Fitzhugh Dirk 200, 306
Fitzhugh Elizabeth aka Elizabeth Palmentier 197-199, 202, 205, 207
Fitzhugh Emily 197, 199, 210, 224, 230, 233-235, 264
Fitzhugh Ernestine 202
Fitzhugh Henry 82, 230-231, 263
Fitzhugh Mary *see Mary Lance*
Fitzhugh Mary Ann aka Mary Lane 232-233
Fitzhugh Sophia 230, 263
Fitzhugh Terrick 197
Fitzhugh Thomas 199
Fitzhugh Valentine 55, 70, 197, 200, 207, 209-210, 221, 254
Fitzhugh Valentine snr 162, 197-199, 202, 204
Fitzhugh William 26, 55, 114, 197, 200, 202, 207, 211, 220-223, 228-230, 232, 254, 266
Fitzhugh Reverand William 230-233, 235
Fitzhugh William Reginald 202
Fitzhugh Chapel 233
Flahault Adelaide Countess of 53
Fleming John 120-121, 269-270
Florence 53

Folkstone Lord 220
Follett Thomas Lisle 52
Fontaine Mr 187-188
Food 35, 91, 143
Foote Edward 7, 10
Ford 51
Ford Captain John 62
Forder Henrietta *see Henrietta de Sourze*
Foulkes Ann 147
Foulkes Arthur 147
Foulkes Mary 147
Foulkes Sarah 147
Foyle George 110
Francis Sir Philip 171
Franklin Benjamin 31
Frederick, Duke of York 244
Frederick, Prince of Wales 18
Freemantle George 122
French 8, 10, 27, 39, 57, 59, 62, 65-67, 69-72, 75, 78, 80, 82-83, 85, 89, 92-93, 96, 111, 122, 126, 128, 143, 164, 167, 198, 207, 210-213, 217, 220-221, 223, 258, 260, 265, 276, 278, 280-281, 285, 288
French Revolution 27, 53, 63, 65- 66, 108, 143, 171
Friend Mary *see Mary Lewin*
Frome 118, 130
Fulham 46
Fuller John 120-121
Furniture 111, 147, 155-156, 220, 242
Fursell John 125
Fusso John 122

Gainsborough earl of 160
Gale Miss 173
Gantlatt John 80
Gardens 5, 26, 92, 118, 125, 141, 155, 160, 173-176, 179, 192-193, 199, 206, 222, 241, 243, 245, 284- 285
Garfield 257
Gatcombe 217, 219
Geagan John 53, 54, 91
Geagan Maria 54
Geagan Maria jnr 54
Geagan Sarah *see Sarah Truss*
Gell Philip 266
George, Prince of Wales, later George IV 108, 111, 244, 262, 287
George I 103
George II 39, 103
George III 27, 30, 35, 40, 63, 75, 101, 112, 124, 167, 262-263
Germany 103
Gervois Clarke 121, 270
Ghent 212

Gibbon Edward 116-117, 128, 152, 289
Gifford Ann 105
Gifford Sir Duke 105
Gifford Eliza 105
Gifford Harriet aka Harriet Mellish 105, 108
Gifford Louise 105
Gifford Maria 105
Gillmore J P 12-13, 34
Gilpin William 22
Glenbervie Sylvester Douglas Lord 103, 108
Gloucester 48
Gloucester Duchess of aka Maria Waldegrave 40
Gloucester Henry Duke of 40
Gloucester Place 219
Glyn Miss 248
Goaters Green 156
Godmersham 245
Goodwood 303, 308
Goosman John 85
Goring Mrs *see Mary Ballard*
Goring Charles 246
Goring Charles jnr 51
Gorton Thomas 48
Goss Mr 39, 46, 277
Goss Mrs 46
Gothic 3-5, 13, 27-28, 41, 47, 106-107, 139, 154, 230
Governess 72, 92-93, 126, 135, 179, 193, 195, 253, 276, 280-281, 284-285
Graham Dr 33
Graham George 262
Graham Margaret 262
Grand Madame aka Catherine Princess Talleyrand 171
Grand George 171
Grant William 139
Granville Dr 36
Gray Thomas 19, 31, 47
Greatheed Bertie 205, 211
Greatheed Lady Mary 205
Greek 197, 235
Green Mr 22
Green Catherine *see Catherine Morse*
Green Edmund 150, 153-154
Green William 179
Greenwich 201
Greenwood Miss aka Mrs Edgar Austen 244
Gregory George 85
Grey Dr 193
Griffith Fanny 305
Griffiths Reverand 180
Grimaldi 224
Grimwood Doctor Thomas 291
Grimwood Miss 291

INDEX

Grote George 179, 187
Grove Anne 97
Grove Place 33, 206
Guillaume Mr 81, 83
Guisborough 169
Gunthorpe Alicia *see Alicia Jackson*
Gunthorpe William 51, 122, 137
Gunthorpe William jnr 137
Gunthorpe Mrs 122
Gustavus Adolphus 102
Gwyn Colonel 70

Hackett Perse 33
Haileybury College 161, 214
Hairdresser 46, 125
Hale Anne aka Nan, Mrs Smelt 170, 194
Hale Catherine 177, 183, 192, 194
Hale Charlotte 71, 90, 93, 177, 192
Hale George 72
Hale George 179
Hale Jane 180, 181
Hale General John 169
Hale Mary 169, 177
Hale Mary *see Mary Lewin*
Hall James Cushen 142
Halton Miss 134, 278
Hamble 72, 74, 238
Hamilton Anne aka Anne Terrick 114
Hamilton Charlotte *see Charlotte Fitzhugh*
Hamilton Emma 101
Hamilton Reverand Dr Anthony 114, 220
Hammersmith 46, 103
Hammond Arthur 56, 227
Hampton John 122
Hancock Eliza 7, 147, 149, 307
Hancock Philadelphia aka Philadelphia Austen 8
Handel 288
Hanover 75, 138
Hanover Square 217, 221
Hardy 80
Hardy Lady 246-247
Hardy Admiral Sir Charles 246
Harrington Mr 46
Harris Frances 76-77
Harris Mrs James 26
Harris Sir James 239, 287
Harrison Francis Sladen 85
Harrison Helena Austen 253, 289
Harrison Samuel 159, 177
Harrow 179, 253
Harrowby Lady Elizabeth aka Elizabeth Terrick 114, 220
Harrowby Lord 220
Hartley Henry Robinson 51, 251

Harvey Admiral 76
Hastings Warren 7-8, 149, 151, 157, 159
Hatsell 238
Havant 51, 174
Hawes William 34
Hawkins James, 24
Hawkins John, 71
Hayes 93
Hayman John 85
Haynes Andrew 43-4, 220, 286
Haynes, Harry 141, 286
Haynes S G 44
Hayward Captain 105

Health 4, 11, 13-14, 23, 29, 31, 35-36, 80, 88, 131-135, 142-148, 166-169, 172, 181-185, 191-196, 200, 207, 212, 219, 221, 235, 243, 249, 255, 257-259, 263, 265, 270-271, 274, 282-285, 288, 304
agues 32
anatomist 39
apothecary & chemist 12-13, 33-35, 99, 191, 236
atrophy 210
blindness 191, 195-196, 204
bilious attack 216
broken bones 145
bronchitis 183
calomel 13, 35-36
cancer 34, 257
chest complaints 34, 200
chicken pox 131-132
cholera 194
colds 191
congestion 34
constipation 35
consumption 33, 69, 210,
corns 191
coughs 12, 28, 32, 34, 173, 191, 193, 257-259, 308
cures 12, 35, 257, 265
deafness 209
dementia 194
diarrhoea 34, 234
dirt bathing 33
doctor 8, 12-36, 38-39, 51, 92-3, 117, 132, 134, 142-3, 167, 184, 191-194, 198, 221, 227-228, 233, 257, 278-279, 284, 292, 308
dysentery 35
epilepsy 32
eye pain 29, 34, 77, 133, 167, 196, 211, 271, 301
fever 2, 31, 34-35, 69, 72, 75, 89, 134, 193, 257, 276

gangrene 257
gravel 32, 99
green sickness 33
headache 259
inflammation 34
inoculation 11, 55, 95, 120, 132, 191-192
invalids 11, 33, 35-36, 80
jaundice 33-34
lameness 285
leprosy 28
lunacy 167
malaria 35, 72
measles 131-132
medicines 12, 30, 34, 35, 133, 191, 257, 271
mental health 166, 265
miscarriage 120, 173-174, 191
mumps 35
nerves 32
palsy 32
paralytic disorders 30, 33
physicians 12, 32-33, 57, 99, 117, 132, 142-143, 167, 184, 192, 257, 270
plague 198
prescriptions 12, 34, 257
props 34, 257
pulmonic 11, 143
putrid fever 2, 12, 134, 257, 308
rabies 31-2, 242
remedies 13, 35, 99, 184, 257
rheumatism 30, 34, 257, 261, 297
rickets 32,
ringworm 313
sea bathing 14, 28-32, 191, 193, 265
scrofula 28
scurvy 28, 32- 34
smallpox 11, 35, 57, 120, 131-2, 134, 137, 191-2, 218, 226, 254
sore throat 191, 257, 308
spa 4, 13-14, 28, 99, 118, 130, 167, 192-194, 229, 245, 260
spasms 34
springs 28-29, 32, 259, 312
stone 32, 99
swan skin cloak 36
syphilis 35
toothache 34, 191
typhus 1, 2, 12, 57, 65, 114, 134, 194, 265
vaccination 11, 137, 192
vomiting 35
war wounds 77
whooping cought 257
wisdom teeth 193
yellow fever 35

Hebolitch Olive 88
Herbert Charles John 162, 169
Herbert Louisa *see Louisa Middleton*
Hertford Lady 108
Hewkel Bernard 252
Heywood Nathaniel 76
Hickey William 158, 171
High Wycombe 53
Highwayman 63, 286
Hill Ann aka Ann Newell 6, 140-143, 147-148, 269
Hill Ann Newell 138, 140, 142-143, 147-148
Hill Reverand Dr Hugh 6, 122, 140-142, 147-148
Hill John 141-142
Hill Robert 71
Hill Roland 184
Hills George 80
Hinton Elizabeth 240
Hinton Jane aka Jane Butler Harrison 120, 134, 237, 239, 240, 276, 278, 289, 306
Hinton Reverand John 120-121, 133-134, 237, 239-240, 271, 276, 278, 296
Hinton Mary 240, 276, 291
Histed Harriet 179
Hoarth Mr 121
Hobbes Thomas 117
Holland Henry Vassall- Fox Lord 80, 106
Holland Miss 91
Hollies 175-179, 190, 195-196
Holsworthy Mrs 91
Holsworth Miss 91
Holy Roman Emperor 104
Honiton 218
Hooker John 237, 244
Hooker Mary *see Mary Austen*
Hooker Sarah Ottley 256
Hooker Thomas 256, 291, 293
Hookey Elizabeth 12
Hookey George 70
Hope Bay 137
Hornby Governor 238
Horne Miss 93
Horsted Keynes 255
Hoskins Mrs 92
Hospital 65, 82, 97, 192, 195, 227, 233, 242
Hotel 25-26, 39, 46, 97, 205
Horses 20, 22, 25, 44-45, 63, 69, 71, 74, 76, 84, 150, 155, 175, 184, 191, 199, 211-212, 218, 240, 253, 257, 271, 284, 286-287
Hort Mrs 301
House of Lords 141
Howard Sir Robert 257

INDEX

Hughes Lady 273
Hudlestone John 157
Hughes Admiral Sir Richard 62, 133, 273, 285
Hughes 285
Hughes Rose 133, 272-273
Huguenot 197-198
Hull 23, 63, 279
Hulton Henry 176
Hunter Mr 270
Hupsman Reverand 141
Hurst 75
Huskett Mr 6
Hutton Dr Thomas 221
Hyde Packet 305
Hyde Mary Anne 251
Hyde Harrison Colin 74, 289
Hyde Park 222
Hythe 176, 205

Impey Elijah 154
India 7, 86, 93, 112-114, 121-122, 145, 150-151, 153-162, 164-166, 171-174, 177, 179, 181-183, 185- 186, 192, 194, 200, 214-216, 218, 248, 253-254, 263, 265, 305
Ingram Miss 29
Insurance 174, 177, 247
Inverary Lord 283
Invasion 57-58, 68, 70-71, 75, 174
Ireland 95, 105, 169
Irward Mr 132
Isaac George, bishop of Gloucester 251
Isaacson Miss 278
Isle of Wight 46-47, 49, 57, 74, 88, 219, 230, 238
Italy 108, 152, 222, 234, 266
Itchen 3, 23, 28, 30, 59, 63, 67, 74-75, 155, 174, 193, 203, 207, 259

Jack and Alice 7
Jackson Mrs 125
Jackson Alicia aka Alicia Gunthorpe 137
Jackson George 205
Jackson John 81
Jackson Josias 45, 73, 136-137
Jackson Margaret *see Margaret Ballard*
Jaffra 35
Jamaica 65, 93, 113, 137-138, 142-143, 147, 149, 151, 153, 162-163, 243
James II 117
James Dr 34, 257
James Mrs 122
Jardain Mr 275
Jeans Dr Thomas 192

Jefferies Mr 297
Jenner Edward 11, 137, 192
Jerningham Edward 162
Jeringham Emily *see Emily Middleton*
Jerningham Sir George 164
Jersey 66, 69
Jewels 158, 166, 287
Johnson Barbara 29
Johnson Elizabeth 80
Johnson George 29, 164
Johnson Richard 159
Johnson Samuel 227
Johnson Thomas 80
Jones Saul 31
Jordan Dorothy 98, 101
Juárez Juan Rodriguez 153
Jumna Doab 161

Kamptee 161
Keate George 47
Keele John 34, 70
Kellow Mr 63, 286
Kelly Mr 261
Kemble Charles 223-224
Kemble Fanny 222, 224-226, 233-234
Kemble John Philip 223, 225
Kensington 111, 184
Kent John 174, 203
Kent 3, 180, 183, 200, 232, 236, 240, 266, 293, 297, 306
Kerr William 206
Kerry 162
Kettle Tilly 151-152, 156
Kew Gardens 206
Killalla bishop of 71
King Mr 77
King Mrs 92, 311
King Lt Andrew 80
Kingdom of the Two Sicilys 220
Kings Bench 159
Kings Somborne 117
Knight Edward aka Edward Austen 151, 237, 247-248
Knight Elizabeth 245, 247
Knight Fanny 11
Knights Place 235
Koch Nils von 190
Kunnison John 24

La Belle Alliance 212
Lady's Magazine 16
Lake Champlain 84
Lambell Mary 36
Lambert Thomas 84
Lance Charles 218

Lance Clara aka Clara Pearce 217-218
Lance David 6, 26, 114, 122, 174, 177, 200-202, 204, 206-210, 212, 214-216, 219, 221, 223, 230, 232, 254
Lance Eliza 202, 213
Lance Elizabeth 201, 207, 263
Lance Emma 202, 209-210, 213, 235, 263
Lance Frances 214, 263
Lance James 218
Lance John Edwin 202, 211-212, 214-220, 229
Lance John Henry 206
Lance Madelina Louise aka Madelina Porcher 217-218
Lance Mary *see Mary Paton*
Lance Mary aka Mary Fitzhugh 113-114, 197-220, 263-265
Lance Mary aka Mary Temple 200
Lance Mary jnr aka Mary Turner 113, 187-188, 202, 209-213, 215-216, 218-220, 264
Lance Mary Ann aka Mary Lane 232
Lance William snr 200-202
Lance Reverand William 201-202, 207, 210, 216
Lance William jnr 202, 210, 214-217, 219, 263
Lance William 218
Lance Islands 212
Lane Anne 156
Lane Henry 218, 232
Lane Henry 232
Lane Mary 232
Lane Mary Ann *see Mary Lance*
Lane Thomas 232
Langa John 205
Langdale Henry 163
Langstone 74
Lansdowne 1st Marquis of 106
Lansdowne Marchioness of aka Mary Arabella Petty 6, 13, 16, 27, 41, 45, 101, 105-111, 266
Lansdowne 2nd Marquis of aka John Petty 5-6, 13, 22, 27, 45, 48, 51-52, 67, 105-107, 109-110, 139, 263
Lansdowne 3rd Marquis aka Henry Petty 106, 108, 110
Laprimaudaye Jane *see Jane Lewin*
Latham Dr John 167
Launce Anne 137
Launce James 137-138
Lausanne 115, 126, 128-129, 239, 267-269, 271-272, 274-275, 277-278, 281, 289
Lavington William 128
Lawrence Sir Thomas 225

Lazarus 303
Le Brun Madame 205
Le Feuvre William James 238
Le Havre 186
Le Vendee 66
Leamington Spa 194
Leeth Alexander 46
Lefroy Anna 255
Legg John 55
Leigh Mr 211
Leigh Hall 174
Lenham James 80
Lere Richard 227
Leroux Jacob 26
Letchmore Miss
Letters 3, 6, 9, 44, 57, 73, 94-95, 102, 114-115, 125-127, 129, 135-136, 145, 158, 169, 178-179, 197, 215, 217, 233-234, 236, 245, 263-265, 267-269, 273-283, 289, 297, 303
Levant 197-198
Leverton Thomas 154
Lewin Anne jnr 172-173, 263
Lewin Augusta 182
Lewin Charlotte 88, 174-175, 178, 185, 187-189, 191, 264
Lewin Diana aka Babington Augusta Diana 182-183
Lewin Edward 175
Lewin Edward jnr 177, 184, 190-191, 193-194
Lewin Elizabeth 194
Lewin Emilius 177, 179, 184, 191, 193
Lewin Frances aka Frances Koch 176-177, 179, 184, 188, 190-191, 193-194, 196
Lewin Frederick 177, 178, 181-183, 190-191, 194
Lewin George 177, 184, 191, 193
Lewin Harriet aka Harriet *Grote* 30, 40, 54, 78, 82, 93, 96, 169, 173-174, 178-179, 184-188, 191, 193-194, 196
Lewin Jane aka Jane Laprimaudaye 181, 183, 194
Lewin John Dick aka Richard Lewin 72, 83, 172, 177-178, 181-182, 193
Lewin Mary aka Mary Friend 184
Lewin Mary aka Mary Hale 71, 72, 86, 93, 113-114, 169-196, 211, 263-265
Lewin Mary aka Mary Marsh 93, 172, 177-178, 180-181, 185-186, 191, 193
Lewin Matilda aka Matilda Rivaz 184
Lewin Octavia 183
Lewin Richard of the Hollies 175, 177
Lewin Richard snr 157, 172, 190
Lewin Richard 157

INDEX 341

Lewin Richard jnr
Lewin Thomas snr 26, 35, 55, 71, 73, 75, 80-82, 88, 93, 169-171, 173, 176, 179, 186, 190, 192, 264
Lewin Thomas jnr 172, 177, 179, 180-182, 190-191
Lewin Thomas 189
Lewin William 145, 175, 177, 180-182, 189-191, 194
Libraries 23, 35, 49, 51
Light Joseph 125
Lind Jenny 184, 187
Linden James 91
Lipscombe Mrs 257, 313
Lipscombe Frances 256
Lipscombe George 22
Lisbon 102
Little Somborne 117
Littlecote 218
Lloyd Reverand Charles 179
Lloyd Mr 211
Lloyd Mrs 211
Lloyd Martha 5, 11, 139
Lockerley 117
Lodgings 4, 18-19, 40, 53, 62, 90, 135, 272-273, 285
Loire 288
Lomer Miss 92
Lomer William 70
London 20, 22, 24-26, 32, 45-46, 51, 71, 94, 96, 103-104, 110, 133, 142-143, 151-152, 154, 158-159, 171-172, 178-179, 196, 198-199, 210, 212-214, 219, 222-224, 226, 228, 234, 244, 258, 261, 265-267, 269, 271, 275-276, 279, 286, 288, 305
Lorrain Claude 235
Louis XVI 63
Love and Freindship 3
Lovelace Ada 233
Lovelace Ralph 233
Lower Titchfield 137
Lucknow 151
Ludgate Hill 166, 287
Ludlow Miss 92
Ludlow Edmund 243
Lydford Giles King aka Mr Lyford 12, 192
Lymington 176
Lyndhurst 75, 238, 292

Macao 223
MacDonald Michael 81
Mackenzie Dr Mordach 198
Mackie Ann Sophy 40, 83, 142, 185, 210, 223

Mackie Dr John 33, 93, 142-143
Mackie John William 143
Mackie Mrs 142
Macklin Thomas 125
Maddison Martin 137, 159, 160
Madras 171, 174, 185, 200, 252
Magdalen College 115, 248, 250
Magdalene Mary 303
Maitland Caroline 248
Mallortie Isaac 26
Malmesbury earl of 76-77, 287
Malthus Thomas 214
Manchester 12
Manila 206
Manners J H 69-70
Manningford 133, 270, 272, 279, 299
Mansbridge 3
Mansfield Park 2
Mant Mrs 296
Mant Alicia 92, 94-95
Mant Frances 92, 296
Mant J A 70
Mant Reverand Richard 82, 94, 296
Marat 5, 27, 108
Marble Hill 256
Marrett Mr 82
Marriage 9, 44, 46, 53, 96, 103, 111, 114, 117, 120-121, 124, 127, 131, 134-135, 137-138, 140-142, 149-151, 154, 160, 163-165, 167, 169-171, 179-181, 185, 187, 189-190, 200-202, 207, 216, 218-219, 221, 232, 238-239, 250, 253, 263-264, 277, 284, 286-287, 297, 305
Marsh Danny 186
Marsh Isabella 186
Marsh Lucy 186
Marsh Mary jnr 186
Marsh Mary *see Mary Lewin*
Marsh Hippesley 186
Marsh Hippesley Charles 185-186
Marsh John 42
Marshall Capt J N 85
Marshalsea 174
Martin Mr John 37, 39, 43, 104, 123, 126, 261, 272, 275, 277, 282
Martin Mrs Mary 98, 104, 261
Martin George Sullivan 172
Mary, Queen 114
Mash Amelay 53, 157
Massena 108
Master of Ceremonies 41, 42-44, 220, 286
Mattheisz Mr F 35
Matthews Miss 92
Maul Mr 34
McCombe Mr 62, 135, 285

McCombe Jack 285
Meade John 142
Mears Roger 62, 285
Mears Reverand Dr Thomas 76, 78-79, 86, 192, 270, 272
Mellish Colonel 108
Mendelssohn 187
Merchants 29, 51, 131, 209, 232
   Auctioneer 51, 73
   Booksellers 19, 35, 51-52, 91
   Cabinet maker 73
   Chapman 25
   Hatter 25
   Hosier 25
   Linendraper 24
   Mercer 46
   Milliner 88, 97
   Perfumer 46, 133
   Ropemaker 71
   Shoemaker 45, 71
Mexico 153
Michell Brigadier General 75
Midanbury 150, 154, 163, 176
Middlesex 93, 117, 147
Middleton Anne aka Anne Morse 55, 100, 113, 140-141, 149-169
Middleton Augusta 161, 169
Middleton Catherine 162, 164
Middleton Charles 161-163, 166
Middleton Charlotte aka Charlotte Beckford 149, 165
Middleton Charlotte aka Charlotte Tucker 151, 160, 164-165
Middleton Eliza aka Eliza Carpenter 162-164
Middleton Eliza aka Eliza Pattle aka Eliza Robson 151, 152, 160, 165
Middleton Emily aka Emily Jeringham 161-163
Middleton Emily aka Emily Purling 162
Middleton Frances 161
Middleton Harriet aka Harriet Purling 161-163
Middleton Hastings 157, 160-161, 163, 165-167
Middleton Henry 161-163, 166
Middleton Henry George 151, 160, 165
Middleton John 149, 151
Middleton Dr John 33
Middleton Louise aka Louise Herbert 161-163, 166-169
Middleton Mary Ann aka Mary Ann Ochterlony 161
Middleton Nathaniel 7, 26, 51, 71, 149, 151-159, 169
Middleton Sophie 161, 169

Middleton William 161, 166
Midshipman 85, 177, 230-231, 281
Mile End 199
Miller John 71
Miller Robert 246
Milligan David 142
Militia 1, 38, 44, 57- 59, 62, 66, 71, 73, 77, 116, 128, 241, 247, 274, 279, 285-286
Minifie Margaret 95
Minifie Susannah 95
Minorca 72
Missing Mr 121, 270
Mitford Mary 260
Moira Lord 69, 72
Molesworth Mr 276, 278
Monkton Dr John 192, 227, 286
Monsey Messenger 57
Montagu Lady Mary Wortley 192, 197
Moodilar Chinniah 174
Moody Miss 269
Moon Charles 12
Moon Rufus 84
Moore Mr 52
Moore Major Henry 71-72
Moore William 158
Morant Catherine 96
More, Hannah 98
Moreland Mr 270
Moreland Mrs 2
Moreland Catherine 2
Mornington Gerald 67
Morresby William 142
Morris Charles 118, 127, 130-131, 255, 269, 311
Morris Charles jnr 131
Morris Elizabeth 131
Morris Emily 131
Morris Emily see *Emily Butler Harrison*
Morris George 131
Morris Melicent see *Melicent 'Milly' Ballard*
Morris Melicent 131
Morris Michael 269
Morris W T 85
Morse Anne see *Anne Middleton*
Morse Catherine aka Catherine Green 150, 153
Morse Edward 153-154
Morse Frances 149
Morse John 149, 152-154, 264
Morse John jnr 150, 154
Morse Robert 150, 166
Morse Sarah aka Sarah Cator 150, 153, 164-166
Morse Sarah aka Sarah van Heelen 149-150
Mottisfont 117

INDEX

Mount Royal 124
Moyes Mr 292
Moyes Mrs 292
Muckross Abbey 162
Mungo 100-101
Munton Antony 173
Munton Hester 173
Murray Elizabeth *see Elizabeth Shirreff*
Murray Mrs Walter 305
Murry 75
Music, musician 38-40, 47-49, 59, 93, 98, 126, 128, 154, 174, 176, 223, 252, 269, 274, 277, 279, 284, 288
Muslin 24, 183, 198, 312
Mylles James 36

Nance Andrew 25
Naples 45
Nash John 212
Nassau Walter 85
Nathan Isaac 98
Naval College 293
Navigation Act 273
Navy 7- 8, 22, 34, 59, 61-64, 74-75, 80-81, 97, 105, 139, 177, 179, 181, 185, 201, 230, 245, 248, 251, 293
Negapatam 172
Nelson Horatio Lord 72, 76-81, 101, 231, 273
Nembhard Ballard Beckford 136
Netherlands 72, 103
Netherton 207
Netley 68, 72, 81, 96, 238
Netley Abbey 2-3, 11, 47, 67, 80, 238, 290
Neufchatal 198
New Forest 16, 47, 76, 238
New Park 176
New Zealand 152
Newbury 302
Newell Ann 6, 70, 100, 113, 135-149
Newell Ann jnr *see Ann Hill*
Newell Bridget 138, 140, 148, 263
Newell Joshua 137-138, 147, 263
Newell Joshua jnr 138
Newfoundland 285
Newlyn James 71
Newspapers 35, 49, 52, 57, 96, 261
Newport 291- 292
Niagra 83
Nicholas Miss 269
Nicholas Robert Boyle aka Robert Boyle-Walsingham 61, 278
Nisbet Fanny aka Fanny Nelson 101
Noel Noel Sir Gerard 159-160, 165, 266
Norfolk 201

Norris Dr 35
North Lord 121
North John Thomas 70
North Baddesley 232
Northanger Abbey 3, 4, 14
Northerwood 124, 269, 275, 279
Nottingham 35
Nursling 33, 69, 75, 96, 176, 206, 247

Ochterlony Mary Ann *see Mary Ann Middleton*
Ocra James 122
Odiham 83
Opera 45, 47, 100
Oporto 273
Orgill George 93
Orleans 73
Orlebar Constantia 32
Ostend 68, 129, 268
Othello 101
Otley William 256
Ottley Mrs M 311
Oudh 7, 151
Owen Mr the elder 32
Oxford 1, 140-141, 219, 231, 248, 250, 304

Paarle 145
Packe Mr 276, 286- 287
Painter 6, 41, 245
Painter Joseph 80
Pall Mall 159
Palmentier Constance 198
Palmentier Elizabeth *see Elizabeth Fitzhugh*
Palmerston Lord 25, 238
Palmerston Lady aka Mary Temple 238
Parker James 80
Parker Tom 12, 14
Parrot Mary *see Mary Weekes*
Parsons George 72
Paris 73, 168, 171, 173-174, 205, 212, 219, 229, 265, 288, 299
Paris Dr J A 35
Park Mungo 137
Pastrycooks 19, 246
Paton Elizabeth 211, 217
Paton George 200
Paton John 200-201, 214
Paton Mary aka Mary Lance 201, 204, 214
Paton Mary 210
Paton Sarah 210
Paton William 206, 212, 214-216
Patterson James 138
Pattle Eliza aka Eliza Robson *see Eliza Middleton*
Pattle Eliza aka Eliza Wakefield 152, 165

Pattle Thomas Charles 165
Paulet earl of 221
Paulet countess of 221
Pavement Commission 21, 37, 110, 139, 241
Payne Mr 305
Payne Mrs 305
Pearce Clara aka Clara Lance 218
Pearce John 218
Pearce Sarah 218
Pearce William 47
Pearson James 27
Pearson Mrs 313
Peers Mr 269, 285
Peers Mrs 92, 285
Peers Newe 227
Pelican Inn 302
Pennsylvania 137
Penny farmer 121, 275
Penshurst 293
Penton Cousin 29, 269, 270
Pera 198
Percival Dr 12
Performers 38-39, 101, 228, 277
Perkins Miss 95-96, 277
Perkins Daniel 95
Perrot Nanny 296, 299
Persia 96, 155-156, 214, 265
Persuasion 54, 185
Perregaux John Frederick 73
Peter Robert 164
Petersfield 83
Peterson Mrs 303
Peveral Mr 134
Peyton Sir Yelverton 56, 71
Phaeton 13, 110, 237, 289
Philip II of Spain 115
Philip V 153
Pickering Thomas 80
Pictures 111, 129, 234-235, 268
Pimlico 168
Pinch Lady 40, 270
Piozzi Hester aka Hester Thrale 121, 205, 228
Piper Mr 283
Pipon Thomas 70
Pirce Richard 85
Pitt George, Lord Rivers 39
Pitt William 78
Plantations 65, 100, 112-113, 122, 136-139, 141, 143-144, 154, 242, 264
   Bryan Castle 138
   Hermitage 137-138, 142, 147
   Hope 29
   Hopewell 238
   Lances Cristine 138

Lodge 147
   Painters 122, 137
   Red Hassell 137, 142
Plattsburg 84
Plaw John 25-26, 68
Plenty Mary 89
Plumer Mrs 181
Poetry 11, 29, 47, 54-55, 98
Politics 3, 57, 99, 113, 116, 120-121, 187, 210, 214, 252, 265, 282
Popham General 218
Poole Captain 278
Poor House 53, 156-157
Porcher Henry 218
Porcher Josias Dupré 217
Porcher Madelina Louisa *see Madelina Lance*
Porcher Sarah aka Sarah Pearse 218
Port Antonio 137
Portchester Castle 83
Porter James 198
Porter Rebecca 194-195
Porteus Mrs 307
Portland 137, 142
Portman Street 234
Portsea 284
Portsmouth 4, 9, 31, 57, 63, 80, 82-83, 172, 205, 207, 293
Portswood 55, 71, 122
Portugal 273
Potter Christopher 62, 63, 285
Potter Mrs 62, 286
Powlett Letitia aka Letitia Follett 52, 53
Powlett Col Thomas 52-53, 70, 157
Powys Lybbe 26
Pratt Samuel Jackson 56
Prescott William 190
Press gang 63-64, 74, 84
Pride & Prejudice 2
Prince Regent *see George Prince of Wales*
Pringle Mrs 92
Prison, prisoners 46, 51, 53-54, 56-57, 66, 68, 72-73, 81-85, 90-91, 97, 152, 159
Protestant 87, 198
Prussia king of 103, 211, 212
Puckler-Muskau Prince Hermann von 111
Pullman Miss 92
Purbeck Mrs 134, 278
Purbeck Elizabeth 95
Purbeck Jane 95
Purling Charles 162
Purling Emily *see Emily Middleton*
Purling Harriet *see Harriet Middleton*
Purling John snr 162
Purling John 162
Purling Nancy aka Nancy Fitzhugh 162, 200

INDEX

Pye Henry 54-55, 71
Pye Sally 188

Quebec 83
Queens College Cambridge 236
Queens College Oxford 117, 141

Races 20, 45-46, 48, 233, 271
Radnor earl of 220
Radnor countess of 220
Radnor dowager countess of 220
Ramsay John 172
Ramsgate 193
Randall William 12-13, 34
Reading 31, 218
Readings 11, 51, 52, 54, 88, 90, 93, 101, 173, 192, 247, 269, 301
Ready Storer 34
Recipes 12, 34, 98, 157, 236, 242-243, 257, 259, 305, 307
Redbridge 74-75
Redcar 191
Refugees 57, 66, 122, 143
Regents Park 212
Remacle Mary 35
Repton Humphrey 203
Rhine 305
Richardson David 47
Richmond duchess of 211, 217
Richmond Vale 200
Ridding Elizabeth Anne 55, 88-90, 98
Ridding John 246
Ridding Margaret 34, 55, 88, 90, 98, 302-303
Ridding Mary 34, 55, 88, 90, 98
Ridding Thomas 3, 13, 34, 83, 85, 88, 90, 98, 135, 243, 245-246, 251
Ridding Thomas jnr 99
Rippington 301
Rivaz Matilda *see Matilda Lewin*
Rivers Lord, George Pitt *see George Pitt*
Robbins J 70
Robertson Captain 283
Robespierre 108
Robson Major Alexander 165
Roe Henry 266
Roebuck Mr 190
Rogers Mr 238
Rogers Mrs 238
Rogers Mary aka Mary Fitzhugh 199-200, 202
Rollestone Mr 288
Rolph Mr 133, 273
Rome 131, 218
Romilly John 163

Romsey 42, 101, 117, 132, 286
Rooke Reverand Robert 87, 134, 286
Rooke Mr 121, 270
Rooke Mrs 134, 278
Rooke Miss 286
Rooke Frances 119
Rooke Giles 275
Rooker Michael 47
Roots Dr 184
Rosa Salvator 235
Rose George 137
Rose George snr 45, 72, 75-76, 136-137
Rotherhithe 63
Rowcliffe John 56
Rowlandson Thomas 49, 64, 66-67
Royal Academy 223, 225
Royal Engagement Pocket Atlas 52
Rule Rushworth 301
Rumbold Lady 90, 176
Rupert, prince 257
Russia 81

Sackville Lord 52
Sadlier Vernon 227
Saffery Thomas Norwood 164
St Andre Nathaniel 39, 51, 227
St Andrew 219
St Faith 201
St George 138, 221
St Helena 85
St Hellens 59, 269
St Kitts 53-54, 145
St Margaret's Bay 137
St Martin-in-the-Fields 220
St Mary College 250
St Mary Clay 186
St Vincent 136
Salter House 118, 130
Salisbury 10, 25, 34, 39, 81, 93, 119, 126, 131, 277, 285, 288, 304
Samaritans 303
Sanditon 2, 14, 92, 259,
Sandwalker 74
Saxby Mary 245
Scarborough 191
Schools 56, 68, 82, 87-88, 91-93, 115, 122, 127, 131, 134, 180, 182, 184, 191, 217, 226, 233, 236-237, 239, 242, 248, 250, 253, 256, 258-259, 273, 275-276, 278, 286, 288, 291, 296, 297, 299, 301, 305
Sciote 197
Scott Admiral 56, 224
Scott Mr 88, 273, 276, 280-281
Scott Mr D 171
Scott Miss 133-134

Scott Reverand James 119
Scudder Richard 179
Sea Fencibles 10, 64, 75, 83
Sea-Bathing 98, 220, 265
Selby Miss 48
Semple Elizabeth 92
Sense & Sensibility 2
Serle Mr 273
Serle Peter 273
Servants 11, 36, 42, 96, 100, 105, 121-122, 157, 185, 192, 199, 205, 287
Seven Oaks 242
Shannon earl of 62
Shawls 24, 102, 183
Shayer William 47
Sheppard William 47
Sheppard 273, 278, 283
Sherer Tom 62, 285
Sherfield English 117
Shergold Elizabeth 91
Shergold Jane 91
Sherlock John 49
Shield Sarah 253
Shipleys 31

Ships 25, 57, 59, 65, 81, 139, 207, 266, 269
  Boreas 273
  Buccleugh 230
  Conquistador 82-83
  Duke 281
  Elephant 72
  Hawke 49
  Henry Addington 206
  Hindostan 221
  Juno 157
  Leander 62
  Mary of Southampton 205
  Nottingham 171
  Nymph 62, 285
  Ocean 80
  Pilot 81
  Prince of Coburg 198, 229
  Princess Victoria 230
  Royal George 59, 269
  Seahorse 7
  Stag 177
  Tartar 230, 231
  Temeraire 83
  Thunderer 61-62, 278
  Unicorn 8
  Victory 59, 77, 269

Shipbourne 236
Shirreff Elizabeth aka Elizabeth Murray 185
Shirreff Lt William, later Rear Admiral 185

Shops, Shopkeepers 16, 18-19, 23, 24-25, 51, 61, 96-97, 277
Short Mrs 96
Sibly Reverand 39, 277
Siddons Cecilia 230
Siddons George 229
Siddons Maria 223
Siddons Sally 223
Siddons Sarah 101, 197, 205, 223-226, 228-230, 233
Siddons William 224, 228
Silvianora 3
Sims Richard 202
Simpson John 159
Simpson Reverand Joseph 119
Sinclair William 138
Skelton Elizabeth 51
Skelton Elizabeth jnr 51
Skelton Mary Mabella 51
Skelton Thomas 51, 78
Skelton William 51
Skinner Miss 291-292
Sladen Catherine *see Catherine Butler Harrison*
Slater Mr 227
Slavery 73, 75, 99-100, 122, 136-139, 142-143, 145, 147, 149, 154, 158, 185
Sloane Hans 120-121, 157, 238, 269-270
Small Lieutenant Francis 84
Smelt Jessie 194
Smelt Anne *see Anne Hale*
Smith Dr 132
Smith Mr of the custom house 272
Smith Miss of Winchester 273
Smith Mrs 276
Smith Captain 248
Smith Private 84
Smith John 34
Smith Samuel 159
Smith Major William 70
Smith William 116
Sotheby William 47
Sourze Antony de 122-123
Sourze Antony de jnr 122
Sourze Charlotte de 123
Sourze Henrietta de aka Henrietta Forder 123
South Africa 145
South Villa 212
Southampton earl of 117

Southampton
  Above Bar 19-20, 23, 33-34, 44, 50, 75-76, 87, 89, 92, 133, 202
  Albion Place 25-26, 70

INDEX

347

All Saints 24, 88, 122, 134, 159, 202-203, 235, 296
Anglesea Place 164, 256
Anspach House 81
Anspach Place 104
Archer Mrs 248
Archer House 160
Assembly Rooms aka Long Rooms 5, 23, 30, 32, 37-40, 43-44, 46, 81, 87-88, 123, 126, 260- 262
Audit House 80, 85, 235, 262
Avenue 22, 68
Back of the Walls 80, 215
Bannisters 26, 198, 222-225, 228, 234
Bargate 5, 20, 28, 58, 111, 245
Beach 22-23, 30, 48, 105, 291, 292
Bellevue 51, 73
Bevis Mount 176, 222
Black Vault 118, 130
Bitterne 199
Bitterne Grove 67
Bitterne Road 203, 212
Brewhouse Lane 205
Brunswick Place 256, 287
Bugle Street 40, 49, 92
Bull Hall 51, 122, 137
Butchers Row 125
Canal Place 34, 73
Castle 5-6, 13, 21, 25, 27-28, 41, 106-110, 139, 266
Castle Hill 273
Castle Lane 27, 134
Castle Square 5-6, 11, 13, 22, 106, 110, 135, 139, 245, 247, 248
Chapel Fair 121, 279
Chapel Mill 62
Chessel Avenue 203
Chessel Cottage aka Little Chessel aka Chessel Lodge 177, 183
Chessel House 6, 26, 174, 202-204, 209, 212
Coffee House Court 286
Cross Guns 81
Cross House 23, 48
Crown Inn 76
Cumberland Place 233, 305
Custom House 85, 123, 272, 282
Ditches 89, 119, 245
Dolphin 3-4, 39, 72, 83, 116, 209, 234, 243, 270, 272
East Street 88-89, 92
Edward VI School 180, 296
Freemantle Hall 122
Freemantle House 121
French Street 44, 78, 91-92, 227, 246-247

Friar's Spring 29
George Inn 19
Gloucester Baths 30
Gloucester House 256
Gloucester Square 34, 92, 95, 192
Goater Alley 88
God's House Almshouse 96, 140
God's House Prison 46, 54, 81, 90, 97
Grosvenor Square 233
Grove Place 33, 206
Guildhall 45
Hamton Court 92
Hanover Buildings 25, 41, 199, 202, 245
Harrison's Cut 259
Hartley Institute 51, 235, 252
High Street 5, 12, 14, 16, 20-22, 24, 34, 37, 45, 50-51, 56, 76, 91-92, 97-98, 118, 125, 130, 132-133, 159, 199, 207, 246-247, 257
Hoglands 25, 241
Holy Rood 35, 95, 122, 140, 148, 192, 199, 202, 210, 278
Houndwell 28
Houndwell Lane 121, 245
Itchen Ferry 30, 67, 74
Lammas Lands 25
Lance's Hill 203, 212
Lansdowne House 106, 110, 247
Linen Hall 104
Little Chessel *see Chessel Cottage*
Little Testwood House 54
Long rooms *see Assembly Rooms*
Love Lane 241
Marland Place 256
Marsh 30, 44, 57, 262, 271
Midanbury 163, 176
Midanbury House 154, 163
Midanbury Lodge 163
Millbrook 35, 75, 77, 140
Military School, Duke of Yorks 68
Moira Place 76
Netley Common 72, 81
New Assembly Rooms 261, 262
Noah's Ark Wharf 118, 130
Northam 59, 60-61, 81, 83, 174, 271
Northam Bridge 203-204, 218
Nursling 33, 75, 96, 176, 206, 247
Nursling Common 69
Old Assembly Rooms 37, 117
Orchard Street 28, 198, 224
Park Place 256
Peartree 95, 194, 212
Peartree Avenue 203
Peartree Church 49, 90, 258
Peartree Green 67

Peartree Lodge 173
Pineapple Inn 73,
Platform 23, 63, 261-262, 279, 286
Portland Street 30, 224
Polygon 8, 23, 25-26, 38, 40, 92, 130, 233, 251, 252
Redbridge 74-75
Ridgeway 66, 173
Ridgeway Castle 26- 27, 172-175, 177, 180, 182-183
Ronceval 104
Royal George Inn 37
St John's hospital 227
St Lawrence Church 76, 78, 89, 91, 118-119, 131-132, 135, 246
St Mary's 121, 303, 305
St Mary's Church 49, 54, 71, 122, 140-141, 148, 198, 241, 255, 259
St Mary Street 241
St Michael's Church 49, 82, 148, 272
St Michael's Square 25, 73, 88-89, 91, 134, 301
St Paul's Church 256
Shirley 68, 72,
Shirley Common 68, 75
Simnel Street 81
South Stoneham 75, 123, 156
Star Inn 20, 24, 31, 46
Stoneham House 121
Sugar House 59, 65, 274
Sun Inn 19
Sydney Cottage 95
Testwood 256
Town Hill Park 140, 154-155, 162-163
Town Quay 19, 48, 66, 82
Trinity Fair 74, 121
University 51, 137, 252
West Gate 104
West Gate Street 85
West Quay 5, 30, 37, 61
Winkle Street 24, 140
Woodmill 67, 68, 71
Wool House 82
York Buildings 33

Southerby Captain 238
Southey Robert 16
Southwark 25
Spain/Spanish 39-40, 57, 80, 82-83, 115, 147, 153
Speed Dr John 32, 134, 192, 278, 292
Speed Mrs 291
Speen 103
Spencer's House 124, 275
Spencer Mrs 132- 133, 270, 272

Spencer Ventham 132
Spilsbury Maria aka Maria Taylor 122
Spithead 59, 269
Spode 187, 209
Spy glass 281
Spriner Miss 278
Stamford 23
Standen Susan *see Susan Butler Harrison*
Stanley Mr 25
Stanley Hans 121
Stephenson Mrs 275
Steventon 3, 8-9, 236-237, 239, 292-293,
Steyning 303
Stibbert General 56
Stock Stephen 71
Stockbridge 117
Stoke Park 193
Stoneyhill Wood 214
Storace Nancy 45
Storace Stephen 45
Store House 22
Stothard Thomas 52
Streat 210, 232, 235
Street Mrs 51, 97
Street Lighting 22
Sturdy John 73-78, 80, 82
Suckett Mr 22
Sugar 29, 59, 65, 112-113, 136-139, 144, 151, 155, 184, 242, 274, 306-314
Summerhill 306
Surinam 206
Susan *see Northanger Abbey*
Sussex 70, 232, 247, 255, 303
Swanage 230
Swanton Miss 303
Swayne Mrs 307
Sweden 102, 179, 184, 190
Sweet 23
Swete John 41-42
Switzerland 212, 281
Sykes Mrs 3

Talantine Monsieur 288
Talbot William 157
Tate George 176, 179
Taunton Mrs 132-133, 270, 276, 284
Taunton Frances *see Frances Cropp*
Taunton Richard 96
Taunton Dr Robert 117
Taylor Mrs 41
Taylor, Elizabeth 97
Taylor Maria aka Maria Spilsbury 122
Taylor Samuel Silver 56, 71
Taylor Sarah 122
Taylor Walter II 61, 97

INDEX

Taylor Walter III 25, 41, 61-62, 71, 96, 122, 245
Taylor Miss 246
Tea drinking 37, 42, 99, 118, 120, 157, 173, 208-209, 238, 246, 269, 272, 289, 291-292, 296, 297, 302
Temple Mary *see Mary Lance*
Templer George 159-160, 165
Thames 46
Thathia fort 161
The Hague 239, 287
The Mystery 7
Theatre 23, 41, 78, 91, 101, 104, 223, 226-228, 261
Thistlethwaite Mr 121, 270
Thomas Lady 305
Thomas Moy 21
Thomas Sarah 88
Thompson John 142
Thompson Mrs 97
Thorpe John 13
Thornton Mr 293
Thrale Mrs *see Hester Piozzi*
Timsbury 117
Tinling William 70, 71
Tiverton 228, 234
Tonbridge 3, 236-237, 243-244, 250, 296, 309, 313
Tonbridge Castle 237, 256
Torbay 29
Toulon 168
Towne Francis 47
Trafalgar 8, 61, 77-78, 80-81
Trench Meselina 73, 100
Trench Richard 73
Trent 219
Tring Mrs 98
Trinidad 122
Trinity College 232
Truss Jeffery John 53-54, 90-91
Truss Mary 90-91
Truss Sarah aka Sarah Geagan 53-54
Tucker Charles 164-165
Tucker Charlotte *see Charlotte Middleton*
Tucker Henrietta Eliza 164
Tucker Marian 164
Tudor Mary *see Mary Cole*
Tumulty William 84
Tunbridge Wells 142, 160, 193, 245, 256
Turin 152
Turk 198
Turner J M W 47, 80
Turner Joseph 125
Turner Mary *see Mary Lance*
Turner Reverand William 218-219

Twining Richard 209
Twiss Horace 224
Twyford 31, 253

Uffington 302
Uniform 1, 71, 73, 76, 88
Unitarian 88, 186, 189, 237, 244

Vamier Mrs 278
Van Heelen Jan Carel 150
Van Heelen Sarah *see Sarah Morse*
Vancouver Islands 212
Vaughan Dr 143
Vernon Charles 160
Vignoles Col. 133, 273-274
Villa 3, 5, 26, 28, 41, 46, 48, 103, 113, 124, 182, 203, 212, 238, 265, 292
Villeniere, Comte Toussaint-Ambroise Talour de la Cartrie de la 66-67
Vimeiro 82
Vincent George 29
Virgin Mary 303
Virginia 117
Voiturier Mr 275

Wakefield Edward Gibbon 152
Wakefield Eliza *see Eliza Pattle*
Walcot 39
Waller Miss 278
Waller Mr 290
Waller Mrs 290-291
Waller Master 290
Walpole Horace 47-48, 102, 120
Wantage 302
Wapshare Charles 10
Wapshare Mary *see Mary Williams*
War 3, 15, 20, 51, 57-86, 108, 121, 171, 173-174, 177, 202, 211, 260, 264-265, 269, 284, 287
Ward Miss *see Mrs Ballard*
Ward Mr 272, 278
Ward Charles 247
Warlock Thomas 125
Warminster 99
Warner Richard 47
Warre James 273, 283
Warres Mr 135
Washington 276, 299
Waterloo 85, 211, 217, 229, 260
Wateridge Elizabeth 256
Wateridge Mary 256
Watson Curate 278
Wavell Jonathan 46
Weather 11, 32, 38, 63, 125, 230, 243, 272, 278-279, 284, 287, 305

Webb Mr 30
Webb Thomas 246
Webster Ann 179
Wedding 119, 141, 190, 240, 249, 255, 259, 303, 304
Wedgwood John 159
Wedgwood Josiah 159
Weekes Abraham 117, 131
Weekes Hobbes 117
Weekes Mary aka Mary Parrot 117
Weekes Melicent *see Melicent Cropp*
Weller Elizabeth 236, 242
Wellington Duke of 85, 211-212, 217, 248
Wells 278
Wells Dr 279
Wells Mr 305
Wells Mrs 279, 293
Wells Fanny 293
Wells George 246, 270, 287
Wemsley Mrs 312
Wesley John 49, 87
West End Common 156
West Indies 50, 62, 69, 74, 100-101, 112, 122, 136, 147, 159, 165, 200, 273
West Wickham 236, 237
Westmoreland 142
Weyhill 119
Weymouth 30, 75
Wherewell 117
White Mrs 134, 277
White Thomas 125
Wickham 236-237
Wickham Mr 192
Widdows Joseph 84
Wightman Robert 33
Wilkes John 29
William 122
William III 117
William IV 111, 262
Williams Private 84
Williams Jane *see Jane Cooper*
Williams Mary aka Mary Wapshare 10
Williams Sir Thomas 7-10
Willoughby de Boke Lord 220
Willoughby de Boke Lady 220
Wills 197, 264
Wilson Private 84

Wilson Alexander 85
Wilson Elizabeth *see Elizabeth Austen*
Wilson Richard 235
Wilson General Robert 310
Wilson General Samuel 310
Wilson Miss 291-292
Wimering 135 *see Wymering*
Wimpole Street 154
Winchester 12, 29, 44, 52, 57, 80, 192, 201, 217, 237-238, 269, 272, 277-279, 284, 290, 291, 296
Winchester College 115-116, 127, 217, 230-231, 233, 250-251, 253, 270, 276
Windows 3, 22, 24, 39, 41, 174, 199, 228
Wine 12, 24, 41, 48, 51-52, 63, 92, 111, 113, 115-116, 118-119, 130-131, 173-174, 183, 199, 207, 239, 242, 257, 279, 306-307, 309-311
Winslade 217
Winston James 227-228
Winterbourne Bassett 252-253
Winthrop 177
Wise Mrs 91
Wise James 139, 143, 145
Wislez Caroline 195
Wiston Park 303
Wodehouse Mr 2, 257
Wollstonecraft Bland 55, 95
Wollstonecraft Mary 95
Wood Mary Challoner *see Mary Ballard*
Woodgate William Frank 240, 313
Woodgate Mrs 306
Workhouse 123, 147, 259
Wormestall Elizabeth 91
Wycombe Lodge 111
Wymering 284, 293
Wyndham William 53
Wynne Mr 282

Yachts & Sailing 48, 105, 175, 204
Yates Reverand 180
Yeates Cavalry Sergeant J 85
Yeoman Mrs 173
Yeomanry 73, 76-77
Young Tobias 5, 40-41, 55, 173, 203, 245
York Sir Joseph 41
Yorkshire 191

www.ingramcontent.com/pod-product-compliance
Lightning Source LLC
Chambersburg PA
CBHW042223250426
43661CB00081BA/2891